The Radio Right

The Radio Right

*How a Band of Broadcasters Took on the
Federal Government and Built the Modern
Conservative Movement*

PAUL MATZKO

OXFORD
UNIVERSITY PRESS

OXFORD
UNIVERSITY PRESS

Oxford University Press is a department of the University of Oxford. It furthers
the University's objective of excellence in research, scholarship, and education
by publishing worldwide. Oxford is a registered trade mark of Oxford University
Press in the UK and certain other countries.

Published in the United States of America by Oxford University Press
198 Madison Avenue, New York, NY 10016, United States of America.

© Oxford University Press 2020

Library of Congress Cataloging-in-Publication Data
Names: Matzko, Paul, author.
Title: The radio right: How a Band of Broadcasters Took on the
Federal Government and Built the Modern Conservative Movement / Paul Matzko.
Description: New York : Oxford University Press, 2020. |
Includes bibliographical references and index.
Identifiers: LCCN 2019033846 (print) | LCCN 2019033847 (ebook) |
ISBN 9780190073220 (hardback) | ISBN 9780190073244 (epub) |
ISBN 9780190073237 (updf) | ISBN 9780190073251 (online)
Subjects: LCSH: Radio in politics—United States. | Radio in religion—United States. |
Radio broadcasting—Political aspects—United States. | Conservatism—United States.
Classification: LCC HE8697.85.U6 M38 2020 (print) | LCC HE8697.85.U6 (ebook) |
DDC 384.54/430973—dc23
LC record available at https://lccn.loc.gov/2019033846
LC ebook record available at https://lccn.loc.gov/2019033847

1 3 5 7 9 8 6 4 2

Printed by Sheridan Books, Inc., United States of America

To Jessica, my love, and George, my bud

To Evelyn Austin Matzko (1918–2018)

Contents

Acknowledgments

Many of this book's best ideas began with offhand remarks by my mentor, Philip Jenkins, whose first spoken words to me were, "We are going to war!" I owe a special debt to Amy Greenberg, who went the extra mile when she did not have to do anything at all. This project ultimately began in a graduate seminar with David Farber and flourished under the generous ministrations of David Watt. The supply-demand metaphor comes from a class with Roger Finke, who has the gift of making every person he talks to feel like the most important person in the world at that moment. Special thanks go to John Matzko, who taught me how to write even when he may wish he did not. Thank you also to Lincoln Mullen, who created the radio station "measles maps"; I am glad you settled in Canterbury.

My research depended on the work of many dozens of archivists and library staff, but I want to honor in particular the kindness of Tim Nutt at the University of Arkansas, Darrin Rodgers at the Flower Pentecostal Heritage Center, Kenneth Henke at the Princeton Theological Seminary Library, and Meredith Sommers at Milligan College, each of whom went above and beyond the call to help me ferret out interesting documents or who took a poor graduate student out for a meal. Also, this project relied on financial support from the following organizations: the Institute for Humane Studies, the Penn State College of Liberal Arts, the Penn State Democracy Institute, the Charles Koch Foundation, the Baylor University Institute for Studies of Religion, the Southern Baptist Historical Library and Archives, and the Billy Graham Center Archives. Finally, I would like to thank my editors—Cynthia Read, Hannah Campeanu, and Jennifer Hammer—for shepherding this book through the publication process.

A portion of chapter three was previously published as "'Do Something about *Life Line*': The Kennedy Administration's Campaign to Silence the Radio Right," *Presidential Studies Quarterly* 48:4 (January 2018): 1–15. Part of chapter six was published as "The National Council of Churches versus Right-Wing Radio: How the Mainline Muted the New Christian Right," in *The Lively Experiment: Religious Toleration in America, from Roger Williams to the Present*, eds. Christopher Beneke and Christopher Grenda (Lanham, MD: Rowman & Littlefield, 2015): 267–286.

Abbreviations

ACA	Americans for Constitutional Action
ACCC	American Council of Christian Churches
ADL	Anti-Defamation League
AFL-CIO	American Federation of Labor and Congress of Industrial Organizations
BFC	National Council of Churches Broadcasting and Film Commission
CCNTB	Citizens Committee for a Nuclear Test Ban
CPUSA	Communist Party USA
DNC	Democratic National Committee
FBI	Federal Bureau of Investigation
FCC	Federal Communications Commission
GRI	Group Research Inc.
IRS	Internal Revenue Service
JCRC	Jewish Community Relations Council
JFK	John F. Kennedy
LBJ	Lyndon B. Johnson
MFN	Most Favored Nation Trade Partner
NAACP	National Association for the Advancement of Colored People
NCC	National Council of Churches
NCCR	National Council for Civic Responsibility
RFK	Robert F. Kennedy
SANE	National Committee for a Sane Nuclear Policy
UAW	United Automobile Workers
UCC	United Church of Christ
WILPF	Women's International League for Peace and Freedom

1

Introduction

"Every Hate-Monger, Radio Preacher and Backwoods Evangelist"

During the 1960 Democratic presidential primaries, John F. Kennedy's campaign faced a significant hurdle in West Virginia. Kennedy had won several other primaries but only in states with significant Catholic populations. Many Democratic Party strategists believed that Kennedy's Catholic faith posed an insuperable barrier to winning the White House, a theory that would be put to the test in West Virginia. If Kennedy proved that he could win in an overwhelmingly Protestant state like West Virginia, then he could win anywhere. The campaign poured resources into the state, buying ads with every major media outlet and sending the president and his photogenic family on a whistle-stop tour, but Kennedy was still losing the state in the polls by a wide margin. The reason "wasn't much of a secret," according to the campaign's internal pollster. "He was a Catholic."[1]

A local campaign official located the source of the problem; if Kennedy lost, it would be because "every hate-monger, radio preacher and backwoods evangelist is being stirred up for an assault which will make 1928 look pale by comparison."[2] That was a reference to the general election in 1928 when Democratic presidential candidate Al Smith, also a Catholic, had lost West Virginia in a nearly twenty-point landslide, roughly the same margin of defeat that the polls were predicting for Kennedy thirty-two years later. As future senator Ted Kennedy told his brother, the problem was not that ardent anti-Catholic "religious extremists" represented a particularly large bloc of votes, but that through their "constant harassing technique" they would make John F. Kennedy's (JFK) candidacy a referendum on religion and thus alienate moderate Protestant voters otherwise sympathetic to the Democratic platform.[3]

Although the campaign did not specify who these "radio preachers" were, the radio preacher with the widest coverage in the state at the time was Carl McIntire, a fundamentalist minister based in New Jersey. He might not have

The Radio Right. Paul Matzko, © Oxford University Press (2020). Oxford University Press.
DOI: 10.1093/oso/9780190073220.001.0001

been a West Virginian, but his radio program aired on three stations there during the 1960 primary, including a station that covered the two largest cities in the state.[4] McIntire opposed Kennedy's candidacy and routinely raised "the question of continued church-state separation" to insinuate that if Kennedy were elected he would give subsidies to Catholic parochial schools and take his foreign policy cues from the Vatican.[5] That prospect alienated many Protestant voters in West Virginia. This was the power of radio broadcasting in 1960; from a relative handful of stations, right-wing broadcasters could reach thousands or even millions of listeners with their criticisms of Kennedy's faith and politics.

Biographers covering Kennedy's 1960 campaign invariably note that he participated in the first televised presidential debates with a haggard-looking Richard Nixon, but what is less well known is that he was the first presidential candidate forced to deal with the phenomenon of conservative domination of independent radio. Conservatives had taken advantage of changes in the radio industry in the 1950s to build an informal network of radio stations spanning the entire country.[6] By the early 1960s, a dozen right-wing broadcasters aired on a hundred or more radio stations nationwide. Several had annual incomes of more than $1 million a year. Carl McIntire had the largest media footprint with a weekly listening audience estimated at twenty million, or one in nine American households.[7]

The election of 1960 marked the first time these conservative broadcasters flexed their political muscle on a national stage. A quick look at chart Figure 1.1, which counts the radio stations that aired McIntire's program, illustrates both the precipitous rise of right-wing radio and the scale of the problem confronting John F. Kennedy.

As the chart indicates, McIntire's radio show, the *20th Century Reformation Hour*, aired on just two stations in 1957, but by 1960 that number had swelled to more than a hundred stations spread across the nation.[8] A near-exponential growth curve meant that these "radio preachers" were no longer just a "backwoods" problem.

Kennedy responded to the crisis in West Virginia by forming a strategic alliance with the National Council of Churches. With forty-five million members, the National Council of Churches was the largest religious organization in the United States. It had its own set of concerns regarding conservative radio preachers—detailed in chapter 6—so it was happy to provide Kennedy with Protestant covering fire. The campaign quickly mailed a selection of pro-Kennedy quotes from National Council of Churches executives

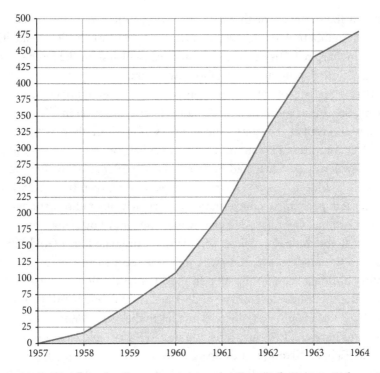

Figure 1.1. Number of radio stations airing the *Twentieth Century Reformation Hour*, 1957–1964.

to every Protestant minister in West Virginia, encouraging them to read the endorsements aloud to their congregations in the weeks leading up to the vote.[9] The tactic helped Kennedy win the West Virginia primary. Kennedy learned two very important lessons from the episode: first, that right-wing radio was a serious political threat, and second, that dealing with these broadcasters required cooperation with allied interest groups.

Kennedy would need that kind of help again. The overriding priority of a first-term president is becoming a second-term president. Kennedy had beaten Richard Nixon in the 1960 general election by the thinnest of margins, just 118,574 votes out of the more than 68 million cast, and he expected an equally tough rematch in 1964.[10] But while the West Virginia crisis was Kennedy's first encounter with right-wing radio, it would by no means be his last. Conservative broadcasting continued to grow during Kennedy's term in office. By 1964 Carl McIntire's program had quadrupled its station count to 480 stations. The threat of right-wing radio had metastasized from a West Virginia problem in 1960 to a national problem by 1964, a situation drawn in sharp relief by the maps in Figure 1.2, which show the radio stations airing McIntire's program during those two years.

These maps are of interest not only for the sheer number of stations dotting the country—and McIntire had at least one station in all fifty states, though never all at the same time—but also for where they were concentrated. Of McIntire's 480 stations in 1964, over half, or 262, were in the South. This New Jersey preacher had built a massive audience below the Mason-Dixon line. Indeed, there is a strong correlation between those states with the densest per capita concentrations of right-wing radio stations—like South Carolina, Georgia, Alabama, Mississippi, and Louisiana—and those states that voted for Republican presidential candidate Barry Goldwater in 1964. To the modern eye, the maps may not seem surprising given half a century of Republican domination in presidential elections in the southern states. But the transition from a solidly blue, Democratic South to a solidly red, Republican South was still in its infancy in the early 1960s. Traditionally, historians have credited that transition first to Barry Goldwater in 1964 and then to Richard Nixon (and campaign adviser Kevin Phillips) in 1968 and 1972. Theirs was a Republican "Southern Strategy" designed to woo disaffected Southern Democrats angry over their party's support for desegregation. Yet as this map suggests, the contours of the "Southern Strategy" were laid down years in advance of either candidate. Right-wing broadcasters prepared the way for the rise of the Republican South.

President Kennedy knew that these broadcasters posed a serious and growing threat both to his legislative goals and to his hopes of re-election in 1964. Within weeks of his inauguration, the administration had already

Figure 1.2. Station map for the *Twentieth Century Reformation Hour*, 1960 and 1964.

begun planning for his re-election campaign. Robert F. Kennedy, the new US attorney general and the president's brother, met with labor union leaders Walter and Victor Reuther multiple times in 1961 to discuss campaign strategy. Robert Kennedy tasked the Reuther brothers with a special mission: find a way to undermine the threat posed by this new political force that had come seemingly out of nowhere, the "extreme right wing." By the end of 1961 the Reuthers hand-delivered a twenty-four-page document titled "The Radical Right in America Today" (colloquially known as the "Reuther Memorandum"). The memorandum warned that right-wing radicals were "better organized than at any time in recent history," were still "growing in strength," and were springing "up like weeds" all over the country. The Reuthers identified some of the usual conservative suspects, including the stridently anti-Communist John Birch Society, but the focus of the memorandum was on right-wing broadcasters.[11] The Reuther Memorandum noted these broadcasters' ability to rouse "vicious local pressure campaigns against teachers or preachers or any one [sic] else who supports anything from negotiation in foreign affairs to governmental programs in domestic affairs."[12] Furthermore, their "pressure tactics on already-timid Congressmen" were already having an effect on the administration's legislative agenda.[13]

An extreme threat justified an extreme response. The Reuther brothers encouraged the Kennedy brothers to use every weapon in the executive arsenal, both licit and not, to silence conservative broadcasting. As this book details, the Kennedy White House would implement each of the major planks of the Reuther plan, using the Internal Revenue Service to target conservative broadcasters with audits and the Federal Communications Commission (FCC) to selectively enforce regulations for radio stations airing right-wing programs. After John F. Kennedy's assassination, the Democratic National Committee picked up the baton and used similar tactics to harass Goldwater supporters in the summer of 1964. Other allied liberal interest groups, including the National Council of Churches, would join the effort in the second half of the 1960s. By the end of the decade, conservative broadcasting was a shell of its former self. The Kennedys' implementation of the Reuther Memorandum slowed the advance of modern conservatism for the better part of a decade. This was the most successful episode of government censorship in America of the past half century.

One might think that so egregious an abuse of executive power with such far-reaching political consequences would attract the attention of historians of the New Right. It generally has not. For example, Jonathan Schoenwald only mentions that "the Kennedy Administration at least considered using . . . right-wing groups as a political tool to help carry the 1964 elections," but he fails to note that the administration went way beyond merely "considering" action.[14] The single best work on conservative broadcasting in the 1960s, by media studies scholar Heather Hendershot, dedicates full chapters to several of the major broadcasters and takes seriously their role in the rise of the New Right. Yet even Hendershot's groundbreaking work only teases the extent of the opposition to conservative broadcasting from the Kennedy administration, the Democratic National Committee, and other interest groups.[15]

This historiographical oversight may be a function of how the story upends our assumptions about the natural positions for the Right and the Left in the drama of American political culture. Scholarly accounts of censorship in modern American history usually feature the suppression of left-wing groups by right-wing politicians, preachers, and businessmen intent on preserving their power and privilege.[16] So it is surprising when the roles are reversed, when conservatives are no longer censors but the censored. Historians may not be as attuned to stories that cut against the expected narrative. Yet understanding the censorship of conservative broadcasters in the 1960s can help scholars historicize the sense of grievance that still persists on the Right today about the perceived liberal domination of the mainstream media.

That sense of grievance is a major theme in historian Nicole Hemmer's recently published book *Messengers of the Right*. Hemmer's main character is broadcaster Clarence Manion, who plays only a supporting role in this book, and she pays greater attention to Manion's publishing endeavors than she does to his radio program. Where *Messengers of the Right* and this book diverge is in regard to the counter–Radio Right campaign. It is almost entirely beyond Hemmer's scope; indeed, she implies that what she calls the "censorship angle"—or accusations of the targeted use of the FCC's Fairness Doctrine against conservative broadcasters—was mostly a figment of overactive imaginations. According to Hemmer, conservative broadcasters had mistaken simple regulatory ambiguity for a conspiracy.[17] Yet as this book shows, there was indeed a concerted campaign to mute the Radio Right using federal regulatory power. This was no mere "angle"; it resulted in a precipitous decline in right-wing broadcasting during the late 1960s.

If one criterion of a movement's importance is the lengths to which its opponents will go to stop it, then conservative broadcasting had been paid

the ultimate backhanded compliment. At its core, this book is an exploration of the importance of the Radio Right through the eyes of its opponents.
Historians should take notice of how often contemporary critics of the New
Right readily acknowledged conservative broadcasters' growing political
power in their private correspondence and internal memoranda. Critics of
the nascent New Right often dismissed these conservatives as "extremists,"
"radicals," and "nuts," but the Kennedy administration believed they posed a
threat serious enough to warrant major executive action.

Taking account of the Kennedy administration's counter–Radio Right censorship campaign ought to change how historians interpret the arc of his presidency. The first accounts of the administration were written by sympathetic
journalists and former staffers, who naturally emphasized Kennedy's positive
accomplishments.[18] But as a result of the sprawling investigations into the
Nixon administration a decade later, scholars received access to previously
classified information about the administration's more unsavory actions.
Looking back through the lens of the Watergate scandal cast the Kennedy
administration in a very different light for revisionist historians in the 1970s
and 1980s. A motif in their work was the willingness of the president and the
attorney general to bend the rules for political advantage. For example, most
revisionist accounts of the Kennedy administration mentioned his fight with
the steel industry in 1962, during which the president and attorney general
used subpoenas, midnight Federal Bureau of Investigation (FBI) interviews,
and an antitrust investigation to intimidate recalcitrant executives and skeptical journalists. The ends justified the means since, in President Kennedy's
own words, "They fucked us. . . . [W]e've got to try to fuck them."[19] Since
the first wave of revisionist work, historians have continued to uncover other
questionable executive actions, including targeted Internal Revenue Service
(IRS) audits and warrantless wiretapping of mobsters, labor union leaders,
and civil rights activists.[20]

In 1971 journalist Victor Navasky described this pattern of behavior as
"an authoritarian capability." In the harsh afterglow of the Pentagon Papers
and Watergate scandals, it was easy to see a precedent in the Kennedy
administration's willingness to brush aside norms and laws, as it did with its
"Get Hoffa" squad." Nobody shed a tear for an organized crime figure like
Jimmy Hoffa, but Navasky worried that future administrations might be
willing to use those same tools to go after other groups, like a "Get Panthers"
squad or a "Get Radical Liberals" squad or a "Get Birchers" squad. Given
later revelations about the FBI's COINTELPRO campaign against the Black

Panthers, as well as the Kennedy administration's anti–Radio Right efforts, Navasky was more accurate in his apprehensions than he could possibly have known at the time.[21] As one biographer later noted while discussing the Kennedy administration's misuse of the IRS, "Luckily for the Kennedys, Richard Nixon's later bid to politicize the IRS . . . was egregious enough that when Congress got around to investigating, it focused mostly on Republican abuses and less on Bobby's."[22]

But by the 1990s, a wave of postrevisionist scholars took a more nuanced approach, acknowledging the administration's excesses while emphasizing personal and political growth over the course of Kennedy's term in office.[23] Historian Peter Ling summarized the postrevisionist vision as the belief that "JFK was a man who grew towards greatness during his presidency. Kennedy was a better president in 1962 than in 1961, and showed still further promise in the summer of 1963, with the test ban treaty and the civil rights bill."[24] Yet this book supports a neo-revisionist understanding of the Kennedy administration. Consider one of the key events Ling cited as proof of Kennedy's personal growth, the passage of the 1963 Nuclear Test Ban Treaty. That was the proximate cause for the White House's sweeping use of executive power to silence the treaty's critics among the Radio Right. Inasmuch as Kennedy "grew towards greatness," it included a growth in his willingness to abuse executive power in order to advance his legislative agenda.

Conservative complaints about hostile treatment were invariably dismissed in the 1960s; indeed, scholars of the time cited those very complaints as evidence of the movement's inherently conspiratorial mindset. For a time, historians followed suit, but the idea of the Right as the natural home for the paranoid began with American social scientists, not historians. They, in turn, borrowed insights from post–World War II European scholars who were seeking to explain the rise of fascism. The key to understanding the Right, according to mid-twentieth-century sociologists like Daniel Bell, was to see it as fundamentally a matter of psychology. The Right flourished among middle-class people who were anxious over challenges to their fragile social status. As originally framed by European scholars, such challenges were primarily economic, but with a little tweaking it was possible for Bell to frame the rise of the American *Radical Right*—the title of an influential edited collection by Bell—as a response to the racial, sexual, and cultural transformations of American culture in the 1950s and 1960s. The conservative reaction to those changes was marked, in historian Richard Hofstadter's words, by a "paranoid style" of politics that saw conspiracies lurking behind every sinister development in American society and which sought an authoritarian strongman that could save the nation.[25] The Right was unified not by shared beliefs or an intellectual tradition, according to this interpretation; it was a product of psychosis manifesting as paranoia.

As historians over the past two decades have increasingly turned their attention to modern conservatism—in response to Alan Brinkley's influential call for scholars to grapple with what he labeled the "orphan" of political history—they widely rejected the social scientific psychologizing of the Right.[26] In part, that was a consequence of the Right's endurance in American politics. It was convenient for Bell and Hofstadter to frame the Right as a temporary recrudescence of America's id during a time of social upheaval, for if it was a "revolt against modernity" then they could "dismiss it as a political force of long-term significance."[27] But after Ronald Reagan's election in 1980, conservatism seemed rather less temporary and the former explanation no longer seemed quite so convincing. As historian Lisa McGirr complained, Hofstadter's "excessively psychological interpretation distorted our understanding of American conservatism" and retarded historical inquiry.[28] Historians began taking conservativism seriously as a belief system, rather than as a mere façade covering up primitive, neurotic impulses. Much of the growing literature on conservatism from the past twenty years can be seen as a tacit rebuttal to the old status anxiety perspective.[29]

Although historians are more inclined to take conservatism seriously as an ideological system than they were a generation ago, the historiography of the New Right has a continuing "What's the Matter with Kansas?" problem, to borrow the title of historian and journalist Thomas Frank's best-selling book.[30] In the book, Frank grappled with the seeming contradiction of Republicans in small-town America voting against their economic self-interest by casting their ballots for the party of laissez-faire economics. Frank thought he had solved the riddle; conservative elites were hoodwinking ordinary voters by distracting them with talk of culture wars, family values, and a range of social conservative issues. Make voters fear gay marriage or abortion rights and they will vote against their pocketbook, or so the argument went. Frank's Kansas thesis continues to be popular in contemporary political analysis, but whatever the concept's utility in the twenty-first century, reading it back into the history of 1960s conservatism is a mistake.[31] Yet some historians have done so because it allows scholars to strip conservatism of its ideological trappings. Instead, it can be reduced, in the words of historian Nancy MacLean, to a "commitment . . . to safeguard the advantages of those long privileged—whether by class, race, gender, religion, or sexual orientation—[while] its leaders have systematically exploited fear and prejudice in order to acquire power."[32]

Yet as chapter 2 details, grassroots conservative activism in the early 1960s thrived in leafy suburbs filled with the families of white-collar professionals, places like Orange County, California, and Dallas, Texas.[33] They were doctors, lawyers, housewives, and engineers living in the economically prosperous Sunbelt, a very different group than the popular caricature of 1960s conservatives as a bunch of frustrated white laborers in the Deep South and the midwestern Rustbelt. Certainly, those voters did exist and they played a significant role in the election of 1968, buoying the surprise candidacy of George Wallace, but they were not the core constituency of the New Right earlier in the decade. Working-class southern whites had a significant role to play in the creation of a new Republican coalition, but it is overly simplistic to reduce the entire story of the New Right to their story.

Even when accounting for the cross-class nature of conservatism, some historians still deny agency to grassroots activists, turning them instead into unthinking pawns of conservative elites. In that vein, Nancy MacLean proposes that "ordinary Americans . . . were not in the driver's seat of this movement . . . [and] had little sense of the conservative leaders' overall project, let alone their strategy for achieving it." Instead, the Right was a product "of organizing by conservative intellectuals and politicians who stirred anxiety about where the country was headed in order to build the power to turn national policy away from the inclusive social citizenship inaugurated in the New Deal."[34] This is a vision of the Right as a top-down, manufactured movement. While on the surface it may appear to be a genuinely grassroots social movement, it is actually a front for the interests of industrial, intellectual, and political elites. Like AstroTurf, it looks real from a distance, but up close you can see that it is plastic.

Few historians are as explicit as MacLean in denying the grassroots legitimacy of the New Right, but the idea is implicit in a new body of work published in the afterglow of the 2007–2008 financial crisis. Historians like Kim Phillips-Fein, Bethany Moreton, Benjamin Waterhouse, and Kevin Kruse have undertaken a "corporate turn" in the study of the Right.[35] Each identifies specific corporate interests that funded right-wing think tanks, periodicals, and even preachers. And there were many connections between the Right and the business world, even in broadcasting. One of the three most influential conservative programs of the 1960s—the *Facts Forum*—was solely funded by Texas oilman and millionaire H. L. Hunt, who inserted advertisements for Hunt-produced household goods in between turgid paeans to the free market system. If Hunt had added a Hollywood celebrity like Ronald Reagan to his show, he would have had a knock-off version of the *General Electric Theater*. All that is to say, while the corporate turn has real historical value, at least some part of its popular appeal comes from the way in which readers have been primed by the financial crisis to blame America's political and economic ills on big corporations, a sentiment that is then read back into the history of the New Right.

Yet this historiographical trend has minimized the contributions of grassroots activists who had little or no connection to corporate interests. Framing the entire New Right as a corporate creation is a mistake. As we will see, chapter 2 describes a national boycott of Eastern European imports led by suburban housewives, who would have taken offense at being called simple-minded dupes. And even among broadcasters, H. L. Hunt's corporate-financing model was an outlier. A majority of the top-earning conservative programs were almost entirely financed by small listener contributions, $1 a month here, $5 a month there, adding up to annual budgets of $1 million or more per broadcaster. Conservative radio's standard fiscal model more closely resembled a National Public Radio pledge drive than it did a corporate front. Again, as with the Reuther Memorandum, it can be instructive to consider what the New Right's most trenchant opponents thought of the movement. The Kennedy administration did target conservative leaders—particularly broadcasters—but that was precisely because of those broadcasters' ability to harness authentic, grassroots outrage and direct it at the administration. The Kennedys and Reuthers respected the irritating resourcefulness of the conservative grassroots; historians should follow their lead.

Yet if the rise of modern conservatism was neither propelled by a primal sense of status anxiety nor merely a product of corporate interests, then what can explain why growing numbers of ordinary conservatives began to engage in grassroots activism during the early 1960s? Historians have assumed that figuring out the origins of the New Right requires identifying which issue or set of issues—opposition to civil rights, feminism, abortion, secularization of education, and so on—activated conservative outrage and stimulated social movement formation.

But there is no *sui generis* idea or issue to which we can link the rise of the Right. Simply put, the answer to the question "Where did the Right come from?" depends on whom and when historians focus their attention.

However, there is a theme that unites all such answers: each explains the rise of conservatism by pointing to a shift in the *demand* for conservative ideas, making outrage over new social or political developments the key to understanding how potential conservatives became actual conservatives. A housewife, previously apathetic about politics, finds a sex education book in her child's backpack and then runs for a seat on the school board, a scenario evoked in Photo 1.1. A small-town businessman opens the newspaper to read about the Supreme Court's decision in *Roe v. Wade* and decides to donate money to a pro-life organization. Framed this way, exposure to a cultural transformation—in this example, the sexual revolution and reproductive rights—alienated a group of people. That sense of alienation created a demand for conservative alternatives, something to explain what went "wrong" in America and what could be done to fix it. The most highly motivated of these new conservative converts were then willing to engage in political activism.

This framework leaves historians to ask which hot-button issues were most effective at stimulating conservative outrage and activism. The hunt for the "correct" issue has led to internecine historiographical squabbles over which issue was most important or most pervasive. This is not to suggest that demand-side explanations of the rise of the Right do not have value. Conservatives did indeed respond to the sexual revolution, the spread of communism, the civil rights movement, and a host of other cultural developments in the mid-twentieth century. The problem is that the other half of the equation—the *supply* of conservative ideas—has been neglected because of the fixation on *demand*.[36]

Ideas do not just float through the ether like spores infecting human hosts in an ideological invasion of the body snatchers. Someone using a mode of distribution must transmit ideas to those people who might be interested. Prior to the twentieth century, ideas spread primarily via print in the form of cheaply printed pamphlets, newspapers, and books, each copy of which might reach dozens or even hundreds of readers. The advent of radio exponentially expanded distribution networks. Each radio broadcast could reach thousands or even millions of listeners, none of whom needed to be literate to understand the message. Radio made ideas cheaper to distribute and more broadly accessible. It did not take long for ideologues and politicians to grasp the inherent advantages of the medium. Huey Long and Father Charles Coughlin used the radio to build grassroots, progressive movements in the 1930s. President Franklin Delano Roosevelt used his radio "fireside chats"

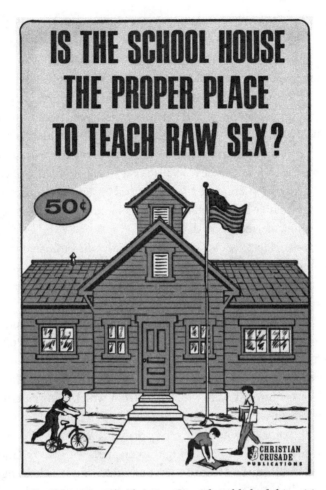

IS THE SCHOOL HOUSE THE PROPER PLACE TO TEACH RAW SEX?

Photo 1.1. Billy James Hargis's *Christian Crusade* published this critique of sex education classes in public schools in the 1960s, predating the peak of the sex ed controversy during the 1970s.

Billy James Hargis Papers, Special Collections, University of Arkansas Libraries.

to bolster popular support for the New Deal. Understanding the surge of progressive sentiment in the 1930s means paying attention not only to external developments like the Great Depression but also to the ways in which a new technology allowed the efficient distribution of progressive solutions for those problems. The ability to *supply* progressive ideas had as important a role to play in the politics of the 1930s as changes in the *demand* for those same ideas.

Similarly, the history of conservative broadcasting in the late 1950s and 1960s has broad implications for how we conceptualize the rise of the New Right. As the major radio networks shifted their attention and investment capital to the new medium of television, radio increasingly became the preserve of small, independent stations that could not afford to be as picky about their programming as the networks had been. Radio broadcasting was newly affordable, and niche political groups were suddenly able to buy timeslots on stations all across the country. Conservative broadcasting was utterly transformed. In the early 1950s not a single, nonnetwork conservative broadcaster aired on more than a handful of stations. Within a decade, a dozen conservative broadcasters aired on a hundred or more independent stations nationwide, most on a daily basis.

Conservative ideas could now be instantly disseminated across the country to millions of listeners, and broadcasters were not just transmitting ideas but also issuing calls to action. With the encouragement of conservative broadcasters, a wave of grassroots activism swept the nation in the late 1950s and early 1960s. In one such instance in 1962, a local Miami boycott of goods imported from Communist Eastern Europe spread to 260 cities in forty-eight states, ultimately forcing Congress to tinker with the Kennedy administration's trade policy and causing consternation in the White House. Actions like the boycott were the "stuff" from which the modern conservative movement was created, and it could happen thanks to the suddenly pervasive presence of conservative broadcasters. The tide of conservative sentiment that reached its 1960s high-water mark with Barry Goldwater's presidential campaign had ridden a wave of right-wing broadcasting.[37]

Parallel to how the boom in conservative broadcasting explains the rise of the New Right at the turn of the 1960s, the censorship campaign to suppress those same broadcasters helps explain the temporary decline of conservatism during the late 1960s. The standard explanation for conservative setbacks after 1964 is that Goldwater's landslide defeat by Lyndon Johnson in 1964 embarrassed the conservative faction of the Republican Party and empowered the moderate faction, which then backed a moderate Richard Nixon in 1968 and 1972. As Donald Critchlow put it, "The election [of 1964] returned the GOP Right to the fringes of the party."[38] It was not until the elections of 1976 and 1980 that conservatives would reemerge from their self-imposed exile and vote for Ronald Reagan. Call this the "demoralization thesis" of the decline of the New Right.

There are alternative explanations for the decline of conservative influence in national politics from 1965 to 1976. On the one hand, historians with an eye on the grassroots have shown that conservative activism never truly ceased during this period. The anti-abortion movement continued to bubble just below the surface, Ronald Reagan was still the popular governor of California, and activists like Phyllis Schlafly were not sitting home twiddling their thumbs.[39] That said, it is true that conservatives were not as visible on the national stage in the late 1960s as they had been earlier in the decade. Conservatism had indeed taken a step back, but it was not a sense of demoralization that had caused it. By 1964 and 1965 the counterconservative broadcasting campaign had begun to take effect. As a result of targeted regulatory attacks, radio stations started dropping conservative programming en masse. Since those programs played such an important role in energizing grassroots activism, it is not surprising that the movement faltered as conservative broadcasting faltered. That was precisely the original intent of the plan concocted by the Kennedys and Reuthers in 1961. The fortunes of grassroots conservatism and right-wing broadcasting were tightly intertwined. Both would falter in the late 1960s, but both would also see a resurgence in the late 1970s with the relaxation of radio and television broadcasting rules, as well as the rise of cable broadcasting.

Focusing on the role of conservative broadcasting also recenters the contributions of radical voices on the Right and in so doing challenges the self-propagated origins myths of modern conservatism. Typically, there are two individuals that historians of the New Right choose as a point of departure: Barry Goldwater or William F. Buckley Jr. Thus, Arizona senator and 1964 Republican nominee Barry Goldwater is called a "towering figure" and his campaign described as the "Woodstock of American Conservatism" (presumably with fewer drugs, less sex, and much worse music).[40] Before Goldwater, or so the story goes, conservatism was a mess, divided into a confusing patchwork of small organizations without clear goals or a sense of broader purpose, at least, that is, until "the senator taught millions of Americans . . . how and why they were conservative Republicans" and "planted the seeds for the future growth of conservative agitation."[41] Goldwater's 1964 campaign was undeniably a major turning point in the history of the New Right, training a future generation of conservative political operatives and boosting conservative influence in the Republican Party.[42]

However, Goldwater was a product of the grassroots New Right, not its progenitor. Years before he discovered his conscience, hundreds of thousands of ordinary conservatives were already engaged in substantial, effective political activism. Indeed, it is not incidental that a conservative broadcaster—Clarence Manion—recruited Goldwater to run for president, assembled his campaign contribution team, convinced a skeptical William F. Buckley to support his candidacy, and arranged for the writing and publication of Goldwater's best-selling autobiography. The order of operations is exactly backward when we start with Goldwater.[43]

If Goldwater has been anointed the "standard bearer" of the New Right, then William F. Buckley has been framed as the prophet preparing the way in the conservative intellectual wilderness of the 1950s.[44] The defeat of conservative senator Robert Taft by the moderate candidate, Dwight D. Eisenhower, in the 1952 Republican primaries had left conservatives on the outside of party power looking in. During this fallow time, or so the story goes, Buckley made conservatism relevant once again by blending elements of classical liberalism with Cold War interventionism and Catholic social conservatism. He and a handful of other likeminded contrarian intellectuals made this "fusionist" conservatism a respectable, mainstream ideology.

Then, in the mid-1960s, when disreputable fellow travelers like the John Birch Society and extremist broadcasters threatened to return conservatism to the political margins through their outlandish conspiracy theories and uncouth rhetoric, Buckley saved the conservative movement by turning his pen against the radicals and purging them from the masthead of his magazine, the *National Review*.[45] By this account, Buckley is the beating heart of the conservative movement, both founder and protector, and his *National Review* is called the "Ur-text of modern conservatism."[46] In the magazine's first issue, Buckley declared that conservatism "stands athwart history, yelling Stop."[47] The problem is that historians have looked to Buckley and done precisely that.

Buckley and his ideological descendants have actively promoted this Buckley-centric narrative of the rise of the New Right. Perhaps the most frequently cited book on the topic is George H. Nash's *The Conservative Intellectual Movement in America Since 1945*. For Nash, the conservative movement was "a movement of ideas" and the men—and it is very much a gentlemen's club—who came up with the ideas are the heroes of the tale. These "purveyors of ideas" were the "architects" of the Right. On the other hand, there were those engaged in "the hurly-burly of everyday politics."

These "extremists of the Right" may have been "energetic" but their "contribution to conservatism as an intellectual force was negligible." Ideas were what mattered, not action. Nash's emphasis is very much in keeping with Buckley's own point of view; he founded *National Review* to "influence the opinionmakers of the nation," not to bother with any "popular and cliché-ridden appeal to the grass-roots." For both Nash and Buckley it was intellectuals who "midwived and implemented the revolution," not those mindlessly energetic, nonintellectual, grassroots types or the radio broadcasters who enabled their activism.[48]

Buckley's marginalization of the "radicals" has had a long half-life because it is politically convenient. On the one hand, that framing allowed Buckley to paint his own branch of conservatism as, to quote Heather Hendershot, "conservative but not extremist" (never mind that on issues of policy substance Buckley and the broadcasters were in lockstep agreement).[49] Rick Perlstein, in a widely read mea culpa after the 2016 election, acknowledged that political historians had bought into this respectability narrative. After all, they were writing about "the *modern* conservative movement, the one that led to Reagan, not about the brutish relics of a more, gothic, ill-formed and supposedly incoherent reactionary era that preceded it." For Perlstein, telling that "respectable tale" meant ignoring the conspiracy-mongering and racist constituent mail that poured into congressional offices during the 1960s.[50] Yet conservative broadcasters constantly encouraged their listeners to join letter-writing campaigns and promoted conspiratorial understandings of current events. Studying the Radio Right in the 1960s is an antidote to that kind of historiographical oversight.[51]

Whatever the reason, it has been easy to exaggerate Buckley's importance because he was, in a sense, the last man standing. The *National Review* remains an influential conservative magazine today; none of the major 1960s conservative radio programs still exist, and most were in serious decline by the 1970s. Yet persistence is only one measure of significance and arguably not the most important given the context. The Kennedy administration decided that conservative broadcasters were a more serious threat than the publishers and then successfully undermined that threat using executive power. Surely that suggests the inverse of the Buckley narrative, that it was "extremist" broadcasters who were the more important factor in the formation of the 1960s Right, important enough to attract the kind of adverse regulatory attention that Buckley himself was spared. As Jonathan Schoenwald has argued, the radicals "acted as a buffer for the responsible Right, deflecting criticism that might have otherwise focused on the hardcore of the GOP."[52] Schoenwald is right, though conservative broadcasters faced much more than mere criticism.

The Buckley-centric analysis of the conservative movement is fundamentally flawed in another way. Ideas do matter, but they do not spread themselves. The Buckley/Nash explanation for the rise of the Right lacks a convincing means of distribution. The closest they come is to point to the *National Review*, giving the magazine a great deal of explanatory freight. As conservative journalist George Will would later say, "Without Buckley, no *National Review*; without *National Review*, no conservative takeover of the Republican Party; without that, no Reagan; without Reagan, no victory in the Cold War."[53] By the transitive power Buckley had personally won the Cold War!

But while the *National Review* had nearly seventy-three thousand subscribers by 1964, a single conservative radio program, Carl McIntire's *Twentieth Century Reformation Hour*, had a listening audience estimated at twenty million.[54] It is true that conservative broadcasters mostly repackaged ideas borrowed from elsewhere, including from Buckley, but it was they who provided the crucial link between rarefied publications like the *National Review* and millions of ordinary activists. Buckley might have been the "architect" of the New Right, but broadcasters were the construction company that hired the workers and assembled the structure. It is long past time to place the "radicals" back at the center of the rise of the New Right.[55]

Although the actions of the Reuthers, the Kennedys, and the Democratic National Committee lie at the core of this book, it is also a political history of religious broadcasting. The two featured broadcasters—Carl McIntire and Billy James Hargis—were fundamentalist preachers in addition to being conservative activists. The political and religious aspects of their public personas cannot be disentangled. While they were part of a movement that upended the post–World War II party system, they also represented a challenge to the informal religious establishment of the mid-twentieth century that was institutionalized in the National Council of Churches.

The National Council of Churches was an ecumenical church council that represented some forty-five million American Protestants. Its leadership tended to be both theologically and politically progressive and they shared every bit of the Kennedy administration's distaste for conservative, fundamentalist broadcasters like Billy James Hargis and Carl McIntire. Indeed, after the Democratic National Committee stopped its direct involvement in the counterconservative broadcasting campaign in 1965, the National Council of Churches picked up where the Democratic National Committee left off. The National Council of Churches was not directly responsible for the changes in the regulatory environment—those can be traced back to the Kennedy administration—but the council would take advantage of those changes to undermine its religious competitors. The informal, mainline religious establishment leveraged its political connections to hobble competing religious groups even while claiming to be champions of religious toleration.[56]

In speaking of religion and the New Right, there is a final point of terminology to be made. Many scholars studying the role of religion in the rise of conservativism have adopted the phrases "New Christian Right" or "Religious Right" to mark the movement off from the rest of a presumably secular Right.[57] Yet the terms only entered common usage after *Newsweek* magazine announced that 1976 was "the year of the evangelical" because of evangelical support for Jimmy Carter.[58] Whether or not the phrases "New Christian Right" and "Religious Right" have utility for explaining the political landscape in the late 1970s and 1980s is a matter for another book, but historians are imposing an alien category when we read that phrase back into the 1960s. This is a mistake also because, as Darren Dochuk has noted, doing so "has helped reify the popular notion that evangelicalism affects the political arena only haphazardly and episodically in contexts of crisis," like a Jack-in-the-Box popping out simply to provide scholars with a colorful anecdote.[59]

Ironically, evangelicals themselves had a hand in walling off the New Christian Right from the New Right proper. Evangelical scholar James Davison Hunter identified "three waves of evangelical political activism"— in the 1920s, the early 1950s, and finally the 1980s—that he treated as discrete phenomena from the rest of the conservative movement. Yet Hunter portrayed the late 1950s and 1960s, the period when the rise of the New Right began, as a time when "theologically conservative Protestants were almost uniformly politically quietistic."[60] This would have been a revelation to religious broadcasters like Carl McIntire, Frederick Schwarz, Billy James Hargis, Fulton Lewis, and their millions of listeners! Even those right-wingers who were not known for their personal religiosity, like Robert Welch, routinely appealed to religious supporters, which in Welch's case meant naming the John Birch Society after an *actual missionary* killed in China by Communist forces during World War II. Scratch the surface of any right-wing archive from the 1960s and religion oozes out.

This book is a political history of religious broadcasting, a social history of grassroots conservatism, a media history of mid-twentieth-century radio, and a prehistory of the Reagan revolution. The Radio Right created a national grassroots movement, forced the White House to listen to housewives who were angry about Polish ham, started the partisan transformation of the Deep South years before the Republican Party thought to try doing so itself, provoked the most intense episode of government censorship of the past half century, undermined the largest religious organization in America, and launched the first wave of mass right-wing radio. In sum, it is the story of how conservative radio left a lasting mark on America in the 1960s–1970s.

2

Polish Ham and the Southern Strategy

How the Radio Right Created a Conservative
Social Movement

Modern observers may take for granted that talk radio is the natural preserve of conservatism; it has been linked to each of the major conservative moments of the past four decades, from the Reagan Revolution in 1980 to the Tea Party movement in 2009. We have become used to a political landscape in which conservative radio broadcasters have the ability to shape the national political conversation in decisive ways. But such was not always the case. Conservative dominance on independent radio was a radically new development in the 1960s, enabling the creation of a new, conservative grassroots that wielded a stunning amount of political influence given the relative youth of the movement. The Radio Right used that influence on behalf of conservatives who felt overlooked by the media and alienated from the federal government. Broadcasters encouraged grassroots activism, including a nearly forgotten boycott of imported Polish ham by suburban housewives, which ultimately forced Congress to defy the Kennedy administration on trade policy. Of even more lasting impact than the boycott was the way that broadcasters aided the partisan transformation of the Deep South by appealing to segregationists. The Radio Right helped turn traditional Southern Democrats into Republicans, making the Republican Party the party of white massive resistance.

This rise of mass right-wing radio was only possible because of a dramatic shift in the radio industry in the mid-1950s. Previously, almost all radio stations were affiliated with large radio networks like CBS and NBC. The networks produced national programming that they then distributed to their local affiliates for a fee. They also had the right to up-or-down approval over local programming decisions. Anything that was too politically, culturally, or religiously controversial was banned. That policy marginalized radical political voices on both the Left and the Right during the first three decades of mass radio, including anti–New Deal populists like Father

The Radio Right. Paul Matzko, © Oxford University Press (2020). Oxford University Press.
DOI: 10.1093/oso/9780190073220.001.0001

Charles Coughlin, socialist labor unions, and the National Association of Evangelicals.[1] But in the 1950s the radio landscape changed as the networks switched their focus from radio to television, pouring investment capital into the new technology and leaving radio to smaller entrepreneurs. Yet at the same moment the number of AM stations in America nearly quadrupled, from about 900 in 1945 to 3,500 in 1960. Almost all of that boom was composed of independent, nonnetwork owners, many of whom owned a single station apiece. In 1945 the four major networks controlled 95% of all radio stations in America. Just seven years later, that percentage had plummeted to less than half, with the percentage continuing to fall throughout the 1950s.[2]

Not only did networks stop applying for new radio station licenses but also they stopped working as hard to sell radio advertising spots. More stations with fewer advertising dollars sloshing around meant that the new small-time, small-town stations had tight monthly budgets. They could not afford to be as picky about programming as the big networks had been in the past. While station owners were not necessarily a politically minded lot, they aired an increasing number of overtly political programs from a wide variety of ideological points of view. Station owners looked at conservatives and Communists and just saw green. This presented formerly niche political groups with the opportunity to cobble together hundreds of independent stations into informal, syndicated networks for their radio shows. Stations constantly dropped and added the programs as their budgets required, but the total number of stations airing conservative programming rose at a rapid pace.

By the early 1960s conservative listeners could turn their radio dial to any of a dozen conservative radio programs that aired on at least a hundred stations nationwide. The conservative broadcasters who benefited from the transformation of the radio industry came from a wide variety of backgrounds, like Robert Welch (candy manufacturer), Clarence Manion (Catholic law professor), H. L. Hunt (Texas oil magnate), and Billy James Hargis and Carl McIntire (fundamentalist preachers). Each had their own particular style, but they all shared a set of conservative priorities: rolling back the New Deal state and taking an aggressive stance against global Communism.

Carl McIntire, in particular, was representative of a group of ordained ministers who took to the airwaves. His radio show, the *Twentieth Century Reformation Hour*, began broadcasting from Collingswood, New Jersey, in 1955. He claimed that Communists lurked behind every sinister development in American society, from nuclear disarmament to sex education. McIntire stoked these fears to a paranoid degree—note the title of one of McIntire's revival meeting brochures, "Stalin's Agents in Camden County"—but beneath his anti-Communist rhetoric was an authentic expression of growing conservative dissent from consensus liberalism.[3] The Eisenhower, Kennedy, and Johnson administrations' support for desegregation, internationalism, and the expansion of the federal government deeply unsettled ordinary conservatives. Since they felt they could not trust the broadcast networks to tell the truth—conservative distrust of the "mainstream" media is not a recent phenomenon—they tuned instead into the *Twentieth Century Reformation Hour* and dozens of similar programs for the real scoop on the news.

The most complete, extant archives of any of the 1960s conservative broadcasters belongs to McIntire, in part because his papers were seized along with his office for nonpayment of taxes in the 1990s. Neither McIntire's family nor his friends had the chance to edit out his embarrassing correspondence or throw away seemingly unimportant financial documents. Given the relative completeness of McIntire's records, it is possible to reconstruct the boom in conservative broadcasting during the late 1950s and early 1960s in remarkable detail. This, not anti-Communism or any other issue of the day, is what explains the rise of the New Right. In 1957 McIntire's radio show aired on just two stations, but by 1964 that number had swelled to 480.[4] To put those numbers in political context, McIntire's station count more than doubled during John F. Kennedy's time in the White House.

McIntire was the largest single conservative broadcaster in the early 1960s, but other broadcasters saw parallel increases in station counts. Billy James Hargis had gone from a single station in Oklahoma in the early 1950s to sixty-eight stations in 1960 and two hundred stations in 1962 (with an additional twenty television stations).[5] Clarence Manion had started with twenty-nine stations in 1954 but was up to more than two hundred stations in forty-one states by 1961.[6] Starting in 1958, oil millionaire H. L. Hunt, seeking to both dodge taxes and fight Communism, plunked his program on three hundred radio and fifty television stations.[7] These bare station totals are impressive, but seeing a program like McIntire's mapped gives an even clearer sense of the national reach conservative broadcasting had. Each of the dots in Figure 2.1 indicates a station that aired McIntire during the Polish ham boycott. You would have to add another 150 dots to that map to portray McIntire at his peak in 1964, but even in 1962 his message of support for the boycott had the potential to reach a majority of American listeners.

Figure 2.1. Station map for the *Twentieth Century Reformation Hour*, 1962.

Prior to the late 1950s, conservative ideas were transmitted primarily through print. Once a week or once a month you would receive a newspaper from your favorite conservative outlet. Carl McIntire himself had a periodical for two decades before he started his regular radio show. It was called the *Christian Beacon*, a weekly newspaper with a circulation of roughly 20,000 in the late 1950s. For the sake of comparison, the *National Review*—William F. Buckley's more famous magazine targeting a higher-brow audience—reached 18,000 at the time (though subscriptions would grow in the 1960s). Those who subscribed to the *Christian Beacon* or the *National Review* were a dedicated core group, but there were strict upper limits to the numbers of people willing to pay for a newspaper subscription, and the total audience was constrained by their reliance on word-of-mouth distribution. Adding together the circulation figures for every major right-wing publication in 1956, no more than 310,000 individuals participated in the print network that distributed conservative ideas (and that figure rests on the implausible assumption of no overlap between subscribers to different publications). That is not an inconsiderable number, but it pales next to the audience potential of radio. Indeed, it was only once conservative radio boomed in the 1960s that print circulation numbers followed.[8]

By contrast, at its peak McIntire's radio show had a listenership of 20 million, or one thousand times as many people as subscribed to his newspaper. Given that the population of the United States at the time was close to 180 million, that would mean that one in nine Americans tuned into the *Twentieth Century Reformation Hour*.[9] Besides the cost of a radio set—which nearly every American household already owned—listening was free. There were no subscription fees. Radio exponentially expanded the ability of conservatives to distribute their ideas to a mass audience by making it cheap, easy, and safe to consume those ideas. You did not have to be a committed conservative activist to turn the radio dial to a conservative program. You could do it in the convenience of your own home, in your car on the way to work, or on a handheld set with headphones on. Holding a right-wing newspaper under your arm visibly branded you as conservative, but radio was anonymous. And that anonymity made it possible for those who may have been previously apathetic about politics or politically moderate to test out conservative ideas without being forced to commit to the ideology. As broadcaster Clarence Manion put it in 1965, "We know from eleven years' experience that, once Mr. Average American gets a chance to find out what is happening to his country, he becomes a dedicated Conservative."[10] Radio was an evangelistic medium for the New Right. A contemporary critic chose a fitting title for his chapter on conservative broadcasters: "The Proselytizers."[11]

From the crack of dawn until late at night you could go an entire day and listen to nothing but conservative programming. During the morning drive, you might listen to a solid hour of attacks on the Kennedy administration's Cuba policy by H. L. Hunt's *Life Line* program. Then you could listen to *Christian Crusade* as Billy James Hargis ferreted out Communist sympathizers at the highest levels of the federal government. Next came Howard Kershner's fifteen-minute weekly sermonizing on "the Christian religion and education in the field of economics."[12] Perhaps your station, particularly if you lived in the South, aired the *Citizens' Council*, the radio home for white massive resistance. During lunch, you might listen to McIntire's *Twentieth Century Reformation Hour* as he applauded the Polish ham boycott. And throughout the rest of the day, one conservative program after another kept up the same basic drumbeat: Communists were everywhere, the Kennedy administration was weak, and only conservative action could save America. There had never been anything like this torrent of conservative programming. Certainly, there were a handful of conservative commentators back during the days of network radio in the 1930s to 1940s, but they generally filled a time slot here or there in the weekly schedule. The idea that there would be hundreds of independent stations running conservative programs all day long would have been utterly alien to previous generations of radio listeners.

Ultimately, it is what happened after conservative listeners turned off their radios that transformed the political landscape of America. Right-wing radio was not just a way of transmitting ideas to potential conservatives; it also made listeners feel joined to a wider movement worth investing their time and money into. Going door to door for a conservative candidate, holding a book club in their living room, and boycotting local grocery stores were all part of a larger effort. A successful movement gives participants a sense of hope that their small, local actions can make a large, national difference. That is what compels people to leave the comfort of polite routine and engage in contentious collective action. That is what makes a conservative social movement that is capable of taking over a major political party and reshaping the political landscape of America. That is what the Radio Right created.

The Polish Ham Boycott

There are many collective actions from the late 1950s and early 1960s that could be used to illustrate the way in which the rise of right-wing broadcasting enabled the creation of a new, conservative social movement. But one of the most compelling is also one that has almost entirely escaped scholarly examination: the Polish ham boycott of 1962. Those few historians who have touched on it have dismissed it as inconsequential. For example, Mary Brennan mentions the original boycott organization, named "the Committee to Warn of the Arrival of Communist Merchandise on the Local Business Scene," as an example of how "organizations concentrating on a particular aspect of a broader cause . . . had only limited support and impact."[13] She makes this point in service of her broader argument that the rise of the New Right could only transpire once conservatives in the Republican Party learned to channel local activism into formal, electoral politics. By downplaying the significance of local activist groups and elevating the importance of party and intellectual elites, this narrative obscures the role of grassroots conservatives in the rise of the New Right.

This portrayal of the New Right runs counter to how scholars assess other mid-twentieth-century social movements; imagine an account of the civil rights movement that dismissed freedom rides, sit-ins, and marches in the

1950s as inconsequential since they did not immediately result in congressional representation or executive action. Political influence can indeed be a product of successful social movements, but those movements are incubated in the kind of local, grassroots activism epitomized by the Polish ham boycott. Although the boycott had humble origins as the brainchild of a Miami chiropractor, within a year it had spread to more than 260 cities in 48 states, convinced Congress to alter trade policy toward Eastern Europe, elicited alarm in the White House, and brought thousands of ordinary activists together into a national political movement.[14] By any reasonable measure of political influence, it was a remarkable success story for the nascent New Right.

The boycott is also an excellent site to explore the relationship between right-wing radio broadcasting and local activism. Broadcasters acted as a kind of megaphone for conservative causes, focusing national attention on previously local issues. Without access to the airwaves the boycott might have remained a matter of minor concern in just Miami or Florida and it is hard to imagine it having the kind of national penetration it achieved. Social movement theory stipulates that successful movements require not only a contentious issue to arouse activism but also a means of organization. Something must gather interested yet scattered individuals together into the movement. Radio broadcasting filled that mobilization role for the Polish ham boycott as it did for right-wing activism more generally.

As tempting as it is to dive into the particulars of the boycott, it is first necessary to understand the Kennedy administration's trade policy with the Eastern Bloc, those Eastern European nations that were allied, often forcibly, with the Soviet Union. Former British prime minister Winston Churchill had famously called the divide between US-aligned Western Europe and Soviet-aligned Eastern Europe an "Iron Curtain" separating free Western nations from those under Soviet domination. Although a vivid image, it was an over-simplification of a far more complicated set of relationships between Eastern Europe and the Soviet Union. Certainly, some nations like East Germany had puppet governments controlled by the Kremlin, but in 1953, with the death of Joseph Stalin, a wave of reformist unrest rippled through the Eastern Bloc. In Hungary that sentiment fueled an independence movement by Hungarian democratic socialists, although Soviet tanks ensured that it was a short-lived experiment. A similar movement in Poland managed, by avoiding outright revolution, to win the country a new measure of political autonomy. Further complicating the picture was Yugoslavia, which had a Communist government under Marshal Josip Tito but avoided alignment with either the United States or the Soviet Union.[15]

President Dwight Eisenhower saw these internal divisions as an opportunity to drive a nationalist wedge between Eastern Bloc nations and the Soviet Union. Autonomy for Eastern Europe meant headaches for Moscow. The carrot was trade with the United States. Eisenhower, and later Kennedy, thought that Eastern European countries—like the Baltic states and Albania—would look at the benefits of exchange with the United States, decide to imitate Poland, and agitate for greater autonomy from the Soviet Union. As John F. Kennedy, then a US senator from Massachusetts, put it, "Other satellites, we may be sure, are watching—and if we fail to help the Poles, who else will dare stand up to the Russians and look westward?"[16] Those tensions were even sharper when it came to Yugoslavia and Marshal Tito, whom Eisenhower called a "thorn in the Russian flesh." The Eisenhower administration funneled World War II–era surplus military equipment to Yugoslavia to keep the country neutral, which really meant, in Eisenhower's words, "Neutral on our side."[17] This "Yugoslaviazation" strategy would show the Eastern Bloc that independence from the Soviet Union meant friendship with the United States, a friendship that came with trade benefits.[18]

Free trade was the crucial component of this strategy. Exporting "soft" power in the form of US-manufactured televisions and radios would buttress military "hard" power by undermining the Warsaw Pact military alliance. In that spirit, President Eisenhower approved Poland for "most favored nation" (MFN) trade status in 1958, followed by Yugoslavia in 1960.[19] "Most favored nation" was a bit of a misnomer given that between eighty and ninety nations were so favored, but it did carry significant trade advantages. Any product exported from a country with MFN status paid the lowest tariff rate negotiated by the United States for that product with any other country. That could mean a tremendous reduction in export costs. With the flick of the president's pen, stores in the United States could now sell goods like Yugoslavian wicker baskets and Polish hams for less than half or a third of what they previously would have had to charge.[20]

Eisenhower and Kennedy had dangled an enticing carrot in front of Eastern Europe, but their strategy faced opposition back home from conservatives interested only in brandishing a stick at Communist-controlled countries. A decade and a half of anti-Communist paranoia had drilled into the American public the idea of a hegemonic, global Communist conspiracy that was centrally controlled by the Soviet Union. This talk of driving a tactical wedge between different varieties of nonaligned Communists, Eastern Bloc Communists, and Soviet Communists fell on deaf ears. When boycotters criticized the R. J. Reynolds Tobacco Co.—which manufactured Camel cigarettes—for using "COMMUNIST TOBACCO" grown in Yugoslavia, they thought it strange to be "aiding the Communists in Europe while our GIs die fighting Communism in Vietnam." While it was easy to criticize such a simplistic understanding of global Communism, President Kennedy could not readily assume the moral high ground. He had campaigned on a hardline anti-Communist platform in 1960—criticizing, for example, the Eisenhower administration for not intervening militarily to stop the Cuban Revolution— and was now reaping an anti-Communist whirlwind after sowing to the wind. Just as he had accused the Eisenhower administration of being soft on Communism as a candidate, now he was the target of those criticizing the government for "*mellowing-Communism*." Kennedy had asked Americans to consume Communist goods, promising them that Eastern European imports would go down as smoothly as smoking a Camel.[21] In effect, boycott proponents were asking why Polish ham and Yugoslavian baskets should be exempted from Kennedy's call to "pay any price, bear any burden, meet any hardship, support any friend, oppose any foe to assure the survival and suc- cess of liberty."[22]

TCTWOTAOCMOTLBS

In January 1962 Jerome Harold, a chiropractor in Miami, started a small protest group with a large name, "The Committee to Warn of the Arrival of Communist Merchandise on the Local Business Scene" (TCTWOTAOCMOTLBS).[23] Journalists could hardly contain their glee when they heard of the organization, making sure to insert the clunky ac- ronym into their ledes whenever possible.[24] Harold was a complete political unknown; being named "Chiropractor of the Year" by one's state licensing board is a compliment, but it hardly signals that the recipient will soon found a surprisingly effective political organization. He was, however, a member of the National Rifle Association, the American Legion, and, later in life, the board of Florida Bible College. Being a conservative and an evangel- ical Protestant would not have predisposed Harold to think well of a liberal Catholic like John F. Kennedy.[25] Although Harold did not give journalists a detailed accounting for his decision to start TCTWOTAOCMOTLBS (henceforth, "the Committee"), the fact that Harold lived near Miami and its large Cuban expatriate community likely played a role, especially so soon after the Bay of Pigs incident. Pictures of Castro were certainly featured in the group's literature, which would otherwise be strange given that the boycott ostensibly targeted Yugoslavia and Poland.[26]

The Committee seized on every critique of the Kennedy administration that it could, including playing on anti-elite prejudice, like when Harold commented that the Eastern European trade deal was "just another example of the fuzzy-minded thinking that goes on in Washington."[27] Washington technocrats might have Ivy League degrees and copious foreign policy experience, but trading with Communist nations while US servicemen fought Communism abroad felt like a basic violation of common sense to conservatives. How could "trade with the enemy . . . possibly weaken the enemy"? Conservatives felt that the State Department was trying to pull one over on them when they defended the trade program as a significant measure to undermine Soviet influence in Eastern Europe while also reassuring the public that the absolute dollar value of the trade was insignificant. It sounded to them like the State Department wanted to both have its Polish ham and eat it too. That logic did not make sense to conservatives, who snarkily made fun of State Department number-crunching expertise by wondering "just how many hams we have to buy from Poland before Khrushchev will set Poland free?" Furthermore, the Committee worried that since "a bullet costs less than a penny," the $85 million in sales of Communist goods could be converted into "a lot of pennies," each a potential bullet aimed at an American soldier.[28]

That concern inspired the following poem, which the Committee frequently reprinted:

> We trade iron ore for canned Polish ham.
> The slave-farmers starve, while our Uncle Sam
> Settles back to enjoy the Communist roast
> As the ore arrives at the Polish coast.
>
> Our State Department encourages this trade
> So, eat up, my Son, it's a cheaper priced grade.
> It's inspected by men from a Communist land
> Who started the war in South Viet Nam.

> They fashioned a bullet from that iron ore
> And to stop it, your son is called to the corps.
> "Killed in action" reads the brief telegram.
> Correction: "Killed in your kitchen by a Polish ham."

The poem's unknown author melodramatically argued that buying a Polish ham was as good as putting a bullet in a Vietcong rifle. Letters from worried parents suggest that the message hit its intended mark. As one mother wrote to broadcaster Carl McIntire, "My son is in Viet Nam. How long must we endure this[?]" She attached her note to a full-color advertisement for "Krakus: World Famous, Genuine Imported Polish Ham." It must have stung when she read the ad copy promising that a ham would make "a much appreciated Christmas Gift," a jarring reminder of her fears about her son's safety in a combat zone during an otherwise festive time of year.[29] Conservative broadcasters like McIntire provoked intense anger among their listeners about the Kennedy administration's trade policies—anger like that mother's anger on behalf of her son—and then channeled that anger in support of the Committee's trade boycott.

The Polish ham boycott took the Kennedy administration completely by surprise. The president had bipartisan support in Congress for expanding trade with Eastern Europe. He had secured the backing of both the Chamber of Commerce and the American Federation of Labor and Congress of Industrial Organizations (AFL-CIO) through promises of a liberal sprinkling of "adjustment assistance" cash.[30] With all the major interest groups on board and elite opinion behind him, the bill should have had smooth sailing through Congress. Confidence was at such a high level that a pro-administration journalist could title his editorial in the *New York Times*, "What Ever Happened to Smoot and Hawley?," a reference to the infamous tariff legislation from the 1930s. The bad, old days of protectionism seemed safely in the past as the Kennedy administration advanced the post–World War II free trade consensus. All Kennedy had to do was institute "a mammoth educational program to show that there is no future in saving the town and losing the nation."[31] If Washington elites had cared to listen at the time, they might have sensed a warning note in that line. The townspeople might not be quite so bullish about giving up their towns to "save" the nation, especially when they thought they were being asked to give up both.

Jerome Harold created the Committee the same month as the publication of the *Times* article in January 1962. By that fall, the organization would

Photo 2.1. This was the Christmas ad for Krakus ham referenced by the distraught mother worried about her son in Vietnam.

open affiliate chapters in 260 cities in each of the lower forty-eight states.[32] The decentralized nature of the Committee's organization helped it take the Kennedy administration by surprise. Jerome Harold controlled only the Miami chapter and played, at most, an advisory role in the creation of other chapters. He focused his efforts on designing pamphlets and cards that could be modified by local groups according to need, as well as distributing a how-to guide for starting one's own boycott chapter. Organizers did not need Harold's permission to start their own group, nor did they have to send any dues back to Miami.

Given such a low barrier to entry and widespread conservative discontent with the Kennedy administration's policy, Committee chapters spread rapidly. The chapter in Alton, Illinois, is typical. Mrs. William J. Droste, a thirty-six-year-old mother of two and a pharmacist's wife from the suburbs of St. Louis, became angry at her neighbors' ignorance about trade with Eastern Europe. After hearing on the radio about Harold's Miami Committee, she wrote to him for information about starting a chapter herself. She felt that if she did nothing "people would not know such things are going on" or that they were "helping to keep [workers in Communist countries] enslaved by buying their goods."[33] Mrs. Droste was not the only suburban housewife to lead a boycott chapter—a topic we will discuss in more detail later—but she is an example of the decentralized nature of the boycott movement.

Most boycott critics, with the exception of the White House itself, as we will see, missed the real source of the backlash. Miami may have been where the boycott movement originated, but it was the Radio Right that introduced the boycott to a national audience. Time and again, as with Mrs. William Droste in St. Louis, local boycott chapters began with the organizer hearing about Harold's Miami Committee on a conservative radio program. Ordinary conservatives, feeling frustration with the Kennedy administration, turned on their radios in the summer of 1962 and heard, finally, that somebody was doing something to challenge Kennedy. They believed that they could trust right-wing broadcasters to tell the real story about what was happening in America, to give flesh to their previously inchoate concerns. It is telling that almost all of the extant primary sources on the Polish ham boycott can be found in the form of listener letters to radio broadcasters.

Although listening to the radio may seem like an impersonal activity—a disembodied voice from a box—listeners clearly felt a vivid, personal connection to their favorite broadcasters. Mrs. Estrellita Capo—long-time listener but first-time writer—filled Carl McIntire in on her successful, one-woman effort to convince a supermarket chain to stop selling Communist goods. She had heard McIntire's full program covering the boycott effort in July 1962. When Mrs. Capo next visited her local A&P Store, she noticed that it stocked Yugoslavian-made folding chairs. She wrote a protest letter to corporate headquarters and the company promised to pull the chairs.[34] Mrs. Capo's letter is interesting not only as an example of the boycott in action but also because of what it reveals about the transmission of the idea for the boycott. She lived in Florida, just a few hours' drive away from Miami, where Jerome Harold had set up the first boycott committee. Yet it was not word of mouth or press coverage that brought the boycott to her attention. It was radio.

Indeed, almost all print press coverage of the boycott began after the movement had already peaked in the late fall of 1962. By that point the major right-wing broadcasters had been trumpeting the virtues of the boycott for the better part of six months. Carl McIntire's first broadcast dedicated to the boycott was on July 2, 1962; other broadcasters like Fulton Lewis and Dale Crowley soon joined in and continued the drumbeat throughout the fall.[35] Letters like Mrs. Estrellita Capo's poured in, crediting the broadcasters with inspiring the decision to act or simply describing what they had accomplished. A husband-and-wife team in Southern California heard McIntire's boycott broadcast and felt compelled to conduct a survey of their local retail stores, all three of which sold either Yugoslavian baskets or Polish tote bags. The manager of one store apologized for the products, but when the couple returned to check several days later they found canned pineapple from Red China, resulting in another tongue-lashing for the poor manager.[36] A boycotter in San Diego, California, wrote to McIntire after a successful protest over "Jugoslav" fruit baskets. "This victory," he wrote, "was probably due to you and your vigilance . . . [in] alerting all of America to this bit of enemy action."[37] The letter writer gave McIntire too much of the credit given that he did not actually start the boycott movement (although the letter writer's misattribution is revealing), but the Miami Committee would later thank Carl McIntire for publicizing their efforts.[38] To borrow an epidemiological term, radio was the primary transmission vector for the spread of the boycott movement. It was the key to transforming a small, local protest contained in just one city into a large-scale, national movement.

Every community that passed a boycott ordinance had at least one local station airing McIntire's radio program, which is not surprising given the general prevalence of stations airing conservative broadcasting. Conservative radio brought local activists like Mrs. Droste in St. Louis, Mrs. Capo in

St. Augustine, and thousands of others around the country into contact with Jerome Harold's Committee in Miami. Radio nationalized local activism. The changing landscape of the radio industry in the 1950s had made possible the rapid expansion of conservative broadcasting. That in turn created the preconditions necessary for the creation of a conservative grassroots that would give the New Right national political influence during the Polish ham boycott in 1962, the election of 1964, and thereafter.

Tips for Hosting a Successful Boycott Card Party

The backing of right-wing broadcasters was necessary for the Polish ham boycott to succeed, but it also needed to offer a compelling product. Consumption in the post–World War II era was not only meant to fulfill the "American Dream" of prosperity and freedom but also designed to be fun. This was the golden age of the product party. When you needed cosmetics or seal-fresh containers, you turned to your local Avon or Mary Kay lady or the Tupperware representative. Their in-home product demonstrations were dressed up as parties (with the added incentive of a "special prize" for the person who agreed to host). Burping plastic and pink Cadillacs were a staple of suburban life in 1960s America. The boycott movement took advantage of this well-worn approach, but instead of demonstrating *for* products, it demonstrated *against* products. If Tupperware and makeup represented the technological progress and ostensible social stability of modern America, then Polish ham and Yugoslavian wicker baskets symbolized the ever-present danger of global Communism.

Still, there was no need for the fight against Communism to be dull. With the proper organization and tactics, even a boycott could be fun. It was in this spirit that boycotters took to calling their protest actions "card parties." The cards themselves were small, two-inch-by-three-inch slips of paper printed on the front with tongue-in-cheek slogans like "Always Buy Your Communist Products at Super Giant" or "This Has Been Inspected for Your Table by a Real Good Communist."[39] On the back, it might commend purchasers for helping to "bankrupt American industry," "deplete America's gold reserve," or "strengthen communism's grip on the captive nations." The boycotters' mission, should they choose to accept it, was to hide these cards all over the offending store. You might leave half a dozen in the restroom, tuck more behind display pieces, and finish by depositing a card in the front breast pocket of every suit coat in the men's department. A Dallas drugstore was forced to issue refunds for shaving kits, over-the-counter drugs, and even a tube of toothpaste because cards had been found carefully inserted into the packaging.[40] One Bullock's manager found more than nine hundred cards scattered about his store. The department store chain was not amused and filed a lawsuit asking for a ludicrous $3 million in damages from the local Committee chapter, as well as a restraining order against its members.[41] While the size of the damages was certainly exaggerated, one goal of the card party was indeed to inflict additional costs on retailers by forcing them to pay overtime to employees searching each shelf or product for the cards.[42]

Careful planning was vital to maximize impact. Given that store managers might call the police—as happened on more than a few occasions—it was important to schedule the card party for peak shopping times. Even if the police did not show, having so many legitimate customers in the store made it harder for store employees to keep an eye on the boycotters and thus snatch up the cards immediately after they were put down. Further preparation meant gathering beforehand to synchronize watches, go over store floorplans, and assign a specific area to each boycotter. Some card parties had as many as forty participants swarming the store; an irate manager or the police might be able to catch one or two, but not everyone.[43] The Miami Committee's guidelines tried to reassure boycotters that it was unlikely that store owners would "prosecute or sue participants" given the bad public relations that would ensue.[44] That did not prevent card party participants in multiple cities from being taken down to the station by the police. But Harold was right about one thing; there's no record of any boycotted store actually pressing charges. A few hours in jail was the worst that the card partier might endure. If anything, that possibility lent the endeavor an air of danger and excitement. They could enjoy the sense of subversion without having to fully pay for the consequences of vandalism or trespassing.

Card party participants were encouraged to gather after the blitz to swap stories about the clever places they had found to hide cards or to chuckle over their near run-ins with store employees or the police. For added fun, the Miami Committee suggested playing a "solitaire" variant of the card party game. A few days after the initial card party, a lone boycotter would return to the site of the crime and leave a few, poorly hidden cards. The goal was to strike "horror" in the hearts of store employees who were worried that they might have been the victim of another large-scale protest and thus be forced to spend hours fruitlessly combing the store for nonexistent

Photos 2.2 and 2.3. Two examples of the cards spread around retail stores during boycott "card parties."
Carl McIntire Papers, Special Collections, Princeton Theological Seminary Library.

cards. Alternately, boycott chapters could try playing "Camera Club," a kind of photo scavenger hunt in which boycotters gathered around a display of Communist-produced goods and snapped pictures of themselves. If the store manager disrupted the photo op, he or she would simply draw even more attention to the protest from other shoppers.[45]

Given how decentralized the boycott movement was and how little archival documentation has been preserved, it is not possible to give precise statistics about how many boycott chapters hosted card parties. However, newspaper articles about the boycott movement invariably mentioned card parties proliferating in small towns and major cities all across the country. Indeed, as we will see later, President Kennedy's personal secretary chose to illustrate the power of the boycott by mentioning card partiers. As a direct-action tactic, card parties were uniquely suited for attracting attention, for what newspaper could resist tales of housewife saboteurs trolling corporate executives? But the boycott also employed other, more typical methods of putting pressure on retailers. They could demand refunds, start letter-writing campaigns, and, in at least one case, sponsor a bonfire of Yugoslavian baskets and invite the local newspaper photographer to attend.[46] No corporate press office enjoys being deluged with letters like the one a Mr. H. D. Bamper wrote to Anheuser Busch complaining about "drinking beer with a Communist tinge" after learning that the company used Yugoslavian hops.[47] Others complained to the Better Business Bureau instead, placing indirect pressure on companies to publicly discuss their purchasing policies.[48]

Although it is possible to reconstruct boycotter tactics from newspaper accounts, there is a detailed, firsthand description of a card party. Mrs. Mildred "Millie" Sakewicz, who lived in the western suburbs of Philadelphia, was an inveterate listener to Carl McIntire's radio show.[49] Mrs. Sakewicz knew her neighborhood well and enjoyed sharing that information with others. In a word, she was a gossip. She had even won a prize ($5) for tipping off her local newspaper about a layoff at the Westinghouse plant.[50] She also happened to be employed at an E. J. Korvette department store. During the mid-twentieth century Korvette filled the gap between the decline of five-and-dime stores and the rise of discount stores like Walmart and Costco. Given their dependence on high-volume, low-margin sales, chains like Korvette stood to benefit the most from cheap Eastern European imports—unless, of course, the boycotters made enough of a fuss that selling such products was no longer worth their while. Millie's store was boycotted in the fall of 1962 and her account of the event is particularly interesting because she was both an insider and an outsider, sympathetic to the boycotters but also a store employee.

It was at Millie's branch that the card partiers stuffed the breast pockets of every suit coat with a card and scattered them throughout the store. When the store manager had two of the partiers arrested, they responded by swarming the store with "carloads" of additional protestors, making such a fuss that the corporate office instructed the local manager not to press charges. That may have had something to do with the corporate switchboard being overrun with calls from customers who promised never to shop at Korvette until all Eastern Bloc goods had been removed. Since the threat of arrest had been taken off the table, the manager gathered the employees and instructed them to remove all the offending goods but only "until things quieted down." At that point, they would put the products back on the shelves. Millie asked McIntire to avoid mentioning that meeting on the radio since her manager would then realize he had a mole among his employees. He would have been especially bothered by Millie's leak of sales figures for that Korvette branch, which dipped by between $118,000 and $125,000 (nearly $1 million in 2016 adjusted for inflation) during the month of the boycott. One card party and a few dozen activists were enough to reduce the earnings of that Korvette store a rather significant amount; indeed, Millie's branch of Korvette, long established in the community, temporarily earned less than a nearby branch that had just recently opened.[51] Carl McIntire's papers do not include a follow-up letter from Millie, so it is not known whether E. J. Korvette weathered the boycott successfully and subsequently returned Eastern Bloc goods to its store shelves, but it is a compelling example of the power that the boycotters wielded.

E. J. Korvette was not the only company to feel the financial pinch from the boycott. A major variety store chain—on the condition of anonymity—admitted to a $100,000 write-down on Yugoslavian baskets alone.[52] Those kinds of losses added up quickly. The Polish Embassy in conjunction with the US Commerce Department estimated that the trade boycott had caused a $5 million drop in trade with Poland over the course of just a few months in 1962.[53] That was a lot of dollars representing a lot of retailers dropping a lot of Eastern Bloc goods. A few retailers defied the boycott, like Bullock's previously mentioned $3 million lawsuit, but they were the exception rather than the rule. By one count, sixty-one major retail chains discontinued all purchases of Communist-manufactured products as a result of the boycott. That included S. S. Kresge (today, Kmart), Diana Stores Corporation (today, Linens 'n Things), Walgreens, Sears Roebuck and Company, F. W. Woolworth and its 3,000 stores, and retail behemoth A&P with its 4,500 stores and $5 billion in total sales.[54] The boycott had won concessions from the largest retailers in the country.

Even Disneyland was forced to promise that it would ban its third-party vendors from selling the products in the future while unconvincingly blaming the mix-up on "obsolete inventory" that had mysteriously snuck into the park's souvenir shops. Many retailers followed Disneyland's example and responded to inquiries with profusely apologetic letters that shifted the blame to someone else. Macy's blamed the State Department itself because it had made a "specific request" to the retailer to buy "a token amount of merchandise from certain Communist countries, the total of which represented less than one-tenth of 1% of our purchases." Sometimes, rather than laying the blame on the government, corporate public relations executives pointed to local store managers for taking too much initiative or blamed purchasing agents who were excessively price conscious. We are so very sorry that one of our employees, "only interested in getting the best values for our customers," got a bit carried away. If we are guilty of anything, it really should be that we try a little too hard to look out for you, oh dearest customer. In any case, the content of your letter was so "very true" and "your expression of your thoughts . . . done so well that they were actually inspiring."[55] Overacting is a vice on the silver screen, but in public relations it can be an absolute virtue.

Inordinate Ordinances

By fall 1962 retailers were hemorrhaging sales from the boycott, but their situation grew even worse by early 1963. Twenty-six town or county councils passed ordinances targeting the retail of Eastern European products. Although the legal specifications differed from place to place, in general the regulations had three components. First, any retailer selling the goods was required to apply for a license to do so and pay a fee ranging from $1,000 to 5,000, a not-insignificant barrier to entry even for chain stores. Second, most of the ordinances stipulated that compliant retailers would also have to prominently display signage announcing that the store was "Licensed to Sell Communist Imports." Some of the ordinances went so far as to require that all official store letterhead and public advertisements include that fact as well. Others forced retailers to tag each individual product with a warning label, effectively giving vigilante card partiers the force of law. Third, storeowners that skirted the regulations could face fines of up to $500 and six months in jail.[56]

Newspaper coverage of the boycott ordinances skewed toward cute or curious examples, like that of the boycott ordinance in Fountain Valley, California. Today, Fountain Valley is a bedroom community for Los Angeles, but in 1962 it was a freshly incorporated town (est. 1957) with just 2,500 people. Its inaugural town council was composed of five men, each of whom listed their occupation as either a farmer or a rancher. In the nineteenth century the area was known as the "Gospel Swamps" for its combination of a high water table and a higher-than-average number of churches. As historian Darren Dochuk has noted, this area of Southern California drew a large number of white southern transplants, who brought with them their plain-folk evangelicalism and small-d "democratic" politics. Like many other Orange County communities, their descendants were skeptical of Communists, labor unions, and anything that smacked of liberalism. Indeed, when the town council met to approve the boycott ordinance, they also enacted a rule automatically dismissing any municipal employee who supported the "introduction of a labor union into any organization or department of the city." The anti-labor rule, like the boycott ordinance, passed unanimously.[57]

Just because Fountain Valley was a deeply conservative town did not mean its business owners appreciated the boycott ordinance. In fact, they were unanimously opposed, albeit "unanimous" in this case means that both store owners in town—there was a gas station and a café—found the rules onerous. The café owner, Joann Dykstra, complained about the "ridiculous" rules to a reporter while throwing three offending Polish sausages to her Weimaraner pup. (No doubt the journalist included that ironic detail because it was a breed created in an area of East Germany that was then behind the Iron Curtain.) The gas station operator identified that the licensing fee was "really a penalty" and protested that "if it's legal to import the stuff into this country, I ought to be able to sell it without a license. They're eating away at our individual rights." He was right. The $1,000 ordinance was a penalty designed to discourage the retail of the products, as was the requirement that the storefront sign announcing his Communist products have at least six-inch-high letters.[58]

The situation in Fountain Valley is humorous because of the low stakes involved, just two stores and three sausages. Add in five loaves of bread and two fish and you are still short a miracle. Yet by no means were such ordinances restricted to small farming communities. Twenty-four towns or cities across the country passed boycott regulations, including Montgomery and Birmingham, Alabama; Columbus, Georgia; Columbus, Ohio; Fort Lauderdale, Florida; and Jefferson Parish, Louisiana.[59]

Twenty-four municipalities is just under 10% of the more than 260 cities in forty-eight states that had boycott chapters, but it is enough to show that the boycott was not just a minor, backwoods backlash but the product of a truly national, grassroots movement that had the ability to sway city councils in major population centers.[60] Furthermore, as Figure 2.2 shows, boycott ordinances had the best chance of passage in areas with high concentrations of right-wing radio stations.

Alabama was tied with Ohio for the state with the most municipal boycott ordinances, so it is not surprising that it led in another metric of boycott success. While there are more than a dozen towns named "Warsaw" in the United States, the residents of Warsaw, Alabama, were not allowed to purchase any Polish ham because the state government had labeled it "diseased, unclean and unfit for human consumption." The intent was expressly protectionist, preventing competition for Alabaman farmers from "foreign imported meats flooding our markets." The man behind the ban was Alabama Commissioner of Agriculture Arvel Woodfin Todd, who perhaps not coincidentally owned a chicken farm himself. (Todd may also have instituted the ban in preparation for his failed bid for the governor's seat two years later.) Whatever his motivations, the self-proclaimed "Todd Plan" was quickly emulated by other state agriculture commissioners, including those of Florida, Georgia, Mississippi, Louisiana, and Tennessee.[61] That the bans

Figure 2.2. Station map overlaid with communities that passed Polish ham boycott ordinances, 1962.

would begin in Alabama is not surprising given that the state's two largest cities, including its capital, had passed boycott ordinances a year prior. The boycott had grown from three sausage links in Fountain Valley to three-quarters of a million pounds of meat in Alabama.

The Boycott Blues

Even as early as 1962 the Yugoslavian and Polish embassies were complaining about the sudden drop in trade volume resulting from the boycotters. Yugoslavia estimated the loss at $3 million, or about 6.5% of their total trade with the United States; up until that point trade had been steadily rising, up by 18% through the first ten months of 1962 alone. And Poland saw a $2.6 million drop in the export of hams alone. The Polish ham boycott had placed the Kennedy administration under serious pressure to revise its trade policy.[62]

Kennedy's solution to the crisis was to try and wait the boycott out while conserving political capital. The boycott came at a particularly inconvenient moment as Congress debated the Trade Expansion Act during September and October of 1962, voting to pass the legislation just a few weeks before midterm elections. The Trade Expansion Act granted the president unilateral authority to lower tariffs by up to 50% without further congressional approval.[63] The bill should have sailed through Congress without significant alterations given the Democratic majority in both houses, but this was after a long summer of increasing boycott pressure. Kennedy did what he could behind the scenes, like commissioning George F. Kennan—an old foreign policy hand and the US ambassador to Yugoslavia—to lobby for the act, but the president avoided publicly supporting the bill. Public support might have endangered other policy initiatives.[64] As George F. Kennan would later say of his boss, Kennedy was worried by the "tenuousness of his majority in the election and the fact that he felt he had bigger fish to fry with Congress."[65] That kind of political capital calculation would not have been necessary prior to the boycott.

To Kennedy's chagrin, when the bill passed in October 1962, it included an amendment revoking MFN status for both Yugoslavia and Poland. It was a sharp if mostly symbolic rebuke to the administration's trade policy. Kennedy could use his newly expanded trade authority to negotiate deals with Poland and Yugoslavia that were similar to MFN status, but the amendment was still an embarrassing political defeat. Kennedy publicly addressed the boycott for the first time two months later at a White House press conference, when he suggested that activists who really wanted to make a difference should join the Peace Corps, not accuse "some merchant [who] happens to have Polish hams in his shop" of being unpatriotic. It was too little, too late.[66]

Three days after the Trade Expansion Act was enacted, the Kennedy administration faced a new foreign policy crisis, albeit one that gave the president a chance to regain face with the public. The act passed on a Thursday and by Sunday the Cuban Missile Crisis was underway. By publicly standing up to Nikita Khrushchev in October of 1962—while secretly granting concessions to the Soviets regarding US missile bases in Turkey—Kennedy defanged conservative critics who had accused the president of vacillating during the Bay of Pigs invasion and advancing Soviet interests through his Eastern European trade policy. Kennedy used this dearly bought political capital to push for a Nuclear Test Ban Treaty during the summer and fall of 1963, a topic we will return to in the next chapter. It also gave him the public support needed to convince Congress to return MFN status to Poland and Yugoslavia, although the bill would not pass until December 1963, a month after Kennedy's assassination.[67]

Having achieved a symbolic victory with the Trade Expansion Act, the pace of the boycott effort slowed after the fall of 1962. Most of the municipal ordinances were not actually enforced; the few cities that attempted to do so found that the courts generally sided with shopkeepers.[68] Regulating interstate and international commerce was, after all, a prerogative of the federal government, not city governments. However, the municipal ordinances were significant not because of their effectiveness in preventing the sale of Eastern European products but as a capstone on the vastly more effective private sector boycott movement. The card partiers had compelled dozens of the largest retailers in the country to drop the offending products, convinced at least two dozen major cities to enact ordinances, and swayed Congress itself into denying MFN status to Yugoslavia and Poland. All of these were temporary victories, but still remarkable given that the movement began with a single Miami chiropractor less than a year earlier.

Anti-Communist Housewife Populism

A demographic analysis of the boycott movement challenges portrayals of 1960s conservatism as the near-exclusive preserve of angry, lower-class, white men. Dan Carter's influential biography of George Wallace, *The Politics of Rage: George Wallace, the Origins of the New Conservatism, and the Transformation of American Politics*, ably captures the anger felt by conservative Southern Democrats toward civil rights reform—which certainly existed—but it is an example of the disproportionate focus in the historical literature on white *male* anger as the primary driver for the rise of the New Right.[69] By focusing on massive resistance, working-class angst, and male anger, this narrative minimizes the roles played by conservative women, the middle class, and issues not directly related to race.

There is a counternarrative from historians like Lisa McGirr, Mary Brennan, and Michelle Nickerson, who argue that while the formal, political leadership of the New Right skewed male, the movement itself was inculcated at coffee klatches, book clubs, and parent teacher association meetings, all spaces dominated by women. A fourth site can be added to that list. A disproportionate number of card party organizers and participants were middle-class women whose involvement in the boycott was an expression of "housewife populism," to borrow Michelle Nickerson's phrase.[70]

These housewives tapped into the tradition of Republican motherhood, which had tasked wives and mothers in the early eighteenth century with instilling domestic virtue. Reformers later in the nineteenth century justified their activism outside the home as part of the effort to inculcate virtue in the national "home." That impulse was wedded with populist anti-elitism around the turn of the twentieth century to target robber barons and slum lords. Conservative housewife populists in the 1960s were inheritors of this tradition, although they targeted unresponsive Washington bureaucrats rather than the predatory rich. The women of the Polish ham boycott saw themselves as a virtuous bulwark against the Communist goods that would corrupt both the nation and the home. Notably, most boycotting housewives signed their letters with "Mrs." By contrast, male writers almost never referred to themselves with an honorific. In the gender structure of the time, being a married woman conferred social status; choosing to write those three little letters in the context of the boycott was thus a political act, a claim of special standing before the body politic.[71]

Simply noting the addresses of the pro-boycott letters that poured into the offices of conservative broadcasters reveals something about the class and gender of card partiers. They came overwhelmingly from the suburbs of major cities, like Chicago, St. Louis, San Diego, Philadelphia, Seattle, Memphis, and New Orleans. Some were employed, like Mrs. Mildred "Millie" Sakewicz, but many were housewives with husbands employed in white-collar professions, like Mrs. William J. Droste, who had married a pharmacist. They were beneficiaries of the post–World War II economic expansion and had new cars, houses, and modern appliances, giving them the time and financial freedom for political activism. Furthermore, their whiteness and middle-class position insulated them from some of the risks of their activism. They could laugh off the possibility of being arrested and jailed, for what police department would imprison a local businessman's wife for the petty crime of putting cards in coat pockets? Privilege may be blind, but it also can enable political activism by lowering the legal barrier to entry.

It was a strategy familiar enough that it became a plot device in an episode of the hit TV show *Maude* that aired in 1972. The titular protagonist of the show, played by Bea Arthur of eventual *Golden Girls* fame, decides to stage a protest of 146 housewives in solidarity with the local grocery store's bag boy who had been arrested for marijuana possession. When her husband objects that she will be arrested herself, Maude confidently declares, "You know darn well they aren't going to put a group of upper middle-class housewives in jail."[72] Yet by the end of the episode, despite Maude's noble intentions, the bag boy is sent to jail. After a moment of head shaking by both Maude and the chief of police over the excessive sentence levied, the audience is allowed to laugh off the tension by retreating into jokes about the grand and yet ineffective actions of liberal women like Maude. The tenor of the episode, despite inviting a surface-level progressive reading, is generally dismissive of the agency of activist women and skeptical of their ability to influence the public sphere in meaningful ways. Yet it is ultimately revealing of the extent to which housewife populism had become an ordinary form of protest during the 1960s while remaining subversive enough that the male producers of the TV show had to resort to ridicule to avoid unsettling the watching audience.

While *Maude*'s depiction of politically engaged yet ineffective housewife activism failed to fully grapple with how much consumer power women wielded, there was an even more timely depiction that fell short of that reality, albeit in a different way. At the peak of the Polish ham boycott in late 1962, Betty Friedan was putting the finishing touches on her book *The Feminine Mystique*. Friedan depicted middle-class housewives as frustrated domestic goddesses. They had the freedom to "choose automobiles, clothes, appliances, [and] supermarkets," but at night they lay beside their husbands asking themselves, "Is this all?" And when friends and neighbors visited, the men sat on one side of the room and "talked shop or politics or septic tanks," while the women could only discuss "how to keep their husbands happy, or improve their children's school, or cook chicken or make slipcovers."[73] *The Feminine Mystique* quickly became a bestselling book and turned Friedan into a national icon for the nascent second-wave feminist movement. She had clearly put her finger on a very real sense of stultification among educated women who had been pushed out of career paths and into more limited suburban horizons.

Yet Friedan's depiction of suburban housewives is very much at odds with what we have seen of card partiers. At a card party the hostess was in command, plotting direct action, assigning targets, and planning for contingencies should the police get involved. Card-partying housewives took center stage, talking politics in the living room while their husbands were relegated to the corner or back patio where they could talk about their silly cars and stultifying corporate jobs. This is not to suggest that Friedan was inaccurate in her portrayal of suburban life but that her portrayal was incomplete. For every frustrated housewife relying on tranquilizers to get through the drudgery and metaphysical ennui of daily life, there was a housewife channeling that frustration into local political activism. For some, that meant joining liberal advocacy groups like the National Organization for Women and pushing for expanded reproductive rights; for others that meant starting a Polish ham boycott chapter and getting out the vote for Barry Goldwater.

Friedan's portrayal of apolitical, frustrated suburban housewives relied on two questionable assumptions. First, Friedan underestimated the political power wielded by housewives who had a disproportionate say over household consumption. Cars, clothes, and houses were given as evidence of the hollowness of the American Dream, as suburbanites sought meaning in the pursuit of material happiness. Yet dollars were also a source of power, a means of exercising political influence outside of formal or electoral politics. Some housewives turned to material consumption as a substitute for career aspirations, a way to try and crowd out internal dissatisfaction, but consumption could also be used to reshape the world outside the household. To borrow a concept from historian Lizabeth Cohen, boycotting housewives were "citizen consumers" who wielded purchasing power as political power.[74]

There is a fascinating exchange between a boycotting housewife and the editor of *Good Housekeeping* magazine that illustrates the gendered and political power of consumption. The magazine had bestowed its "Good Housekeeping Seal of Approval" on several Eastern European imports.[75] Mrs. Alice J. Miller, of Portland, Oregon, wrote Wade Nichols, the magazine's editor-in-chief, to complain about its endorsement of Polish hams. Nichols had been hired by *Good Housekeeping* to guide the aging women's magazine in a more progressive direction. He featured stories about women who successfully and winsomely balanced both domestic and career obligations. Indeed, it was under Nichols's leadership that *Good Housekeeping* published Betty Friedan's 1960 article—"Women Are People, Too!"—which she would subsequently expand into book form as the *Feminine Mystique*.[76]

Yet Nichols's letter to Alice Miller betrays little of that progressive sentiment. After briefly defending the safety and cleanliness of imported Polish ham, Nichols challenged Miller to stop trying "to legislate as an individual" and instead "accept the thoroughly considered conclusions of our Congressional and Executive leaders." It went without saying that those leaders were almost all men. The tenor of the letter implied that Nichols thought Mrs. Alice Miller a silly woman with ideas above her station; Nichols missed no opportunity to patronize Miller, defending the magazine's position by referring to this "immensely involved matter" involving arguments that "filled thousands of pages of the Congressional Record."[77] Why would Nichols write such a stern response to a subscriber like Mrs. Miller? He recognized that the boycott had the power to disrupt congressional and executive policymaking, something that may have made him uncomfortable because it meant that women were using their power over domestic consumption to influence male-dominated formal politics. Gender progressivism might have helped sell copies of the magazine, but boycott activism would not receive *Good Housekeeping*'s seal of approval.

Friedan erred not only by dismissing the power of consumption but also in downplaying the significance of local political activism. She pooh-poohed women who discussed how to "improve their children's schools." Yet as the next decade of conservative politics revealed, school boards and parent teacher associations were vital sites of gendered political activism. In one famous example, a West Virginia housewife named Alice Moore would lead a revolt in 1974 in Kanawha County against state textbook standards using massive rallies, wildcat strikes, and school shutdowns. Textbook controversies are now a staple of local politics as school board members across the country routinely call for bans on books that are too sexually explicit, historically revisionist, pro-socialist, or any of dozens of other criticisms.[78]

The significance of local, gendered activism might have escaped Betty Friedan in 1963, but it was not lost on President Kennedy. In the fall of 1963, as the president prepared for his re-election campaign, White House aide

Myer Feldman sent Kennedy a lengthy memorandum outlining the threat from the "radical right." Feldman worried that while it was possible to gather information about major conservative broadcasters and organizations—like Carl McIntire and the John Birch Society—it was almost impossible to calculate the "membership and finances of local right-wing organizations scattered around the country that harass local school boards, local librarians, and local government bodies" despite being "a formidable force in American life today." Feldman specifically mentioned the "card party movement" as an example of this kind of grassroots activism that had thus far slipped under the Democratic Party leadership's radar.[79] The steps the president would take to undermine this threat is the subject of the next three chapters, but for now suffice it to say that card party housewives had seized the attention of the White House itself through their persistent activism.

The boycott is just one example of a consistent pattern of disproportionate female influence in conservative activism during the 1960s. That pattern emerges in sharp relief from listener letters sent to conservative broadcasters, the largest collection of which are contained in the papers of Carl McIntire. The typical listener was middle-aged, married or widowed, and a mother. For example, McIntire's files include two folders stuffed with letters from listeners who had written in to protest after their local radio station stopped carrying the *Twentieth Century Reformation Hour*. Of the 163 letters received from those cities in the weeks following the cancellations, female listeners wrote 125 and men just 38.[80] That same pattern, albeit not quite as heavily skewed, showed up in donation totals. In a random sample of donor letters from July 1959 to December 1960, women contributed fifty-four of the eighty-nine checks received.[81] Donating money and launching letter-writing campaigns was par for the course. As Mrs. Lila Hughes of Odessa, Texas, said in her letter to McIntire, "I have been asked, 'Why do you get all het [sic] up about it? You can't help matters any.' I know I can't do anything but try to learn, and speak up about what I have learned."[82] Throughout the 1960s conservative women learned new forms of political activism while speaking up loudly enough to be heard in far-off Washington, DC.

Card Parties as Social Movement Formation

Whatever the scope of its effects on international trade policy and electoral politics, the Polish ham boycott should interest historians because of what it reveals about conservative social movement formation during the mid-twentieth century. Movements like the boycott were the "stuff" from which modern conservatism was created. The rapidity with which a local group could be catapulted onto the national stage by right-wing broadcasters shocked liberal policymakers in 1962, so much so that they took rather extreme measures to silence those broadcasters, as detailed in the next three chapters. But before moving on to the anti-broadcasting campaign, it is worth considering how a relatively brief event like the boycott contributed to something much bigger, the rise of modern conservatism as a durable force in national politics.

For many boycotters this was the first time they felt connected to a broader movement. For example, Jeanne Thomas, a longshoreman's wife in Seattle, had listened to Carl McIntire's boycott broadcast in July 1962. Her husband then discussed the boycott with a friend who worked for a furniture rental company and who subsequently saw crates marked with "Made in Yugoslavia" in the warehouse where he worked. The arc of the boycott went from local (Miami) to national (radio) and back to local (Seattle) again, a pattern that repeated all over the country. It was this sense of connectedness to a broader movement that gave Jeanne Thomas the courage necessary to "step up my efforts in combatting this communism, socialism and internationalism."[83] Only someone with a sense of ownership in a movement would go to the lengths of many of these boycotters. They would visit stores repeatedly, carefully checking each shelf for the offending products. They spent time and effort organizing card parties and launching letter-writing campaigns directed at congressmen and corporate headquarters. They had fully bought into the cause and sought to convince friends and neighbors to do likewise.

But for a social movement to get off the ground its participants need at least a taste of success. The boycotters got a full three-course meal, complete with appetizer (card parties), entree (boycott ordinances), and dessert (repeal of MFN status). Think of how intoxicating it must have felt to single-handedly force an entire department store chain to change its policy. Take Mrs. Estrellita Capo, the St. Augustine housewife mentioned previously, who spoke up and convinced her local A&P store to change its policy. That would have counted as a thrilling victory by any measure, but the specific circumstances heightened the sense of accomplishment. Two weeks after sending her letter to A&P corporate headquarters in New York City, Mrs. Capo heard the doorbell ring. It was with "great surprise and joy," she wrote later, that she opened the door to find the local A&P store manager, who informed her that the offending products would be "immediately removed." By joining the boycott movement a Florida housewife had forced a company with 4,500 stores and $5 billion in sales to change its policy and send a representative to issue an apology in person. As Mrs. Capo, in her understated way, confided to Carl McIntire about the experience, "I can't tell you how happy it made me feel."[84] If you want to create an army of activist foot soldiers, giving them that sense of empowerment is a good first step.

Experiences like that made boycotters feel invincible. When told by the head of the local boycott committee that he was concerned the government would come after them for their activities, Dale Crowley Sr., a radio evangelist in Arlington, Virginia, responded, "I dare the State Department to lay a hand on you." Not only did Crowley participate in an arguably illegal action, in this case blanketing a Super Giant grocery store with cards, but also he made no effort to conceal his identity, taking to the airwaves on a local radio station to encourage listeners to flood the switchboards of Super Giant headquarters with phone calls. Super Giant threatened prosecution—they had identities and a confession after all—but Crowley was confident it was an empty threat. He was right.[85] If sixty major retailers had already backed down because of the boycott, why would you not feel supremely confident that Super Giant would make sixty-one?

Success in one conservative campaign often led to involvement in others. Multiple letter writers, having heard Carl McIntire's program for the first time in connection to the boycott, then asked for additional information about other conservative causes. In social movements, as in life, one thing leads to another. For example, after Jeanne Thomas, the longshoreman's wife in Seattle, pledged herself to "step up [my] efforts" in the fight against socialism and internationalism, she asked for additional literature produced by McIntire's program. Specifically, she requested a pamphlet calling for the repeal of the federal income tax via constitutional amendment. That amendment was known as the "Liberty Amendment" and had been first proposed nearly twenty years before by an anti–New Deal newspaper reporter; in 1959 arch-conservative Representative James Utt (R-California) introduced the amendment in Congress and ultimately succeeded in getting it ratified in nine states. There was a logical connection between the boycott and opposition to the income tax; if the federal government could give Communist-produced goods with one hand, it could also take a share of the taxpayer's earnings with the other. When right-wing broadcasters introduced Jeanne

Thomas to the boycott, they were also providing her with an entry point into the conservative movement as a whole.[86]

It is worth taking a step back and considering whether these card partiers were participating in a true social movement. Social movement theory, which originated in sociology departments in the 1970s, traditionally focused on progressive movements like second-wave feminism and the black freedom struggle. For something to be considered a social movement it needed to feature an underrepresented group making rights-based claims using tactics outside the formal political process. Since conservative activists tended to be privileged—disproportionately middle class and white—early social movement theorists generally excluded them from analysis even when they otherwise acted exactly like members of social movements. A new generation of sociologists in the 1990s began paying more attention to conservative social movements, but such groups are still often framed in reactionary terms as responses to progressive (read, "more authentic") social movements.[87] They were always the "anti": anti-abortion, anti-feminist, anti-gay, and so on.

The Polish ham boycott is a poor fit for that schema. The boycott was against something, certainly, but the decision to allow the import of Eastern European products was not a reaction against a countervailing social movement. Rather, the card partiers believed that their opposition to the Eastern Bloc trade had been discounted by unelected State Department officials and a president whose popularity ratings had sunk to new lows after the Bay of Pigs debacle. It struck them as essentially undemocratic, allowing them to frame themselves as a marginalized group fighting against the political establishment. They were white, middle class, and privileged, but those attributes did not automatically grant political influence. So they resorted to contentious collective action (à la card parties), which subsequently won them the influence needed to push for changes via the formal political process (congressional revocation of MFN status and municipal boycott ordinances).

That would not have been possible on a mass, collective scale were it not for conservative broadcasting. To use social movement language, radio broadcasting enabled the "mobilization" of conservative dissent into social movement action. Sociologist Charles Tilly defined mobilization as "an increase of the resources available to a political actor for collective making of claims."[88] The combination of a sudden decline in the cost of radio broadcasting and the rise of independent station ownership in the late 1950s made it possible for conservatives to much more efficiently forge an activist network. Previously, they had been forced to rely on newspaper and other printed media to spread their message, but radio could reach an even wider audience at a lower price point. Furthermore, broadening the audience made it easier to raise money. As Carl McIntire's previously discussed finances show, donations to radio programs were individually insignificant but impressive in the aggregate. The rise of conservative broadcasting increased available resources both by lowering the cost of distributing conservative ideas and by making it easier to solicit contributions.[89]

To switch from the language of sociology to that of economics, resource mobilization can be thought of as a shift in the supply of a point of view. Conservative broadcasting made it easier to spread conservative ideas, thus sparking the rise of the New Right. Historians specializing in the rise of modern conservatism have traditionally focused on the demand side of the equation, looking for the right combination of hot-button issues that finally ignited conservative dissent. Yet while changes in the demand for conservative ideas certainly deserve consideration, they are only half the equation. Political historians should give more consideration to the ways in which changes in the supply of conservative ideas—whether induced by technological innovation, regulatory changes, or industrial development—propelled the movement's surprising advance in the early 1960s. As the next five chapters detail, it did not take long for those opposed to the conservative movement to realize that they needed to reverse the process, for if resources could be mobilized via broadcasting, then undermining broadcasting was the key to demobilizing the New Right.

The Radio Right's Southern Strategy

Whatever one thinks of the politics involved, the stories of housewife-led boycotts, accounts of mildly subversive card parties, and readings of dramatic anti–Polish ham poetry can have a certain underdog charm. But it is important to remember that to be conservative in the early 1960s almost invariably meant support for Jim Crow segregation. As historian Elizabeth Gillespie McRae has shown, conservative housewife populism in a white supremacist social order also meant organizing grassroots action to protect the home from miscegenation, desegregation, and integration.[90] On the other side of the ideological spectrum, civil rights activists, who often lacked the protective shield of racial or socioeconomic privilege, paid much higher costs for their social movement engagement. A white, conservative, suburban housewife might avoid prison for her card party in the clothing department at a Woolworth store, but her black counterpart protesting segregation at the Woolworth lunch counter would face potential consequences that ranged from severe to life-threatening.

By the early 1960s, each of the major conservative radio broadcasters supported white massive resistance to desegregation. For some, like Billy James Hargis in Oklahoma and H. L. Hunt in Texas, the South was their home and they found it easy to inflame white fears about desegregation to attract listeners. Yet most of the other major broadcasters, including Carl McIntire, did not have deep southern roots. McIntire fits the profile of those whom historian Joseph Crespino has labeled "national conservatives." They did not place as high a priority on maintaining southern white supremacy and Jim Crow–style segregation, although they were willing to ally with southern whites for whom it was a top priority.[91]

Yet while Carl McIntire and other national conservatives had previously avoided much mention of race and civil rights, appealing to an expanding radio audience of southern white supremacists meant taking a harder stance against desegregation than had previously been the case. The prize for doing so seemed worth it. As previously mentioned, Carl McIntire's *Twentieth Century Reformation Hour* had more stations in the South than in the rest of the nation combined, going from 61 to 262 stations in the South alone from 1960 to 1964. Defending segregationists gave broadcasters like McIntire the opportunity to frame themselves as sympathetic allies in the fight for states' rights against a tyrannical federal government. In exchange, the involvement of nonsouthern broadcasters allowed southerners to claim, albeit unconvincingly, that their complaints were not purely regional or racially motivated.

The fact that Carl McIntire, a lifelong Republican from New Jersey, was the most widely heard conservative radio broadcaster in the Deep South in the early 1960s is striking. Indeed, Republicans, including Clarence Manion and eventually Billy James Hargis, dominated the top tier of conservative broadcasters. For many white southern listeners, most of whom came from families that had voted for Democrats for generations, the first time they may have ever seriously considered listening to a Republican for political advice was when they tuned into their favorite Radio Right program.

Affiliation with a political party is notoriously inelastic. Americans are significantly more likely to change religions than they are to swap party membership.[92] The partisan transformation of the Deep South required a powerful ideological motivation, but white supremacy and massive resistance alone were not enough to transform the political affiliation of the South. After all, even two decades after the Dixiecrat revolt in 1948 had brought intraparty tensions over segregation out into the open, most white southerners either remained Democrats or voted third party. The number of white Republicans remained vanishingly small until, quite suddenly, it did not.

For reluctant Democrats and stranded Dixiecrats to make the jump to becoming card-carrying Republicans required something in addition to a commitment to white supremacy. In this regard broadcasters served a vital function in the partisan transformation of the Deep South. They made it possible for white southern segregationists to imagine that the Republican Party, which many had hated their entire lives, could really be relied upon to be the new home for massive resistance to desegregation. The Radio Right, composed disproportionately of Republican broadcasters and white Southern Democratic listeners, eased that transition process between party identities by privileging ideological consistency over party loyalty.

To provide just one example, note the partisan composition of a possible Goldwater White House cabinet slate half-seriously proposed by Carl McIntire in the summer of 1964. Those listed were divided between Democrats (Edwin Walker – Defense; George Wallace – Attorney General; Westbrook Pegler – Labor) and Republicans (Barry Goldwater – President; Carl McIntire – FCC; William F. Buckley – USIA; Robert Welch – CIA; J. Bracken Lee – Treasury). Party affiliation aside, all of them were radically conservative. Conservative radio gave listeners the chance to imagine a certain fluidity in party affiliation before actually making the change. In other words, the Radio Right prepared the way for a Republican Southern Strategy almost a decade before Kevin Phillips—Richard Nixon's campaign strategist—thought to call it that.[93]

But before the Radio Right could play its role in the partisan flipping of the Deep South, the Deep South would transform the racial politics of the Radio Right. McIntire's appeal among southern segregationists would have been surprising to those familiar with his early career, when he rarely mentioned topics like segregation or civil rights either in his publications or on his radio program. One notable exception was a 1940 article in the weekly paper that McIntire edited comparing Jim Crow laws in the South to the Nazi persecution of Jews in Germany, which is hardly the first comparison one would expect to come to mind for an ardent segregationist.[94] That said, as a college student in segregated Missouri in the 1920s, McIntire had expressed his preference for maintaining segregation, answering "false" when asked if "the restrictions placed upon negroes in railway trains, restaurants, etc., should be removed." On the other hand, he checked "doubtful" when asked if "the white race is mentally, morally and physically superior to any other race" and supported the invitation of George Washington Carver to speak to the college student body.[95] McIntire was certainly not a progressive when it came to race, but neither was he a hardliner by the standards of the time.

For McIntire, and for many white southerners, that relative apathy began to change in the late 1940s when the Democratic National Convention officially inserted a pro–civil rights plank into the party platform. Two weeks after a convention walkout by pro-segregation Dixiecrats, McIntire, although a Republican, privately wrote to US senator and Dixiecrat sympathizer Tom Connally (D-Texas). McIntire praised Connally's "fight against the so-called Civil Rights Program" while complaining about the centralization of federal power and the violation of states' rights.[96]

This was fairly standard rhetoric for supporters of segregation. Yet what is interesting about the letter, besides being McIntire's clearest and most public opposition to desegregation to that point, is what it reveals about his priorities. Opposition to civil rights qua civil rights was only the opening to the letter, most of which was dedicated to other topics. He complained extensively about the Federal Council of Churches—the precursor to the National Council of Churches—and its support for civil rights while asking for Connally's support for McIntire's lobbying efforts with the Federal Communications Commission on behalf of fundamentalist radio broadcasters. McIntire was praising Connally on segregation to beg a favor. In other words, McIntire's opposition to desegregation was as much instrumental as it was a matter of racist belief. The logic went like this; people McIntire despised—liberal clergy, for example—supported desegregation and therefore he would oppose it. This would be the pattern behind McIntire's opposition to the civil rights movement throughout the 1950s and 1960s.

In addition, McIntire's increasingly overt and vehement support for segregation had mutual utility for both him and his growing base of southern listeners. Thumping the pulpit for segregation meant more listeners, more radio stations, and more donations for McIntire. For massive resisters, support from nonsouthern broadcasters was used in the (failed) effort to deflect accusations of racist intent. This mutually beneficial exchange can be illustrated by McIntire's relationship with Arkansas governor Orval Faubus. As the federal government slowly started to enforce the US Supreme Court's decision to integrate schools in *Brown v. Board of Education* (1954), Southern

Democratic politicians pushed back. Governor Faubus, although previously having a reputation as a racial moderate, blocked the integration order for Central High School in Little Rock by calling out the Arkansas National Guard. It was a calculated move to win support from segregationist hardliners for Faubus's re-election campaign and it gained the governor national newspaper headlines.[97] McIntire wrote an effusive, public letter to Faubus praising his "stand for freedom and the constitutional rights of our states."[98] Faubus returned the compliment, paying to have McIntire's endorsement placed in the state's paper of record.

To illustrate how both Faubus and McIntire benefited from that endorsement, consider the response of an Arkansas woman who signed her letters as Miss Emmetta Germaine. Germaine saw McIntire's endorsement of Faubus in the paper and sent a clipping of it to the preacher along with a letter complaining about civil rights activists who were visiting local churches and refusing to leave until arrested by the police (a protest tactic nicknamed a "pray-in"). Those protests, combined with several recent prosecutions of mixed-race couples—Germaine used scare quotes when one defiant white woman proclaimed her "love" for her black partner—was enough to convince her that "segregation must be the answer until once more 'Morals' are taught and not Humanism [in public schools]." She was particularly annoyed by how the situation was unsympathetically portrayed by "the 'northern' papers written by 'foreign' reporters." But now she could be confident that McIntire, although a northerner, was on her and Governor Faubus's side.[99] By taking a hard line against desegregation, McIntire had become an honorary southerner in the eyes of Miss Emmetta Germaine and had thus become worthy of her financial support.

In his response letter, McIntire told Germaine that he wished his program was on a radio station that she could listen to. When McIntire wrote in 1958, he had no stations in Arkansas. By 1963, he had three stations, including one on the outskirts of Little Rock where Germaine lived. Vocal support for segregation won broadcasters like Carl McIntire listeners like Miss Emmetta Germaine. Her letter is just one of the hundreds of letters from southern listeners preserved in McIntire's papers, which are only a tiny sample of those that he received over the course of his career. Segregation was the bedrock on which the southern expansion of right-wing radio was built.

McIntire would pursue similar relationships with other prominent segregationist politicians, including Strom Thurmond and George Wallace. After receiving McIntire's endorsement, Wallace named McIntire an "Honorary

Lieutenant Colonel Aide-de-Camp in the Alabama State Militia." McIntire returned the favor by taking a choir to serenade Wallace in his hospital bed after the failed assassination attempt on his life in 1972.[100] This courtship between politicians and broadcasters went both ways. In March 1964 US Senator Strom Thurmond (D-South Carolina) sent Carl McIntire a donation for his radio program. McIntire responded with on-air praise for "the tremendous work" Thurmond was "doing for God, humanity, and our Country"; indeed, when the senator reached the five-and-a-half-hour mark of his record-setting filibuster of the Civil Rights Act of 1964, McIntire uttered "a quiet prayer" for him, comparing him to Moses standing with arms upraised while his people fought the Amalekites.[101] Of course, their exchange of letters was grist for the next several episodes of McIntire's radio program.

McIntire was not alone in pursuing this endorsement strategy. Oklahoma-based broadcaster Billy James Hargis invited George Wallace to give the keynote address at the annual Christian Crusade Convention in 1969.[102] By publicizing these relationships, conservative broadcasters were able to win new fans among southern conservative Democrats. These endorsements by political celebrities were a form of marketing; they signaled that if you liked Faubus, Wallace, or Thurmond and their stance against desegregation, then you would like what you heard if you tuned into McIntire's *Twentieth Century Reformation Hour* or Hargis's *The Christian Crusade*.

However, as segregationist anger peaked in the 1960s, it meant that conservative broadcasters needed to match their fevered rhetoric in order to continue to keep listener interest. For example, in 1964 McIntire published an open letter, pictured below, to Martin Luther King Jr. as a response to King's own famous "Letter from a Birmingham Jail." McIntire posed as the voice of reason between King's "anarchy" on the one hand and "the rabid segregationist" on the other, but all McIntire succeeded in doing was to show just how little he understood the situation on the ground in the South. In one breathtakingly audacious line, McIntire asked how King was "going to win the respect . . . of your white neighbor when you seek to use the policeman's club against him." Instead, if King just "followed the word of God," he "would not even have the problem of police brutality."[103] Given that logic, it is not surprising that four years later McIntire would essentially blame King for his own assassination, calling out "the so-called nonviolent approach" for breeding the "hatred" and "ill will" that "has borne its evil fruit in our nation."[104] Again, this kind of rhetoric was common among segregationists in

Photo 2.4. Carl McIntire authored this pamphlet in response to Martin Luther King Jr.'s "Letter from a Birmingham Jail."

Carl McIntire Papers, Special Collections, Princeton Theological Seminary Library.

the 1960s, but it is striking coming from McIntire since it reveals how much his views and rhetoric had evolved since the 1940s to match those of his most racist southern listeners.

Ultimately, historians can harmonize the Radio Right as both the inculcator of a genuine social movement and a key player in the transformation of the Republican Party into the party of white racial backlash.[105] As shown with the Polish ham boycott, broadcasters did energize grassroots activism from those who felt ignored by Congress and overlooked by the national media. At the same time, conservative broadcasters expressly appealed to the racist priorities of white southerners who saw desegregation as a violation of their right to live in a society predicated on white supremacy. Segregationists in the Deep South felt alienated from the national Democratic Party as it slowly embraced a pro–civil rights platform; the Radio Right eased the transition of these disaffected Democrats into the Republican Party, which renewed their access to the formal routines and levers of political power after a decade or more of declining formal influence. In any event, both card partiers and segregationists represented a threat to the Kennedy administration's legislative agenda and his hopes for re-election in 1964. As the next chapter details, the growing influence of the Radio Right convinced the president that decisive executive action was necessary.

3

Seven Days in May

How the Kennedys Learned to Stop Worrying
and Love the Radio Right

The year 1964 was a good year at the movie theater box office for political thrillers. Moviegoers who liked a bit of dark comedy mixed in with their intrigue could see *Dr. Strangelove or: How I Learned to Stop Worrying and Love the Bomb*, which held pole position at the box office for most of February. An insane Air Force general, obsessed with "precious bodily fluids," launches a rogue nuclear attack on the Soviet Union in retaliation against the USSR's insidious plot to fluoridate American water supplies (at the time an obvious reference to the anti-fluoridation conspiracy theories popular with the radical Right). Nuclear carnage was also the subject of October's *Fail-Safe*, in which a technical error leads to an imminent, unavoidable US strike on Moscow. To prevent a full-scale Armageddon, the US president orders the tit-for-tat nuking of New York City to assuage the Soviet premier. Both *Dr. Strangelove* and *Fail-Safe* were dark fantasies that tapped into very real American worries about a third world war.

There was another political thriller released in 1964 with a very different tenor than that of *Dr. Strangelove*'s comedy or *Fail-Safe*'s pathos. *Seven Days in May* was a self-serious, thinly fictionalized depiction of another Cold War phobia: military insurrection. As *The Nation*'s film reviewer wrote, "[The movie is] simply dramatizing the plausibility of a military takeover in this country."[1] As the movie opens, the United States and Soviet Union have just signed a nuclear disarmament treaty. Public opinion is divided over the treaty, and protesters and counterprotesters clash in front of the White House. Air Force General and Chairman of the Joint Chiefs of Staff James Mattoon Scott testifies at a congressional hearing that he believes that the Soviets will renege on the treaty and bomb America once the United States disarms. When the president ignores his warnings, he and the other joint chiefs of staff plot a coup to scuttle the treaty. Through the heroism of President Jordan Lyman and several military officers, the conspiracy is uncovered and the plotters

The Radio Right. Paul Matzko, © Oxford University Press (2020). Oxford University Press.
DOI: 10.1093/oso/9780190073220.001.0001

forced to resign from their positions. The movie made a tidy $3.4 million on a $2.2 million budget and its star-studded cast—Kirk Douglas! Burt Lancaster! Ava Gardner!—garnered two Oscar nominations.

The plot and characters had been ripped from the headlines. Soon after his election, President John F. Kennedy faced two crises concerning civilian control of the military. The movie's General Scott was based on an Army general named Edwin Walker. President Lyman was, of course, John F. Kennedy. Lyman's confidant, the drawling southern Senator Clark, was reminiscent of Arkansas Senator J. William Fulbright. Movie reviewers at the time noted the similarities, like *The New Republic,* which wrote, "Under different names they are all on the front page of your newspaper." The comparisons became even more apt once Kennedy signed a Nuclear Test Ban Treaty with the Soviet Union in the fall of 1963, only two days before production began on *Seven Days in May.* Indeed, the movie producers displaced actual anti–nuclear test ban treaty protesters in front of the White House to make room for the movie extras playing fictional nuclear test ban treaty protesters.[2]

None of this was a fortuitous accident. The authors of the book the movie was based on—which sold more than two million copies and spent forty-nine weeks on the *New York Times* bestseller list after its release in October 1962—were Kennedy supporters.[3] When movie president Lyman's confrontation with General Scott climaxes with the line "Every now and then a man on a white horse rides by and we appoint him to be our personal God," it was written in imitation of a speech given by President Kennedy at the Hollywood Palladium in November 1961. Unsurprisingly, Kennedy enjoyed the book and gave the director and crew special access to the White House to help with set design. Partly that was because Kennedy thought another fiasco on the scale of the Bay of Pigs might give some of his generals the idea of turning the novel into nonfiction. The movie was, as *Variety* magazine put it, "an exploration of what could conceivably happen momentarily."[4]

As will become clear in later chapters, the Kennedy administration's counter–Radio Right campaign shows that the controversies over civilian control of the military were only the surface problem. The true danger to the Kennedy administration's domestic and foreign policy agenda was right-wing broadcasting, which had the ability to magnify minor hiccups into national scandals. The movie *Seven Days in May* gives a minor role to a character that played a much more prominent role in the book that the movie was based on. In the book, a television commentator named Harold McPherson holds Nuremberg-like patriotic rallies with the traitorous General Scott. That character bears an uncanny resemblance to a real-life conservative broadcaster named Billy James Hargis. During the spring of 1963, Hargis sponsored a series of political rallies, named Operation Midnight Ride, that featured General Edwin Walker, who was then considering a third-party bid for the presidency in 1964. In response to this and other Radio Right threats, the Kennedy administration orchestrated a behind-the-scenes campaign to mute the offending broadcasters. To do so, they needed the assistance of their labor allies, particularly the Reuther brothers at the United Auto Workers. In a secret memorandum written at the end of 1961, the Reuthers proposed using targeted Internal Revenue Service (IRS) audits and Federal Communications Commission regulations to stem the tide of money flowing to right-wing broadcasters.

This chapter introduces each of the major players in the counterconservative broadcasting campaign and outlines their motives for getting involved. The Kennedy brothers thought silencing the New Right was the key to re-election in 1964. The Reuther brothers were interested in removing an anti-labor thorn from their side. Yet while the Kennedys and Reuthers designed the counter-Right strategy, the group with the most to gain, and which had engaged with the problem of conservative broadcasting for the longest, was the National Council of Churches. The National Council of Churches had an impressive institutional edifice, but conservative broadcasters tapped into a simmering tension between conservative parishioners and liberal clergy. They were worried about the New Right before Kennedy's election and they would continue the fight long after his death.

The Air Force Manual Scandal

Although fears of a right-wing military coup may seem bizarre today, they were rooted in two very real controversies over civilian control of the military in 1960 and 1961. Both involved the overzealous application of a 1958 directive from the National Security Council. During the Korean War, the US Joint Chiefs of Staff had been unpleasantly surprised by how poorly American prisoners of war responded to Communist psychological conditioning. They would come home and continue to parrot the Communist propaganda that had been drilled into them under torture. That phenomenon inspired journalist Edward Hunter to coin the term "brainwashing," which put a pithy name on a very deep-seated American fear.[5]

The military's fear reflected American public opinion. After more than a decade of Communist hunting by the House Un-American Activities Committee, the average American had decided that Communists could be anyone and anywhere. Popular novels and films like *The Manchurian Candidate* (1959) traded on that fear (and director John Frankenheimer would go on to direct *Seven Days in May*). To allay those concerns, President Eisenhower instructed the Department of Defense to educate the troops about the threat of Communism to the American way of life. The military needed, in the words of Senator William Proxmire, to be "indoctrinated in freedom."[6] The military gave generals broad discretion in creating classes and training manuals for the soldiers under their commands. Given the lack of central oversight for the initiative, it did not take long for some of those generals to step on toes, especially when they started pointing fingers at alleged Communist front organizations back home.

On February 10, 1960, a reservist serving at Mitchel Air Force Base in New York showed an anti-Communist training manual to his pastor, who quickly sent it up the chain of command to James Wine, then an executive in the Office of Interpretation at the National Council of Churches of Christ (NCC).[7] Wine shared the document with former NCC president Eugene Carson Blake and they read page after page accusing NCC clergymen of being "card-carrying Communists!"[8] They were shocked that an Air Force general, using government resources, was teaching his soldiers that the largest association of Protestants in America was a Communist front organization.[9]

Much of the material cited in the manual came from a Disciples of Christ preacher in Tulsa, Oklahoma, named Billy James Hargis. The manual's author was Homer Hyde, a lowly civilian employee of the Air Force, but Hyde had cribbed much of its content from Hargis's publications.[10] Hargis promptly took advantage of the controversy, flying to Washington, DC, to meet with various conservative congressmen, including Senator Strom Thurmond, and issuing a statement to the press saying that the NCC "has done more to nurture Communism than any single organization in the United States" (while admitting that he had not yet read the very manual that he was defending). All press is good press for those in the business of stirring up outrage, and Hargis quickly offered a two for $1 special on the pamphlets cited by the Air Force manual, including *The National Council Indicts Itself on 50 Counts of Treason to God and Country*.[11]

Hargis had been on the NCC's radar for several years as one of a group of radio preachers who attacked the NCC on the air. The two worst offenders were Hargis, whose broadcast ministry started in 1948, and the previously mentioned Carl McIntire, whose *Twentieth Century Reformation Hour* began broadcasting from Collingswood, New Jersey, in 1955. The NCC was their favorite target. To Hargis and McIntire—both fundamentalists who believed in the inerrancy of the Bible, the deity of Christ, and blood atonement—the NCC's championing of liberal theology represented a deviation from true Christianity. The errors of the NCC seemed so egregious to McIntire that he called for a second Protestant Reformation that would fight back against the "ecumenical blitz" of liberalism.[12]

Their criticisms of the NCC typically blended fundamentalist doctrine and anti-Communist rhetoric. For example, Hargis and McIntire criticized the NCC for sponsoring visits by Eastern Orthodox clergymen from the Soviet Union, noting that only state-sanctioned clergy were allowed to visit, and when they did, the Russian clergy lied about the existence of religious persecution in Russia.[13] By sponsoring these sanctioned clergy, McIntire and Hargis reasoned, the NCC had abandoned unsanctioned and persecuted Russian Baptists. In a typical protest at the airport where a visiting group of Soviet clergy had landed in the summer of 1956, Carl McIntire and two hundred demonstrators waved banners reading "Go Home, Servants of the Devil," "Give Real Freedom of Religion in the Ukraine," and "Only the Stupid Believe You and the Traitors Support You." McIntire, as editor of his own small religious newspaper, claimed press access to get into the news conference, took control of the microphone, and read a lengthy statement written by Russian Baptists.[14]

At first, the NCC's leadership was not inclined to take McIntire and Hargis very seriously. The two men did not have large formal followings. Hargis was the pastor of a single church and McIntire's quasi-denominational organization, the American Council of Christian Churches (ACCC), claimed to represent just 120,000 members, or "perhaps ½ of 1% of American Protestantism."[15] The NCC could not, however, take comfort in those statistics, for as small as McIntire's and Hargis's churches and denominations were, they had booming radio ministries reaching millions of listeners. McIntire aired *Twentieth Century Reformation Hour* over just two stations in 1957, but he was on over two hundred stations by the start of 1961. Hargis aired on more than two hundred stations by 1963, with fifty-five of those stations added in 1961 alone.[16] By the early 1960s they had graduated from minor irritant to major threat, routinely staging embarrassing direct actions like the one portrayed in Photo 3.1.

Photo 3.1. Carl McIntire holds a protest sign in front of the Riverside Church in New York City, a National Council of Churches (NCC) affiliate. McIntire also issued a "Christian Manifesto" demanding reparations from the NCC for its alleged mistreatment of conservative Protestants. It was done in imitation of civil rights activist James Forman's protest at Riverside a few months earlier, which had led to a "Black Manifesto" demanding reparations for the NCC's complicity in white supremacy.

Carl McIntire Papers, Special Collections, Princeton Theological Seminary Library.

The NCC began receiving reports that parishioners were listening to, and being persuaded by, these "unprincipled purveyor[s] of hate" who were, in the words of one flustered clergyman, "poisoning the minds of our people who believe anything if told often enough."[17] Faced with this level of indignation, the NCC reassured their local clergy, in the words of a pastor from Michigan, that they would "make the radio and TV stations realize that they must not continue to allow such attacks to be made against Protestant Churches, [and] their leaders and Councils, over the air."[18] A regional executive in the NCC wrote to the organization's president, "I hope . . . that the Council does not underestimate this attack. . . . It does play into the hands of our laymen who are against the Church speaking out on economics and political issues."[19] McIntire and Hargis had tapped into a strong current of internal opposition to the NCC's political and religious agenda.

Laypeople all over the country heard conflicting messages. From the radio each weekday, they heard that the NCC was full of Communists; from the pulpit on Sunday morning, they were reassured that this was not so. They did not know whom to trust, so they wrote J. Edgar Hoover. The Federal Bureau of Investigation (FBI) maintained a confidential file of the letters that poured in. Church deacons and elders wrote, telling the FBI that they would pull their churches out of the NCC if the accusations were true. A Christian Church pastor wrote to say that he had told his parishioners to ignore the "prophets of discord on the air" but complained that they would not believe him; might the FBI have some conclusive evidence to disprove the accusations? One Episcopal chairwoman expressed her confidence in Hoover's integrity—"*The only man* or organization that the diehards would admit were [*sic*] not corrupted were you and your F.B.I."—and offered to send him her superlative blueberry pie if he responded promptly. The FBI wanted to avoid getting involved in this sticky situation; an FBI administrator wrote, "The Air Force got themselves into this and the FBI shouldn't be used to get them out of it."[20]

The FBI was not being helpful, but the NCC saw the scandal as an opportunity to force its "pastors for the first time in their lives to interpret [advocate for] . . . the National Council."[21] Public declarations of support rolled in from all quarters, from the United Presbyterians to the Polish National Catholic Church. The Massachusetts branch of the American Civil Liberties Union wrote to condemn the manual, as did the editor of *The Christian Century*, Harold Fey. Fey also offered the help of one of his staff journalists, who, with the aid of the Anti-Defamation League, could compile a detailed study of each of the right-wing agitators, something that the *Century* could do from its "independent position" without seeming partisan. The NCC did not pursue Fey's offer to "build an affirmative climate of opinion" for cooperative Christianity.[22] The time for study was past.

Instead, the NCC launched a media blitz. Within two days of the re-servist showing the manual to his minister, James Wine had held a press conference with two hundred journalists. The press conference was an at-tempt to shape the media narrative on the controversy, something further aided by an advance briefing for sympathetic journalists, particularly those who attended NCC-affiliated churches.[23] Wine also made sure that the major papers and news wires, including the Associated Press, United Press International, and *New York Times*, received thank you notes after they ran favorable stories, especially when they emphasized the size of the NCC in comparison to its "small but vocal dissident opposition."[24] Within a month, the NCC's media campaign had garnered favorable editorials from 106 dif-ferent periodicals.[25]

But the NCC was not satisfied with a mere war of words. For the NCC to deal a serious blow to right-wing broadcasting, they needed allies. They turned to their contacts in the US Congress, seeking a congressional order to the Federal Communications Commission that would bar the airwaves to the sort of attacks made by McIntire and Hargis. James Wine traveled to Washington, DC, to meet with sympathetic congressional representatives and to secure commitments from the presidential hopefuls as well.[26] Wine met with Representative Richard Bolling and arranged, with the approval of powerful Democratic Speaker of the House Sam Rayburn, for a dozen con-gressional speeches defending the NCC following the Easter recess.[27]

As mentioned in the introduction, one of those speakers was Massachusetts Senator and Democratic presidential candidate John F. Kennedy. Kennedy entered his Senate speech into the *Congressional Record* on April 17, three weeks prior to the vote in West Virginia. In the speech, Kennedy pro-nounced, "Our Government cannot—directly or indirectly, carelessly or intentionally—select any religious body for either favorable or unfavor-able treatment." He also defended the NCC's record in the fight against Communism and dismissed the NCC's critics as those "who want to silence the views of the National Council because they do not share those views."[28] With this speech, which was Kennedy's strongest statement on the separa-tion of church and state to that point, he had won a valuable ally in the NCC just in time for the West Virginia primary, as previously discussed.

After West Virginia, Kennedy also gained a new special assistant for reli-gion (a forerunner of later generations of "faith-based" White House liaisons). Campaign strategist Ted Sorenson had decided that Kennedy needed a "top Protestant" with "political know-how" to liaise with the NCC and to field interview requests from religious newspapers. That "top Protestant" was none other than James Wine, who left the NCC's Office of Interpretation to work as Kennedy's special adviser on religion.[29] By employing Wine, the Kennedy campaign cemented its close relationship with the NCC (and Wine would later be rewarded with a plum ambassadorship to Luxembourg). The "hate-monger radio preachers" might not have been able to defeat Kennedy in the West Virginia primaries, but they had pushed him into a strategic alliance with the largest Protestant organization in the country. It was Kennedy's first encounter with right-wing broadcasting, but by no means his last.

General Edwin Walker and Pro-Blue

By the end of 1960 it seemed that the NCC, with the help of presidential candidate—and now president—John F. Kennedy, had wrapped up the Air Force manual controversy with minimal political fallout. The secretary of the Air Force had issued an official apology and the manual was recalled. Still, the incident served as a warning that some military officers were using their anti-Communist indoctrination programs to advance partisan ends. But the problem would resurface in 1961; less than a year after the Air Force manual scandal, Major General Edwin Walker's military education efforts became the center of a new controversy.

Walker had served in the military with distinction for three decades. During World War II, he fought in the Anzio landings, at Monte Cassino, and in the invasion of southern France. Later, he trained Rangers at Fort Benning and fought with them at Heartbreak Ridge during the Korean War.[30] While commanding an army division in West Germany, Walker developed what he called the "Pro-Blue" anti-Communist training program, which consisted of lectures, a recommended reading list, and discussion groups. The Pro-Blue program drew criticism when, during the 1960 election, Walker distributed a voter guide produced by the conservative think tank Americans for Constitutional Action to those troops who asked for absentee voting ballots. Unsurprisingly, few liberal Democratic politicians made the ACA's list of recommendations. Furthermore, Walker described Harry Truman and Eleanor Roosevelt as "definitely pink" in a speech to the troops. Prominent newsmen Edward Murrow and Walter Lippmann, on the other hand, were "confirmed Communists."[31] Pro-Blue was an echo of the Air Force manual controversy; in both cases an ardently anti-Communist general used materials from right-wing publications to attack Democratic politicians and allied interest groups.

In April 1961 *Overseas Weekly*, the unofficial newspaper of the US Army in Germany, broke the story, which was promptly picked up by major papers back in the United States. The US Senate's armed services subcommittee immediately opened an investigation into the allegations. As a result, the Army removed Walker from command and placed him on paid leave until the end of the hearings. In November, the committee recommended that he be formally reprimanded for conduct unbecoming an officer.[32] Walker, sensing a political opportunity, resigned in protest. In his final statement to the committee, he said that he would "find other means of serving my country in the time of her great need," but that to do so he "must be free from the power of little men who, in the name of my country, punish loyal service to it."[33] Congressional Democrats and the White House were just happy to see him go and accepted his resignation.

Although the administration had pushed out Walker, their concerns over his right-wing enablers continued to grow. Conservative broadcasters like Billy James Hargis, Kent and Phoebe Courtney, and Clarence Manion lionized Walker as a martyr for freedom. The Courtneys rushed a fawning biography, *The Case of General Edwin A. Walker*, into print, claiming proof that the attack on Walker "was planned in Moscow" to "soften up America for ultimate surrender to the International Communist Conspiracy!"[34] Conservative military veterans embraced Walker as one of their own. The chairman of the "Americanism Committee" at the New York County Council for the Veterans of Foreign Wars wrote Walker to tell him that they had adopted the Pro-Blue curriculum for their own educational outreach, calling it a "Liberty Bell" and a "well ordered assembly line to turn out apostles of, and for, America."[35] Walker might have been just a disgraced former general were it not for the right-wing broadcasters who turned him into a conservative *cause célèbre*. Walker was the latest in a long line of Douglas MacArthur knockoffs; ever since MacArthur had accused the Truman administration of insufficient rigor in the fight against Communist China, conservatives had been on the hunt for their own version of Dwight D. Eisenhower, a popular military hero turned successful politician, albeit one with more conservative political principles.

Walker sought to turn his newfound popularity into a political career. Even as the investigation was under way, Walker began giving stump-like speeches, especially in his native Texas. At the "American Eagle Crusade for

Truth" rally in Dallas, Walker lambasted congressional Democrats as "a class of men who believe that in 'One World' of 'Peace' and 'Internationalism,' U.S. Sovereignty and independence are obsolete." Unlike them, Walker declared, "I refuse to accept the 38th parallel or our present terms of surrender. I stand with Travis *to die*, for Sam Houston *to conquer*."[36] That was red meat for a crowd of conservative Texans. The enthusiastic reception he received at these rallies convinced Walker to run for political office. He aimed first at the Texas gubernatorial election in 1962—coming in a disappointing sixth in the Democratic primary—but then set his sights on a presidential campaign during the election of 1964.

Kennedy's "Man on Horseback" Speech

President Kennedy had Edwin Walker on his mind when he gave a speech on right-wing radicalism at the Hollywood Palladium on November 18, 1961. An aide, possibly Myer Feldman, drafted the speech to counter the "mug-wump, Know-Nothing pocket of resistance on the right."[37] The speech is quite clever, alluding to conservatives without ever naming names. In the speech, Kennedy deplored those on the conspiratorial "fringes of our society who have sought to escape their own responsibility by finding a simple solution," a critique of anti-Communists who blamed all the nation's ills on Communists coming out of the woodwork. But Kennedy's most enduring line singled out Walker for those in the know; he described conservatives as those who "look suspiciously at their neighbors and their leaders" and who "call for 'a man on horseback' because they do not trust the people."[38]

Kennedy's use of the phrase "a man on horseback" is both revealing and quite old. In one of Aesop's fables a man on horseback steals a hare from a hunter without consequence; the hunter, helpless to intervene, pretends it was meant as a gift all along. In 1903, an anarchist publisher named Ross Winn turned the fable into a metaphor for military dictatorship in which a general, astride his steed, enforces his every whim on the nation. Winn had in mind President Theodore Roosevelt, whom he called a "fake rough rider with opulent eyeglasses and mastodonic dental furnishing."[39] However, where Aesop and Winn had meant the metaphor as a cautionary tale, others found the prospect of a decisive leader who could singlehandedly turn America around quite appealing. That was what was on conservative Texas newspaper publisher Ted Dealey's mind when, on a visit to the White House in 1961, he blurted out, "We need a man on horseback to lead this nation and many people in Texas and the Southwest think that you are riding Caroline's tricycle." Dealey went on to tell Kennedy that "you and your administration are weak sisters." (Several years later both lines would show up in the script of *Seven Days in May* spoken by the central villain in criticism of the John F. Kennedy–esque fictional President Lyman.)[40]

President Kennedy was not amused by Dealey's comparisons. When Kennedy echoed Dealey's "man on horseback" line in November 1961, he was referencing another Texan, General Edwin Walker. Earlier that evening, Walker had spoken at Hollywood High School before leading a march the ten blocks down to the Palladium to protest Kennedy's speech. Indeed, Walker may have been picketing outside the venue at the very moment Kennedy uttered the "man on horseback" line.[41] It was life imitating art imitating life. But Kennedy did not stop there. These men and their followers were those who "find treason in our churches, in our highest court, [and] in our treatment of water." The church reference was a nod back to the Air Force manual scandal. Without using the words "conservative broadcasting" or naming a single person, Kennedy had pointed to broadcasters in general and Billy James Hargis specifically as the potential enablers of an anti-Communist military coup. No one else fits the description. It was Hargis who was at the center of the Air Force manual scandal and who subsequently organized Edwin Walker's campaign rallies. Kennedy's concern over the ties between Walker and conservative broadcasters was not just a ploy to get donors to give to his re-election campaign. Immediately following the "man on horseback" speech, Kennedy commissioned one of his aides to prepare confidential weekly briefings on the activity of right-wing broadcasters to be circulated only among top White House staff.[42]

With the backing of the Radio Right, Walker posed a threat to Kennedy's re-election chances should the general make a third-party bid in the presidential election of 1964. Conservative broadcasters Kent and Phoebe Courtney had commissioned fourteen-inch-by-twenty-two-inch placards for Walker supporters to carry at his rallies emblazoned with "WIN WITH WALKER" and "WALKER FOR PRESIDENT."[43] Walker fanned the flames by routinely critiquing both parties, telling crowds that they had "no more choice in their party system than the Russians."[44] Walker kept his name afloat as long as it looked like liberal Republican Nelson Rockefeller would win the nomination. Once the conservative Barry Goldwater won in an upset, Walker backed off.[45] Whether Walker or Goldwater, Kennedy could plan on facing at least one "man on horseback." Walker may have had more medals, but Goldwater was himself a general in the Air Force reserves.

If Walker had run for president, he would not have been a serious electoral threat, but the Kennedy campaign anticipated another closely fought election against Rockefeller like they had faced against Richard Nixon in 1960. After all, Kennedy's margin of victory in the popular vote was a measly one hundred thousand votes, fewer even than sixth-place Walker had won in the Texas gubernatorial race alone. Walker looked to be a major threat as a spoiler among pro-segregation, conservative Democrats and Dixiecrats in the South, which was the audience for his December speeches in Texas and Mississippi. In hindsight it is clear that worries about Walker were quite reasonable given that Nixon would beat Humphrey in 1968 when George Wallace captured enough conservative Democratic votes to take Mississippi and most of the Deep South. Furthermore, Wallace would do it with a disgruntled military general as his running mate, although in his case it was Air Force General Curtis LeMay, not Army General Edwin Walker. But it suggests that Walker could have played that spoiler role four years earlier.

The Reuther Memorandum

John F. Kennedy's "man on horseback" speech coincided with the internal release of a confidential, anti-conservative strategy document that had been in the works for at least six months. In April 1961, just days after the Pro-Blue scandal had erupted, US Attorney General Robert F. Kennedy met with Walter Reuther, then President of the United Auto Workers (UAW) and arguably the most prominent voice for organized labor in the country. Walter Reuther had supported Lyndon Johnson over Kennedy in the 1960 Democratic primaries, but he quickly backed the winning horse once Kennedy pulled ahead. Indeed, all three "Brothers Reuther"—Walter, Victor, and Roy, each members of the UAW leadership—offered Kennedy their help.[46]

A mere three weeks after John F. Kennedy's inauguration, Roy Reuther sent a memo to Robert F. Kennedy with recommendations for the 1962 midterm elections and Kennedy's 1964 re-election campaign.[47] At Walter Reuther's meeting with Robert F. Kennedy in April 1961, they further discussed the 1962 midterms and the 1964 re-election campaign; Walter did not go into any more detail about what was said at the meeting but he did say he would "be following through on the matters we discussed."[48] A few weeks later, Walter Reuther would meet with John F. Kennedy, who had said he was "anxious" to see him, but neither left any record of what was said in that meeting, although the president did ask Walter to continue to send him "whatever ideas you might have."[49]

Those ideas would take form in the Reuther Memorandum, but before discussing that document, it is worth mentioning the source of the Reuther brothers' long-standing interest in right-wing radio. Opposition to labor organization and support for right-to-work laws were staples of conservative broadcasting, like when Carl McIntire convinced more than six hundred clergymen to sign a statement decrying union shops for theft because union dues were collected regardless of whether individual workers supported the union.[50]

But the Reuthers had a particular antipathy for Billy James Hargis. They first encountered Hargis in 1958 during the heated gubernatorial race in California between Republican Senator William Knowland and Democratic California Attorney General Edmund "Pat" Brown. Knowland ran on a right-to-work platform, which Brown opposed. As the campaign heated up in mid-September, the Brown campaign pounced on Knowland's wife after she praised a pamphlet written by a man named Joseph Kamp. Kamp was an old anti–New Dealer, but in 1958 he was writing for Billy James Hargis and the *Christian Crusade* broadcast. Hargis also invited Kamp to review books for his weekly paper and republished some of Kamp's literature, including " 'We *Do Not* Believe in God' Said Walter Reuther," as well as the offending pamphlet recommended by Knowland's wife, "Meet the Man Who Plans to Rule America."[51]

Brown immediately blasted Knowland for allying himself with "elements that would not stop at imposing a Fascist dictatorship over the American people."[52] Walter Reuther also responded to the controversy, calling Kamp a "convicted hate-monger who went to prison because of his un-American activities." Reuther went so far as to compare those businessmen who gave money to Kamp to industrialists in prewar Germany who had supported Hitler.[53] Reuther had even more reason than most for disliking Kamp. Twenty years earlier in 1937, Kamp had authored a booklet on Walter Reuther—using some of Reuther's pro-Soviet letters from his time in Russia—sarcastically titled "Join the CIO . . . and Help Build a Soviet America."[54] The antipathy between Walter Reuther and Kamp lingered even after the deaths of both men. When Victor Reuther wrote his brother's biography nearly twenty years later, he began his discussion of right-wing politics with Joseph Kamp.[55] Kamp, and by extension Hargis, were ground zero for the Reuther brothers' campaign against conservative broadcasting.

Ultimately the Kamp controversy was not really about Kamp. Pat Brown bashed Knowland over the head for his association with the "poison-pen peddler" all the way up until the election; anybody who supported Knowland "obviously either condones or subscribes to the Senator's covert class-hate mongering." All the while, Brown could piously opine about how "for too long many self-seekers for public office . . . have been running on platforms of invective and insult."[56] Brown had found a winning issue and Kamp was the gift that kept on giving. The chairman of the Democratic National Committee got several days of headlines out of the scandal when he demanded that President Eisenhower and Vice President Richard Nixon repudiate Kamp.[57] Nixon promptly did so and asked that Republican donors stop financing "screwball" pamphleteers like Kamp.[58]

The Kamp scandal would linger on into the election of 1960. Kamp himself faded into obscurity after 1958, but his former employer Hargis kept the anti-labor tradition going. Throughout the summer of 1960, Hargis repeatedly attacked the American Federation of Labor and Congress of Industrial Organizations (AFL-CIO), the UAW, and Walter Reuther. The week before the election, he echoed Kamp's rhetoric, saying that a Kennedy victory would do to the United States as a whole what the Reuthers had done to Michigan. He accused Walter Reuther of practicing "chicanery and violence as a swifter and more sure method of attaining power" than the democratic process.[59]

Hargis was not the only one with a long memory. The UAW helped keep the legacy of Joseph Kamp alive, running pro-Kennedy campaign ads in the *New York Times* and other major papers that condemned "hate group propaganda" from the likes of Kamp.[60] There was no connection between Nixon and Kamp in 1958, let alone 1960, but the Reuthers had learned an important lesson during the Kamp scandal. Using "radical" right-wingers to tar and feather mainstream Republicans was an easy way of scoring political points. Even if the charges did not stick, it shifted the focus of the debate for days or weeks, preventing the candidates from effectively asserting their own platform.

The Reuthers got the chance to propose that strategy to Robert Kennedy in person in early November 1961. On November 8, Victor Reuther and Joseph Rauh, the UAW's longtime general counsel, sent Walter and Joe Reuther an abbreviated draft of what would later be called the "Reuther Memorandum" so that Walter would have something in front of him when he met with Robert Kennedy.[61] This earlier draft of the memo encouraged Kennedy to take the offensive in the military censorship controversy. Remaining on the defensive and responding to questions about the "muzzling" of General Walker would play into conservatives' hands. Instead, the president should highlight the "real problem of other Walkers in the Armed Forces."[62] Two weeks after Walter passed these thoughts on to Robert Kennedy, John F. Kennedy did as they suggested and gave the "man on horseback" speech.

Later that month, while drafting the full memorandum, Victor Reuther revealed something of the Reuthers' overarching strategy to Walter in a note titled "Right Wing activities and new political opportunities." Victor noted that Richard Nixon was "deeply concerned" about right-wing groups "siphoning off" donations that would otherwise have gone to "regular GOP conservatives." Victor suggested they "breathe new life" into their proposals for new campaign finance regulations now that Nixon and the Republican establishment were in a more receptive mood. But what really excited the Reuthers was the hope that the rise of right-wing extremists would "create sharper and deeper divisions within the Republican Party and make the more liberal wing feel even less comfortable in the GOP house." A major political realignment was on the horizon and the Reuthers knew whom to thank: "Perhaps the Birchites may yet perform a useful service."[63] The Reuthers were right about that political realignment, although they have not received much credit from historians for their insight. By focusing public attention on the radical Right, the Reuthers and the Kennedys aided the radical conservative takeover of the Republican Party and helped drive liberal Republicans into the Democratic fold.[64]

Victor sent the final memorandum—from now on referred to as the "Reuther Memorandum"—to Robert Kennedy in December 1961 "pursuant to your conversation with President Reuther."[65] The Reuther Memorandum was a twenty-four-page document outlining the threat the Right posed to the Kennedy administration and the measures that the Reuthers believed the Kennedy administration should take to combat the Right. The memo began by praising Kennedy's "man on horseback" speech at the Hollywood Palladium but argued that "speeches without action may well only mobilize the radical right." The Reuthers estimated that the number of Americans affiliated with conservative groups numbered in the millions. As a measure of their radicalism, Senator Goldwater was considered to be on the left boundary of what the Right considered acceptable; indeed, even Billy James

Hargis would receive significant criticism from fellow conservatives when he declared for Barry Goldwater in 1964.[66] A movement in which Barry Goldwater was the voice of reason scared the Reuthers badly.[67]

Unsurprisingly, the memo highlighted conservative "infiltration" of the military and briefly mentioned Edwin Walker, but the three groups that the memo called out as the true leaders of the movement were Robert Welch's John Birch Society, Fred Schwarz's Christian Anti-Communism Crusade, and Billy James Hargis's Christian Crusade. They noted that Hargis could claim an annual income of more than $1 million and that the movement as a whole pulled in perhaps twenty times that. Fred Schwarz was an Australian medical doctor and pastor who caught the attention of Carl McIntire in 1950. McIntire had invited Schwarz to the states for a two-month speaking tour; a few years later Schwarz immigrated to the United States to make a career of it.[68] Schwarz held multiday anti-Communism "schools" all over the nation, although his base of operations was Orange County, California. Schwarz's schools had become so popular that when he held one in St. Louis in 1961, he got sponsorships from the *St. Louis Globe Democrat*, the mayor of St. Louis, and even both of Missouri's US senators, including Stuart Symington, one of Kennedy's old foes from the Democratic primary in 1960 and someone Kennedy had considered for vice president. Worse, when Schwarz held a rally in Los Angeles in late August 1961, he filled the Hollywood Bowl (seating capacity sixteen thousand), convinced actors like John Wayne and Jimmy Stewart to attend, and televised the proceedings on thirty-three stations in six states. Four million Americans may have watched.[69] That November, the Schick Safety Razor Company paid for one of Schwarz's schools to be condensed and shown as a three-hour television broadcast in New York City.[70] Newspaper accounts of the rallies emphasized the relative youth of the attendees. Many future foot soldiers of the Reagan revolution got their first taste of politics as teenagers at one of Fred Schwarz's schools.

Hargis, Schwarz, and Welch engaged in the usual hyperbolic attacks on the Kennedy administration. The Reuthers acknowledged that the Right was also a problem for establishment Republicans, like Richard Nixon, but their threat to President Kennedy's agenda was far more severe. "Treason in high places is their slogan," the memo noted, "and slander is their weapon." They told people not to trust the government and they possessed the power to move "the national political spectrum away from the Administration's proposed liberal programs at home and abroad." These radicals were making previously unthinkable policy positions reasonable to the average American voter.

Radical had become the new normal. In response, the Reuthers outlined specific steps for the Kennedy administration to take "to contain the radical right from further expansion and in the long run to reduce it to its historic role of the impotent lunatic fringe."[71] Among those recommendations, the Reuthers reiterated their desire to see President Kennedy and Secretary of Defense Robert McNamara go on the offensive in regard to the military censorship controversy. They also called for toning down anti-Communist rhetoric by Democrats, which had gotten used to a kind of rhetorical arms race with Republicans during the McCarthy era.

The more significant and controversial recommendations called for political action, not just a change in rhetoric and calls for voter education. First, the Reuthers recommended that Robert Kennedy add conservative groups to the attorney general's list of subversive organizations. Although the list had been instituted in 1947 with the mandate to include both fascistic and Communist organizations, the list was populated almost exclusively by liberal groups during the 1950s. It had become, as the memo elegantly put it, "a Good Housekeeping seal for the radical right." Conservatives had brandished the list against ordinary liberals who had unwittingly joined Communist front organizations. The Reuthers wanted Kennedy now to return the favor. Furthermore, they thought that the FBI should announce an investigation of right-wing groups—the headlines would have an "immediate, salutory effect"—and send informants to infiltrate them and build a case for congressional hearings. It would be McCarthy all over again, just directed at the Right rather than the Left. Better yet, if conservatives resisted the investigation, as the Communists had before them, nothing would "reveal to the public the true nature of these groups" better than "defiant resistance to their government."[72]

Robert Kennedy did not follow through in regard to the subversive list, likely because it was the most public of all the recommendations. Adding conservative groups to a list would have had a high political cost when those groups cried "political suppression," enraging the conservative base in time to turn out for the midterm elections. It was simply not a politically viable measure.

The memo's second and third major recommendations, however, were. Both involved interrupting the flow of money to right-wing groups, which "should be dammed to the extent possible." These groups claimed federal tax exemption as educational groups. Educational corporations were not supposed to engage in partisan politics, but the IRS had neither the means nor the inclination to investigate every group that applied. But if the Kennedy administration could revoke even a few tax exemptions, they "might scare off a substantial part of the big money now flowing." The Treasury Department should be encouraged to begin "undercover operations" to find tax violations by these organizations, their founders, and their donors.

The final measure the Reuthers proposed was using the Federal Communications Commission (FCC) to combat right-wing access to the airwaves. The memo specifically calls out Hargis's *Christian Crusade,* which aired on seventy radio stations, some of which gave him free "public service" time. Victor Reuther, whose office was in Washington, DC, could listen to Hargis's show six days a week on a local station. He had even heard Hargis tell his listeners that Gus Hall and the Communist Party USA had filled the Kennedy administration with Communist staffers. Victor's recommendation was that the FCC should "encourage stations to assign comparable time for an opposing point of view on a free basis." This was a decent summation of the equal time portion of the FCC's "Fairness Doctrine," although the memo does not use the phrase. The UAW had a particular interest in the matter given that the FCC was currently investigating a Cincinnati station that had sold time to the right-wing *Life Line* program but which had not allowed the UAW to buy time for a pro-labor program.[73]

These final two major recommendations had the advantage of not being easily traceable back to the administration. Both the IRS and the FCC had the legal right to investigate the abuses mentioned in the memo. It was simply a matter of two federal agencies enforcing regulations that had been long neglected. It would be all but impossible for conservatives to prove that they were receiving targeted, unfavorable treatment—that is, as long as nobody was foolish enough to put the plan down on paper. If something like that were leaked to the conservative groups in question, it would be a public relations nightmare! And that is precisely what would happen in the summer of 1963. But between the fall of 1961 and the leak of the Reuther Memorandum two years later, the threat posed to the Kennedy administration by right-wing agitators like Edwin Walker and Billy James Hargis continued to grow.

Operation Midnight Ride

Within a month of Kennedy's Palladium speech, Edwin Walker had officially started his foray into politics. First, Walker had to reassure white southerners of his segregationist bona fides. That was because in 1957 Walker had commanded the paratroopers ordered to Little Rock, Arkansas, by President Eisenhower to rebuff Governor Orval Faubus.[74] Walker later expressed regret for obeying the order, but being the face of a federal military occupation damaged his reputation among segregationist hardliners. Walker began his rehabilitation efforts with a speech in Jackson, Mississippi, in December 1961. He flattered the crowd by crediting Mississippi with "the preservation of the Union" by "standing for its own sovereignty" during Reconstruction. It was, he said, a true "model of freedom from Oppression and Reconstruction—from the tyranny within our own white race."[75] Walker had hit all the right segregationist and racist notes, but white supremacists needed to see if his actions backed up his rhetoric.

So in September 1962, Walker headed to the University of Mississippi where civil rights activist James Meredith was attempting to enroll as the school's first black student. The Kennedy administration, after failing to broker a compromise with Mississippi Governor Ross Barnett, pressed ahead, sending military police and US marshals to Oxford to enforce the integration order. Walker had been in town for several days and loudly supported Barnett and segregation while also, variously, attacking Kennedy's Cuba policy and criticizing the Supreme Court's recent ruling on public school prayer.[76] The day before Meredith's enrollment, Walker had gone on television and encouraged Mississippians to "rally to the cause of freedom in righteous indignation, violent vocal protest, and bitter silence under the flag of Mississippi at the use of Federal troops."[77] Walker later clarified that he opposed actual violence, but his choice of words at the time sounded ominous. On September 30, Meredith tried to enroll, Governor Barnett withdrew state police, and in the ensuing chaos two journalists were killed and several soldiers were shot at by rioters. An Associated Press journalist reported witnessing Walker leading a mob of students in a charge against US marshals. It was front-page news the next day.[78]

Walker denied the allegations, saying he had actually encouraged the students to peaceably protest but that the students would not listen to him.[79] Whatever the truth of the matter, Robert Kennedy, who as Attorney General was in charge of the US marshals, had Walker arrested the following day and charged with sedition and insurrection. Walker's arrest certainly prevented him from further involvement in the riots, but Kennedy then turned the situation to partisan advantage. He had Walker, a potential rival to his brother in the next election, in the custody of the Justice

Department. It was an opportunity too good to pass up. The Justice Department claimed, with no substantiation, that it "held some doubt as to General Walker's competence to stand trial" and ordered him to undergo ninety days of psychiatric evaluation to determine if he was mentally competent.[80] Within eight and a half hours of his arrest, Walker had been flown out of state to a federal medical center, strip-searched, and placed in isolation in a maximum-security ward.[81]

Billy James Hargis leapt to Walker's defense, dedicating a full issue of the *Weekly Crusader* and multiple broadcasts to the case. He worried that if Walker could be detained for psychiatric evaluation on the basis of his extreme political points of view, who was to say that any other conservative might not be next? He complained, with more vehemence than accuracy, that liberals were ignoring Walker's plight and suggested that "if Martin Luther King had been so treated, every liberal newspaper in the nation would have launched a front page crusade."[82] After applying legal pressure, Walker walked free after two weeks in detention and the criminal charges against him were quickly dropped.[83]

The detention of Edwin Walker reveals, again, the extent to which the administration worried about the Right and the lengths to which it would go to marginalize Walker and his radio allies. It also played directly into white southern apprehensions about an unchecked federal government willing to bend the laws to desegregate the South. Furthermore, the episode illustrates how right-wing broadcasters magnified Walker's influence. He was a regular speaker for shows like the *Manion Forum,* the *Christian Crusade,* and the *Twentieth Century Reformation Hour.* Simply put, each time Walker spoke on one of these shows, his message was amplified by hundreds of radio stations all over the nation.

While part of Walker's appeal for right-wing broadcasters was his hardline stance on segregation, Walker's criticisms of the Kennedy administration's foreign policy were an equal draw. Walker was an ardent anti-Communist who believed that the president's failure to support the US-trained invaders at the Bay of Pigs in Cuba had categorically disqualified him from being president. (In an odd coincidence, the controversy over Walker's "Pro-Blue" curriculum erupted on April 16, 1961, and he was suspended from active duty the next day on April 17, 1961; April 17 was also the day of the Bay of Pigs fiasco.) Again, Walker knew what his audiences wanted to hear. For example, during his Jackson, Mississippi, speech in 1961, he assured the crowd that the Communists were particularly afraid of the free citizens of Mississippi,

Photo 3.2. Billy James Hargis sold copies of this pamphlet at Operation Midnight Ride rallies.

attacked the United Nations as "ornate, Asiatic, and Atheistic," and accused the Kennedy administration of being the latest in a long line of "Potomac Pretenders—New Dealers, Fair Dealers, Red-Herrings, [and] Co-existers."[84] Anti-Communism, anti-internationalism, and disgust for John F. Kennedy? Check, check, and check. Walker's views were by no means exceptional since militant anti-Communism was a basic conservative tenet, but having a former general offer those critiques gave them added weight.

Billy James Hargis quickly capitalized on Walker's anti-Communist obsession. Hargis had himself said that if Castro remained in power, then the Communists would "use Cuba as the base for the conquest for the remainder of Latin America and then the overthrow of the government of the United States."[85] Although Hargis had nothing but contempt for a Communist dictator like Castro, he never met an anti-Communist dictator he did not approve of. Hargis got his picture taken with Syngman Rhee in South Korea, defended the newly formed Republic of Rhodesia, and even befriended Rafael Trujillo, the anti-Communist dictator of the Dominican Republic. Hargis went to Dominica at Trujillo's invitation and on his dime in 1958 but without first obtaining clearance from the State Department, leading to a flurry of annoyed reports from the FBI.[86] After Trujillo's assassination in 1961, Hargis—annoyed by media coverage that focused on Trujillo's brutal suppression of political dissidents—memorialized him as an anti-Communist stalwart.[87]

In the spring of 1963, Hargis and Walker teamed up for a twenty-two-state campaign they called "Operation Midnight Ride."[88] Instead of warning that the British were coming, Walker and Hargis would sound the alarm about Communist infiltration of the federal government. One if by Congress, two if by White House. Speculation about Walker's possible third-party candidacy reached a fevered pitch. During each of the thirty-four rallies, Walker would discuss some point of Kennedy's foreign policy—the need for another invasion of Cuba one week, the danger of nuclear disarmament the next—while Hargis preached about the threat of domestic Communism. They certainly made no secret of their spite toward John F. Kennedy. When Hargis would introduce Walker at the rallies, he often started with the line "His [Walker's] noble qualities were demonstrated, not in losing P.T. boats . . . but in victories won on the battle-field against our enemies."[89] Hargis was attempting to subvert one of John F. Kennedy's particular strengths as a candidate. Kennedy had captained a patrol torpedo boat in the Pacific during World War II and been injured when his boat was struck by a Japanese destroyer. Kennedy's heroism in keeping his crew together after the sinking was frequently mentioned in campaign literature; but now Hargis was slyly implying that the incident was actually Kennedy's fault in the first place.

Like a presidential campaign, Operation Midnight Ride provided fliers, posters, and audio tapes for radio announcements to local sponsoring committees, which were then told to contact local branches of the Veterans of Foreign Wars and the American Legion among other groups. However, Hargis made it clear that he did not want any sponsors "associated with rabid anti-Semitic or anti-Catholic activities."[90] It simply made no business sense to alienate possible allies in the war on Communism and the Kennedy administration. Foreshadowing the Wallace campaign in 1968, Hargis and Walker concentrated their rallies in the Deep South with occasional forays into the Rustbelt cities of the Midwest.

Approximately thirty thousand people paid $1 or $1.25 to hear Walker and Hargis during the campaign. The typical rally consisted of eight hundred to a thousand people jammed into a small, civic auditorium for about three hours. Between ticket sales and book receipts, the campaign raised between $80,000 and 85,000 split between Hargis and Walker.[91] More important, each stop generated media attention as local and state newspapers covered the rallies in detail and national papers reprinted the highlights.[92]

Local businesspersons and civic boosters sponsored the rallies, including Birmingham Mayor Arthur Hanes and Public Safety Commissioner Eugene "Bull" Connor, who presented Hargis and Walker with keys to the city.[93]

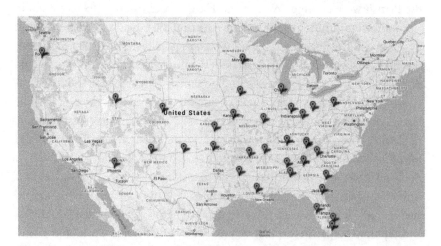

Figure 3.1. Map of Operation Midnight Ride stops, 1963.

In Greenville, South Carolina, the Bob Jones family—which ran a private, fundamentalist (and segregationist) school named Bob Jones University— sponsored the rally, although they held it off-campus, perhaps to insulate Walker from the school's well-known anti-Catholicism.[94] In Des Moines, the committee chairman was Robert D. Dilley, a leading manufacturer of loose-leaf binders, the author of *Message for America: A Handbook for Those Who Will Defend Freedom*, and eventual American Party candidate for the governorship of Iowa. He offered to introduce Walker to the chamber of commerce, brought him to speak to an assembly at Drake University, and got him a two-hour interview slot on "Russ Levine's Hawkeye Nite Line Show" after the rally.[95] In tiny Bunker Hill, Illinois, the town's sole physician headed the committee. In Birmingham and several other cities, radio station owners sponsored the rallies and provided free advertising.

Sometimes rallies were sponsored by doyens like Rosalind Kress Haley, a formidable figure in the business and social scene of Savannah, Georgia. Haley—whose father had founded the S. H. Kress & Co. chain of department stores—ran several gift shops, opened a conservative reading room, hosted a radio program, served on the county board of education, raised three children, served as a delegate to the Republican National Convention, and led a chapter apiece of the Daughters of the American Revolution, the John Birch Society, and Young Americans for Freedom. At age sixty, while volunteering for the Goldwater campaign, she met and married a fellow volunteer, the cattle rancher and historian J. Evetts Haley. Ronald Reagan would later appoint her as a delegate to the United Nations Educational, Scientific and Cultural Organization (UNESCO); she promptly drafted a report that led the United States to withdraw from the organization.[96] She was the kind of person who got things done. While the absolute numbers that attended the Operation Midnight Ride rallies may not seem significant, a few thousand like Rosalind Kress Haley were enough to move mountains, or at least enough to secure a nomination for a radical right-winger like Barry Goldwater.

Operation Midnight Ride almost ended a month early on April 10, 1963, when Lee Harvey Oswald attempted to assassinate Walker while he was at home taking a break from the rallies. Oswald shot Walker with the same rifle he would later use to kill President Kennedy, but the bullet shattered on the window frame and Walker's wound was not serious.[97] He returned to the campaign trail with Hargis a month later. What is most intriguing about Oswald's assassination attempt is his motive. Oswald's wife later testified that when he returned home the night of April 10 he told her that he had shot at

General Walker. When she questioned his right to kill Walker, Lee Harvey responded, "Well, what would you say if somebody got rid of Hitler at the right time?"[98] Lee Harvey Oswald believed what many on the Left thought at the time, that there was a real possibility that Edwin Walker might lead some kind of military insurrection if not stopped. The United States seemed merely a putsch away from a fascistic, military dictatorship. Oswald simply carried that belief to its logical, albeit extreme, end.

Oswald was not the only person keeping an eye on Walker during Operation Midnight Ride. The FBI sent informants to several rallies. The FBI began tracking Hargis in 1957 when "Billy James HARGUS [sic]" criticized Eisenhower's foreign policy on border radio station XEG in Monterrey, Mexico. Stations like XEG were a haven for broadcasters excluded from American airwaves, including right-wingers like Hargis, infamous "goat gland doctor" John R. Brinkley, and "the Mexican Nightingale" Rosa Dominguez.[99] They were hotbeds of quackery, political radicalism, and cross-border cultural innovation. By being just across the border, these stations escaped FCC regulation and their unlicensed, high-power broadcasts reached as far north as the Dakotas at night. It is not hard to imagine why the FBI would be concerned about an American national using Mexican radio to accuse Secretary of State John Foster Dulles of being pro-Soviet.[100]

Once Hargis held a rally with both Walker and Strom Thurmond in attendance, the FBI became much more active. The conference was held in Tulsa, Oklahoma, in January 1962. The FBI's report, which went up the chain to J. Edgar Hoover, also noted Hargis's role in the Air Force manual scandal.[101] The FBI began sending informants to Hargis's meetings, especially when they overheard anti-Hargis chatter from their sources in the Communist Party USA and various socialist parties. Multiple informants attended rallies during Operation Midnight Ride, evincing a particular interest in Walker's mental state. One informant reported that Walker appeared unstable only when photographers and reporters were present, but was "very lucid" and "quite normal" while addressing the group.[102] The FBI was worried that Walker, Hargis, or one of their followers would advocate violence at the upcoming civil rights march in Washington, DC, in August 1963. The informants were asked if they saw weapons at the rallies and if Hargis and Walker had expressed an opinion about the march, but none reported seeing any firearms and the most Hargis and Walker ever said about the march was to wish that the attorney general had the gumption to stop it.[103]

Operation Midnight Ride drew to a close in May 1963. Walker remained a regular at Hargis's annual conventions and on the anti-Communist speaking circuit, but he did not run for president in 1964. If Walker had been a better public speaker, he, rather than George Wallace, might have been the most infamous third-party candidate of the 1960s. But Walker had a wooden delivery behind the podium and was awkward both in person and with the press.[104] He had spent his military career being respected for his rank; retail politics did not come naturally to him. Furthermore, Goldwater was conservative enough to assuage right-wingers like Walker and Hargis (although only just). Yet as Walker's presidential aspirations petered out, two new developments sparked right-wing outrage.

The Nuclear Test Ban Treaty

The first development was the Kennedy administration's final push for a Nuclear Test Ban Treaty with the Soviet Union. It had been a campaign issue for Kennedy in 1960, although not a particularly contentious one given that Nixon also supported a ban on atmospheric testing. In September 1961 during a speech to the United Nations, Kennedy challenged the Soviet Union "not to an arms race, but to a peace race—to advance together step by step, stage by stage, until general and complete disarmament has been achieved."[105] That same month Congress passed legislation establishing an independent US Arms Control and Disarmament Agency (ACDA). From 1961 to 1963, the new agency published a series of booklets—including contributions from the likes of United Nations representative Adlai Stevenson and Secretary of State Dean Rusk—advocating for far more than a ban on atmospheric nuclear testing. The booklets laid out a three-stage plan that would end with complete nuclear disarmament, the abolition of all national armed forces, and the creation of a United Nations peacekeeping force as a replacement.[106]

The more radical proposals had no serious political support in Congress, but that did not stop conservatives from blaming the Kennedy administration for having unrealistic goals in the ongoing disarmament talks with the Soviets. There was plenty of breathless hyperbole in reporting on the talks, not all from right-wing outlets. "US TO PROPOSE END OF NATIONAL ARMIES" screamed the front page of the *Los Angeles Times*.[107] One conservative columnist summarized the plan as "one, two, three bingo. The U.N. Rules the world."[108] And, as expected, conservative congressmen lined up in opposition. Senator John Tower criticized disarmament proponents for their "childlike faith"; they were marching off the same cliff as arms controls advocates had after World War I. It was, Tower said, "national suicide."[109] Broadcaster Dan Smoot wrote a parable comparing negotiations with Russia to law enforcement sitting down and supping with organized crime.[110]

In the 1960s, like today, hyperbole made for punchy soundbites, but there were also calmer, more reasonable critiques of the Nuclear Test Ban Treaty from the Right. *National Review* editor William F. Buckley, Brent Bozell, and World War I fighter ace Eddie Rickenbacker formed the short-lived National Committee against the Treaty of Moscow, arguing against a policy of appeasement toward the Soviet Union.[111] Clarence Manion dedicated a half dozen of his radio shows to the topic, inviting guests like California Congressman Craig Hosmer to comment. Hosmer told Manion's audience that he opposed a treaty because the administration had stripped out enforcement mechanisms after the Soviets protested. The final treaty would ban all but underground nuclear tests and require even those to remain contained. Yet the treaty had no mechanism for inspecting underground test sites, and several posttreaty Soviet bomb tests likely violated the agreement.[112]

President Kennedy again had a political problem on his hands. He had pushed radical conservative officers out of military leadership in 1961, but now he had retired Rear Admiral Chester Ward routinely lambasting him on Clarence Manion's radio program while General Walker stumped across the Midwest with Billy James Hargis. Worse, people listened to them. In a March 1962 poll, 67% of Americans approved of all nuclear testing, even atmospheric testing. Things improved from the Kennedy perspective the next year—the Cuban Missile Crisis was a godsend for disarmament advocates—and by July 1963 the ratios had started to flip with 52% of Americans supporting an atmospheric test ban.[113] That was still an uncomfortably close popular margin, especially since the anti–test ban crowd was the more energized position. Lawrence O'Brien, one of Kennedy's personal assistants, reported that constituent mail split almost fifteen to one against the test ban.[114] Treaty approval required a two-thirds vote of the Senate, and while the Democrats controlled sixty-six Senate seats, they could not rely on conservative Southern Democrats with such lackluster poll numbers.[115] Something needed to be done to goose public opinion. What the administration came up with would hinge on action by the FCC, but that is a discussion for chapter 4.

The Reuther Memorandum Leaked

The second development in the summer of 1963 that outraged conservatives was the leak of the Reuther Memorandum. You would think that such an inflammatory document would be leaked by a conservative sympathizer in the Kennedy administration, but it actually came from an unexpected source. Two journalists, Donald Janson from the *New York Times* and Bernard Eismann from CBS, published a book, *The Far Right*, earlier that year. The book was a critique of various right-wingers, including Billy James Hargis, Fred Schwarz, and Robert Welch. The authors had included a summary of the Reuther Memorandum to show that the tide had turned against the "Far Right."[116] They did not include the entire memorandum, although given their substantive quoting from the document, someone had clearly given them a peek at the memo. Despite the two journalists' liberal sympathies, they had unwittingly exposed the Kennedy administration to significant embarrassment.[117]

Conservatives seized on the document's existence as proof of liberal skullduggery. First, though, they needed to get their hands on a copy. In June 1963, letters inquiring about the Reuther Memorandum started trickling into both Robert Kennedy's and Walter Reuther's offices. The trickle soon became a flood. Victor Reuther's assistant warned him, "You might want to start to keep a file of this kind of material because there will be a lot of it."[118] Outraged conservatives wrote in saying that they had heard from Billy James Hargis or Edgar Bundy about Walter Reuther's plot, no doubt concocted in the depths of the Kremlin, to persecute the Right and "Sovietize" America. But not all the letters came from conservatives. Kennedy supporters wrote in to complain about conservatives in their workplace, neighborhood, or church fabricating what were surely slanderous allegations about some memorandum. Might the attorney general confirm that the document was a fake so they could silence these pesky right-wingers? A high school English teacher in Virginia was appalled when his "so-called Sunday School class" was "almost turned into a Republican rally" over "an alleged 16-page memo from Walter Reuther." He was used to being "surrounded by these idiots," but he would not mind some help with a rebuttal by confirming that no such document existed.[119] Another Kennedy supporter had heard Bundy on the radio and wrote the White House worrying that such allegations would not "lie dormant in the fertile soil for lunatics in So. Cal."[120]

Photo 3.3. After its leak, copies of the Reuther Memorandum were widely reprinted by conservative groups and given an anti-Communist gloss.
Billy James Hargis Papers, Special Collections, University of Arkansas Libraries.

Nor would they. What the letter writer had heard was a rebroadcast of Edgar Bundy, who had gone on television station KTTV in Los Angeles in July to discuss the Reuther Memorandum with Emmy-award-winning news anchor George Putnam. Always media savvy, Bundy teased the memorandum for his audience, giving a few damning quotes and promising to reveal the entire document at an upcoming rally.[121] Every major conservative broadcaster followed suit, dedicating entire broadcasts to the memorandum. Once Bundy got his hands on a copy—likely from conservative Congressman James

Photo 3.4. A cartoon in Carl McIntire's newspaper, *Christian Beacon*, dramatizing the actions proposed in the leaked Reuther Memorandum.
Carl McIntire Papers, Special Collections, Princeton Theological Seminary Library.

Utt—the document spread quickly. Hargis reprinted the memo and offered it for sale ($.50 a copy or, for a limited time only, fifteen copies for $5.00). After initially planning a response—the stencils for a counterattack ad were already cut—the Reuthers decided to stay silent and direct all questions to the attorney general. It must have smarted for Walter to have to grin and bear Hargis's attacks, which were ready-made for radio. Fundamentalist ministers do like a good alliteration. Hargis labeled Walter Reuther a "ruthless, reckless, lawless labor goon," a "persistent prevaricator," and a "double-talking, rabble-rousing opportunist, who glibly repeats the fallacious fulminations of his Red-tinged ghostwriters."[122]

Given how useful the Reuther Memorandum leak was to conservatives, it is reasonable to ask why the Kennedy administration gave out copies. It was not for wanting of trying to avoid doing so. They resisted for a time, not even responding to inquiries about the memo for more than a month after it was leaked. The delay gave them breathing room, time to figure out how to respond.[123] At first, Robert Kennedy favored simply denying the memorandum's existence. Kennedy's press secretary wrote him in June to double-check "that there is no foundation to the report" in Janson and Eismann's book. (Embarrassingly, the press secretary was forced to admit just four days later that he was one of Janson and Eismann's sources.) Kennedy responded in the margins, "I know nothing about it."[124] By July, Kennedy's tune had changed as the volume of mail increased and his office began receiving requests from congressmen. The story was too believable and its authors too credible for people to believe that the document did not exist at all. The longer they delayed, the guiltier they seemed. One of Kennedy's assistants noted that Senator Robert Byrd, a conservative Democrat but loyal to the administration, was "hot after this thing; they think we're trying to cover up."[125] It is one thing to ignore requests from congressmen in the other party, but quite another to stonewall a prominent member of your own party. The attorney general's office subsequently secured the memorandum from the UAW and released copies to the first 1,200 who had written in to ask for it.

The official explanation that accompanied each copy of the memorandum was that Robert Kennedy had not requested it from the Reuthers. It was merely "an expression of the writer's ideas and thoughts on a topic of current interest." Far be it from Kennedy to discourage "those who have views respecting matters of national concern from communicating their views to him."[126] Apparently, Walter Reuther was just some guy who happened to "have views." Since denial had not worked, the attorney general's new strategy—outlined in an internal memo to Kennedy that November—was to admit its existence but to deny that he had solicited, disseminated, or implemented the memo.[127] Kennedy took the advice to heart, shortly thereafter claiming to not having read the memo, this despite five months of controversy, constant conservative criticism, and thousands of photocopies.[128]

A week later the controversy was completely subsumed by the assassination of John F. Kennedy in Dallas. Conservative broadcasters would dredge it up periodically over the next few years, but accusations of a Kennedy-sponsored conspiracy to shut down right-wing broadcasting had no hope of gaining any traction after the president's death. Since then labor historians have shown little interest in the Reuther Memorandum. The files on the controversy, and the memo itself, have been part of Walter's and Victor's papers since the 1970s, yet the memo makes no appearance in Nelson Lichtenstein's otherwise excellent biography of Walter Reuther.[129] Lichtenstein focused on labor politics, and since the brouhaha over the memo came mostly from conservative circles, it may have fallen into a blind spot. In any case, the memo certainly validates Lichtenstein's book title, *Walter Reuther: The Most Dangerous Man in Detroit*. For the Right, Walter Reuther proved to be a very dangerous man indeed.

It is not surprising that Robert Kennedy's story changed repeatedly regarding the memo. It did, after all, look bad. Walter Reuther never publicly discussed the memo, but after Walter's death Victor included a copy in *The Brothers Reuther*. Victor's account is brief, barely a page in a book that somehow finds room for five pages on the intricacies of a small tractor exchange program with Cuba. Although brief, Victor's account differs dramatically from Kennedy's. According to Victor, John F. Kennedy had asked for Robert's advice about how to deal with the many death threats he had received from conservatives, particularly conservatives from Texas. Robert then asked Walter to "put some concrete suggestions on paper." Victor also believed that at least some of their suggestions were implemented by the attorney general. His only regret was that they had not implemented even more of the recommendations, for if they had then "the American tragedy that began with the two Kennedy assassinations, the murder of Dr. King, and continued with the Nixon election might have been avoided."[130] (Reuther did not elaborate on how exactly a crackdown on the Radio Right would have stopped assassinations committed by two left-wing individuals.)

More important, for Robert Kennedy's denial of soliciting or even reading the memo to be accurate, Victor would have to be mistaken. Fifteen years had passed between the creation of the Reuther Memorandum and the publication of *The Brothers Reuther*, so a simple mix-up of memory is possible, except that, as already discussed, letters between the Reuthers in the fall of 1961 show that Walter met on multiple occasions with both Robert and John F. Kennedy. Furthermore, he had used an early draft of the memorandum as the basis for those conversations. Victor Reuther's version of the story has more documentary evidence behind it and has the added benefit of being more believable.

Robert Kennedy and Victor Reuther also disagreed over whether the Kennedy administration had ever actually implemented the memo's recommendations. That is a much more difficult question to answer because the only people who knew the truth of the matter asserted beyond the shadow of a doubt, Robert and John F. Kennedy, were murdered before the decade was out. It is also hardly the sort of thing that the two brothers would have detailed on paper or on tape, even prior to Watergate. Given that frustrating silence, one must look at their actions and those of their inner circle of advisers and operatives after the fall of 1961. As chapters 2 and 3 have shown in detail, the Kennedy brothers had motive aplenty for wanting the Radio Right silenced; but whether the Kennedys used the means available to them to undermine the Right is the subject of chapter 4.

4

Just Because You're Paranoid Doesn't Mean They Aren't After You

Putting the Reuther Memorandum to Work

On November 21, 1963, historian Richard Hofstadter lectured at Oxford University on "the paranoid style in American politics."[1] The paranoid, Hofstadter argued, saw "the fate of conspiracy in apocalyptic terms." They believed that they were the last bulwark of civilization against a coming chaos perpetrated by a secretive, powerful, and imagined enemy. Hofstadter traced the paranoid style through American history from the anti–Masonic Party to the John Birch Society. He made no attempt to hold back his scorn for the people mentioned, going so far as to suggest that the paranoid's espousal of morality and purity were the projected "fantasies of true believers" who needed "strong sadomasochistic outlets." This was not an uncommon belief about conservatives among left-wing intellectuals and artists at the time; Stanley Kubrick's film *Dr. Strangelove*, released just a few months later, featured the character of General Jack D. Ripper, a sexually frustrated obsessive who was paranoid about protecting Americans' "precious bodily fluids." Hofstadter ended his lecture with pseudo-scientific musings about "a persistent psychic phenomenon" that affected "a modest minority of the population."[2]

The lecture could not have been more auspiciously timed. The very next day on November 22, President Kennedy was assassinated in Dallas. Lee Harvey Oswald was certainly no right-winger, but in the immediate aftermath of the shooting many liberals assumed that paranoid conservatives were somehow responsible. Hofstadter's ideas received further attention the following year during the presidential election when the lightly edited lecture was published in *Harper's Magazine*. Although the essay only briefly mentioned Barry Goldwater, it was clear that Hofstadter considered the conservative senator and presidential hopeful to be afflicted with the paranoid style.

The Radio Right. Paul Matzko, © Oxford University Press (2020). Oxford University Press.
DOI: 10.1093/oso/9780190073220.001.0001

Hofstadter's analytical lens has had a long half-life. Accusations of being prone to the "paranoid style" continue to be flung about in political discourse today. But as popular as Hofstadter's ideas about conservatism remain among pundits, they have fallen out of favor with academics. The growing body of literature on conservatism from the past fifteen years can be seen as a tacit rebuttal to Hofstadter's view.[3] Yet while Hofstadter's theory has been widely rejected by political historians because he portrayed conservatism as a mere neurotic tic, a more fundamental problem with his portrayal remains. When Hofstadter gave his lecture in the fall of 1963, conservatives did have much to be legitimately worried about. The Reuther Memorandum was finally bearing fruit.

By the fall of 1963, three of the major recommendations of the Reuther Memorandum had been implemented. The first recommendation was fulfilled by the Reuther brothers themselves. As soon as the ink on the Reuther Memorandum had dried, the Reuthers had funded the creation of an information clearinghouse that would provide opposition research on conservatives to Democratic congresspeople and liberal interest groups. The other two recommendations were discharged by the Kennedy administration. Starting in late 1961, the Internal Revenue Service (IRS) began a targeted campaign of audits of right-wing organizations with the encouragement of the White House and the attorney general. Then in 1963 the Federal Communications Commission (FCC) clarified its Fairness Doctrine rules in such a way as to empower liberal interest groups at the expense of conservative broadcasters. As this chapter will show, these three actions set the stage for the censorship of the Radio Right.

Group Research Inc.

The Reuther brothers had never planned to leave the fight against the Right solely in the hands of the Kennedy administration. The Kennedys were to implement "affirmative Administration policies and programs" that would "set the backdrop against which private activity is most likely to succeed." Then, in a footnote in the Reuther Memorandum, the Reuthers called on private interest groups in the press, the church, labor, and the media to join the government in the effort "to identify and expose the radical Right."[4] In January 1962, a month after sending Robert Kennedy the memorandum, the Reuthers made good on their promise—likely relayed in person by Walter Reuther at his November meeting with Robert Kennedy—to create a "clearing house of information" on right-wingers. The new organization, which was given the appropriately bland name Group Research Inc. (GRI), would provide opposition research to all "those fighting the extreme right-wing."[5]

Joe Rauh, Victor Reuther, and several other United Auto Workers (UAW) administrators formed GRI's executive committee and they asked Wesley McCune to be its public face and research director. McCune was a safe choice. After law school he had worked briefly for the National Labor Relations Board before embarking on a career as a journalist, writing for *Newsweek* and *Time* with a particular interest in agricultural policy. In 1953 he joined the Democratic National Committee as their agricultural research specialist, and in 1956 he joined the National Farmers Union as director of public relations. He was a labor man and a Democrat through and through.[6]

The GRI's initial 1962 budget of $30,000 came entirely from union sources, split three ways between the UAW, the American Federation of Labor and Congress of Industrial Organizations (AFL-CIO), and contributions from union affiliates. After the 1964 election, the AFL-CIO pulled its funding and GRI's financial situation looked grim until the Democratic National Committee took up the slack and became the organization's largest contributor.[7] Their investment paid dividends in opposition research. GRI maintained an extensive directory of right-wing groups and individuals, which they offered to liberal congresspersons and interest groups for a small fee. For instance, say you wanted to know more about the strange former B-list Hollywood actor and General Electric shill that had recently addressed your local chamber of commerce. Submit your request for "Ronald Reagan" to the GRI and they could give you all the dirt on Reagan's radical connections, from speaking at a Fred Schwarz crusade to spearheading the American Medical Association's anti-Medicare campaign, "Ronald Reagan Speaks Out Against Socialized Medicine."[8]

GRI's files came in handy during the 1964 election season. To justify his budget to the UAW and Democratic National Committee, McCune generated a confidential list of all the requests he had received in the prior year. No fewer than eighty-six congresspersons (exclusively Democrats) had requested files on right-wingers, as had more than a hundred liberal interest groups. For example, GRI helped Robert F. Kennedy with his run for a US Senate seat in New York following his resignation as US attorney general in 1964. Kennedy faced Republican incumbent Kenneth Keating, a political moderate who tried to distance himself as much as possible from the Republican Party's conservative wing. He even refused to endorse the Republican presidential nominee that year, conservative Senator Barry Goldwater.[9] This meant that Kennedy stood to benefit if he could tie Keating to the "radical" Right and muddy his moderate reputation. GRI helped him do that.

The Kennedy campaign submitted multiple requests to GRI for information exposing Keating's true conservative colors, requests with titles like "ACA Ratings on Sen. Keating" and "1961 ACA award."[10] The Americans for Constitutional Action (ACA) was a conservative think tank founded in 1958 to counter the liberal group Americans for Democratic Action.[11] With information from GRI in hand, the Kennedy campaign recruited an ally, New York City Mayor Robert Wagner, to release the bombshell news a month before the election. The "ultra-conservative" ACA had given Keating an award in 1961, a distinction he shared with none other than Strom Thurmond and Barry Goldwater himself.[12] Keating protested that he had not been informed of the identities of the other award winners, but the charges stuck. Kennedy subsequently won the election by ten percentage points (which was slightly disappointing given that Lyndon Johnson demolished Goldwater in New York by 68% to 31%).

Many of the requests submitted to GRI asked for information about right-wing broadcasters. The names of Carl McIntire, Billy James Hargis, the John Birch Society, and other broadcasters pepper the thirty-six pages of requests. A group like the Presbyterian Appalachian Broadcasting Council could get full station listings for Carl McIntire from GRI, handy for when their parent organization, the National Council of Churches, asked their affiliates to use Fairness Doctrine complaints to push right-wing religious broadcasters off the airwaves. GRI was as interested in right-wing broadcasting as its clients were. The first issue of their newsletter featured an article about Billy James Hargis.[13] Yet while information gathering was useful at every stage of the anti–Radio Right campaign, more direct action was needed.

Death by Taxes

The second major recommendation of the Reuther Memorandum was for the Kennedys to choke off the supply of money to the Right by ordering the Internal Revenue Service (IRS) to audit right-wing broadcasters, repeal their tax exemptions, and thus drive off their donors. Ironically, these were the same tactics used during the 1950s to squash radical left-wing groups. For example, in 1954 the IRS had secretly audited the Communist Party USA (CPUSA), levied massive fines against it, and promptly seized all of its major assets and padlocked its offices. In 1967, after thirteen years of legal wrangling, the IRS realized it might lose the CPUSA's counterlawsuit and settled.[14] Despite the setback, the IRS had truly won; their tactics scared off donors and members and helped turn the CPUSA into a shell of what it once was. Victory even in defeat would have been a fitting motto for the IRS. The Kennedys simply took the weapons used against the Far Left and brought them to bear on the Far Right.

There is substantial documentary evidence tying the White House to this systematic campaign of IRS audits of right-wing organizations from 1961 to 1965. The campaign is a major subject in the late historian John A. Andrews's book *Power to Destroy: The Political Uses of the IRS from Kennedy to Nixon.* Andrews did the mind-numbing work of submitting Freedom of Information Act requests and slogging through the Church Committee's reports to reconstruct the IRS's "Ideological Organizations Project." It is a remarkable work on an agency that resists examination.[15] Yet although Andrews dedicates an entire chapter to the IRS's scrutiny of Billy James Hargis, the question of why it was that Hargis received special attention is beyond the scope of the book. Andrews mentions John F. Kennedy's "man on horseback" speech briefly, but then falls back on generalities when describing the president's concerns about the Right in 1961. Andrews was also content to simply assert a link between the IRS audits and the Reuther Memorandum. By taking a closer look at the archives of the Reuther brothers and the Kennedy administration, we can confirm that connection.

The timing of the IRS's audit campaign, called the "Ideological Organizations Project," is damning. As mentioned in chapter 3, Walter Reuther shared some of his ideas about the Radio Right with Robert Kennedy at a meeting during the second week of November 1961.[16] A few days later on November 16, John Seigenthaler, who was Robert Kennedy's administrative assistant, contacted Mitchell Rogovin, the IRS commissioner's assistant and legal adviser, to inquire about the tax-exempt status of "four or five organizations generally considered to be right-wing" and to ask whether they had been audited recently.[17]

Seigenthaler was Robert Kennedy's special projects man, someone whom he could trust to get things done off the books. He had worked as Robert's assistant during the 1960 campaign and stayed in the position after the election. In his own terms, his job was to help Kennedy to "dis-associate himself from politics, insofar as he could," by working with the Democratic National Committee to distribute political favors.[18] As we will see later, one of those favors would be paid out to E. William Henry in the form of the chairmanship of the FCC. Seigenthaler functioned for Robert in much the same way as Robert himself functioned for his brother. Robert wanted to be John F. Kennedy's man on the ground, someone who could implement controversial policies while acting as a buffer against crit-icism of his brother. If an action went sour, he could take the political fall.[19] Seigenthaler did the same for Robert, contacting the IRS on his behalf and later testifying before a congressional committee and denying any know-ledge of his actions. (When confronted with the fact that his appointment calendar showed multiple calls to Mitchell Rogovin in November of 1961, Seigenthaler claimed that he did not remember the subject of any of the calls although he was absolutely certain he had never discussed the Right with Rogovin.)[20]

Those "four or five" right-wing organizations were not identified by the US Senate's Church Committee.[21] However, a note from Seigenthaler to Rogovin later in November shows that one of them was Fred Schwarz of the Christian Anti-Communism Crusade, who was one of the conserva-tive broadcasters prominently featured in the Reuther Memorandum.[22] Two days after Seigenthaler's phone call, President Kennedy gave his "man on horseback" speech in Los Angeles. At a news conference at the end of the month, Kennedy fielded a question about campaign finance reform in light of contributions to "Right-Wing extremist groups." Kennedy responded with concern that some donors were diverting taxable funds to tax-exempt groups, although he "was sure the Internal Revenue System examines that."[23] He did not mention the fact that he could be confident that the IRS would do so because his brother's administrative assistant had told them to.

The Kennedy brothers had a reliable ally at the IRS. President Kennedy appointed Mortimer Caplin, one of Robert Kennedy's former law professors, as the new IRS commissioner. The Attorney General had chosen Caplin for the position because he wanted a discreet ally who would bend the rules to help him take down organized crime. (Indeed, the IRS helped the Justice Department raise its mob indictment totals from just 19 in 1960 to 687 in 1964.)[24] Caplin later explained of his philosophy as commissioner, "If the president is interested in a particular program, you would certainly in some instances give attention to some area he's interested in. . . . [I]f the president should call, and you feel that he has a reasonable request, you will be compliant."[25]

The day after the president's news conference, the IRS's assistant commissioner in charge of compliance sent a clipping of the president's statement at the news conference to three people: the head of the IRS audit division, Mitchell Rogovin (Caplin's legal adviser), and John Seigenthaler at the attorney general's office. Rogovin was ordered to come up with a list of groups to be "examined," to use the president's words. In three weeks he had compiled a list, which he sent to the head of the IRS audit division "for your use in making the referred to sample checks." Again, a copy was sent to John Seigenthaler at the attorney general's office. There were eighteen groups on the list; all were conservative. Number one on the list was Billy James Hargis's *Christian Crusade*, but most of the major right-wing groups and broadcasters made an appearance on the list, including the John Birch Society, H. L. Hunt's *Life Line*, and Fred Schwarz's Christian Anti-Communist Crusade.[26] To summarize, on November 29 the president had signaled his desire for the IRS to check the tax exemption compliance of right-wing organizations. Within three weeks, the IRS's Rogovin had come up with a list of right-wing groups and ordered the audit process to begin, being careful all the while to keep Seigenthaler and the attorney general's office in the loop. There is no dearth of documentary evidence showing coordination between the Kennedy administration and the IRS's right-wing audit program.

Rogovin was selected as the lead investigator for the audits. The presence of so many conservative broadcasters on the list was no accident. Rogovin would later claim that the chosen groups had been selected merely because they were "ideological" groups that sought "to educate the public in currently controversial fields" through "mass media."[27] But it did not take long for the IRS to realize that an audit campaign exclusively targeting right-wingers might look bad if the list were leaked. So in March 1962, the national office of the audit division officially replaced the words "right-wing organization" with "political action organization" in order "to avoid giving the impression that the Service is giving special attention to returns filed by taxpayers or organizations with a particular political ideology." IRS Commissioner Mortimer Caplin would later say of the revised list, "We recognized the sensitivity of just going after [the] right wing, so we wanted to add both left- and right-wing groups for balance."[28] The audit program was even given a scrupulously nonpartisan name, the "Ideological Origins Project." Of course, the IRS was primarily targeting the Right, but a little change in terminology was an easy way to divert suspicion. For the sake of appearances, the IRS also added ten left-wing groups to the list and trimmed the right-wing groups down to twelve. This list of twenty-two organizations was then forwarded to the secretary of the Treasury and Robert Kennedy, who signed off on the project.[29]

At first blush, this seems like an equitable division between Left and Right. After all, when JFK called IRS Commissioner Caplin in July 1963, he told Caplin "to go ahead with [an] aggressive program—on both sides of center."[30] And at an internal IRS meeting three days later, Rogovin charged his agents to "go up the middle." Still, he followed those words with a charge to "first deal with right-wing groups." Words are cheap. Actions are telling. The White House asked Rogovin to give updates on the project multiple times during 1962–1963. The White House had hoped that the IRS could complete its audits and make its recommendations by October 1963, but Rogovin needed more time.[31] That summer the list of targeted groups was revised yet again. Rogovin added several additional conservative broadcasters, including Carl McIntire, and dropped almost all of the remaining left-wing organizations. His source for deciding which groups to add was none other than GRI, bringing these two wings of the Reuther Memorandum strategy into direct contact.[32]

Rogovin sent a copy of the revised list to Robert Kennedy, but the Ideological Origins Project was still proceeding too slowly. On August 20, 1963, Robert Kennedy went to the IRS in person to meet with Rogovin and encourage haste. Kennedy brought along a strange plus-one, E. William Henry, the newly minted chairman of the FCC. Henry's presence at that meeting will take on added significance later in this chapter, but for now suffice it to say that this was a highly unusual meeting of officials from three distinct executive agencies. After receiving an update on the status of the various investigations, Robert Kennedy asked for an expedited ruling on the tax exemption of *Life Line*, a conservative broadcast sponsored by Texas oil man H. L. Hunt. Rogovin promised it within six weeks and Kennedy left after charging Rogovin to keep him "personally advised" of its progress.[33] John F. Kennedy echoed this interest in October 1963, telling a friend that he was frustrated that rich conservatives had their already light tax burdens made even lighter by deductions for their contributions to "ultra-right" broadcasters. The worst offenders named by Kennedy? Jean Paul Getty and H. L. Hunt.[34] If there are any remaining doubts about the partisan bent of the Ideological Origins Project, consider the fact that of the final twenty-four groups audited, the IRS decided to revoke the tax exemptions of fifteen. All fifteen were conservative.[35]

This kind of close contact and information sharing between the White House, the attorney general, and the IRS was irregular and likely illegal but not uncommon. The only other possible explanation for the Ideological Organizations Project is that it was the product of an exuberant, rogue IRS faction seeking to curry favor with the administration. However, all the available pieces of evidence point to it being a plan hatched by the Kennedy administration based on advice given by the Reuther brothers. When Robert Kennedy sat down with Walter Reuther in November 1961,

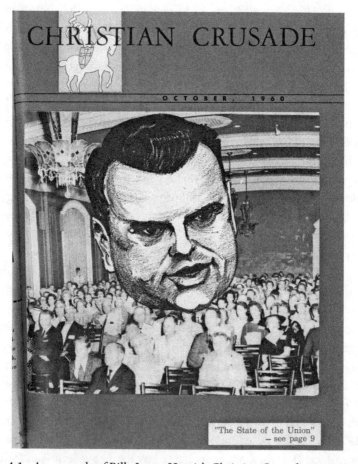

Photo 4.1. An example of Billy James Hargis's *Christian Crusade* magazine including this cover drawing of Hargis as a giant, floating, disembodied head.
Billy James Hargis Papers, Special Collections, University of Arkansas Libraries.

it was Reuther who told him to use IRS audits to combat the Radio Right. Days later, Kennedy's assistant contacted the IRS about scheduling audits for right-wing broadcasters, including one of the men featured in the Reuther Memorandum. Both Kennedy brothers showed unusual interest in the project and received regular updates from the IRS. When the project progressed more sluggishly than expected, Robert Kennedy pushed for an accelerated audit on H. L. Hunt's *Life Line* program, another of the groups featured in the Reuther Memorandum. The Reuthers had suggested the IRS as a means to stem the flow of contributions to right-wing broadcasters and the Kennedys had followed through. The only question that remains is whether their plan worked.

The IRS versus Billy James Hargis

One of the groups that had its tax exemption revoked by the IRS was Billy James Hargis's *Christian Crusade*. The investigation began in April 1962 when the national IRS office sent its prettified list of "political action organizations" to its branch offices. The Tulsa branch office assigned an agent to Hargis's case, but, much to the frustration of the national office, the local agent would not recommend revoking Hargis's tax exemption. Indeed, four times in a row from 1962 to 1964 the agent returned a "no charge report" on the *Christian Crusade*. His reasoning was simple. Neither Hargis's rhetoric nor the relevant tax code had changed since the IRS granted the *Christian Crusade* a tax exemption back in 1952. After each "no charge," the national office instructed the local agent to look again and look closer. Memos from the branch office show some confusion among the local agents about why the national office was pushing this case on them, especially since the national office did not inform them of the partisan purpose of the Ideological Organizations Project. They were explicitly told that the IRS did "not have a 'drive' going on" but was merely "making more examinations of this type [of] organization throughout the country."[36] The memos do not reveal whether local agents swallowed the line they were being fed.

Rogovin and the national office were in an awkward position. They did not want to tip their hand and risk exposing the true purpose of the project, but their cautiousness was keeping them from getting the tax exemptions revoked. So they took over the case themselves. This was an unusual step, typically used only when a local branch or agent was suspected of corruption, which was not the case with the agent assigned to Hargis. They did so through a little sleight of hand, ordering the branch office to ask the national office for "technical advice," even telling them how to word their request.[37] Unsurprisingly, once the national office got its hands on the case they recommended that Hargis's tax exemption be revoked in November 1964. They also ordered the *Christian Crusade* to pony up more than $100,000 in back taxes. Worse yet, contributors to the *Christian Crusade* could no longer claim the money they had donated as a tax deduction.

Once the investigations went public, conservative outrage towards the IRS was swift and predictable. Carl McIntire, despite a falling out with Hargis several years earlier, came to Hargis's defense with a special issue of the *Christian Beacon* (and multiple reports on the *Twentieth Century Reformation Hour*). In the issue, Hargis defended himself by saying he had never supported a particular candidate for public office. He had certainly criticized many candidates, but he had not told his listeners whom to vote for. He was ideological but nonpartisan. Most of his self-defense consisted of pointing out the hypocrisy of the situation. After all, there were many liberal tax-exempt organizations that had gone several steps further than he had but without consequence. For example, the mainline *Christian Century* had run a series of editorials just before the 1964 election discouraging its readers from voting for Barry Goldwater.[38]

Hargis frequently repeated variations on this argument over the next several years. In 1967 he cited President Lyndon Johnson encouraging a group of mainline Methodists to get involved in politics in order to address social problems. Hargis then listed the many specific, liberal political positions that the National Council of Churches had advocated for during the 1960s.[39] Hargis, McIntire, and other right-wingers suspected a double standard between how the IRS treated groups that supported administration policies versus those that did not. A comic in Hargis's paper had an "Internal Revenue" cop biffing a chubby, beatific Hargis over the head with a billy club and yelling, "You're too political!" Meanwhile a mob composed of beatniks, thugs, and sanctimonious clergymen looked on holding signs reading "Defeat Goldwater" and "Repeal Taft-Hartley Act."[40]

Hargis challenged the ruling in court. The IRS argued that Hargis was guilty of "advocacy of a political point of view on a variety of topics," including income tax, urban renewal, and education. He had even encouraged his listeners to write their congressmen with their concerns about these issues. The IRS held that this kind of activity was "only remotely, if at all" concerned with educational or religious ends. The Federal Tax Code did indeed prohibit tax-exempt organizations from influencing legislation or intervening in political campaigns on behalf of a candidate.[41] Yet the IRS had traditionally given relatively wide latitude on those requirements for nonprofits. Organizations could advocate for political issues, just not for particular pieces of legislation; likewise, they could criticize or praise candidates for public office as long as they did not specifically tell their audiences for whom to vote.

When the case wound its way up to a US district court, the judge sided with Hargis and called the IRS's investigation "arbitrary as well as discriminatory" and a denial of due process. Not only did the judge find the IRS's behavior irregular, but also he believed that Hargis was truly motivated by his religious beliefs, noting that he was an ordained minister, that the organization's constitution was explicitly religious, that Hargis's political views flowed out of his view of biblical prophecy, and that he conducted regular religious revival meetings. The IRS might find Hargis's religion and politics distasteful, but that was not grounds for dismissing his religion as inauthentic. With only one exception, the judge found that Hargis had never advocated for a particular piece of legislation or candidate. This did not constitute grounds for revoking his tax exemption. The IRS appealed the ruling to the US Supreme Court, which remanded the case back to the district court.[42]

Hargis had won, but at great cost. It was 1972 when all was said and done. Eight years of court battles had taken a toll. During that time, many individual contributors to the *Christian Crusade* and other right-wing organizations reported having their tax deductions denied by the IRS.[43] And some of the other right-wing broadcasters were not so fortunate. *Life Line*, which was sponsored by H. L. Hunt, had its exemption revoked as well. But when it went to court it lost because it did not have the additional protection of being a religious organization. Neither Hunt nor Smoot was a minister. They just talked right-wing politics, and as far as the IRS and the Kennedys were concerned, that was the wrong kind of politics. The IRS scolded *Life Line*, saying that "aside from occasional individual broadcasts which may have been educational," as a whole the program was "essentially political commentary consisting largely of unsupported opinion and conclusions" and thus lacked "sufficient factual or other development of the subject matter to qualify as being instructional." As a result, Hunt withdrew his financial support and within a few years the program was a shell of its former self.[44] Although Hargis's *Christian Crusade* escaped the fate of *Life Line*, his victory was essentially pyrrhic. As with the CPUSA a decade earlier, the IRS may have lost the battle to revoke Hargis's tax exemption, but it had still won the war to slow contributions to right-wing broadcasters. It was the process that mattered—lengthy, expensive court battles and intimidated donors—not ultimate victory or defeat.

The Federal Communications Commission and the Ideal of Fairness

The IRS's Ideological Organizations Project had struck a major blow against right-wing broadcasting, but it did not force them off the airwaves. Silencing conservative broadcasters would require the cooperation of the FCC, which had theoretically vast if functionally limited oversight over the content of broadcasting. The Radio Act of 1927 had explicitly barred the FCC from censorship, but it had also required all licensed stations to operate in the "public convenience, interest, or necessity." There was an innate tension between these two mandates that would fuel a great deal of controversy over the next half century. If the FCC decided that certain broadcasters violated the public interest and subsequently barred them from the airwaves, how was that different than censorship?

Free speech qualms aside, the "public convenience, interest, or necessity" line was taken by progressives on the FCC as a sweeping warrant for action against the commercialization of radio. They were alarmed by the large corporate networks that had taken control of the preponderance of broadcasting in the United States. In the early 1940s, FCC Chairman James Lawrence Fly and Commissioner Clifford Durr developed a set of regulations called the "Blue Book," which would have required stations to air more educational programs, cut down on the number of sponsored programs, and offer balanced treatment of political issues. The major networks considered this censorship, an attempt by the FCC to control the content of their broadcasts. When the Blue Book was released, the network heads raised hell, nicknaming it the "Red Book." The FCC quietly backed down.[45]

In 1959 the FCC tried again to introduce similar reforms, this time calling it the Fairness Doctrine, which had three components. First, it stipulated that stations that gave airtime to one candidate for political office had to offer "equal time" to opposing candidates. Congress quickly passed legislation affirming the policy as both parties looked ahead to the first mass televised presidential election in 1960; neither party wanted the other to have an advantage. Congressional debate focused only on this single component of the Fairness Doctrine, but in codifying the part it had validated the whole, or so the FCC would later argue. The second component was a requirement that stations notify any victims of "personal attacks" and offer them airtime to respond to those attacks. The personal attack rule would be a source of recurring controversy, as we will see, but it was at least relatively easy to define. Either a program attacked a person or group or it did not. The third component of the Fairness Doctrine was less clear. In a single sentence in the 1959 rewrite the FCC required stations "to afford reasonable opportunity for discussion of conflicting views on matters of public importance."[46] The goal was balance in on-air editorializing, but the standard ("reasonable") was too vague to be the basis of concrete action. Even with the 1959 overhaul, the second and third components of the Fairness Doctrine needed clarification before they could be of much practical use.

These two components of the Fairness Doctrine—the personal attack and balanced editorializing rules—would remain unenforceable until the FCC clarified the Fairness Doctrine in 1963. This had not stopped the FCC from hassling station owners in the past—from opponents of the New Deal during the 1930s to labor unions and suspected Communists following World War II—but the FCC had only haphazardly enforced its standards prior to the 1960s. What changed was the nature of station ownership; as the major networks turned their attention to the higher profit margins and fat advertising contracts of television during the 1950s, growth in radio became the preserve of small, independent operators who struggled to break even from year to year. Unlike the networks, these station owners could not afford to be fussy about who bought airtime from them. They might not have liked conservative broadcasters like Carl McIntire and Billy James Hargis, but at least they paid in cash. By syndicating their programs across hundreds of these independent stations, conservative broadcasters were able to reach the kind of national audience that had previously been reserved for network customers. Yet these ad hoc networks were vulnerable because they lacked the lobbying heft and cohesion of the major networks.

To take advantage of that vulnerability, the Kennedy administration first had to fill the FCC with sympathetic commissioners. The first of the new commissioners was Newton Minow, whom John F. Kennedy appointed as FCC chairman in January 1961. Minow was a dependable choice, a New Frontiersman who had campaigned for Kennedy during the 1960 election and who was a personal friend of Robert Kennedy. As fellow FCC commissioner and Kennedy appointee Kenneth Cox later put it, "If Newt called the White House and wanted to talk to the President, he could talk to the President."[47] That was no insignificant measure of access in an organization the size of the federal government. Minow's short tenure was marked by his clashes with the major television networks. Soon after his appointment he gave the most famous speech—or, perhaps the only famous speech—in FCC history before the National Association of Broadcasters. Minow decried the poor state of television broadcasting, calling it "a vast wasteland" filled with "game shows, formula comedies . . . blood and thunder, mayhem, violence, sadism, murder, western bad men, western good men, private eyes, gangsters, more violence, and cartoons."[48] Instead of broadcasting in the public interest with educational and informative programming, station owners were instead obsessed with making money without regard for the merit of what they aired.

Conservative groups immediately saw a threat in Minow's ideas, particularly his belief that broadcasters had an obligation to uphold the "public interest" when they selected programming. One of Ayn Rand's earliest newsletters called out Minow. His advocacy for the public interest was nothing more than a gauzy tissue covering "the right of some men (those who, by some undefined criterion, are *the public*) to sacrifice the interests of other men (of those who, for unspecified reasons, are *not* the public)." Most Americans, Rand said, had been distracted by Minow's sideshow pitting "Westerns *versus* spelling-bees," when the real threat came in Minow's criticism of "those few of you who really believe that the public interest is merely what interests the public." Rand feared that enlightened technocrats and sympathetic community leaders would squelch nonconformist voices under the guise of protecting the "public interest."[49] The conservative magazine *Human Events* rewarded Minow's efforts with the nickname "Little Caesar."[50]

Conservative hyperbole aside, communications scholars like Allison Perlman have long since argued that the idea of the public interest is not a "singular, knowable thing." Rather, it is a site of "social conflict over control of the airwaves," a battlefield among groups all claiming that their particular interests are the public interest. It is, as Perlman notes, simultaneously a fight "over cultural resources and for political recognition."[51] Newton Minow had a vision of the public interest in broadcasting that emphasized educational content over entertainment, contained fewer commercials, and promoted civil conversation about current events and political issues of the day. The major networks had a vision of the public interest as quite literally the programs that interested the public; and since the public preferred westerns to educational programming, that must then be the public interest. Of course, the networks also argued that commercials were necessary to give the public the high-quality programming they wanted for "free" (and also for the networks to turn a healthy profit). On the other hand, small, independent station owners were typically too busy trying to meet the monthly budget to worry about abstractions like the public interest.

Finally, conservative broadcasters were suspicious of the definitions of the public interest provided by both the major networks and Newton Minow. They shared Minow's worries about cultural and discursive decay—albeit blaming rather different factors for that perceived decline—and favored education over entertainment. At the same time, they felt they had been shunned by the major networks, which they accused of being biased toward liberal causes and politicians. The Radio Right broadcasters truly believed that they were serving the public interest by warning ordinary citizens about the bad policies of the Kennedy administration and organizing political resistance. Thus, the debates over the public interest in radio in the 1960s were multivariate, divided among competing interests, and promised significant social and political rewards for the winners.

Minow's "Vast Wasteland" speech had shocked the major broadcasting networks, but he quickly became frustrated with his inability to convince the moderate old guard of the FCC to enact substantial reforms and resigned in June 1963. (By "old guard," consider that Commissioner Rosel Hyde had been appointed to the original Federal Radio Commission in 1928 by Secretary of Commerce Herbert Hoover!) The major networks were never seriously in danger, especially after Minow's resignation, but small station owners could not be so blasé. In his resignation speech, Minow, who had never met an expansive metaphor he did not like, compared the commission's work to venturing into a "vast and sometimes dark forest, where FCC hunters are often required to spend weeks of our time shooting down mosquitoes with elephant guns."[52] He proposed that Congress empower the president to appoint a single administrator to take charge of the FCC, thus freeing the commission from bothersome policy disagreements. Congress did nothing of the kind, but before resigning, Minow convinced John F. Kennedy to appoint Kenneth Cox and E. William Henry to the FCC, giving the New Frontier faction the numerical edge it needed. The mosquitoes were in trouble.

Kenneth Cox was the most vocal proponent of tighter government regulation of broadcasting on the commission. Cox did not believe that "the profit motive provides an incentive for the kind of programming the public needs."[53] Since broadcasters were just chasing entertainment dollars, the FCC should force them to air more substantive programs. Of course, Cox's definition of "substantive" differed quite drastically from that proffered by conservatives. One annoyed listener—who signed his name as "Hooray for Agnew!"—told Cox that he should resign and get a job as a garbage collector since he was "well suited for such work."[54] Cox did not take his advice. Prior to joining the commission he had served as a counsel for the Senate Commerce Committee as the protégé of its powerful chairman, Senator Warren Magnuson (D-WA).[55] Cox's connection to the Senate Commerce Committee will become significant later, as will his membership in the United Church of Christ.[56]

Cox's allies—Minow, Magnuson, and Nicholas Zapple—lobbied the Kennedy administration to give Cox his seat on the FCC.[57] Cox was actually John F. Kennedy's first choice to replace Minow as chairman, but squabbling between the House and Senate Commerce Committees meant Kennedy needed a compromise candidate. He asked Robert Kennedy if he knew of anyone, Robert turned to Seigenthaler for advice, and Seigenthaler recommended E. William Henry. Ironically, Kennedy had once offered Seigenthaler's job to Henry, though he had turned it down because it was insufficiently prestigious. But when Seigenthaler came calling with the FCC commissioner slot several months later, Henry responded affirmatively (though only after securing a promise that he would eventually be elevated to FCC chairman).[58]

Henry, like Cox and Minow, had campaigned for John F. Kennedy during the 1960 election, serving as a liaison between the Kennedy campaign and the Democratic National Committee. Before joining the campaign, Henry had worried about his lack of political experience, but Robert Kennedy reassured him that he was simply looking for "people who are loyal, reasonably bright, and willing to work hard." [59] All three attributes were true of Henry, and like many New Frontiersmen—who were disproportionately freshly minted law school graduates or, as Henry put it in a letter home, "young caballeros"—he was also eager for reform in Washington.[60] His first push as chairman was to enforce lapsed FCC rules regarding what percentage of broadcasts could be dedicated to commercials. He also wanted to ban canned laughter, "extreme violence," and overly loud commercials.[61] But like Newton Minow before him, Henry quickly realized how limited the FCC chairman's power really was; in response to his proposals, Congress considered a bill that would have shorn the FCC of significant oversight authority. The bill was sponsored by a conservative Southern Democrat, whose loyalties were prioritized in exactly that order. Being a fellow Democrat did Henry no good; as he complained to a friend, "I might as well be a Republican."[62] Henry had no choice but to back off.

Still, Henry's star was rising. Henry, Cox, and Frederick Ford formed the core of the liberal, reform-minded wing of the FCC, nicknamed the "rumpus group" for doing a "good job at making itself heard."[63] Two commissioners were opposed to these reforms, Robert E. Lee and Lee Loevinger. The remaining two commissioners, Rosel Hyde and Robert Bartley, were moderate swing voters, but they would mostly back the reform faction during Fairness Doctrine rulings. After the early, unsuccessful clashes with the major networks, Henry and Cox realized that reforming the broadcasting industry would have to take place at the margins. The networks were too big, had too many lobbyists, and could call in too many favors from sympathetic congressmen. Right-wing broadcasters, on the contrary, were small, divided, and vulnerable. The tool that Henry and Cox would use was the Fairness Doctrine and they had presidential warrant to do so. When Henry was appointed chairman in May 1963, President Kennedy told him, "It is important that stations be kept fair."[64] Kennedy's injunction to Henry was in line with the Reuther Memorandum, which had called for the FCC to counter right-wing broadcasts by taking "measures to encourage stations to assign comparable time for an opposing point of view on a free basis."[65] This was the essence of the Fairness Doctrine.

Why was it so "important that stations be kept fair" in the summer of 1963? President Kennedy did not tip his hand to Henry, or at least he left no record of it. But given the administration's involvement in the IRS audit project, it is likely that Kennedy had the Right wing on his mind when he spoke those words to Henry in May 1963. Indeed, that May marked the end of Edwin Walker's and Billy James Hargis's Operation Midnight Ride campaign, as well as the moment when the debate over the Nuclear Test Ban Treaty started to heat up. All the major right-wing broadcasters, including Hargis, Carl McIntire, and Clarence Manion, blasted away at the treaty throughout 1963, reaching a fevered pitch that summer. If there was ever a moment for Kennedy to pull out all the stops and go after the Radio Right, the summer of 1963 was it.

"Clarifying" the Fairness Doctrine

On July 16, Henry appeared before the House Commerce Committee to discuss the FCC's plans to reinforce the Fairness Doctrine. Henry outlined the standard justification for FCC oversight of fairness in programming, that stations were not licensed "exclusively for the private interest" of their owners but "to serve the community generally and the various groups which make up the community." As part of that responsibility, Henry believed that station owners should air programs that deal with "controversial issues of interest to his community, and in doing so . . . be fair." The problem that arose was when station owners preferred programming that reflected their own political positions and ideas, not those of the entire community. Unless the FCC stepped in to force stations to air the various sides of controversial issues, it would be "difficult, if not impossible to achieve fairness." The FCC could, however, take a step in the right direction with new regulations, the most significant of which would have required stations to notify every person or organization attacked on the air, mail them a transcript of the attack, and then offer them airtime—free of charge, if necessary—to respond to those attacks. It was obvious to everybody involved that the rule changes would have major political ramifications. Henry himself stated that he hoped that the new rules would be put in place in time for "any actions taken" to be "applicable for the 1964 election."[66]

   In his testimony, Henry portrayed the FCC as an impartial referee evenhandedly applying the rules. However, Henry's desire to push through stricter Fairness Doctrine rules before the 1964 election was not politically impartial. When the FCC issued its clarification of the Fairness Doctrine on July 26, it clearly targeted right-wing broadcasters. The FCC, with a certain pomposity, had declared that it looked "to substance rather than to label or form" when deciding whether stations complied with the Fairness Doctrine, but these nods toward impartiality were really pleasant-sounding fictions disguising partisan intent. The next sentence revealed which groups the FCC was really concerned with. "It is immaterial," the statement continued, "whether a particular program or viewpoint is presented under the label of 'Americanism,' 'anti-communism,' or 'states' rights,' or whether it is a paid announcement, official speech, editorial or religious broadcast." These were all labels and forms embraced by conservatives. A liberal cause is mentioned at one point in the document but in a rather different light. While discussing the responsibility of stations to air editorials on controversial issues of public importance and to do so fairly, the FCC gave the example of the civil rights movement. If a station aired an editorial in support of segregation, then it must offer "similar opportunities" to those who favored desegregation.[67] In sum, the FCC's new rules on the Fairness Doctrine were designed to advance liberal speech while placing limits on the unbalanced expression of conservative speech.

The July 26 clarification ended up doing rather less clarifying than it intended. In keeping with Henry's statement before the House Commerce Committee, the July 26 clarification required station owners who aired personal attacks to notify the persons or groups attacked and to give them "a specific offer of his station's facilities for an adequate response." Likewise, if a station supported a particular candidate or political position, it had to give the other side "a comparable opportunity for an appropriate spokesman to answer the broadcast." Yet the ambiguity of these rules would lead to great confusion among licensees. Did "specific offer" mean that stations could merely offer to sell response time to the offended parties? Or did they have to give away that response time without charge? And how much time exactly constituted "an adequate response"? Furthermore, who decided the appropriateness of a spokesman?[68] Broadcasters were left even more confused about the Fairness Doctrine than before.

Liberal interest groups immediately jumped on the FCC's clarification, delighted that the commission had finally taken their side. The widespread confusion actually played to their advantage; as long as the Fairness Doctrine criteria remained ambiguous, it made threats of FCC complaints all the more dangerous. Compliance would be in the eye of the beholder and the beholders were a bunch of Kennedy appointees. The next day on July 27, the Washington Human Rights Project, a pro–civil rights organization, mailed all of its members selections from the statement. Since the FCC had made "clear reference to programs such as '*Life Line*,' Billy James Hargis, and White Citizens' Council broadcasts," it was "absolutely essential" that Washington Human Rights Project members immediately contact their local stations and request response time. Since most southern station licensees were up for renewal in the spring of 1964, the Human Rights Project noted, those Fairness Doctrine complaints would carry extra weight.[69]

The Citizens Committee for a Nuclear Test Ban

The first blow struck against conservative broadcasting following the July 26 clarification came from a group that had been cooked up in the White

House. During the summer of 1963, the White House began having serious concerns about one of their allies in the push for a nuclear test ban treaty. SANE, or the National Committee for a Sane Nuclear Policy, had started in 1957 with a small group of pacifists who favored total nuclear disarmament and by 1963 had grown to include prominent liberal activists like Martin Luther King Jr., Benjamin Spock, and Walter Reuther. From 1962 to 1963 SANE issued a series of newspaper advertisements encouraging public support for the test ban, ads with shock ledes like, "Your children's teeth contain Strontium-90."[70] Ban nuclear testing or your children's teeth will turn radioactive! Yet as the treaty negotiations drew to a close, the Kennedy administration worried that SANE veered too far to the Left and would alienate political moderates. SANE advocated total disarmament of both nuclear and conventional weapons, a much more radical (and politically risky) position than a simple ban on above-ground nuclear testing.[71]

Thus, on August 7 the president held a planning meeting at the White House for a new group created to counter charges of excessive liberalism among treaty supporters. Kennedy ally (and SANE member) Walter Reuther was present at the meeting, but the new Citizens Committee for a Nuclear Test Ban (CCNTB) would highlight its Republican members, all of whom had ties to the Eisenhower administration.[72] The CCNTB would be the public, bipartisan face of the administration's pro-treaty push. (Though the White House continued to coordinate efforts behind the scenes with SANE, the UAW, and eighteen other liberal interest groups.) The CCNTB's first order of business was to hire Ruder Finn, a public relations company specializing in aiding Democratic candidates and liberal interest groups. The CCNTB began publishing ads in major national newspapers, while Ruder Finn coordinated "localized" news releases highlighting how passing the treaty would benefit regional interests. The CCNTB also reached out to religious groups, including the National Council of Churches, asking them to organize letter-writing campaigns.[73]

The president of the CCNTB was James J. Wadsworth. Wadsworth could have been a poster child for the liberal East Coast Republican establishment that conservatives constantly complained about. He was a fourth-generation public servant, educated at Yale and Bowdoin, and once received a farm as a birthday present. Under President Eisenhower he served as Deputy Chief of the US delegation to the United Nations. From 1958 to 1960, he had been involved in early negotiations for the Nuclear Test Ban Treaty with the Soviets and the British.[74] Wadsworth was the perfect man to head up the committee.

As a Republican, he provided the committee with nonpartisan cover; as a liberal Republican, he despised the right-wing broadcasters who threatened to take over his party.

Immediately following the CCNTB's meeting at the White House on August 7, Wadsworth started sending letters to radio stations that aired conservative shows attacking the test ban treaty, especially those airing the *Manion Forum*, the *Christian Crusade*, and *Life Line*. For example, Wadsworth wrote to station WQIZ in South Carolina asking for airtime with which to respond to Clarence Manion's position on the treaty, or, as it was likened by Manion's guest Rear Admiral Chester Ward, a Soviet trap "set to weaken us for the final kill."[75] Wadsworth asked the station to air, free of charge, a fifteen-minute response put together by the CCNTB. The response included a lengthy excerpt from President Kennedy's July 26 address, carried by the major networks, encouraging public support for the test ban treaty.[76] WQIZ complied but made no bones about its displeasure at being compelled to do so. In the opinion of the station's owner, the test ban treaty "stinks and smells to the high heaven of communist infiltration." If the treaty passed the Senate, it would only be because of "misinformed people like your stinking committee." Still, he would give Wadsworth the airtime because "even a dog deserves this."[77]

Station WGCB—which will play a featured role in the next chapter— responded with more grace but still declined to air the response without charge. The owner, John Norris, offered to sell the CCNTB airtime at the same rate as he had sold it to Clarence Manion. Wadsworth responded that the CCNTB could not afford to purchase the airtime and reiterated his request for free time. Without saying as much, Norris insinuated that Wadsworth was lying. He noted that the CCNTB could boast the support of the chairmen of American Airlines and Eastman Kodak. Surely, they could afford the measly $100 or so it would cost to reimburse a small, independent radio station for the airtime used? After all, the CCNTB had just recently purchased a full-page ad in the *Washington Post*.[78]

The exchange between Wadsworth and station WGCB highlights a major ambiguity within the FCC's July 26 clarification of the Fairness Doctrine. Station owners understood that they were required to provide balanced coverage of major political issues and that sometimes doing so required inviting interest groups to respond to arguments from the other side. But the question remained, who was responsible to pay for the airtime? Did the mere act of airing a program that criticized the test ban treaty obligate stations to give airtime gratis to supporters of the treaty? If the FCC ordered stations to provide free response time, it would give liberal advocacy groups a powerful tool to counter right-wing-dominated independent radio.

The CCNTB is significant to our story because it was the first organization to take full advantage of the FCC's new push to enforce the Fairness Doctrine. Although the Reuther Memorandum had not specified the creation of a front organization, the fact that both Walter Reuther and the Kennedys were present in the Oval Office at the genesis of the organization, that the committee made its move so quickly after the FCC's Fairness Doctrine clarification, and that it dedicated so much of its effort to fighting the Radio Right certainly points to the CCNTB being an extension of the Reuthers' original plan.

The Cullman Doctrine

The FCC had given the CCNTB an invaluable weapon against the Radio Right; the CCNTB would soon return the favor. A month after the Fairness Doctrine clarification, FCC Chairman Henry got the chance to establish a position on paid versus free response time. Two stations just outside Birmingham, Alabama—WKUL in Cullman and WARF in Jasper—had aired programs from *Life Line* attacking the Nuclear Test Ban treaty. They promptly received a request for free response time from Wadsworth and the CCNTB. The stations then wrote to the FCC asking if they were obliged to give the CCNTB free response time or if they could just offer them a paid time slot. They also asked the FCC if their responsibility to offer response time extended only to local groups with a presence in their coverage area and not to national groups from New York or Washington, DC.

Henry, writing on behalf of the FCC, replied on September 18. The policy statement in this letter would become known as the Cullman Doctrine. Henry made it clear that stations that failed to obtain a paid response from a local group could not "reject a presentation otherwise suitable to the licensee" and "thus leave the public uninformed." In this case, that meant the Cullman stations would have to give the CCNTB what they had asked for. Henry did caveat his response slightly. The station owners had argued in their letter that the pro-treaty position had been covered in other programming. Henry noted that the FCC had no complaints to the contrary in their files on WKUL and WARF and if, in their "good faith judgment," they believed the listening public had been sufficiently informed of both sides of the issue, then they could deny the request for response time and still be in compliance with the Fairness Doctrine.[79] It was a risk they were free to take but a risk nonetheless.

It is not clear how WKUL and WARF responded to the FCC's ruling—whether they aired the CCNTB response or not—but the ruling set a significant precedent. Stations that aired programming that touched on controversial issues could not be one-sided in their presentation, no matter the personal beliefs of the owners. They had the right to reject requests for free response time, but only if, it was strongly implied, they had a clear record with the FCC. If, on the other hand, interest groups had lodged complaints with the FCC about a particular station's one-sidedness, that station would not receive the benefit of the doubt. In such a case, an FCC investigation was possible and could even result in the denial of a broadcasting license renewal. In effect, the Cullman Doctrine expanded the FCC's rules on personal attacks to cover controversial issues of public importance. Free response time used to be reserved for targets of personal attacks. Now any group could make a claim if it felt its views had not been adequately represented. It should not be a surprise that the ruling opened up a new battleground for partisan advantage. After all, has any political party or interest group ever felt that media outlets for the opposing side treated them fairly? Of course not.

The Cullman Doctrine left independent radio stations in a bind. On the one hand, the FCC had told them that they could rely on their own "good faith judgment" in regard to balance in broadcasting controversial issues. Yet although that sounded reassuring in theory, it still left stations with no fixed criteria for gauging compliance with the Fairness Doctrine. If enough complaints against the station were filed, it might face a lengthy and expensive FCC investigation that would be painful even if the station were to be cleared in the end. The subtext of the Cullman Doctrine, whether intentional or not, was that stations refused requests for free response time at their own risk. As a result, all but the most ideologically driven or financially desperate station owners did the math and began turning down conservative programs. That included the original Cullman, Alabama area stations; WKUL and WARF chose not to continue their relationship with Carl McIntire when his contract expired at the end of 1964.

Right-wing broadcasters were predictably outraged by both the July 26 clarification of the Fairness Doctrine and the Cullman Doctrine. Billy James Hargis's *Christian Crusade* passed a resolution at its annual convention condemning the Fairness Doctrine as an "increasing, unlawful, and unconstitutional interference with freedom of speech."[80] Immediately following the Cullman ruling, Clarence Manion dedicated a weekly broadcast to the Fairness Doctrine under the headline "Do you want federal censorship for your local radio station?" From Manion's perspective, the hunt for perfect "fairness" on the air was a waste of time. If the number of commercials or the political balance was a problem, why, all the listener had to do was vote with the dial. Self-regulation by the forces of supply and demand were infinitely preferable, he averred, to "the inevitable alternative . . . uniform Federal control of all radio and television programming." It smacked of Soviet "jamming" of Western radio signals, not of the marketplace of ideas.[81]

Manion did not use the phrase "chilling effect," but that was what he feared would be the result as station owners dropped the *Manion Forum* to avoid airtime requests or Fairness Doctrine complaints. Furthermore, he thought it suspicious that only right-wing programs had been the target of Fairness Doctrine complaints while the pro-administration "liberal line that flows in constantly over the three big networks" continued unabated. President Kennedy could appeal directly to the people with the blessing of the FCC, but when one of his conservative opponents opened his or her mouth it was automatically considered unfair or unbalanced.[82] Popular conservative columnist Edith Kermit Roosevelt echoed Manion's suspicion, calling the July 26 clarification "a squeeze-play to eliminate television and radio broadcasts which conflict with [the] government line." Station owners, eager "to avoid such bothersome and costly" regulations, would simply eliminate right-wing programs and leave the airwaves to pro-administration voices.[83]

It was not only right-wing broadcasters who were concerned. Conservative members of Congress agreed and multiple congresspersons contacted E. William Henry to ask for an explanation for why the July 26 clarification had singled out right-wing ideas. It also struck some as an example of bureaucratic overreach as the FCC was "legislating rather than administrating." Congress had not passed new legislation expanding the Fairness Doctrine, so why was the FCC doing just that during an election season?[84] Another congressman forwarded a constituent letter by the son of an independent station owner complaining that the "FCC is fast becoming an iron-clad dictator." The FCC's new rules would stifle political speech, he claimed. Indeed, even political satire and comedy might be under threat because humor was often "based on [the] belittlement of a person, a subject, [or] a circumstance."[85] Such humor would now be considered personal attacks and could trigger Fairness Doctrine complaints. Even congresspersons sympathetic to the purposes of the Fairness Doctrine, like Representative Bill Brock of

Tennessee, worried that Henry had gone too far, that "the medicine offered may kill the patient."[86]

Henry waited to respond to most of the inquiries until after *Broadcasting* ran an article reporting a possible link between the FCC's actions and the recently leaked Reuther Memorandum.[87] He could safely ignore wild accusations from conservative broadcasters but not when the industry magazine of record took them seriously enough to reprint them. Henry denied any connection to the Reuther Memorandum, telling letter writers that he had never even laid eyes on the Reuther Memorandum let alone made it the basis of FCC policy; "any contrary assertion is entirely without merit."[88] Likewise, he denied targeting right-wing broadcasting for special treatment, stating that stations "will not have their licenses placed in jeopardy should they choose to broadcast either liberal or conservative viewpoints."[89]

But Henry's congressional correspondents wanted more than simple denials. So he adopted another tack. His responses to questions about the free response time provision and the possibility of a chilling effect on political discourse were studies in evasion. Republican Senate Minority Leader Everett Dirksen asked for a firm yes or no on whether stations could reject requests for free response time. Henry responded very differently, and more ambiguously, to Dirksen than he had in his Cullman Doctrine ruling several weeks earlier. It was, he wrote, an issue on which "the licensee has wide discretion, subject only to Commission review for reasonableness." Dirksen expressed his dissatisfaction with the answer, but Henry stopped responding to his letters.[90] The correct answer was quite simple and clearly outlined in the Cullman Doctrine. Yes, if licensees aired a program giving an opinion on a controversial issue of public importance and could not find a sponsor for the other side of the question, then they must give the respondent free time. However, spilling out technically correct but unhelpful legalese was an effective means of stonewalling Dirksen and other congressional Republicans.[91]

In similar fashion, Henry downplayed the possible chilling effect of the Fairness Doctrine on political discourse. He reassured Representative Bill Brock that he was "confident that any limiting effect [the Fairness Doctrine] might temporarily have on the discussion of controversial issues is more than offset by the public's right to hear both sides of a controversy."[92] He did not deny that there might be a chilling effect, but he thought it was worth it for the sake of balanced discussion of issues. That was of course an easy thing to say when the affected discourse came from people whose views he found distasteful. Still, Henry believed he was successfully walking "the narrow path between the legal prohibition against censorship . . . and our statutory duty to require that the nature of the service rendered by each licensee is in the public interest."[93] Henry had placed his finger on the conflicting mandates of the original Communications Act of 1934 but thought he had balanced them properly. Conservatives thought differently.

Henry also frequently mentioned in his responses that the July 26 clarification had been a unanimous decision of the seven commissioners, both Republican and Democrat. Clearly, this could not be a partisan plot to suppress conservative political speech. It is true that the entire commission had upheld the principle of the Fairness Doctrine in theory, but when it came time to put teeth into the enforcement of the Fairness Doctrine, Henry would fail repeatedly to win the backing of the commission. He lost a series of four-to-three votes in 1964 and early 1965. After expressing his frustration to an ally he wrote, "I . . . only hope that some day [sic] we'll get a majority here which will vindicate my position." He did not have to wait much longer. In April 1965, President Lyndon Johnson appointed James J. Wadsworth— the previously mentioned former president of the Citizens Committee for a Nuclear Test Ban—to the FCC. Wadsworth was a Republican, but he would be a strong advocate for the Fairness Doctrine on the commission, giving the pro–Fairness Doctrine faction the upper hand. Henry would not be on the FCC much longer, but his replacement was liberal wunderkind Nicholas Johnson, at that time the youngest person ever appointed to the commission and Henry's equal in antipathy toward right-wing broadcasting.[94] A decisive pro–Fairness Doctrine majority had finally been secured and, as chapter 6 details, it would put some teeth into Fairness Doctrine enforcement in 1967.

Following the Archival Trail to the White House

Conservatives blamed the FCC's new Fairness Doctrine push on the White House and the Reuther Memorandum. Certainly, the FCC's July 26 clarification and the Cullman Doctrine were in line with the strategy outlined in the Reuther Memorandum, but it is necessary to consider whether the overlap is correlation or causation. After all, FCC Chairman Henry might simply have been acting out of the same general fear of right-wing radicalism that was pervasive among liberals during the early 1960s. Connecting the FCC's enforcement of the Fairness Doctrine to the Reuther Memorandum requires evidence tying the policy shift back to the White House. As previously mentioned, John F. Kennedy had told Henry when he nominated him for FCC Chairman, "It is important that stations be kept fair," but that statement is too general to be damning. There is, however, more concrete evidence.

On August 13 the Oval Office tape recorders caught John F. Kennedy mentioning the FCC in relation to a major right-wing broadcaster. Kennedy was speaking with Myer Feldman, his primary legal adviser and close personal aide. During the 1960 election, Feldman had been in charge of the campaign's opposition research effort gathering dirt on Richard Nixon; his collection of Nixon's gaffes was nicknamed the "Nixonpedia." It was no surprise, then, that the president tasked Feldman with checking in on the IRS's progress in the Ideological Organizations Project throughout 1961 to 1963.[95] Although the tape recording of Kennedy and Feldman's Oval Office meeting only captures part of their conversation and alludes to other meetings that were not recorded, it does point to Kennedy's interest in using the FCC to combat right-wing broadcasting.

On August 13, Kennedy proposed that Feldman meet with Robert Kennedy and FCC Chairman E. William Henry to discuss how the "Federal Communications Commission ought to be able to do something about *Life Line*." (*Life Line* is the previously mentioned conservative broadcast sponsored by oilman H. L. Hunt.) Feldman assured Kennedy that the FCC is "going into it," which was certainly true given the FCC's July 26 statement on the Fairness Doctrine. These small snippets of a conversation connect John F. Kennedy's interest in right-wing broadcasting to action by the FCC. Furthermore, there is a link to the IRS. Kennedy responds to Feldman's assurances with a somewhat garbled "but of course, then the tax people."[96] Although Kennedy did not explicitly mention the IRS, the circumstances suggest that that was his meaning. Just a week later, Robert Kennedy would contact the IRS asking for an accelerated audit of *Life Line*.[97] "The tax people" meant those IRS agents and administrators doing the bidding of the president and attorney general with the Ideological Organizations Project. Although Feldman and Kennedy's conversation is short, it connects the Kennedys to actions by both the IRS and the FCC against conservative broadcasting.

It also aligns with a series of memorandums that Feldman drafted for the president in the days following their taped conversation. Two days after their conversation, Feldman had worked up a summary of the right-wing threat for the president with recommendations for further action, pulling his statistics and descriptions of conservative organizations from Group Research Inc.'s files. He estimated that the Right as a whole pulled in between $15 million and $25 million a year, aired programs on more than a thousand radio stations, and produced a truly "enormous amount of direct mail." Feldman gave the president three examples of threatening right-wing organizations. The John Birch Society had started "gearing to political purposes," had a hundred thousand members already, and had forty full-time organizers adding new local chapters. If it were not stopped, the society could become the Right's version of the labor movement's get-out-the-vote operation. Carl McIntire was the next person mentioned because he aired the *Twentieth Century Reformation Hour* on an estimated four hundred to five hundred stations and was then raising funds to get to six hundred. Finally, the memo fingered H. L. Hunt, that "frank champion of plutocracy," who aired *Life Line* on three hundred stations. In keeping with President Kennedy's recorded wish that "the tax people" would do something about *Life Line*, the memo focused on the tax deduction claimed by contributors to the program, including the large annual deduction claimed by the Hunt Food Company itself.[98]

Feldman's second memorandum to the president, weighing in at more than 140 pages, detailed dozens of conservative groups—including all fifteen of the conservative groups that the IRS was then investigating and which would have their tax-exempt status repealed—and noted their major donors. But it was not the large corporate donors that worried Feldman the most. What gave him pause was the "average American who supports one, or several, Right-Wing organizations by small contributions, by work, and by the purchase of books, pamphlets, and tape recordings, and who places his dollar bill in the collection basket at a Right-Wing rally." These grassroots conservatives supplied "the mass base without which the Right-Wing movement would be ineffective," as well as the movement's "day-in-and-day-out" activism.[99]

Indeed, the conservative housewives discussed in chapter 2, who had organized boycotts of goods imported from the Communist bloc, received a backhanded compliment in Feldman's memoranda. Feldman wanted an example of right-wing extremism and settled on the "card party movement" that "invade[d] supermarkets which sell Polish hams." Feldman's worry was that this kind of local activism often escaped the purview of Democratic Party strategists because the movement was just too dispersed to collect accurate data on. Still, it had real political power. Conservatives were constantly "harass[ing] local school boards, local librarians, and local governing bodies."[100] Grassroots activism was the beating heart of the New

Right. Democratic leaders might pooh-pooh the conservative grassroots in public—DNC chairman John Bailey dismissed them as "grandmothers dressed in cowgirl costumes passing out Barry Goldwater buttons"—but in private they were less sanguine.[101] Feldman's worry about local activists belies the dominant narrative of recent histories of the New Right that portray the movement as an artificial, top-down fabrication of industrial interests. Of course, the Right had its fair share of corporate backers, but it was this grassroots, bottom-up activism that gave the Kennedy administration fits in the early 1960s. And it was a form of activism that was being energized by right-wing broadcasting. If the Kennedys could take out the broadcasters, the local activism might die down on its own.

Feldman's memoranda also confirm that his taped conversation with the president two days earlier had revolved around finding ways to combat right-wing broadcasters. He concluded that more information on the Right's finances, methods, and literature was needed. More concretely, he believed that inquiries should be made into the fact that right-wing nonprofits were "using tax-exempt funds for political purposes." He also noted that the "Federal [sic] Communications Act" was being violated whenever there was not "a fair presentation of both sides of a question," a reference to the Fairness Doctrine.[102] Feldman had more or less restated the major recommendations of the Reuther Memorandum.

The White House tapes, Myer Feldman's memos, and the timeline of August and September 1963 all point to a connection between the administration, the IRS's Ideological Origins Project, and the FCC's Fairness Doctrine push. On August 13, President Kennedy told Myer Feldman to meet with Robert Kennedy and E. William Henry because he thought that "the Federal Communications Commission ought to be able to do something about *Life Line*."[103] In his August 15 memorandum, Feldman recommended action on unfair broadcasting and political contributions to right-wing organizations, especially *Life Line*. On August 20, Robert Kennedy met with Mitchell Rogovin at the IRS to ask for an accelerated audit of *Life Line*, preferably completed prior to the Senate hearings on the Nuclear Test Ban Treaty. On August 21, Rogovin met with Myer Feldman at the White House and referenced his meeting with Robert Kennedy and E. William Henry. On August 22 the letter from stations WKUL and WARF, which had aired an anti-treaty program by *Life Line*, landed on Henry's desk. On September 18 Henry issued a sweeping extension of the Fairness Doctrine that directly benefited the pro-treaty push for Senate confirmation of the Nuclear Test Ban Treaty.

Although the timeline and the White House tapes suggest that Henry was privy to the administration's plan, it does not necessarily follow that he had read the Reuther Memorandum. Henry need not have known that he was carrying out the plan envisioned two years earlier by Walter and Victor Reuther. He was simply complying with the wishes of his political patrons. Yet if we take a step back, the scenario that I have just described in detail is really quite shocking. A sitting US president, annoyed by opposition to a favored piece of legislation, created an interest group to lobby for its passage. He ordered the IRS to audit his political foes while encouraging the FCC to scrutinize their unbalanced use of the airwaves. The FCC then revised its regulations in such a way as to ensure free airtime for the president's front organization. It is one of the greatest acts of bureaucratic strong-arming in American history.

The July 26 clarification of the Fairness Doctrine had set the stage for ten years of partisan warfare over control of the airwaves. Despite Henry's protestations of equitable intent, both conservative broadcasters and liberal interest groups saw the FCC's rulings as a major precedent for anti-conservative activism. The "chilling effect" feared by conservatives and hoped for by liberals would be further tested by the FCC and in the courts. Although President Kennedy was assassinated and would not see the Reuther Memorandum plan come to full fruition, the administration's actions to combat the Right did not fade away. With the encouragement of the Democratic National Committee, both the IRS's Ideological Origins Project and the FCC's selective enforcement of the Fairness Doctrine would continue. The regulatory framework called for by the Reuther Memorandum had been put in place, launching a veritable land rush as liberal interest groups staked their claims to the airwaves.

5

"The Red Lion Roars Again"

The Fairness Doctrine, the Democratic National Committee, and the Election of 1964

After Kennedy's assassination in November 1963, the counter–Radio Right campaign might have been left rudderless at a crucial moment. President Lyndon Johnson had always been a marginalized figure in the Kennedy White House and he had no involvement in the planning or implementation of the Reuther Memorandum. Robert Kennedy continued as attorney general until the fall of 1964, but while he was willing to act as his brother's hatchet man, he was under no such obligation to Lyndon B. Johnson, whom he personally despised. Implementation of the Reuther Memorandum plan might have ended right then, but into the void stepped the Democratic National Committee (DNC) and DNC Chairman John Bailey. Bailey had been involved in multiple stages of the Reuther Memorandum's planning and implementation. And he grasped the political possibilities latent in the Fairness Doctrine once the Citizens Committee for a Nuclear Test Ban had successfully used it to extract free airtime from stations over the Nuclear Test Ban Treaty controversy.

As befitting a former political machine boss, Bailey thought big. The DNC would double down on the Reuther Memorandum's tactics while greatly expanding the counterconservative broadcasting campaign. Bailey assembled a team of DNC operatives who would use the Fairness Doctrine to ensure Lyndon Johnson's landslide victory over Barry Goldwater in 1964. The plan worked well; the only conservative station owner to challenge the Fairness Doctrine lost in a US Supreme Court case that validated the doctrine for the next twenty years.

The Boss: John M. Bailey

Before becoming the chairman of the DNC, John M. Bailey had dominated Democratic politics in Connecticut during the 1950s. Like other municipal

The Radio Right. Paul Matzko, © Oxford University Press (2020). Oxford University Press.
DOI: 10.1093/oso/9780190073220.001.0001

political machines of the mid-twentieth century, including the Kelly-Nash machine in Chicago, Bailey could rely on the near-total support of his white ethnic Catholic constituents and he was not afraid to get his hands dirty squelching the old-boy network of white Anglo-Saxon Protestants who had previously controlled the state party. Bailey was also an early supporter of Kennedy's political aspirations. In a 1956 memorandum to then–Democratic presidential nominee Adlai Stevenson, Bailey argued that John F. Kennedy should be named Stevenson's vice presidential running mate to woo Catholic voters in battleground states.[1] The suggestion was rejected (and Stevenson subsequently lost all the northeastern battleground states in question), but Bailey would again back Kennedy in the 1960 Democratic primaries and be rewarded for his support with the DNC chairmanship in 1961.[2]

Later in his chairmanship, Bailey would be criticized for both his rough political tactics and his support for the Vietnam War. For example, historian and lifelong Democrat Henry Steele Commager wrote to Bailey in 1968 bemoaning "the puerility of your remarks and the ruthlessness of your tactics" and calling him "an echo of President Johnson, only rather a bad one."[3] When Lyndon Johnson pulled out of the election in 1968, Bailey left party leadership as well. Still, Bailey served the Democratic Party well in the early 1960s, overseeing the Democratic surge of 1964 as the party expanded to its largest majorities in either chamber since the New Deal forty years earlier. Presidential historians of the Kennedy and Johnson administrations have long appreciated Bailey's role in the electoral success of the Democratic Party in 1960 and 1964, but his tactical use of the Fairness Doctrine to intimidate Goldwater supporters in 1964 has been almost entirely overlooked. The most thorough history of the DNC during Bailey's chairmanship dedicates only two sentences to the topic.[4]

During the fall of 1963, Bailey shared the Kennedy administration's apprehension of the Radio Right. Conservative broadcasters were a particular concern out west, the only region of the country that overwhelmingly backed Nixon in 1960. Kennedy had won only Nevada and New Mexico, which gave him just seven out of the seventy-nine total western electoral votes.[5] Just as important for Bailey were the upcoming congressional elections. Democratic control of the US House of Representatives might not hinge on the thinly populated Intermountain West, but the party could ill afford to lose any of the eight western Senate seats up for grabs in 1964 if it wanted to keep its near super-majority in the Senate. In the end, the Democratic Party won six of the eight contests, albeit by much thinner margins than the presidential election, like in Nevada where the incumbent Democrat beat a surprise conservative Republican challenger by a mere forty-eight votes.[6]

Gale McGee (D-Wyoming) was one of the Democratic senators facing re-election that year and he worried about the influence of right-wing broadcasters in Wyoming. In August 1963 he sent a memorandum listing those concerns to Myer Feldman at the White House. Feldman promptly forwarded it to President Kennedy along with his own previously discussed memoranda. McGee argued that right-wing broadcasting had found a willing audience in the West because of westerners' isolationist views and "the remnants of a 19th Century rugged individualism." The Republican-controlled state legislature in Wyoming had recently passed a right-to-work law and resolutions condemning the United Nations and US foreign aid. Indeed, the state was so conservative that McGee had heard Republicans grouse that moderate Republican Nelson Rockefeller was "as bad as McGee."[7]

Conservative broadcasters were equally infatuated with the western states albeit for a more practical reason. They got a "bigger bang for [their] buck," in McGee's words, in the thinly populated western states; after all, a Senate seat from, say, Wyoming counted just the same as one from more a densely populated state like New York. In his letter to Feldman, McGee complained about the usual cast of conservative characters, including Clarence Manion and the Courtneys, but he worried most about Carl McIntire's *Twentieth Century Reformation Hour* and H. L Hunt's *Life Line*. "It would," he wrote, "be difficult to exaggerate how the concentration of these programs in limited population areas ultimately captures the public mind." He was right to worry. By 1964 Carl McIntire aired on seven of the twenty-nine radio stations in Wyoming, blanketing most of the state, especially the (relatively) densely populated southeastern corner of the state, as shown in Figure 5.1.[8]

The situation was not entirely hopeless. McGee believed that the rise of the Right could be turned to the Democratic Party's advantage. Political moderates found the Right's extremism repugnant, and since the conservative wing was part of the Republican Party, it could be used to tarnish the Republican Party as a whole and push independent voters and moderate Republicans to vote for Democrats. Thus, writing in 1963, McGee cautioned the Kennedy administration to delay launching the anti-conservative campaign until 1964. He believed that the Right was "the winning issue for 1964." He wanted the administration to keep them "alive and kicking for a year" and then announce a congressional investigation in the summer of 1964 that would "blow these fellows out of the water" by publicly disclosing their finances.[9]

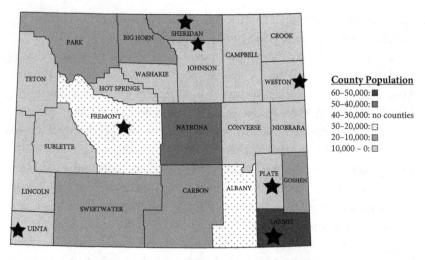

Figure 5.1. Map of Wyoming election returns and *Twentieth Century Reformation Hour* stations in 1964.

McGee's idea for a congressional investigation would have to wait until 1965—it is a major topic of chapter 7—but his worries were shared by the DNC. On September 19 to 20, 1963, the DNC hosted the Western States Democratic Conference in Salt Lake City with representatives from thirteen states, including Gale McGee and John Bailey. California Governor Edmund Brown, who as we discussed in chapter 2 had tangled with the Right wing in 1958, also spoke at the conference, condemning conservatism as being full of "racists, warmongers, hatemongers and apostles of non-think."[10] The keynote session was dedicated to combating the spread of political extremism in the West. The conference was an annual tradition, but it took on added resonance because Republican presidential candidate Barry Goldwater hailed from Arizona. As Idaho Senator Frank Church lamented to the attending press, "We westerners bear a special responsibility for Barry Goldwater." He called for Democrats to "surmount the tide of nonsense" coming from the Right, which did "not represent the calm voice of conservatism" but "the frantic voice of fanaticism." John Bailey, however, had a different person on his mind when he condemned Republicans who can "rely on oil-rich millionaires."[11] It did not take much sleuthing for reporters to figure out that Bailey was referring to oilman and broadcaster H. L. Hunt. By highlighting the wealth of the other side's supporters, Bailey could paint the opposition as being out of touch with the will of the people.

With the help of Wesley McCune and Group Research Inc., the DNC distributed a booklet to the several hundred conference attendees further outlining the dangers of the Right. The booklet included the map shown in Photo 5.1 and contained half a dozen articles—including hard-bitten pieces like "Far Right—Fanatics or Lunatics?"—but the highlight was a map showing the location of every radio station in the West that aired conservative programs, including the H. L. Hunt–funded program *Life Line*. It was the influence of conservative broadcasting that particularly concerned McGee, Church, and Bailey, not Goldwater's candidacy or even conservatism per se. The DNC knew that the fortunes of the Right were tied to its presence on the airwaves.[12] If they could silence the Right on the air, electoral success would follow.

The Bagman: Wayne Phillips

The DNC's first step was to find someone to take point on the counter-Right campaign, which it did in Wayne Phillips. Phillips, who had worked for ten years as a *New York Times* reporter, joined the Kennedy administration in 1961 as a special assistant to the director of the Housing and Home Finance Agency. He also handled several publicity assignments for the White House like organizing a pro-Medicare rally at Madison Square Garden that was headlined by the president and was televised on all the major networks. But on October 17, 1963, Phillips was summoned to the White House by Kenneth O'Donnell to discuss a more sensitive assignment. Phillips distinctly remembered the odd juxtaposition of meeting with O'Donnell in the Roosevelt Room while the president entertained Yugoslavian dictator Marshal Tito across the hallway in the Oval Office. O'Donnell was one of Kennedy's closest personal assistants, a member of the so-called Irish Mafia trio of assistants that had been with Kennedy since the beginning of his political career in 1946 (along with David Francis Powers and Lawrence F. O'Brien). Indeed, he had roomed with Robert Kennedy at Harvard, where both played collegiate football, and he later worked with Robert Kennedy on the Senate Labor Rackets Committee.[13] In short, O'Donnell had the deepest confidences of both John and Robert Kennedy.

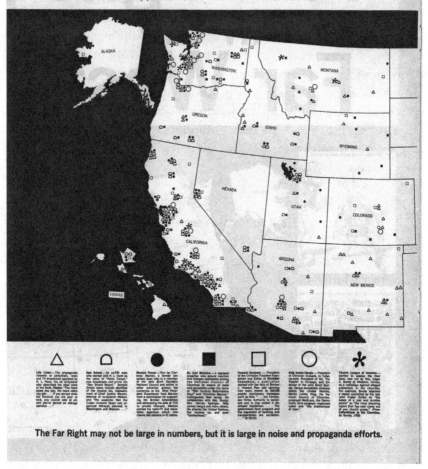

Far Right Fallout in the Far West

Each dot indicates the broadcast point of radical right programs which give aid and comfort to the Republican Radicals. The airwaves of the west are badly poisoned. Some of these programs are sponsored. Some are carried as a "public service" by the station.

See the Key for where and what.

The Far Right may not be large in numbers, but it is large in noise and propaganda efforts.

Photo 5.1. This map of stations airing conservative programs accompanied Senator Gale McGee's (D-Wyoming) report to Myer Feldman on the "Right-Wing Movement" in the US West.

John F. Kennedy Presidential Papers, John F. Kennedy Presidential Library and Museum.

O'Donnell informed Phillips of the Federal Communications Commission's (FCC's) recent clarification of the Fairness Doctrine and told him to meet with Nicholas Zapple, then counsel for the Senate's Communications Subcommittee, "to see if it could be used to provide support for the President's programs."[14] Zapple had significant influence with the FCC as counsel to the US Senate Commerce Committee from 1949 to 1975. When Zapple spoke, he had the backing of powerful Senate Commerce Committee Chairman Warren Magnuson and Communications Subcommittee Chairman John Pastore. Indeed, when Zapple later wrote to the FCC in May 1970 asking for an additional clarification of the Fairness Doctrine, the result was an enhancement of the equal time rule called the "Zapple Doctrine." Previously, stations only had to give equal airtime to political candidates themselves. The Zapple Doctrine extended that requirement to their supporters as well, a useful rule during a tough midterm election year featuring a number of Republican upsets of Democratic incumbents. In fact, the Zapple Doctrine would outlive the Fairness Doctrine by a quarter century; the FCC only struck it from its regulations in 2014.[15] Nicholas Zapple and the Senate Commerce Committee have an important role to play later in this story, but for now suffice it to say that Phillips had been recruited by two very well-connected individuals.

Zapple was more than happy to help Phillips "fight the lunatics of the Right."[16] He gave Phillips copies of both the FCC's July 26 Fairness Doctrine clarification and the Cullman Doctrine. Phillips then visited the office of public relations firm Ruder Finn to get a copy of the letter that the Citizens Committee for a Nuclear Test Ban had mailed to stations when requesting free response time. He next turned to Wesley McCune and Group Research Inc. for a list of stations airing right-wing broadcasters. List in hand, Phillips started monitoring local conservative broadcasts from his home, listening for attacks on specific organizations or government programs. For instance, during the fall of 1963 Phillips contacted the president of the National Housing Conference, a prominent lobbying group supporting public housing policies, to notify him of a "particularly virulent attack against Federal housing programs" by H. L. Hunt's *Life Line*. Phillips then asked him to write the offending stations and ask for response time under the terms of the Fairness Doctrine. Through this and similar efforts with the National Council of Senior Citizens and the National Farmers Union, Phillips secured over five hundred free response programs for interest groups allied with the DNC.[17]

Phillips may never have heard of the Reuther Memorandum, but his operations in the fall of 1963 represented the next step in the administration's implementation of the memorandum's recommendations. The test case for the Reuther plan had been the Citizens Committee for a Nuclear Test Ban's use of the Fairness Doctrine during the passage of the treaty in September 1963. Just a month later Phillips was tasked with using the strategy to support another administration policy proposal. President Kennedy wanted Congress to authorize a cabinet-level department of public housing modeled on the Housing and Home Finance Agency (HHFA). With the tacit support of the White House, Phillips, himself an HHFA employee, taught a key administration ally how to use the Fairness Doctrine to mitigate conservative opposition to public housing.[18] Kennedy was assassinated before the effort could bear much fruit, but the Johnson administration ultimately secured approval for the new Department of Housing and Urban Development in 1965.

The Propagandist: Fred Cook

In January 1964 Kenneth O'Donnell rewarded Wayne Phillips for his efforts with a new position as Director of News and Information for the DNC. Phillips was tasked with overseeing the DNC's Fairness Doctrine push. His first action was to hire Fred Cook—a freelance writer and a personal friend from his days at the *New York Times*—to write an article condemning right-wing broadcasting. Cook regularly churned out books on politics, including a biography of Franklin Delano Roosevelt (a "valiant leader"), a takedown of J. Edgar Hoover's Federal Bureau of Investigation (FBI) ("the police state looms on the horizon"), and an apology for Alger Hiss (whose trial was the "most callous outrage ever perpetrated for base political advantage in America").[19] Cook, in other words, was a liberal with a reliable track record.

In fact, Walter Reuther had previously selected Cook to ghostwrite his biography for an *Encyclopedia Britannica* series titled "Great Lives for Young Americans." Reuther was reassured by his assistant that "Cook is on our side" and "he will do a sympathetic and understanding job."[20] Case in point, Cook told Reuther that he had no interest in the controversial letter that Victor and Walter Reuther had sent home while working in the Soviet Union in 1934. Conservatives frequently republished the letter, which was full of praise for the Soviet system and ended with a call to "carry on the fight for a Soviet America."[21] The letter had become a political liability for the Reuthers and Cook knew to steer well clear of it.

Cook had caught the eye of both Walter Reuther and the DNC with a forty-two-page article on "ultra" conservatives written for a special issue of *The Nation* in the summer of 1962. The article did not say anything particularly original—conservatives were "rabid," "bankrolled by industrial millions," and leading America down "The Road to Fascism"—but it demonstrated that Cook would be a willing and useful instrument in the DNC's campaign.[22] Early in May 1963 Wayne Phillips commissioned Cook with writing, on the DNC's dime, a new article focusing specifically on conservative broadcasters. Cook eagerly accepted because, as he told an interviewer a decade later, he was disturbed by "the way the media is weighted . . . towards arch-conservative principles" and because he felt that the likes of Billy James Hargis were "hysterical hate makers" who promoted "a demonic sort of concept."[23]

In less than a month Cook had finished "Radio Right: Hate Clubs of the Air" using materials he pulled from Group Research Inc.[24] He called out the usual suspects, including Carl McIntire, Clarence Manion, Billy James Hargis, and H. L. Hunt, insinuating that these "merchants of hate" were ultimately responsible for the assassination of John F. Kennedy because they had created "a climate of hate and unreason in which the unstable inevitably are incited to violence." Conservatives had as good as pulled Oswald's trigger that day in Dallas through their vitriolic attacks on the president and his policy. Countering right-wing broadcasters was not only one's patriotic duty but also a way of honoring Kennedy's memory.[25]

Wayne Phillips asked the editor of *The Nation* to publish Cook's article alongside a map of every radio station in the nation airing right-wing programs (see Photo 5.2).[26] Phillips then sent a copy of the article to each of those 1,300 stations. It was accompanied by a letter from DNC Vice Chairman Samuel C. Brightman, who notified station owners that "all of these programs have repeatedly attacked the candidates, programs, and policies of the Democratic party" and warned them that requests for response time would be forthcoming should they continue to air the offending conservative programs.[27] Phillips also distributed copies of Cook's article to state and local Democratic organizations with instructions on how to use the Fairness Doctrine to their advantage.

Photo 5.2. The National Council for Civic Responsibility distributed this map of stations airing the top conservative programs.
Clarence Manion Papers, Chicago History Museum.

The Inside Man: Martin Firestone

Phillips made another smart hiring decision prior to the DNC's opening salvo. In Cook he had found a reliable propaganda voice, but he needed someone with technical and legal expertise on the team. He found his man in Martin Firestone, a Columbia Law School graduate who joined the FCC after the 1960 election and who was a close ally of FCC Chairman E. William Henry. While with the FCC, Firestone's office had reviewed all station license renewal applications and was also responsible for enforcing the Fairness Doctrine.[28] During 1963 Firestone had taken point on one of Chairman Henry's pet projects, a regulatory test case in Omaha that was intended to convince television stations to air more locally produced public service programs. Henry and Firestone wanted stations to determine their programming based on surveys of local religious organizations, educators, ethnic groups, business chambers, and labor unions. Henry concluded that "members of the public need and are entitled to help from the Commission and the broadcaster . . . in articulating their own needs."[29] But the effort failed because the television industry saw it as an indirect government programming mandate and thus a violation of the FCC's promise not to tinker with broadcasting content.[30]

Firestone resigned from the FCC in February 1964 to become the in-house counsel for a private television interest group that needed help navigating the Fairness Doctrine and other FCC regulations.[31] Resigning also freed Firestone to volunteer for Phillips, giving the DNC an enthusiastic insider with a special connection to the FCC chairman. Firestone knew how to squeeze the maximum benefit out of the Fairness Doctrine and would prove a valuable asset to the DNC's campaign. Furthermore, Firestone handled the campaign's correspondence and was skilled at deflecting questions from already bewildered station managers using a wall of legalese and thinly veiled threats of FCC action.

The Job: The Summer of '64 Campaign

With Fred Cook's article in hand and Martin Firestone's expertise on board, Phillips and the DNC were ready to launch their campaign. They barraged stations airing right-wing programs with requests for response time. After Clarence Manion criticized federal urban renewal programs on the air,

Firestone secured 108 free broadcasts for the DNC. When Dan Smoot compared the Democratic National Convention to the "Munich Beer Hall Coup," he just gave the DNC another thirty-one broadcasts. And when Smoot doubled down after the Gulf of Tonkin incident by accusing Lyndon Johnson of being willing to do anything to win the election, "even contrive a war if necessary," the DNC claimed another thirty-three.[32] Other liberal organizations joined the feeding frenzy. When *Life Line* complained about poverty programs in June, the National Rural Electric Cooperative Association convinced 101 stations to air a response broadcast by Sargent Shriver, the front man for Lyndon Johnson's "War on Poverty."[33]

Not satisfied with answering only direct attacks, Phillips and Firestone became rather inventive in justifying responses from the DNC in reprisal for attacks on other liberal groups and individuals. For example, when Carl McIntire invited former General Edwin Walker to speak on his show, Walker attacked Carl Rowan, the Director of the United States Information Agency, both for being black and for supporting the civil rights movement.[34] The DNC had no direct grounds for requesting response time. As Firestone noted, "the program was actually a personal attack on Rowan," who evinced no interest in offering a response. So Firestone "interpreted the statements to be an explicit attack upon the nature and quality of the Presidential appointments of the Democratic administration and its handling of foreign affairs through the U.S.I.A." In the DNC's opinion, a conservative attack on any one member of the administration or any of its agencies constituted an attack on the administration as a whole, thus justifying the DNC's demand for response time. Bluff or not, the DNC got sixty-one offers of free time out of the gambit.[35]

In response, frustrated station owners complained to the FCC, but their sternly worded letters filled with impotent threats accomplished little. For example, the manager of station KWFS in Eugene, Oregon, one Marvin Steffins, wrote the FCC and listed the five warnings that they had received from Martin Firestone and the DNC in the span of just eight months. Steffins did not know how right he was when he blamed the "infamous Reuther Memorandum" for the wave of Fairness Doctrine complaints his station had received. "The Democratic Party," he wrote, "using the unreserved power of the Democratic administration is now on record with a determination to silence all opposition." He further compared the DNC's actions to those of the Federalist Party in the eighteenth century when "it, too, drunk with power" had passed the Alien and Sedition Acts. Steffins warned that the Federalist Party learned the error of its ways when the party "died very suddenly" after the election of Thomas Jefferson in 1800; if the Democratic Party wanted to avoid the same fate it should reconsider their campaign against right-wing radio. Steffins may have correctly diagnosed the source of the campaign, but his letter was all bluff and bluster. Like most stations, KWFS and Steffins ultimately knuckled under and offered free response time.[36]

The DNC had gained hundreds of hours of free airtime and successfully flustered station managers who aired conservative programs. Each individual claim for time did not amount to much, a few dozen broadcasts, but in the aggregate they had a significant impact. The true success of the DNC's strategy is revealed by internal memoranda in the months following the election. In January 1965 Chairman John Bailey reported to the rest of the Democratic National Committee on Phillips's success in obtaining more than 1,700 free broadcasts.[37] In the crucial final week before the election, the DNC had snagged 234 broadcasts, each lasting between fifteen and thirty minutes.[38] However, as Phillips noted, "more important than the free radio time . . . was the effectiveness of this operation in inhibiting the political activity of these Right Wing broadcasts." Conservative broadcasters had continually attacked first Kennedy and then the Johnson administrations, but after the DNC initiated its campaign, these kinds of attacks "virtually disappeared" as broadcasters learned to steer clear of direct criticism of Lyndon Johnson. Notably, Phillips addressed his comments to Richard Maguire, the DNC treasurer and the man in charge of fundraising for first John F. Kennedy and then Lyndon B. Johnson.[39]

Martin Firestone also believed that the campaign had been a major success. Like Phillips, Firestone was most impressed with the "collateral benefits" of the DNC's campaign, not just the sheer amount of airtime. He believed that "the constant flow of letters from the Committee to the stations may have inhibited the stations in their broadcast of more radical and politically partisan programs." Furthermore, he believed that pressure on the stations translated into pressure on the program producers themselves, "thereby keeping them from becoming too extreme in partisan political matters." Yet for Firestone, Phillips, and the DNC leadership, using the power of a federal bureaucracy with the intent of inhibiting the speech of their political opponents was not partisan behavior. Without a hint of irony, Firestone concluded that despite "the rather low level to which this campaign descended, our letter writing campaign kept even more mud from being slung on these programs."[40] Of course, what is "mud" from the perspective of one side of the partisan divide is reasonable complaint to the other.

The reason that the DNC's campaign worked, according to Firestone, was that conservative programs aired mostly on "small rural or semi-rural" stations with "little or no political affinity" for conservatism. These stations were, however, "in desperate need of broadcast revenue" and right-wingers paid in cash. Only a few of the stations had dropped conservative programs as a direct result of the DNC's election push, but Firestone believed that a year-round effort would lead to drops on a massive scale. By making "the broadcast of these programs bothersome and burdensome (especially if they are ultimately required to give us free time)," the DNC could put a real dent in the number of stations willing to air right-wing broadcasters.[41]

For example, three small stations in northwestern Alabama, known as the "Tri-W Network," dropped McIntire as soon as they received a complaint from the DNC in July 1964. Interestingly, one of the three stations was located in Jasper, one of the two towns (along with Cullman) that had given birth to the Cullman Doctrine less than a year prior. The Tri-W stations were not affiliated with the stations involved in the FCC's Cullman Doctrine decision, but the speed with which Tri-W dropped McIntire may have had something to do with their local knowledge about the FCC's push for Fairness Doctrine enforcement.[42] Tri-W's decision to drop conservative programming anticipated a trend through the rest of the decade. As other liberal interest groups learned to imitate the DNC's Fairness Doctrine strategy, station owners decided that accepting conservative cash was no longer worth the hassle of Fairness Doctrine compliance.

The Front: The National Council for Civic Responsibility

The DNC's Fairness Doctrine strategy may have succeeded beyond even their grandest expectations, but John Bailey was not the kind of chairman to put all his eggs in one basket. Even as Wayne Phillips and Martin Firestone were sending out equal time demands in the summer of 1964, the campaign advanced on another front. With the blessing of John Bailey and funding from the DNC, a front organization was created to publicly protest the Right's influence on the airwaves. The National Council for Civic Responsibility (NCCR) was the bipartisan, respectable face of the counter-Right campaign. Through an odd turn of events after the election, the NCCR's backers were exposed and the group subsequently fizzled out. Although a failure, the story of the NCCR highlights the lengths to which the DNC was willing to go to undermine conservative broadcasting.

This section on the NCCR pulls heavily from interview notes in the papers of Fred Friendly, a former CBS News producer who compiled the information for his 1975 book *The Good Guys, the Bad Guys, and the First Amendment*.[43] By 1975, the Pentagon Papers and Watergate scandals had shaken the confidence of the journalistic community in the executive branch. Traditionally, the press corps had shown a great deal of deference to the White House by not covering personal scandals and by parroting the official line on policy. However, the Johnson administration's heavy-handedness with media coverage of the Vietnam War had alienated journalists like Friendly, who resigned as president of CBS News in 1966 when the White House pressured the network into airing reruns of *I Love Lucy* and *The Andy Griffith Show* instead of showing a US Senate hearing about the Gulf of Tonkin incident.[44]

Friendly worried that journalists had abrogated their fundamental responsibility to tell the truth no matter the political consequences. The same spirit that motivated *Washington Post* journalists Carl Bernstein and Bob Woodward to doggedly investigate the Watergate burglary inspired Friendly to unearth the true story of the NCCR. Those involved in the sordid affair were willing to talk with Friendly out of a sense of guilt that the kinds of tactics they had used against Goldwater in 1964 had prepared the way for Nixon's dirty tricks in 1972. As Friendly wrote of one interviewee, "[He] has, like the others, serious questions of guilt about his own involvement although he claims that he didn't know it had anything to do with the Fairness Doctrine."[45] While Friendly was the first person to write about the NCCR, he could only tease a connection between the NCCR and the White House. The Kennedy administration's involvement in the Internal Revenue Service (IRS) tax audit scheme, the FCC's clarification of the Fairness Doctrine, and the creation of the Cullman Doctrine were beyond the scope of Friendly's sources. Scattered in archives around the country are major pieces of the story that were not available to Friendly. This section of the book both broadens and deepens Friendly's account.

One fact that escaped Friendly was a meeting that occurred between Walter Reuther, John Bailey, Lawrence O'Brien, and Kenneth O'Donnell in January 1964 in which they planned the creation of the NCCR.[46] They left behind no records of their conversation at that meeting, but O'Donnell would hire Wayne Phillips as the DNC's director of news and information just days later. Bear in mind that it was O'Donnell who had met with Phillips in the White House the previous October and who had outlined ways in which the FCC's new Fairness Doctrine rules might be "used to provide support for the President's programs."[47] Phillips's initial efforts that

winter had borne fruit and Reuther, Bailey, O'Brien, and O'Donnell had decided Phillips was the person to oversee the next step in the counter-Right
campaign.

That next step came with a meeting between Wayne Phillips and Bill Ruder
in March 1964.[48] They met in the offices of the eponymous Ruder Finn, a
New York public relations firm that specialized in supporting Democratic
politicians and liberal interest groups. Indeed, it was Ruder Finn that had run
the pro–Nuclear Test Ban Treaty ad campaign back during the fall of 1963
at the suggestion of the president himself. The cozy relationship between the
firm and the administration began with Bill Ruder, who had served as an
Assistant Secretary of Commerce until Kennedy's assassination.[49] Ruder Finn
could be trusted both to do good work and to keep quiet. After the meeting
with Phillips, Ruder Finn started work "almost immediately [on] proposals
for an independent organization to combat right wing radio activity."[50]

The Patsy: Arthur Larson

Ruder Finn had some time to work with—the plan was not to unveil the new
organization until after the Democratic National Convention in August—
so the first order of business was selecting a respectable figurehead for the
council. Although this time it involved creating a front for the DNC rather
than for the White House, Ruder and Finn still patterned the NCCR after
the Citizens Committee for a Nuclear Test Ban. In both cases the logical
candidate for the top position needed to be someone with unimpeach-
able, bipartisan credentials, preferably a moderate Republican if one could
be found. That criteria nixed their initial top candidates, poet Archibald
MacLeish, broadcast journalist Edward Murrow, or economist John Kenneth
Galbraith.[51] And while Republican diplomat James Wadsworth had filled
that role nicely for the Citizens Committee for a Nuclear Test Ban, putting
the same token Republican in charge of sequential front organizations would
not have been a strong play.

Ruder, Phillips, and Bailey settled instead on Arthur Larson, another
former Eisenhower administration staffer.[52] Larson had been director
of the United States Information Agency during the mid-1950s before
serving as President Eisenhower's chief speechwriter until 1958. During his
time in the White House, he and other "Modern Republicans" had clashed

with the rising conservative faction within the party. The animosity only grew as Barry Goldwater rolled toward the Republican nomination in 1964. At first, Larson thought that the best course of action for reasonable Republicans was to ignore the Right, but the "Niagara of noxious literature" being published during the election season, including Barry Goldwater's book *Conscience of a Conservative*, forced Larson to take the threat more seriously. He only regretted not getting involved sooner.[53] In September 1964 Larson formally endorsed Lyndon Johnson. Larson was almost too good to be true for the DNC, a moderate Republican who hated conservative Republicans enough to hold his nose and endorse a Democrat for the presidency. He was the perfect mark. Albert Landa, a former NCCR staffer, described Larson as a "weak, vain man who didn't know what was going on." Another insider called him a "stuffed shirt who hadn't done his homework."[54] Whatever his personal failings, these comments make clear the disdain that DNC operatives had for Larson. His desperation to save the Republican Party from a conservative takeover kept him from asking too many questions about the organization he fronted or where the money for it came from.

The NCCR now had its chairman, but it still needed members, so Ruder Finn came up with a Who's Who of prominent individuals who had joined or donated to liberal causes in the past. Among those who agreed to join were Archibald MacLeish, historians Jacques Barzun and Oscar Handlin, National Association for the Advancement of Colored People Director Roy Wilkins, and former National Council of Churches President Eugene Carson Blake, along with dozens of other educators, literary figures, and clergy.[55] They even got a signature from former IRS commissioner Mortimer Caplin, who was responsible for launching the targeted audits of right-wing broadcasters. While having influential members is all well and good, the lifeblood of any advocacy group is donations, and donors want tax write-offs. Applying for tax-exempt status with the IRS would have been straightforward, but they might not have gotten a ruling until after the election was over and doing so would have meant publicly disclosing financial information. And that might have exposed the fact that the DNC was funding the ostensibly nonpartisan NCCR to the tune of $50,000. That would not do, so Phillips and Bailey looked for another option. If they could find a defunct organization with tax-exempt status, they could effectively merge the groups and avoid financial disclosure.

They settled on the Public Affairs Institute, an advocacy group founded in 1948 with money from the Congress of Industrial Organizations. The institute began with the goal of being "a sort of Brooking Institution of the labor movement," but after a few years the money ran out and the organization ceased operations. The man still technically in charge was a retired Hoover administration bureaucrat and part-time cattle rancher named Dewey Anderson. Anderson met with Bailey in Washington, DC, and they agreed to merge the organizations. The NCCR now had its tax-exempt status, and even though Anderson knew the arrangement was fishy—later acknowledging that it was a "tax front" or "tax dodge"—it also made his organization relevant once again. Besides, Anderson thought he was advancing a worthy cause by combating extremism on both the Left and the Right.[56]

With funding, tax exemption, members, and a leader now in hand, the NCCR was ready to go public, which it did with a full-page ad in the *New York Times* that proclaimed "Six Reasons Why You Should Worry About Extremism in the U.S. Today." Half of those reasons dealt with extreme conservative views—like wanting to impeach Supreme Court Chief Justice Earl Warren and working to undermine Social Security and the federal income tax—but the other half focused on the newfound influence of right-wing groups on the airwaves. Conservatives were spending $10 million a year on more than seven thousand weekly broadcasts across the country, a 1300% increase since 1958.[57] The NCCR promised to monitor all broadcasts made by the ten largest conservative broadcasters, including Carl McIntire, Billy James Hargis, Clarence Manion, Dan Smoot, and the John Birch Society. With the help of Group Research Inc., they would tape each program so as to easily identify attacks and demand response time.[58]

Conservatives responded to the NCCR's launch with as much vim and vigor as one might expect. One small group in Pasadena called "The Network of Patriotic Letter Writers" declared that the NCCR was an "embryonic Gestapo." Billy James Hargis accused the NCCR of adopting "smear activities and Hitler-type techniques" while simultaneously, and somewhat confusingly, blaming "[Walter] Reuther and his Marxist disciples" for the group.[59] For once, Hargis was on the right track; the NCCR's announcement came just weeks after the existence of the "Reuther Memorandum" was reluctantly confirmed. Even so, major news outlets had no interest in doing stories based on unverified claims made by extremist groups. The NCCR scandal attracted little attention outside of a smattering of articles in conservative magazines like *National Review*.[60]

Things Fall Apart

As it turned out, conservatives need not have worried. The NCCR imploded in rather spectacular fashion without any outside help. The flood of expected donations to the council never materialized, and once Lyndon Johnson had secured re-election the DNC lost any interest in subsidizing the council. They designed the NCCR to be a single-shot pistol, not a long-range rifle. Financial stress brought other tensions to the surface; within a few months Dewey Anderson and the DNC handlers fell out over the organization's use of funds. Anderson thought money had been wasted on black-tie affairs at fancy hotels and so felt justified taking part of the DNC's seed money as compensation for startup costs that he said he had paid out of his own pocket. The DNC accused him of theft and considered a lawsuit, but all talk of going after Anderson in court ended once he leaked embarrassing information about the organization to a newspaper columnist. These public revelations forced Arthur Larson to confront the fact that he had been duped into working for a front organization. He then threatened to sue the DNC but was dissuaded by Wayne Phillips, who pointed out that further airing of their dirty laundry would just make Larson seem even more foolish. No legal action came of the Mexican standoff between Anderson, Larson, and the DNC, but the organization was finished anyway.[61]

Mutual recriminations followed. Larson had to write each of the NCCR's members and explain the scandal over taking money from the DNC for a supposedly bipartisan organization. While it was certainly true that Larson "personally had no knowledge of this and no way of knowing it," admitting so to several hundred prominent Americans must have stung. And having to offer the thin excuse that he was resigning immediately because of the onerous workload (and not the scandal) was not much better.[62] The fact that Larson's biographer decades later was forced to rely on newspaper accounts of the NCCR suggests that the episode was so embarrassing that Larson did not save any relevant personal correspondence.[63] Larson would later describe himself as "naïve," express regret at being a "tool of the D.N.C.," and say he "would never do it ******* again."[64] Larson and Dewey Anderson agreed on that much. Anderson felt like he had been made "a patsy." Both men had allowed their antipathy for the Right to blind them to the "seamy, sleazy" side of the operation, but that sort of "end justifies the means" logic only held so long as the true end was not in sight.[65]

The collapse of the NCCR did have a silver lining for the counter-Right campaign, albeit on a different front. In August 1964, before settling on the merger with Dewey Anderson, the NCCR had informally contacted the IRS to ask whether the tax exemption application process could be expedited in time for the election. The person they contacted was Mitchell Rogovin, the IRS legal counsel who had worked with IRS Commissioner Mortimer Caplin on the Ideological Organizations Project. Now Caplin, his former boss, was a member of the NCCR and "engaged in activities not too far out of line with our ideological study," albeit on the other side of the partisan divide. It was awkward because the IRS was at that moment trying to revoke the tax exemptions of the very groups being targeted by the NCCR. People might start asking embarrassing questions if it looked like the IRS was picking sides. Furthermore, the law banning tax-exempt organizations from engaging in political activity had been introduced in 1954 by then Senator Lyndon Johnson, now the person who stood to benefit most from selective enforcement of the regulation against pro-Goldwater groups. To Rogovin's relief, the conflict of interest resolved itself with the NCCR's demise.[66]

Loose Ends

There was one final loose end from the NCCR that would not tie up so neatly. Fred Cook, who Phillips had hired in 1963 to write the "Hate Clubs of the Air" article for *The Nation*, had also been hired to write copy for the NCCR. His assignment—accompanied by a $1,500 advance check from Ruder Finn—was to turn the article into a book highlighting Goldwater's connections to the Right.[67] It was the DNC's response to the publication of several bestselling pro-Goldwater, paperback books in early 1964, like Phyllis Schlafly's *A Choice Not an Echo*, which sold 3.5 million copies in six months.[68] Reports poured into the DNC about the negative effect these "hate books" were having on voters. Lawrence O'Brien, who stayed on after Kennedy's assassination as Johnson's campaign manager, even had an airline stewardess buttonhole him on a plane to ask questions after reading all three of the books. O'Brien was most disconcerted by the fact that the stewardess was "not a Birchite or a conservative" and had voted for John F. Kennedy in 1960. These books were both energizing the conservative base and alienating potential Democratic voters.[69]

To make sure that Cook's *Goldwater: Extremist of the Right* would make a splash, Wayne Phillips, on behalf of the DNC, ordered 72,250 copies or almost half of the book's total advance. The publisher, Grove Press, sold the books to the DNC at cost, charging only $0.12 a copy rather than the cover value of $0.75. Yet by election time the DNC had not paid the balance due despite multiple entreaties from Grove Press, which resorted to hiring an attorney in January 1965 and threatened a lawsuit. As is often the case with presidential campaigns, the Johnson campaign was in debt and a host of creditors were clamoring for payment. Still, the prospect of having the DNC's subsidy for the book exposed in court was unpalatable and the DNC finally paid in full.[70] Cook received a 5% royalty from book sales, which when combined with his advance was a tidy sum for two months of work.

The book also attracted the ire of Billy James Hargis, who had supported Barry Goldwater's campaign. Several weeks after the election Hargis dedicated one of his programs to roasting not only Cook's book but also the author himself. He accused Cook of being fired from a position with the *New York World Telegram* for making a false charge against a New York City government official.[71] Hargis went on to complain about Cook's liberal perspective in his books and articles, but it was the lying charge that outraged Cook, which he saw as a "calculated campaign of considerable dimensions aimed at damaging my reputation."[72] He had indeed been forced to leave the newspaper, but it was another journalist with whom he was partnered who had concocted the false accusation of bribery, not Cook. The incident had deeply impaired Cook's journalistic career, but Cook was not the prime instigator. He even obtained a letter from the New York City district attorney clearing him of fabricating the false charge.[73]

If the Fairness Doctrine had not existed, Cook's only recourse would have been to take Hargis to court for slander. Victory in court would have been far from a sure thing. After all, Cook had indeed made a false charge against a city official even if he had not concocted the charge himself. Furthermore, Hargis had based his criticism of Cook on a *Newsweek* article; a court might have reasonably inquired whether Cook should have gone after the magazine rather than one of its readers.[74] But if Cook had little chance of winning in court, the Fairness Doctrine conveniently provided a lower bar to clear. Under the doctrine the truth of the matter asserted was completely irrelevant. So long as a personal attack was made, the offended party could demand response time from radio stations.

In public, Cook took grave offense at Hargis's accusation, but, in private, he burbled with glee contemplating the damage he could inflict on stations airing Hargis's program. He told Wayne Phillips that he would "dearly love to break these bastards down," especially given how "very righteous and stuffy" they could be.[75] For example, when a recalcitrant station in Tennessee finally gave in to Cook's demands, he forwarded the station's acquiescence on to Phillips—just "for chuckles"—and patted himself on the back while wondering "who killed Cock Robbin in Dayton, Tenn.?"[76]

The DNC and Wayne Phillips were happy to help Cook extract his pound of flesh. Phillips paid for Cook's health insurance coverage, a boon for the freelance journalist. More important, Phillips also provided Cook with Group Research Inc.'s file on Hargis, including a list of all radio stations airing his program.[77] In return, Cook kept Phillips apprised of which stations cooperated or resisted, cleared his response time request transcript with Phillips, and asked for tactical advice when necessary. For example, several stations acceded to Cook's response time requests but then stipulated that he would have to pay for the airtime himself. Cook expressed his frustration to Phillips: "Do you have any idea about the best tactics to follow in these cases? I hate like hell to let them get away with it—and, of course, I'm not going to pay them."[78] Phillips responded by sending Cook a copy of the Cullman Doctrine, which outlined the responsibility of stations to provide free response time to victims of personal attacks if they were not willing to pay themselves.[79]

Armed with that knowledge, Cook started working directly with the FCC, identifying which stations they needed to send Fairness Doctrine complaint notifications to and which had complied with his requests.[80] Confronted by Cook's Fairness Doctrine complaint, many stations complied promptly, letting Cook air his five-and-a-half-minute response without charge. One station manager even described himself as a long and "active adversary of the Far Right." He wished Cook good luck and hoped only that "the Federal Communication people are going to make him [Hargis] pay thru the nose for his broadcasts." Whether out of political sympathy or financial distress, several dozen radio stations belonging to minor, regional networks had already dropped Hargis's show in August and September, likely because of the DNC's direct pressure campaign that summer. Several more followed suit in the immediate wake of Cook's Fairness Doctrine request.[81]

Not all stations complied and several sent half-hearted complaints to the FCC before buckling under relatively light pressure. Some resisted because they misunderstood the rapidly evolving Fairness Doctrine regulations. When Cook contacted the stations in early December 1964 asking for free response time, the Cullman Doctrine was only two months old and the complaints from the Citizens Committee for a Nuclear Test Ban were still being adjudicated. Thus, station KHEP in Phoenix, Arizona, rejected Cook's equal time request because they believed it "applicable to political candidates only."[82] The station's management were thinking of the original purpose of the 1959 Fairness Doctrine, which was to require that stations that aired one political candidate provide equal time on the same basis to opposing candidates. Neither they nor the attorney they specially hired to advise them on Fairness Doctrine compliance understood the Cullman Doctrine.

KHEP did offer to sell Cook response time, but Cook would not pay so he had the FCC send the station a formal notice about their Fairness Doctrine violation. In response to the FCC, station management said that they had been suspicious that Cook's request was part of "a planned harassment of the stations that carry Rev. Hargis' broadcast in connection with an article Mr. Cook had written for *The Nation*." They were right, of course, but their complaint fell on deaf ears. After all, the FCC chairman had actively worked with the White House to strengthen the Fairness Doctrine in order to use it against right-wing broadcasters like Hargis.[83] KHEP's reference to Cook's article in *The Nation* is a testament to the reach of the DNC's summer of 1964 campaign. The DNC had enclosed a copy of Cook's article "Hate Clubs of the Air" with the warning letter that they sent to every station in the nation airing right-wing programming. KHEP had taken notice and posited a connection between that letter and Cook's request for time several months later.

In any case, KHEP found Cook's response tape lacking, both in terms of its technical quality and because in his response Cook volleyed epithets back at Hargis—calling him a "demagogue" and a "fanatic"—rather than simply stating what Hargis had gotten factually wrong. The station manager wondered if airing Cook's response would give Hargis the right to respond to the response and so on and so forth, a succession of free responses stretching all the way into the distant radio horizon. After several more months of waiting, the FCC finally told KHEP in unambiguous terms that they had to give Cook the response time for free unless he was willing to pay. (He was not.) On November 15, 1965, almost a full year after Hargis had first accused Fred Cook of being fired for lying, Cook finally got his response aired on KHEP. There is no record of whether the station's listeners had any clue what Cook was talking about.[84]

The Mark: John Norris

While KHEP held out for the better part of a year before capitulating, one station in Red Lion, Pennsylvania, with the call letters WGCB ("The World for God, Christ and the Bible"), surpassed all others in recalcitrance. Its owner, eighty-one-year-old Rev. John M. Norris, was a minister in the Bible Presbyterian church, the small denomination founded by Carl McIntire. His son, John H. Norris Jr., had left a career as a chemical engineer to help his father run WGCB-AM, WGCB-FM, and short-wave station WINB. Norris Jr. was also a board member at Carl McIntire's Faith Theological Seminary. Indeed, Norris would convince McIntire in 1965 to mortgage the school for $425,000 and use the proceeds to buy radio station WXUR, leading to the controversial battle between McIntire, the National Council of Churches, and the FCC that is the subject of chapter 7. By 1964 McIntire's program aired on more than four hundred stations, but back in 1958 WGCB was just the second station in the nation to give McIntire a shot. Many independent station owners accepted right-wing cash with some reluctance, but the Norrises were true believers. They carried conservative shows out of ideological affinity, not just because they were a source of cash flow.[85] Besides McIntire's show, the Norrises also carried Dan Smoot, Billy James Hargis, Clarence Manion, and H. L. Hunt's *Life Line*.

In the summer of 1964, months before they clashed with Fred Cook, the Norrises had placed themselves in the crosshairs of the DNC. Norris Sr. read in *Broadcasting*, the industry trade journal, about the DNC's ongoing Fairness Doctrine campaign. He realized that WGCB was not included on the DNC's master list of stations airing the nine "Hate Clubs of the Air" since they had not received a cease-and-desist letter. Norris took the oversight personally and contacted Marvin Firestone at the DNC asking to be placed on the list post haste. Tongue firmly planted in cheek, Norris acknowledged a personal debt to the DNC; he only aired seven of the nine offending programs. But he reassured Firestone that he would "take immediate steps to secure these [two programs] also." After all, it was vital that WGCB be as "complete as possible in our presentation of basic American views." Someone had to counter the "one-sided and slanted news which is put out by the wire-services and by the big-city newspapers on the side of socialism," and Norris wanted to do his part.[86]

Whatever momentary satisfaction Norris felt at provoking the DNC, he quickly had reason to regret proffering his station as a target. For their part, the DNC was more than happy to return his bluster with a barrage of requests for response time. The DNC added WGCB to its list and sent the Norrises half a dozen requests for response time between July 1964 and March 1965. It began with a complaint by Samuel Brightman, the deputy chairman for public affairs at the DNC, whose name was on the initial salvo of letters. Brightman took offense at Carl McIntire's accusation that the DNC was trying to intimidate stations into dropping conservative programs. It is possible that Brightman was not fully privy to the DNC's summer Fairness Doctrine campaign—he was just a spokesperson and his name does not pop up on the relevant internal correspondence—but otherwise McIntire had correctly identified the source of the campaign. As shown previously, Wayne Phillips and Martin Firestone had expressly hoped that the DNC's campaign would result in hassled station owners dropping conservative programs. Still, even if McIntire had been able to prove his accusation—which he was not— accuracy did not matter under the personal attack rule. Courts might require proof of libel, but the FCC only needed an offended party. After a flurry of correspondence, McIntire decided to air Brightman's response on his own time, saving WGCB the expense of giving the DNC man a slot.[87]

The DNC followed up the Brightman success with a complaint regarding McIntire's previously discussed attack on Carl Rowan. It then lodged a complaint against Clarence Manion's skepticism about federal urban re- newal programs. Next up was *Life Line* for criticizing US foreign aid to Eastern Europe. The DNC finished with a trio of letters demanding response time contra Dan Smoot, who had attacked social security, the Johnson administration's education policy, and the creation of the Department of Housing and Urban Development.[88] These final three letters were written by Wayne Phillips, who may have taken a special interest in WGCB given his previous employment by the Housing and Home Finance Agency. Indeed, it was back in the fall of 1963 that Phillips had first field tested the Cullman Doctrine by securing free airtime for pro–public housing lobbying groups, so he was on familiar ground.

Norris responded to each request with an offer to sell airtime to the of- fended parties, but he thought it manifestly unfair that an independent sta- tion with a monthly budget in the thousands be required to give time to the DNC, which had spent millions on television and radio buys during the 1964 campaign.[89] Norris refused to cooperate because he suspected that "the whole business of demanding 'free time' is designed to 'snow-ball' to such an extent that we will no longer be able to accept 'paid time' because of all the demands that will be made for 'free time.'" Norris was right to suspect malicious intent from the DNC, but he had not quite hit the nail on the head. The DNC did not need to replace anywhere near *all* paid time to successfully pressure stations into dropping conservative programming. Hyperbole aside, the tenor of Norris's letters had changed greatly after just a few months of correspondence with the DNC. The exultant defiance from the summer was long gone, replaced by complaints of never having "known such harassment as has been directed at me."[90]

Norris needed to take the threat of Fairness Doctrine complaints seriously because his station's license had the misfortune of coming up for renewal in September 1963, which was just a month after the FCC had first signaled its intent to crack down on Fairness Doctrine violations. For twenty months WGCB operated in limbo as the FCC took the unusual step of granting the station a month-by-month permit while it reviewed a litany of Fairness Doctrine complaints against all three of Norris's stations. Norris seemingly caught a break in February 1965 when the DNC stopped pressing its complaints against WGCB with the FCC. The commission subsequently cleared Norris but noted that he would have been forced to comply had the DNC not dropped the matter.[91]

Norris then hired an attorney and sued the DNC and the FCC for harassment, demanding an outrageous sum of $5 million in compensation. He argued that the Fairness Doctrine violated the First, Fifth, Ninth, and Tenth Amendments to the US Constitution by impinging on free speech, taking airtime "property" without due process, and delegating law-making authority to the FCC. Furthermore, by forcing WGCB to give airtime to a political party during an election season, the FCC had forced the station to violate the Federal Corrupt Practices Act, which barred corporations from contributing to political campaigns on the federal level. After several months of legal back and forth, a US district court judge dismissed Norris's lawsuit as frivolous.[92] Norris could have appealed the decision to the US Supreme Court, but a more promising opportunity to challenge the Fairness Doctrine had presented itself in the form of Fred Cook.

WGCB had aired Billy James Hargis's attack on Fred Cook in November 1964, so in December Cook sent Norris a form letter asking for response time. But the letter arrived smack dab in the middle of Norris's clash with the DNC and he was in no mood to comply with any requests for free time, especially not from the author of "Hate Clubs of the Air." That summer Norris had bragged to the DNC about collecting all nine of the "Hate Clubs," but by December he faced Fairness Doctrine complaints for comments made by at least five of those conservative broadcasters. An embattled-feeling Norris wrote back to Cook and refused his request for free response time. The best he could do was to offer to sell Cook airtime at the going rate. If he gave airtime away to every person who asked for a response to a personal attack, well, it would ultimately "remove all broadcasting from the realm of free enterprise, leaving only government subsidized and controlled radio," a prospect he thought even Cook might shudder at. For example, if the personal attack rules were applied to automobile advertisements, Norris reasoned, then General Motors and Ford might tie themselves up in an escalating spiral of attacks and responses over the question of which company truly manufactured the "best car" (and, by so claiming, imply that the other manufacturer did not).[93] Norris was speaking with his usual hyperbole, but he had touched on an unintended consequence of the Fairness Doctrine's personal attack rule. Ultimately, station owners were on the hook for the cost of any feud between broadcasters and public figures. And if that cost became sufficiently burdensome, stations owners might decide to drop all potentially controversial programming.

Cook had no interest in paying for time and so, after consulting with Wayne Phillips at the DNC, he officially lodged a Fairness Doctrine complaint against WGCB. The FCC, with typical bureaucratic haste, ruled almost a year later in October 1965 that the station had violated the Fairness Doctrine. Norris tried to defend himself by arguing that Cook had started the entire affair with a personal attack on Hargis in his magazine article "Hate Clubs of the Air." The FCC rejected Norris's defense; Cook may very well have kicked off the dispute, but that was beyond the purview of the commission. All that mattered to them was that Hargis had taken to the airwaves to respond to the attack because the Fairness Doctrine applied to a "broadcast licensee irrespective of the position which may be taken by other media on the issue involved."[94] From the commission's perspective, it was also a matter of "elemental fairness" that WGCB give Cook the chance to respond to Hargis's personal attack. Cook deserved an eye for an eye even if he had poked first. The FCC also worried that without the Cullman Doctrine requiring stations to give free response time for personal attacks, then broadcasters would impugn public figures willy-nilly and, in effect, hold their reputations hostage. Offended parties would have to pay just to clear their own names, which would turn personal attacks into "an opportunity to obtain additional revenues."[95]

Norris, of course, did not share the FCC's paranoia regarding hypothetical, predatory radio station owners. The FCC did suggest that Norris could appeal to the court system if he felt that the ruling was unfair. It was at this very moment that Norris's lawsuit against the DNC stalled in court. So Norris changed tracks, suing the FCC for its handling of the Cook complaint in a case that would make it up the chain to the US Supreme Court. It was the first direct legal challenge to the Fairness Doctrine to make it so far.

Bringing the First Amendment to a Radio Fight

Norris's arguments in *Red Lion Broadcasting Co. v. Federal Communications Commission* were similar to those in his original case against the DNC. First, he alleged that the FCC's criteria defining what exactly constituted a violation of the Fairness Doctrine were vague and thus a violation of the Fifth Amendment's guarantee of due process. The so-called vagueness doctrine had been used to overturn legislation since it was first coined by Justice Sutherland in 1926 to condemn laws so vague that "men of common intelligence must necessarily guess at its meaning and differ as to its application."[96] A law that poorly defined either a criminal offense or the penalties to be assessed for breaking it could easily be applied in a discriminatory or arbitrary fashion. Vague laws were potential cudgels that could be wielded against those holding unpopular views. Norris and his attorneys argued that the Fairness Doctrine, which was filled with language like "reasonable opportunity" and "contrasting views of all reasonable elements," was unconstitutionally vague because the standard of "reasonableness" was in the eye of the beholder, which in this case was whoever happened to be in charge of the FCC. What was "reasonable" could change as easily as a vacancy on the commission.

But in its ruling in June 1967, the US Court of Appeals in the District of Columbia rejected Norris's vagueness argument. Although the Fairness Doctrine was created in 1959, it appealed to the original language of the 1934 Communications Act, which had called for the FCC to advance the "public interest, convenience, or necessity" over the airwaves. Congress had delegated regulatory authority over defining the "public interest" to the FCC, so the commission had not exceeded its bounds, and since regulating radio intrinsically entailed "complicated factors for judgment," any greater precision would prevent the commission from doing its job.[97] The US Supreme Court would uphold that logic in its own 1969 decision.

If either court had had access to more information, they might have decided very differently. After all, in July 1963 the FCC had attempted to clarify its Fairness Doctrine rules—a tacit acknowledgment of its overly vague standards—and did so by explicitly condemning only conservative rhetoric and causes. And when the rules were subsequently enforced in the fall of 1963, leading to the adoption of the Cullman Doctrine, they exclusively targeted conservative broadcasters critical of the Kennedy administration's push for a Nuclear Test Ban Treaty. In other words, with the active encouragement of the executive branch, a regulatory agency had pushed for an interpretation of a vague regulation that would privilege pro-administration speech at the expense of anti-administration speech. Doing so was both arbitrary and discriminatory. But the court of appeals did not have access to White House tapes or DNC internal correspondence, so it seemed to them like the Fairness Doctrine was being applied equitably.

Even though appealing to the Fifth Amendment had been a failure for Norris in court, it was the First Amendment on which he pinned most of his hopes. Norris alleged that the FCC was guilty of prior restraint, that it effectively censored speech by making station owners fear "subsequent punishment" should they air a broadcaster "speak[ing] out in opposition to governmental action or policy" and not then give "free time commensurate with the paid time to voice the contrary view." This created an onerous financial burden on station owners and discouraged them from speaking freely. Indeed, when they first obtained a station license, owners had to essentially agree to become the "first censor" of their own content; if "their censorship is not to the liking of the Commission," they could lose their license when it came up for renewal, as was the case with WGCB's own license renewal application. The FCC might not be directly censoring speech, but it indirectly incentivized station owners to avoid staking out positions on controversial issues of public importance.[98]

Both courts curtly dismissed the charge of prior restraint. Circuit Judge Edward Tamm noted that since stations "are not required to submit any broadcaster material to the Commission, or any other government agency, prior to broadcast," by definition it could not be prior restraint. Broadcasters had wide latitude in selecting programs, personnel, and format in order to comply with the public interest mandate. Besides, it was obvious to Tamm—so much so that it seemed "almost superfluous" for him to point it out—that the FCC could not be censoring broadcasts because the law prohibited it from doing so. The FCC had not broken the law because the law said it could not.[99]

The Supreme Court avoided any (almost) superfluous discussions, but it did concur with Tamm's dismissal of the prior restraint charge. Speaking for the court, Justice Byron White mooted that evidence of "self-censorship" would "indeed be a serious matter." After all, the ostensible purpose of the Fairness Doctrine was to encourage robust conversation about controversial issues of public importance. If it instead caused licensees to "actually eliminate their coverage of controversial issues," then "the purposes of the doctrine would be stifled." However, White was comfortable upholding the Doctrine because the FCC had assured him that self-censorship was "at best speculative" and "the fairness doctrine in the past has had no such overall effect." If self-censorship became an issue at some point in the future, then the court could revisit the question. White felt comfortable leaving the matter in the capable hands of the FCC, which had the "authority to guard against" stations dropping all controversial coverage and which was "not powerless to insist that they [stations] give adequate and fair attention to public issues."[100]

White never questioned whether the FCC's take on self-censorship as "at best speculative" might be at least a bit self-interested. The agency was a party in the case, after all. Given the FCC's active involvement with the DNC's and White House's counter–Radio Right campaign, White had essentially just expressed his confidence in the dedication of the fox to guard the chicken coop. That said, *Red Lion* was the first direct challenge to the constitutionality of the Fairness Doctrine, so it was easy for White to perceive the WGCB case as an isolated exception to generally fair conduct by the FCC. The court would not overrule the FCC without a clear pattern of obvious misconduct.

Norris's inability to get traction in court for his First Amendment complaint was partly a function of the fact that the courts had defined First Amendment protections very differently for radio speech versus print or other kinds of speech. On the airwaves, it was the listener's right to hear that was "paramount" over the broadcaster's right to speak. In response to critics of this logic who complained that regulating speech violated station owners' First Amendment rights, the courts argued that the higher purpose of the First Amendment was "to preserve an uninhibited marketplace of ideas in which truth will ultimately prevail, rather than to countenance monopolization of that market, whether it be by the Government itself or a private licensee."[101] In other words, the goal of the First Amendment in regard to radio was to create a marketplace of ideas from which hearers could freely sample. As long as regulation of radio speech promoted that marketplace of ideas, it was permissible for the court to ignore the face-value meaning of the amendment itself. The end—a robust marketplace of ideas—justified any regulatory means.

This inventive constitutional logic was justified by an appeal to radio spectrum scarcity.[102] Unlike newspapers or books, the number of which was limited only by reader interest or the availability of capital investment, the number of radio stations was naturally limited by the radio spectrum. Each station needed to have exclusive access to a particular radio frequency, or else it would overlap with another station and result in cacophony. Any given area had X number of frequency slots available for Y number of potential stations and X is a finite number that may be smaller than Y. Since the goal of the First Amendment was to promote a marketplace of ideas, the courts worried that any one point of view might monopolize all frequencies in an area. This logic led to a number of anti-network monopoly regulations by the FCC and several subsequent Supreme Court decisions, including *NBC v. United States* in 1943. It also was used to justify the Fairness Doctrine, which would never have survived a First Amendment challenge in the world of print media. Yet since the danger of monopoly was ever present on the limited radio frequencies, or so the logic went, the FCC should take an active hand in making sure that all—or at least all *reasonable*—points of view be heard by the public.

The scarcity principle has aged poorly since the 1960s with the rise of essentially limitless modes of communication like cable broadcasting and the Internet. Indeed, the FCC itself has repudiated the principle repeatedly, including in 1985 when the commission decided to stop enforcement of the Fairness Doctrine.[103] But there are legal scholars today who question whether the logic made sense even prior to the internet age. Justice White was right about one thing back in 1969; by the 1980s the courts and the FCC would find that the Fairness Doctrine had a "chilling effect" on speech and disproportionately affected political views that were "unorthodox, unpopular, or unestablished." Officially, the Fairness Doctrine, and the *Red Lion* case that validated it, is dead, but its corpse shambles on in debates over the regulation of the internet.[104]

The future unraveling of the Fairness Doctrine was cold comfort for the likes of John Norris and the conservative broadcasters he aired in the 1960s. Even granting the validity of the scarcity principle, the effect of the Fairness Doctrine was anything but the creation of a robust marketplace of ideas. Indeed, the express purpose of the White House's and DNC's employment of the Fairness Doctrine was to curtail anti-administration speech from conservative broadcasters. They did not truly want a greater diversity of radio speech; they wanted to use Fairness Doctrine complaints to harass

independent station owners into dropping conservative programming altogether. They wanted a smaller marketplace of ideas. In privileging the
public's right to hear over broadcasters' right to free speech, the FCC had
secured neither and undermined both. By their own standards, Justices
Tamm and White should have sided with Norris against the FCC. Instead,
they carved out an exception to the First Amendment large enough to fit a
radio tower through.

Of course, the justices did not understand what was really going on behind the scenes. To them it appeared to be a minor spat between a freelance
journalist and an independent station owner, a perfect low-stakes opportunity to test the constitutionality of the Fairness Doctrine. In reality, the DNC
was using Fred Cook as a kind of front in a manner similar to the way it
had used the NCCR. Both were cutouts meant to disguise DNC involvement and to deflate any potential charges of seeking partisan advantage. As
already mentioned, the DNC helped Cook find health insurance and paid
him generously for his anti-Goldwater material, as well as the copy he wrote
for the NCCR's publications. Cook's Fairness Doctrine push was possible
only because of station lists that the DNC had worked up during its summer
of 1964 campaign. When Cook found himself running up against a tactical
wall as stations offered only paid and not free response time, it was the DNC
that informed him about the Cullman Doctrine and helped him hit all the
right notes when he filed Fairness Doctrine complaints. Finally, when Norris
refused to give Cook free response time, the DNC forwarded Cook their own
correspondence with the recalcitrant station owner. The file folder—which
is marked "Trouble File" in handwriting other than Cook's—remains in his
papers today and contains letters that Cook otherwise would have had no
way of obtaining. Whereas the DNC had failed to keep the provenance of the
NCCR a secret, they had greater success with Cook. The court system had
been thoroughly hoodwinked.

One line from the Supreme Court decision hints at an additional blind
spot in Justice White's thinking. When discussing the "speculative" nature of
Norris's complaint about self-censorship, White wrote that "the communications industry, and in particular the networks, have taken pains to present
controversial issues in the past, and even now they do not assert that they
intend to abandon their efforts in this regard."[105] White's logic is predicated
on the idea that the proper criterion for measuring the constitutionality
of regulatory changes is the effect on network radio. The major networks,
with their fleets of lawyers and lobbyists, could do a much better job turning

"speculative" fears into established fact. Absent organized representation, independent stations like Norris's outfit were an afterthought. The FCC would repeatedly take advantage of this legal blind spot. As chapter 7 discusses in greater length, when the commission sought targets for regulatory enforcement, it carefully chose smaller stations.[106]

The FCC knew that it did not have to take John Norris's bluster seriously. Senator Gale McGee—who, as previously discussed, encouraged the Kennedy administration to act against conservative broadcasters back during the fall of 1963—received a letter from John Norris in November 1965. Norris had read that the Senate Commerce Committee, on which McGee sat, was opening an investigation of "extremist" broadcasting. The fruit of that investigation is a major subject of the next chapter, but for now suffice it to say that Norris was not happy to hear about the Senate getting involved. With typical hyperbole, Norris compared it to something that might happen in the Soviet Union or "other dictator countries." McGee did not even bother responding to Norris's letter. Instead, he promptly filed a Fairness Doctrine complaint with the FCC against WGCB. An attorney in the FCC's compliance division forwarded the letter to FCC Chairman E. William Henry with the sardonic note, "The Red Lion Roars Again."[107] Norris had named his corporation Red Lion Broadcasting after a fearsome animal, but the FCC knew that this particular lion was toothless.

Norris was clearly out of his depth. The defiant tone from 1964 and 1965 was long gone by 1967, when in a sign of his increasing desperation Norris wrote President Lyndon Johnson to ask for a meeting. He appealed to Johnson for help not as his president but as a fellow broadcaster.[108] Johnson did indeed have significant interests in radio back in Texas where multiple stations were owned in Lady Bird Johnson's name, but it is impossible to imagine Johnson sympathizing with Norris. After all, Johnson had saved the FCC from Congress's threatened abolition of the commission back in the 1940s because he knew that a friendly FCC would help him acquire favorable radio frequencies, which he then parlayed into political influence and a not insignificant family fortune.[109] Norris got a form letter in response, so in his next request he namedropped Robert F. Kennedy as someone who had also "expressed interest concerning the problems of broadcasting."[110] Norris clearly did not know that Robert Kennedy was one of the individuals most responsible for WGCB's travails or that Johnson hated Kennedy almost as much as Kennedy despised Johnson. Norris's desperate letters to the White House may have given some secretary cause for a good chuckle, but they did not result in a meeting, let alone any executive action.

Thus, in 1969, when the Supreme Court sided eight to zero with the FCC in *Red Lion Broadcasting Co. v. FCC*, Norris was forced to either give Fred Cook free response time or lose his station license. In a terse letter Norris offered Cook fifteen free minutes in the timeslot normally reserved for Billy James Hargis.[111] Given that it had been more than four and a half years since the offending broadcast had aired, Cook declined the offer. Still, he could not resist twisting the knife just a little, spending much of his letter reminding Norris that the whole mess could have gone away if he had just complied all those years ago; as Norris was "doubtless aware," his was the only station that tried to resist the FCC's order, as if four and a half years and thousands of dollars in legal fees were not enough to jog Norris's memory.[112]

Defanging Norris was a nice capstone for the DNC's campaign to push conservative broadcasters off the airwaves. However, the DNC would not replicate its 1964 efforts during the next election cycle. That may have been in part because of opposition from conservative Southern Democrats. As previously discussed, right-wing broadcasters had vastly expanded their station footprint in the South in the early 1960s, implementing their own version of the eventual Republican Party "Southern Strategy." That approach paid dividends in the form of sympathetic, southern politicians. One Democratic congressman reassured an outraged constituent that the DNC's action "can not [sic] be condoned" but must be the "result of the ill-advised judgment of some person within the Committee" rather than the position of the Democratic Party as a whole. He promised to take the matter up with DNC Chairman Bailey.[113] But while right-wing radio broadcasters had won allies among southern congressional Democrats, by this point in time the Democratic Party's national leadership was quite experienced at ignoring the complaints of its southern members.

More important, the DNC no longer needed to carry the Fairness Doctrine baton because other liberal interest groups were willing to take point on the campaign. With the possible exception of the NCCR, the DNC's Fairness Doctrine push from 1963 to 1965 was an unmitigated string of successes. Thousands of hours of free airtime had been secured for liberal causes and stations had begun dropping conservative programming entirely to avoid the hassle. McIntire's radio program alone lost nearly 10% of its stations in just one year, going from 480 stations to 438 from 1964 to 1965. Yet as significant as those victories were, they paled in comparison to what was to come in the next several years.

6

Outsourcing Censorship

How the National Council of Churches Silenced
Fundamentalist Broadcasters

The Democratic National Committee (DNC) relinquished leadership of the counter–Radio Right campaign in 1965, but the infrastructure of the campaign remained in place. The tactical use of the Fairness Doctrine to extract free airtime and to intimidate radio stations had been proven to work twice over, first with the Citizens Committee for a Nuclear Test Ban and then with the DNC's summer of 1964 campaign. The Fairness Doctrine itself had been refined and expanded, and was even then receiving legal validation in a series of court cases. All that was needed for the counter-Right campaign to continue was an organization that could replace the DNC, a role that the National Council of Churches (NCC) was happy to fill. During the late 1960s the NCC would greatly ratchet up the pressure on radio stations airing conservative broadcasting. Two such stations, WLBT in Jackson, Mississippi, and WXUR in Media, Pennsylvania, fought back and lost their station licenses for their pains; hundreds more stations preemptively dropped conservative programs altogether.

Over the past decade, scholars have been paying closer attention to the history of mainline Protestantism, a loosely defined collection of denominations which, by the mid-twentieth century, claimed more adherents than any other religious tradition in America. Mainline clergy tended to be more theologically and politically liberal than their counterparts in evangelical churches (or, for that matter, than their own parishioners).[1] When discussing the mainline during the 1960s, the new historiography emphasizes the prophetic role played by the NCC and other ecumenical organizations as they protested the Vietnam War, advocated for nuclear disarmament, and campaigned for civil rights legislation even as mainline pews slowly but steadily emptied of parishioners. This sympathetic view of ecumenical Protestantism can spill over into effusive declarations like that of theologian Gary Dorrien, that the mainline

The Radio Right. Paul Matzko, © Oxford University Press (2020). Oxford University Press.
DOI: 10.1093/oso/9780190073220.001.0001

"served as guardians of America's moral culture," "preserved the idea that the USA was a nation with the soul of a church," and "helped to liberalize American society."[2] This glossy depiction of ecumenical Protestantism elides over the willingness of mainline leaders to fight hard (and even dirty) in defense of their claim to represent the soul of America. At times, the mainline's defense of liberalism could be profoundly illiberal.[3]

Although the NCC remained the largest religious organization in America in the 1960s—its forty-five million members was more than the Catholic Church's forty-two million—it had peaked.[4] Nobody in the NCC's leadership could have imagined how rapid its decline in membership would be over the next half century, but they did worry at the time about the many parishioners and even entire churches that were leaving the association under the influence of conservative, religious broadcasters. It is no accident that it was in this moment, as the NCC felt a growing sense of anxiety about its status in American society, that the term "mainline" was first defined in its modern sense as a shorthand for liberal Protestantism. The term evoked the wealthy, well-connected suburbs along the Main Line railroad west of Philadelphia, which contained many NCC-affiliated churches; it was also home to one of the most infamous right-wing radio stations in the country, station WXUR in Media, Pennsylvania, which from 1964 was owned and operated by none other than Carl McIntire. As Photo 6.1 shows, WXUR's signal gave him an immense potential audience in the greater Philadelphia area. But the NCC's leadership would not let McIntire's ownership of WXUR stand.

A Pyrrhic Victory

But before we discuss the NCC's fight against McIntire and WXUR in the second half of the 1960s, we first need to return to 1960 and the aftermath of the Air Force manual scandal. The NCC had won that fight; the offending manual had been removed, congressional support rallied, the favor of a future president secured, and a deluge of favorable media attention followed. Yet the NCC could not rest on its laurels. At a meeting of the NCC's general board in June 1960, James Wine argued that winning the "temporary battle" over the manual would not suffice; although the NCC had "removed an excrescence"—the manual—the "fundamental problem" remained unresolved. The fundamental problem, which Wine labeled an "apparent conspiracy," was that McIntire and Hargis still had influence that reached into the NCC's

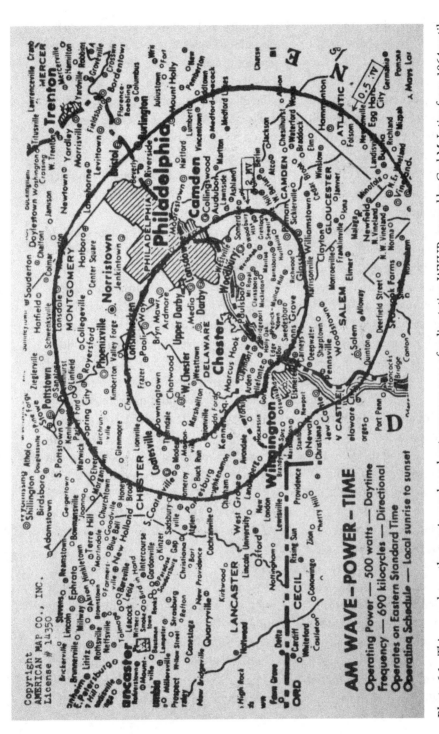

Photo 6.1. This map shows the maximum broadcast coverage area of radio station WXUR, owned by Carl McIntire from 1964 until the Federal Communications Commission denied him a license renewal in 1974. Note that it includes most of the western suburbs of Philadelphia along the Main Line railroad route.

Carl McIntire Papers, Special Collections, Princeton Theological Seminary Library.

own pews. These "purveyors of half truths" and "perverters of fact" were the "willing tools of any person or group that will pick up the tab for their activities." So long as these broadcasters continued to speak, they would "forestall efforts to achieve fuller social justice" in America and continue to violate the freedom-of-religion clause in the First Amendment to the Constitution. Wine noted that conservative broadcasters complained of unfair treatment in the press and by radio stations, but he denied that this had anything to do with the NCC. It was instead a testament to the American "sense of decency" and "sense of fairness." All the NCC had to do was publish the facts and "public opinion in its forceful fashion . . . will drive these people into the black holes of oblivion."[5]

Wine's portrayal of the situation was typical, if fanciful. It became standard during the 1960s to accuse conservative broadcasters like McIntire and Hargis of being cogs in a vast, right-wing conspiracy controlled by rich businessmen who wanted to discredit liberal reformers. In a similar vein, Eugene Carson Blake told the *New York Times* that "support for slanderous accusations against liberal churchmen normally comes from the people who combine conservative theology with conservative economics and politics, specifically including wealthy men of the far right." Their goal, Blake continued, was to turn the NCC into "a tame, kept church such as all totalitarian states attempt."[6] Yet McIntire and Hargis received nothing from corporate interests, instead relying almost entirely on small, voluntary contributions from listeners. Likewise, as the incredible boom in McIntire's radio station count during the early 1960s shows, public opinion had indeed spoken "in its forceful fashion," but it was to validate the appeal of conservative broadcasting, not to drive it into oblivion. The *Twentieth Century Reformation Hour*, heard on 108 stations in 1960, aired on 480 by 1964. It was clear that the NCC could not count on the American people's sense of decency to end these right-wing attacks.

The NCC's broadcasting arm also faced worrisome financial headwinds. The NCC's radio outreach had long been almost completely dependent on "sustaining" airtime given to them without charge by the networks. Starting with the Communications Act of 1934, the Federal Communications Commission (FCC) had mandated that all radio stations dedicate some portion of their weekly programming to news, religion, and educational shows. Given that such programs were not in particular demand, stations usually placed them in the least favorable timeslots of the week, either late at night or early on Sunday morning. While these scraps of airtime were hardly primetime, they were, according to FCC fiat, free. The NCC, as the representative of the vast majority of Protestant churches in America, received the bulk of this free airtime, in contrast to broadcasters like McIntire and Hargis, who had to purchase almost all of their own airtime.

Getting all its airtime gratis gave the NCC's Broadcasting and Film Commission (BFC) a huge advantage over conservative broadcasters. It also had an initial advantage in fundraising. The BFC relied on budgeted amounts levied from its member denominations—$10,000 from the Methodists, $20,000 from the Presbyterians, and so forth—while McIntire and Hargis raised the entirety of their annual budgets from voluntary, individual contributors. Indeed, the rise of conservative broadcasting in the late 1950s correlated precisely with a decline in listener contributions to the BFC. Voluntary contributions to the BFC peaked in 1956 and declined each year thereafter.[7] Religious radio listeners were voting with their donor dollars; conservative broadcasters were winning in a landslide. From 1964 to 1966 the BFC averaged an annual income of approximately $250,000; Carl McIntire, alone, averaged $2,040,000 in annual receipts during the same period.[8] Moreover, the financial disparity was worsening as the BFC began to hemorrhage money in 1959; the deficit grew year by year into an annual loss of $140,000 by 1966.[9] Because of that loss, the BFC shuttered its West Coast office, started paying bills from its endowment, and began asking the major networks not only for free airtime but also to reimburse the BFC for production costs.[10] The networks were not receptive.

These were desperation moves. The NCC, representing forty-five million Protestants, was being dwarfed on the airwaves by the likes of McIntire, whose American Council of Christian Churches could claim at most 120,000 members.[11] The NCC's position on the airwaves vis-à-vis any single conservative broadcaster was already bad by 1960 and growing worse with each year. But by relying on denominational membership statistics, historians have missed the very real and present danger that fundamentalist broadcasters posed to the NCC. Thus, historian Elesha Coffman dismisses Carl McIntire and the anti-NCC organizations because they had "few members, little money, and even less credibility."[12] In reality, conservative broadcasters had huge audiences, large budgets, and a great deal of credibility with their listeners.

While the BFC had particular reason to worry about the Radio Right, the NCC as whole was starting to see conservative broadcasters transform lay disgruntlement into support for outright secession. The First Baptist Church of Wichita, Kansas, by a majority vote of its 4,300 members, had left its parent denomination and the NCC in 1960 because of the influence of conservative broadcasters. The denomination sued for control of First Baptist's building in a case that went all the way to the Kansas Supreme Court. Although the denomination finally won the case and kept the now mostly empty building, it was a public relations disaster.[13] More churches threatened to follow suit.

Some NCC executives urged caution in dealing with the Radio Right. From their point of view, conservative broadcasting was "an intellectual virus which has to run its course." If they simply ignored the broadcasters, the problem would remain "localized" and would eventually go away on its own. But the hardline faction in the NCC argued that ignoring the Radio Right was what had gotten them into trouble in the first place. If the Air Force manual scandal had proven anything, it was that a forceful response was the best course of action. Thus, Methodist Bishop John Wesley Lord asked the NCC to commission "shock troops to meet the attacks of the virus." The Radio Right threat could no longer be ignored because "the attack is from within as well as from outside."[14] Lord was saying that the NCC could not trust its own laypeople because of a fifth column of conservative radio listeners within NCC churches.

This internal debate also hinted at a deeper motivation for the counter-attack. The NCC had an interest in maintaining its position as the informal religious establishment of America. Warren H. Turner Jr., then the vice president of the NCC, wanted the BFC to take action because there was "beginning to be a mood of respect for the Church in this country" after the NCC had forcefully responded during the Air Force manual scandal. The NCC had never appeared to be stronger than it was in the early 1960s. The member denominations were hitting new highs for membership and offerings. Certainly, none of the people sitting in the room that day could have imagined the coming collapse of the Protestant mainline; most of the member denominations would be barely half their 1960s size within a generation. Yet at least some of the board members appear to have had an inkling that the tide was turning. To ignore the Radio Right was to ignore the surge of conservative evangelical sentiment among American churchgoers in the mid-twentieth century.

Regulator of Last Resort: The Federal
Communications Commission

The NCC could not compete in the marketplace with McIntire, Hargis, and other conservative broadcasters, so they turned to the FCC for help. Just before leaving to join the Kennedy presidential campaign, NCC executive James Wine met with FCC Chairman Frederick Ford to discuss how the commission might help the NCC maintain its dominant position in religious radio. Ford—an Eisenhower appointee charged with cleaning up the reputation of the FCC after a string of scandals during the 1950s involving payola and rigged game shows—told Wine that the FCC would soon be setting up a new agency responsible for monitoring broadcasts to ensure that any editorializing on current events represented diverse viewpoints.[15]

With Chairman Frederick Ford's promise of a new monitoring agency in hand, Eugene Carson Blake began calling for local pastors and regional councils "to lead counter-attacks" against conservative broadcasters while warning them that this would be an extended time of "battle."[16] The militant language betrays the manner in which Blake linked success in this struggle with the long-term prospects of the NCC. James Wine—befitting a public relations executive in the Office of Interpretation—used gentler language, encouraging pastors to "enlighten" station managers as to their responsibility to broadcast in the public interest.[17] The goal of this push, as Wine explained to a confidential informant, was to make radio stations "watch their p's and q's concerning some kinds of broadcasts that they carry because it is a very risky business," a goal made easier by McIntire's insistence on publishing the call letters of the stations he aired on.[18] To help local pastors, the NCC typed up a form letter—addressed in this case to the town of "Anywhere, New Jersey"— that they could address to any station airing McIntire or Hargis.[19]

Going to the FCC offered another important benefit; conservatives could not then accuse the NCC of trampling on their First Amendment rights. Wine wrote, "We take some satisfaction in this process"—the FCC's promised new monitoring agency—"because it would be better for the regulating agency to take action than to have us file complaints with running the risk of suggesting any restriction of freedom of speech."[20] In other words, the NCC would reap the benefits of the FCC's censorship without having to bear the onus of being the censor themselves. However, the planned FCC monitoring agency proved ephemeral. Setting up such an agency would have required Congress to approve a massive expansion in the agency's personnel and budget. Furthermore, FCC Chairman Frederick Ford, whose idea the agency had been, stepped down as John F. Kennedy came into office. (Ford then joined the board of directors of the BFC.) The FCC, stocked with Eisenhower appointees, had no interest in pushing for a measure that would benefit liberal interest groups. It would not be until July of 1963, after the appointment of two key liberals—Kenneth Cox and Chairman E. William Henry—that the FCC would propose any serious action to uphold the Fairness Doctrine.

The United Church of Christ Takes the Lead

Once the FCC clarified the Fairness Doctrine on July 26, 1963, the NCC could finally take direct action against the Radio Right. However, the NCC's efforts to support the Fairness Doctrine push would not come through the aegis of the BFC. As the BFC's board members had previously discussed among themselves, it would be a public relations disaster for the NCC itself to be caught trying to mute conservative broadcasters. Instead, two individual board members of the BFC would lead the charge under the cover of other organizations. Their efforts culminated in two, separate campaigns, one led by Charles Brackbill and the Greater Philadelphia Council of Churches, the other sponsored by the United Church of Christ's (UCC's) Office of Communications and its director, Everett C. Parker.

In 1935, Everett Parker had graduated from the University of Chicago. Over the next several years, he worked for the radio department of the Works Progress Administration in Washington, DC, ran a radio station in Louisiana, held an internship with NBC's public service division in New York, and pastored a Congregational Christian church in Chicago. As an undergraduate, Parker had briefly dabbled with socialism, but he remained highly involved in progressive politics for his entire career. Besides being an enthusiastic New Dealer, he had produced campaign ads for the infamous "Kelly-Nash Machine" that dominated Chicago-area Democratic politics during the 1930s. Indeed, his proposed PhD thesis discussed the control that the broadcasting industry had over the newly formed FCC, a flaw that Parker spent his career trying to correct. During this formative period of Parker's life, he realized just "how important the Church could be in influencing public policy through radio."[21]

He would have the opportunity to influence public policy because of his involvement with the UCC's Office of Communication. When the UCC leadership realized in 1957 that a large minority of Congregationalist churches rejected the merger with the Evangelical and Reformed Church, they asked Parker, a former Congregationalist minister himself, to lead the newly organized Office of Communication and bolster lay support for the denominational merger. Because of the way the UCC was structured, the Office of Communication remained Parker's virtual fiefdom until his retirement in 1983, answering only to the UCC's president. Parker had a great deal of influence outside the UCC as well, serving as the founding director of the Joint Religious Radio Commission (1945), which was the predecessor of the BFC.

Parker was a cosmopolitan—well traveled, well educated, and well regarded—and he knew it. He had nothing but disdain for "these fundamentalist commercial preachers" that preached a "theology of greed." His opinion of consumers was not much better since it seemed that consumers wanted nothing more than shallow entertainment. So long as "the consumer was not a real person"—by which he meant that consumers were not socially conscious—someone responsible, someone rather a lot like Everett C. Parker in fact, needed to "force upon the people some factual material, some honest interpretation."[22] Parker saw the greatest need for honest interpretation in regards to the civil rights movement. The Congregational Christian Church had a long history of supporting equal rights for African Americans going all the way back to abolitionism, a tradition that Parker fully supported. (Visitors to the UCC headquarters in Cleveland, Ohio, will see that the denomination's support for the civil rights movement remains a particular point of pride. Pictures of civil rights activists standing with UCC leaders cover the walls and the lovely chapel is named for the Amistad.)

During the Montgomery bus boycott of 1956–1957, Parker and several other UCC leaders met with Martin Luther King Jr., who asked, "Why don't some of you do something about the way we're treated on radio and television?"[23] The UCC decided to prioritize the fight against pro-segregation stations in keeping with one of the new denomination's earliest official statements, the "Call to Christian Action in Society," adopted in the summer of 1959. In the document, the UCC asked its members to support a broad range of liberal policies, including nuclear disarmament, the United Nations, organized labor, farm subsidies, environmental conservation, poverty reduction, and the like. Parker's fingerprints were all over the document, especially in its critique of American society for its "selfish indulgence" by private consumers, the "concentrations of power, controlling the channels of information," and the way in which entertainment dulled people's sense of crisis regarding the world's problems. Special attention, however, was paid to race relations as the UCC called for the end of segregation "in church life, in housing, in employment, in education, in public accommodations and serv- ices, and in the exercise of political rights," essentially listing the rights that would be secured five years later in the Civil Rights Act of 1964.[24]

The First Test Case: WLBT

Parker needed a test case, a station that violated the FCC's July 26, 1963, order that stations fairly represent the views of local black leaders and organ- izations. Ideally, the targeted station would be "a powerful group that would feel it because we were hitting them in their pocketbooks."[25] Parker settled on WLBT-TV in Jackson, Mississippi, owned by a subsidiary of the Lamar Mutual Life Insurance company, controlled in turn by the wealthy Murchison family. The two Murchison brothers, John and Clint Jr., were larger-than-life characters: Texas oilmen, founders of the NFL's Dallas Cowboys, and owners of a famous pirate radio station in the Baltic Sea.[26] They were also committed racists and made WLBT-TV over into their own image. For example, the sta- tion editorialized against James Meredith's fight to integrate the University of Mississippi, urging its listeners to "go out to Oxford and stand shoulder to shoulder with Governor Barnett and keep that nigra out of Ole Miss."[27] Furthermore, in a town that was more than 40% black, the station did not em- ploy any (nonjanitorial) black staff, gave no sustaining time to black clergy, and never used titles—Mr., Mrs., etc.—for its black interviewees despite never failing to identify their race. WLBT was in clear violation of the FCC's July 26 statement. More important, from the perspective of the UCC, WLBT did not have the heft of one of the networks despite the Murchisons' wealth; as an independent station, WLBT was vulnerable. Henry Geller, one of the FCC's in-house counsels during the WLBT case, had a tongue-in-cheek rule for determining which stations the FCC could go after, the "three outhouse rule."[28] If a station was large enough to have three outhouses, the FCC would look for easier prey. Only the networks owned headquarters large enough to need multiple bathrooms. WLBT only had one.

First, Parker met with FCC Chairman E. William Henry, who encouraged him to file a complaint with the FCC about WLBT. Parker needed signers from Jackson—for it would look inauthentic for a Chicagoan to complain about WLBT—and convinced Aaron Henry, president of the Mississippi conference of the National Association for the Advancement of Colored People (NAACP), and Robert L. T. Smith, an officer of the Mississippi Freedom Democratic Party, to join the complaint.[29] The primary difficulty with their petition was that FCC rules gave standing at its license renewal hearings only to those with a material interest in the hearing's outcome. Parker, Henry, and Smith were not representing a competing local radio station and thus had no standing.

The principle of standing stemmed from a time when regulatory agencies were "seen as the embodiment of the public interest" and a "victory of the people over the vested interests."[30] In this progressive vision, impartial bureaucratic experts were the embodiment of the public interest. An agency like the FCC could be trusted to fairly rule on the needs of local communities. Of course, bureaucrats are not impartial, but the rules on standing remained in force. Parker challenged that principle, arguing that the best way to discover the will of the local people was to ask the local people. Yet because Congress had set up the FCC, the FCC believed it was up to Congress to change the definition of standing and the commission voted five to one (with Henry as the lone dissenter) for WLBT on the basis of the UCC's lack of standing. The FCC made a concession, however, renewing WLBT's license for a single year, instead of the usual three years, in recognition of the station's bad track record in not hiring black employees or representing the point of view of the black community. The UCC would have another chance at challenging WLBT's license the next year.

The UCC was not the only organization interested in taking down WLBT. The American Federation of Labor and Congress of Industrial Organizations (AFL-CIO) joined the UCC's complaint on April 16, 1964, protesting that WLBT "used its facilities to encourage opposition to organized labor," that its station manager was a member of the pro-segregation White Citizens Council and the John Birch Society, and that it aired anti-Johnson and pro-Goldwater editorials.[31] The AFL-CIO had been gunning for WLBT's license ever since its failed attempt to organize the Storkline Furniture Corporation's wood cabinet plant in Jackson. The AFL-CIO lost the unionization vote by a slim margin, 677 to 703. They felt that unfriendly editorials by local papers and stations, including WLBT, had swayed the result by pointing out, for example, that the union in question, the United Brotherhood of Carpenters and Joiners of America, was under Senate investigation for bribery and embezzlement.[32] The FCC's July 26th statement gave the AFL-CIO a way of punishing WLBT for its role in defeating the organization drive.

The AFL-CIO's complaint backfired, however, as many Jackson-area union locals protested the attack on WLBT, including an umbrella group for local chapters, the Jackson Building and Construction Trades Council. The blowback took the state and national AFL-CIO leadership by surprise, although at the heart of it was the fact that the AFL-CIO had attacked not just WLBT's stance on labor but also its stance on segregation. None of the local union resolutions baldly stated that they had a problem with the AFL-CIO's alliance with an anti-segregation group like the UCC, although one local representative made his motives clear when he said that WLBT served the people of Mississippi without discrimination "unless it be the National Shows which are becoming overloaded with Negro entertainers." The pressure proved too much and two weeks after joining the UCC's complaint, the AFL-CIO backed out, saying that its "objections to the renewal of the licenses to these stations do not relate to racial matters."[33]

Although abandoned by the AFL-CIO, both the American Civil Liberties Union and the BFC filed *amicus curiae* for the UCC's complaint.[34] Still, the FCC rejected the initial complaint for lack of standing, so the UCC's chances of success looked grim. In 1965, when WLBT's temporary license renewal was up, the UCC challenged and lost. In 1967, they tried again, and again lost. Because the UCC lacked standing, the FCC had to take WLBT's management at its word that they had improved their outreach to the black community by hiring a handful of black employees and giving airtime to black clergymen. During that third attempt, Parker went to Washington, DC, to meet with Paul Porter, the lead counsel for WLBT and a former chairman of the FCC during the 1940s. Porter threatened Parker, saying, "I can keep this case going for 11 years and I can bankrupt the United Church of Christ" if the UCC did not back off its appeal. Parker responded, "Paul, if you do this, if you push it to 11 or 15 years and if you died and I die, the United Church of Christ will still be in this case." (Later in life, Parker enjoyed retelling a subsequent moment of poetic justice, that Paul Porter had "choked to death on a fish bone" in a DC restaurant..)[35] Parker's bravado notwithstanding, the UCC needed a miracle to win.

It found its miracle worker in Warren E. Burger, then chief justice of the US Court of Appeals for the District of Columbia. First, in 1966, Burger ruled that the UCC had standing before the FCC, giving them the opportunity to dispute WLBT's presentation of the facts. After three more years of investigation and appeals, in June 1969—just three days before Burger left the appeals court for the US Supreme Court—he directed the FCC to revoke Lamar Life

Insurance Corporation's license for WLBT.[36] The FCC gave a UCC-sponsored group control of the station in 1969. The group would eventually win permanent control of the license in 1974 with the help of a $300,000 loan from the Methodist Board of Missions to satisfy the FCC's capital requirements.[37] The cost to Lamar was as great as the victory was for the UCC. Lamar lost the station license, worth millions on the open market, and lost the station's annual profit of approximately $314,000.[38]

The logical question at this point is to ask what the WLBT ruling has to do with broadcasters like Carl McIntire and Billy James Hargis. Directly, there was no connection; McIntire and Hargis were radio broadcasters, while WLBT was a television station. But indirectly, the decline of conservative, religious broadcasting in the 1960s accelerated with the WLBT decision. The fact that the public now had legal standing before the FCC meant that listeners could testify at FCC hearings, not just file complaints. This gave the UCC and the NCC the platform they needed to silence McIntire and Hargis. Through its success with WLBT, the UCC convinced donors it could change the dynamics of the broadcasting industry and it would drastically expand its efforts to combat on-air right-wing extremism in 1968. Parker also pointed to the victory as proof that the BFC should "help educate local groups in understanding the WLBT decisions."[39]

Hunting Bigger Game

One such local group was the Greater Philadelphia Council of Churches, which would take its challenge of conservative, religious broadcasting all the way to the US Supreme Court. Back during the Air Force manual scandal, no local council had wanted more to take down Carl McIntire than the Greater Philadelphia and New Jersey Council of Churches. McIntire was their noisy neighbor, taping the *Twentieth Century Reformation Hour* at his home church in the Philadelphia suburbs, Bible Presbyterian of Collingswood, New Jersey. Charles Brackbill, then director of the New Jersey Council's Broadcasting and Film Commission and an executive in the Presbyterian synod of New Jersey, in particular could not stand McIntire.[40] Brackbill had graduated from Princeton Theological Seminary in 1948—the same institution that McIntire had briefly attended before leaving in protest over the seminary's liberal theology—and had pastored churches in New Jersey for seven years. Brackbill had had plenty of opportunity to observe McIntire's ministry and he was embarrassed that "some of the worst 'non-Council' broadcasting in the country originates in New Jersey," singling out Carl McIntire, who "from his kitchen in Collingswood . . . daily spews forth his invectives against Eugene Carson Blake" and the NCC. Brackbill lumped McIntire in with the likes of Pentecostal evangelist and healer A. A. Allen as irresponsible broadcasters who had "undoubtedly lifted millions of dollars from New Jersey Christian pockets." Brackbill's first effort to counteract the likes of McIntire and Allen was to browbeat a local radio station into dropping Allen's program. He acknowledged that passing judgment on other broadcasters put the NCC in a "very difficult and ticklish position" vis-à-vis the freedom of speech, but that would not stop Brackbill from attempting to do to McIntire what he had done to Allen earlier.[41]

At the height of the Air Force manual controversy, James Wine had commissioned the Greater Philadelphia and New Jersey Council of Churches to monitor McIntire's *Twentieth Century Reformation Hour* and to look for evidence of attacks on the NCC. They found plenty of incriminating material, so much so that they warned Wine to take his Miltown (the then-popular tranquilizer colloquially known as "mother's little helper") before listening to the recordings.[42] Brackbill offered Wine additional advice, suggesting that this was the time for a "Truth Crusade" against "psychopaths" like McIntire. "The time has come," Brackbill suggested, "to fight it out legally with these masters of innuendo." The difficulty, however, was that "a frontal attack is what these birds welcome most" given how adept McIntire and Hargis were at turning every controversy to their own advantage. What Brackbill truly wanted was a lawsuit against a station that, "properly reported" by the NCC's friends in the media, "would get everyone's attention fast." Still, the NCC had to take care not to be "officially connected with any imagined suppression of free speech" and should leave those efforts to local councils. An unofficial connection to actual suppression of free speech would have to do. At the time of the Air Force manual scandal, Brackbill recommended only that Wine reserve a hospitality suite at the upcoming National Association of Broadcasting's annual meeting to meet the movers and shakers in the industry, even if "nothing very direct could be said."[43] The idea of making an example of a radio station never went away, but it would be several more years before the Greater Philadelphia Council of Churches could take Carl McIntire to court.

Brackbill's ideas found a sympathetic audience at the BFC, which elected the young, bold Brackbill to its board of managers in 1961. It was a smart choice; Brackbill knew who the real threats to NCC broadcasting were and was willing to baldly state things that other executives would only speak of in whispers. During his acceptance speech, Brackbill told the board that the time had come to be realistic about the threat posed by conservative broadcasters and their millions of listeners and millions in income. The financial position of the BFC was grim, not least because "much of the money we crave for our kind of programming is going into their [conservative broadcasters'] pockets—from members of our churches." Just as significant was the decline of network radio, which meant less free sustaining time for the NCC. Brackbill advocated devolving authority and funds from the BFC to the local councils, which could better take advantage of the new FCC rulings.[44] In a speech to council broadcasters later that year, Brackbill returned to these themes. He acknowledged his audience's frustration with "diminished audiences," "lowered income," and "loss of stations," telling them that it was not the NCC's fault. Conservative, religious broadcasters were responsible. Admittedly, he wished that they could just "somehow mysteriously or magically . . . push a button and get network affiliates and independent stations to drop non-National Council religious programs."[45] While not quite magical fantasy button material, the FCC's Fairness Doctrine was the next best thing.

Yet this happening two years before FCC Chairman enhanced the Fairness Doctrine rules in 1963, so the FCC would prove the weak link in Brackbill's initial plan. In February 1961, Brackbill held a broadcasting conference and invited BFC Director S. Franklin Mack to address the New Jersey Council of Churches. Mack applauded their efforts to contact station managers about the Radio Right, but noted that the FCC had not yet denied a license to any station for "program deficiencies." Still, he had hope that this would change given the "new mood in both the government and the Commission" following the election of Kennedy.[46] That hope was rooted in the new FCC monitoring agency promised by Chairman Frederick Ford who had spoken to the BFC earlier that month.[47] However, that hope proved misplaced. Ford's new monitoring agency, as discussed earlier, never got off the ground.

Although Brackbill's initial plan fizzled out in 1961, the NCC reaffirmed his vision in 1964 by promoting him to associate chairman for planning.[48] Because of his position at the BFC and his ties to the Philadelphia-area councils, Brackbill would be the central player in the next phase of the BFC's counterattack against conservative broadcasters. First, the BFC stepped up its courting of the FCC. Frederick Ford, the former FCC chairman who was now a director of the BFC, joined the NCC's Government and Industry Committee along with Brackbill and Everett C. Parker. They were the lobbying arm of the NCC and one of their first actions was to send Robert Edwin Lee—director of the BFC's West Coast office and author of *Inherit the Wind*, the Broadway play that was a thinly veiled critique of fundamentalism and McCarthyism—to meet with the FCC commissioners in Washington, DC.[49] There is no record of the discussion at that meeting, but the following year four of the seven FCC commissioners spoke at a Washington Council of Churches meeting on broadcasting, the first time so many commissioners had attended an NCC-affiliated event. BFC Executive Director William F. Fore lauded the meeting for being "extremely helpful in establishing two-way communication between local religious broadcasters and the FCC."[50] The desire for "two-way communication" seems to have been mutual. A year later, Fore reported back to the board of the BFC, in a confidential report, that "many members of the Federal Communications Commission . . . are deeply interested in us as a force in the public arena of discussion, expressing quite openly their hope that we can be an ally in some of the FCC efforts to achieve more responsible broadcasting." And once the UCC won standing in the WLBT case that year, the FCC began to attach greater significance to the opinion of the BFC.[51]

Yet despite the warmth between the BFC and commissioners E. William Henry and Kenneth Cox, they failed to change FCC regulations to further favor the NCC's broadcasters. For example, in June 1964, the FCC considered a change to the reporting form for license applicants and invited the NCC to testify at the hearing. Fore, Brackbill, and S. Franklin Mack (representing the BFC, the United Presbyterians, and the UCC, respectively) spoke for nearly an hour. All three men supported the FCC's rule change, which would have tweaked a pre-existing requirement for licensees to ascertain community needs and tailor their programming accordingly.

The FCC had first issued a community ascertainment rule in 1960, telling licensees to "make a positive, diligent and continuing effort, in good faith, to determine the tastes, needs, and desires of the public" when choosing programming. That was it. The FCC issued no further guidance of which groups licensees should contact or what exactly "diligence" looked like; nor did they include any enforcement mechanisms for stations that failed to make the attempt. In the words of media scholar Kim A. Smith, the agency "struggled to define and implement the ascertainment process with little success."[52] In part, this was because the FCC did not want to be seen as requiring stations to air any particular kind of programming, since that would smack of censorship. Instead, the FCC charged station license holders with reaching out to an undefined number of local community groups, asking them about their programming preferences, and then incorporating that advice in an unspecified way. The rules were so generic as to be unenforceable even if the FCC had included a realistic enforcement process.

In 1957 and again in 1961, the BFC had proposed that the FCC give more guidance on community ascertainment. In particular, the BFC had suggested adding questions to the ascertainment form asking stations which specific religious programs they planned to carry and noting what percentage of that religious programming would air on a commercial or a sustaining basis. This was notable because the vast majority of conservative religious broadcasters paid for their time (commercial), while all NCC programs relied heavily on free airtime (sustaining). Adding that question to the community ascertainment form would have given the BFC extra leverage in negotiating free airtime for itself with local radio stations. After the FCC's first attempt at ascertainment in 1960, Charles Brackbill had sent a memo to all New Jersey Council of Churches pastors telling them to write their local stations and remind them that the NCC was "the representative body for Protestantism in the area" and to offer advice on which religious programs the stations should include in their line-up.[53] But the ill-defined and unenforceable nature of the FCC's rule kept the letter-writing campaign from having any noticeable effect.

The BFC hoped for a different outcome with the FCC's proposed ascertainment rules in 1964. While acknowledging that the rule change would "tend to require more broadcasting staff time," they held "that this is part of the price the licensee must pay for his franchise, and is the kind of price all responsible citizens must pay to keep our pluralistic democratic society viable and responsive to the needs of the public."[54] It is not hard to imagine why the BFC advocated making other people pay a "kind of price" to keep broadcasting responsive to the needs of the NCC; it is equally obvious that station owners, represented by the National Association of Broadcasters, were not interested in paying any price at all. The proposed measure failed, although FCC Chairman Henry met with Fore to thank the BFC for its support. (The FCC would eventually enact stronger community ascertainment rules in 1971, although enforcement was typically pro forma and the rules mostly benefited large, nationally-recognized organizations at the expense of small, local groups.)[55]

Local Counterattack

The BFC's appeal to the FCC had failed once again, but the second half of Brackbill's counterattack succeeded precisely because the BFC took a hands-off approach to local efforts. Brackbill had called for devolving the counter–Radio Right campaign to local councils in his acceptance speech; he followed words with action by personally founding broadcasting divisions for both the New Jersey and Greater Philadelphia Council of Churches. Like it or not, he said, "*the local broadcaster is now in the driver's seat*" (emphasis original).[56] During his term as director of planning for the BFC, Brackbill continued to promote his vision of a decentralized model of NCC broadcasting. There were two major benefits to having local councils sustain the BFC's campaign against conservative broadcasters. First, as Brackbill argued in his acceptance speech, local councils had a better chance of receiving airtime from independent stations. During the 1940s and 1950s, the NCC had become dependent on nationally-syndicated programs that ran on the major networks; the NCC had the backing of ABC, NBC, and CBS, and so they were content to let the crazy fundamentalists scrabble for the leavings. In the 1960s, however, network sustaining airtime steadily decreased and the number of network stations plateaued. Brackbill hoped that local efforts could take up some of that slack. Second, the NCC's long-standing argument before the FCC was that local, community groups were best suited for determining whether a licensee had served the public interest. It would be inconsistent to make that argument and then throw the public weight of the NCC against a local station.[57] Third, having local councils counter conservative broadcasters helped the NCC avoid accusations of censorship by giving it plausible deniability. The BFC could claim that it had nothing to do with putting pressure on stations and that the complaints had organically bubbled up from local ministers. As long as Brackbill dictated BFC policy, the NCC's coordination of the counterattack would stay behind closed doors.

Despite the BFC's tactical restraint, the NCC and its affiliated denominations maintained an aggressive strategic stance against McIntire and the conservative broadcasters. For instance, Richard Goode, an executive in the broadcasting division of the United Presbyterian Church (UPC), wrote a guarded letter to Eugene Carson Blake (former NCC president and an executive in the UPC) about McIntire. The Presbyterians wanted to distribute an official letter along with a response program to its local broadcasters, something to scare stations away from airing McIntire's show. Goode never mentioned McIntire by name, preferring "this man," "the man," and various personal pronouns. For example, Goode hoped the letter would "force this man off the air in most market areas"; so long as the letter was "tough, legal, and ideally signed by legal counsel," it "should scare the hell out of the broadcaster when he gets it." The UPC would demand that stations notify the UPC whenever McIntire attacked the denomination or Blake. Then, since station managers "do not KNOW what [McIntire] is going to say tomorrow," they would have to ask him to speak only from prepared notes. That in turn would "compel [McIntire] to sit down in front of a typewriter," "seriously complicate his movement around the country and the world," and "add considerably to his overhead and expenses if he is forced into distributing scripts with his tapes." Best-case scenario, scared station managers would drop McIntire outright. Worst-case scenario, McIntire would find himself hobbled by the script requirements. A petty revenge was preferable to none at all. Goode reassured Blake, "We have nothing to lose and everything to gain."[58]

Although the BFC would foreground the efforts of local councils and member denominations in the fight against conservative broadcasting, the BFC continued to organize efforts behind the scenes. When Everett Parker brought a new UCC initiative to the attention of the BFC in 1966, the BFC approved the proposal—subtly titled "EXTREMISM '67" and consisting of a former FBI agent giving tips on combating right-wingers—but "it was the consensus of the group that it should probably be distributed by a non-BFC agency and not be under the auspices of the NCC." Local councils would be encouraged to sponsor the program by writing local stations and demanding they air it for free under the Cullman Doctrine, while the BFC itself would only send a private letter of appreciation to the UCC commending its efforts.[59] This was the recurring pattern in all post-1963 BFC efforts, private collaboration while local councils and affiliates did the public work.

The NCC ramped up its efforts during the election season of 1964 as right-wing darling Barry Goldwater faced off against Lyndon Johnson. Conservative broadcasters drew extra scrutiny for their support of Goldwater. The DNC's attempts to intimidate conservative broadcasters during the election have already been discussed, but for the NCC the timing was perfect. The BFC had been planning the counteroffensive since that summer; James Richards, director of broadcasting at the Kansas City Council of Churches, had written William F. Fore and alluded to "the BFC plans for fall." Fore confirmed that the BFC planned to monitor McIntire and had prepared a series of counterprograms. At that time, Fore discouraged the Kansas City

Council of Churches from prematurely invoking the Fairness Doctrine when speaking to local stations, but that strategy would change in the fall.[60]

As fall 1964 began, a flurry of NCC-affiliated publications ran articles encouraging local ministers and councils to respond to conservative attacks. For example, a September editorial in the Methodist *Newspulse* detailed the FCC's *Primer on Fairness* (an expansion upon its July 26, 1963, clarification statement) and cheerfully welcomed "the end for Billy Joe Hargis, Carl McIntire, Dan Smoot and others." Yet the FCC would only take action while investigating complaints for the public, so "individual laymen and clergymen must rise to the defense of those who are attacked" and write their local station managers. Pressuring the stations would force conservative broadcasters to temper their attacks, which would in turn hinder their fundraising, for "how many of the Smoot, Hargis, and McIntire supporters would continue to buy air time for them at $50 to $100 per day per station, if deprived of the joy of hearing their boys do what they do best?"[61]

These articles coincided with a rise in local council activity. The BFC's canned programs—including an interview of Eugene Carson Blake by media personality John Cameron Swayze—proved a hit. William Fore recommended that local councils use the short programs in combination with their own specific, one-minute rebuttals of conservative attacks.[62] James Richards at the Kansas City Council of Churches, now given the go-ahead by the BFC, wrote Fore of their success using the Swayze-Blake interview. Richards had written a local radio station and asked only "whether Dr. McIntire is being fair . . . [or] really promoting a fantastic and irresponsible lie" about the NCC? Technically, Richards never mentioned the Fairness Doctrine in his letter, although his repeated use of the word "fair" and his reassurance that he considered the station manager to be a "responsible broadcaster" were a pointed reminder of the unused stick even if only the carrot was on display. The station immediately conceded, giving Richards ten minutes of free airtime.[63]

Other groups adopted a more belligerent tone. Garnett Phibbs, the executive director of the Toledo Council of Churches, wrote a local station manager regarding his biased news reports and "slanted interviews." Phibbs did not doubt that "like B.O. and halitosis, your best friends are the last ones to tell you," but if the bias continued, he promised that the station would find itself in trouble "when license-renewing time rolls around." The station reluctantly complied; Phibbs exulted to the BFC that he had made "Brother O.H. Bertram eat crow enough to call and ask what he could possibly do about this." (Bertram was a minister in the conservative Lutheran Church—Missouri Synod; his program aired on ten radio stations and a dozen television stations during the 1960s.)[64]

However, not all of these local efforts were successful. Often, station managers would reject requests for response time saying that they felt no obligation to offer free airtime when the conservatives had purchased theirs. For example, station WTOT informed the Florida synod of the UPC that its "station policy does not permit us to give you equal time for rebuttal when Mr. McIntire is required to pay for his," noting that McIntire paid $8.10 per program while the local ministerial association received four free hours each week.[65] This confusion over what exactly the Fairness Doctrine required was a function of its basic ambiguity, which specified only that stations offer their "facilities for an adequate response." This ambiguity meant that the BFC's counteroffensive from 1964 to 1966 had mixed results with limited, local successes matched by the intransigence of many stations managers who were uncertain what the FCC really required.

The Second Test Case: WXUR

However, these local efforts to convince stations to give free response time were strictly minor skirmishes compared to the BFC's primary campaign against the Radio Right. In November 1964, the Greater Philadelphia Council of Churches began its eight-year mission to deny a radio station license to WXUR, the McIntire-owned station in Media, Pennsylvania. It made sense for Philadelphia to be the focal point of the NCC's campaign. McIntire's base of support came from the metro area and it was where he held most of his political rallies and protests.

Likewise, the greater Philadelphia area was vitally important to several of the major liberal Protestant denominations. Religious historians often call these denominations the "mainline" churches, yet there has been little study of where the term came from. Thus, historian David Hollinger writes that liberal Protestant "churches were often called 'mainline' because of the social power they had achieved" and leaves it at that.[66] But what was it about the term "mainline" that evoked social power, and how exactly did it become attached to the major liberal, Protestant denominations?

The term originally had no religious connotations whatsoever. It referred instead to the "Main Line," the name of a well-traveled passenger rail line running through the western suburbs of Philadelphia in the late nineteenth century. Those suburbs, seeded with the households of railroad executives, became synonymous with wealth and privilege, as instantly recognizable as someone in the early twenty-first century saying "the Hamptons." Wealthy benefactors endowed ornate church buildings, colleges, and seminaries like Palmer, Eastern, Bryn Mawr, and Haverford. With Princeton Theological Seminary on the other side of Philadelphia, the region could lay claim to being the epicenter of American Protestantism. It is no surprise, then, that even as the "Main Line" railroad stopped carrying passengers in the late 1950s, the term would take on a different significance, first, as a shorthand for wealthy, educated, religiously active Philadelphians, and second, for the larger community they sustained and represented.[67]

The term did not enter common religious usage until the 1960s, as shown in the chart in Figure 6.1, generated by Google's Ngram viewer.[68] The first mention of the term in a major newspaper was in the *New York Times* on March 28, 1960. The article, "Extremists Try to Curb Clergy," discussed the Air Force manual scandal in which a conservative Air Force general had used conspiratorially anti-Communist materials from broadcaster Billy James in a troop training manual. In particular, the *New York Times* article accused broadcasters, including Hargis, Carl McIntire, and Fulton Lewis, of fomenting dissatisfaction among wealthy, conservative laypeople within the NCC. Notably, the only such individual named in the article was millionaire oilman J. Howard Pew, who financed a broad range of fundamentalist

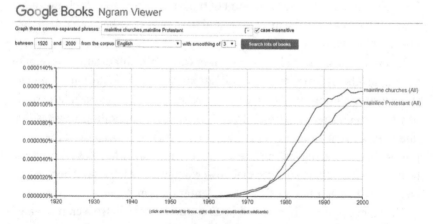

Figure 6.1. Google Ngram for "mainline churches" and "mainline Protestant."

and evangelical causes and who lived and attended a mainline church in a western Philadelphia suburb along the old Main Line railroad.[69]

It was the Air Force manual scandal, if you will remember, that had convinced the NCC to throw its significant support behind John F. Kennedy in the 1960 West Virginia primary. It is no coincidence that the first national use of the term "mainline" would be used in conjunction with that scandal. The battle between the NCC and conservative, fundamentalist broadcasters like Billy James Hargis and Carl McIntire began in earnest in 1960. In other words, the word "mainline" in its religious usage was forged in the conflict between conservative broadcasters and the NCC, a conflict that raged the hottest in the greater Philadelphia region. This was the context in 1964 when Carl McIntire decided to buy radio station WXUR located in Media, Pennsylvania, a hamlet west of Philadelphia that was a stop on the old Main Line railroad.

McIntire's reasons for buying WXUR were straightforward. He had become frustrated with his dependence on independent radio stations. Syndication meant a lack of control and while a few station owners were overt McIntire sympathizers, for most owners it was simply a pecuniary relationship. Enough pressure from local community groups or the FCC and cost-benefit logic could persuade them to either drop McIntire's program or significantly raise his daily rates. In 1964 McIntire received the first of many cancellation notices from stations mentioning their fears of FCC action. Jack Black, a manager with the "Tri W" network's three stations in northwest Alabama, informed McIntire that they had received pressure from the DNC during its summer of 1964 campaign. Black ended McIntire's broadcast because a radio station "that dares to utter a criticism against any person or any group" put itself "in an impossible predicament."[70]

McIntire worried that the DNC's campaign was a harbinger of further pressure on stations airing conservative broadcasters. Similarly, Democratic Alabama congressman George Huddleston Jr., who represented the congressional district where the "Tri W" network was located, wrote the DNC demanding a reason for the intimidating letters. The DNC's Samuel Brightman responded by baiting McIntire into attacking the DNC yet again. Brightman noted that the DNC's letter had simply stated that the listed programs, including those of McIntire, Hargis, and Manion, were "known to repeatedly attack the candidates, programs, and policies of the Democratic Party." Brightman said that the DNC's letter was "merely a reminder" to the stations to be fair when they carried "broadcasts dealing with controversial issues of public importance." Surely such a measured letter could not be construed as an attack on conservative broadcasting per se?[71]

McIntire took the bait. On his next radio show he accused the DNC of attacking his program, which of course it had, but only on paper until that moment. Attacking someone in print was protected free speech; make the exact same attack on the airwaves and you were in violation of the Fairness Doctrine. The DNC promptly responded by demanding response time to McIntire's attack on its own attack. Huddlestone forwarded Brightman's response to McIntire, although it is doubtful that McIntire found any consolation in proof that he had been duped. McIntire wrote back to Huddlestone complaining that stations were dropping the *Twentieth Century Reformation Hour* on the advice of their lawyers. Worse yet, even stations too poor to afford legal counsel had decided "to simply play 'Rock and Roll' or Country Music and be free of FCC headaches." His show was "suffering and suffering greatly from this."[72]

In response, Carl McIntire decided to buy his own radio station. He would prove to weak-kneed station managers that they could safely ignore Fairness Doctrine complaints. Fortuitously, Brandywine-Main Line Radio, owners of station WXUR in Media, Pennsylvania, was facing bankruptcy and willing to sell the station to McIntire. WXUR reached all of Philadelphia, its suburbs, and Wilmington, Delaware. The price was $450,000, a significant amount of capital for McIntire to raise. Although his annual revenue topped $2 million a year in 1964, almost all of that went to salaries, airtime, and other overhead. McIntire scraped together what he had in his accounts—$25,000 in cash—and paid the balance with a $425,000 mortgage on Faith Theological Seminary, which was located at Lynnewood Hall, a grand, albeit decaying, mansion on the edge of Philadelphia. McIntire provided collateral for the mortgage with a $100,000 life insurance policy on himself.[73] McIntire had staked a great deal on the success of WXUR.

The pending license transfer outraged the Greater Philadelphia Council of Churches and its allies. It was obvious to anyone who had ever heard the *Twentieth Century Reformation Hour* that McIntire attacked his opponents in almost every broadcast. Technically, he had never violated the Fairness Doctrine, but that was simply because the Fairness Doctrine applied to station licensees, not to broadcasters. The Greater Philadelphia Council of Churches knew McIntire would violate the Fairness Doctrine early and often, so they sent a formal complaint to the FCC protesting the license transfer. Francis Hines, the director of broadcasting for the Greater Philadelphia Council of

Churches, wrote FCC Chairman E. William Henry objecting that McIntire's persistent attacks on the Roman Catholic Church, the NCC, the United Nations, and the FCC itself made him "a dangerously divisive force wherever he is or is heard." Hines's argument—that McIntire's divisiveness made him dangerous—was standard Cold War rhetoric in domestic American politics. Whenever radicals, whether from the Left or Right, challenged the status quo, the moderate middle accused them of weakening the American consensus and making the nation vulnerable to Communist infiltration. It was the standard argument among segregationists, including McIntire, who accused civil rights leaders of disrupting American unity and thus playing into Soviet hands.[74] Here, Hines turned the logic against conservatives, accusing them of undermining the religious and diplomatic institutions that acted as a bulwark against Communism. Indeed, the threat McIntire posed to American harmony was so severe that although the Reverend Hines "would not deny any man the right to free speech," he would make an exception in this case because free speech "carries with it a responsibility for the truth which I do not believe Mr. McIntire exercises."[75] Only true speech deserved constitutional protection.

Dozens of other churches, denominations, and community organizations joined the Greater Philadelphia and New Jersey Council of Churches' complaint and echoed Hines's logic. The Reverend Frederick Fritsch, from Trinity Lutheran Church in Havertown, asked the FCC to deny the transfer to "this apostle of discord" because "men who make statements and accusations backed up by phony documentation should not be allowed to create a false image and thus undermine our beloved country."[76] Many of the letter authors recognized the dissonance between their repeated affirmations of the freedom of speech and their request to deny a radio station license to McIntire. Frank Stroup—a self-described "ardent believer in the right of free speech" and an executive in the Philadelphia synod of the UPC—"hesitate[d] to ask that his application be turned down." Yet he did so anyway because "when I consider the use to which Dr. McIntyre puts freedom of speech it appears to me that he does not exercise it responsibly."[77] The letter writers also betray a more mundane motivation for supporting the complaint, a desire to remove an obstacle to the success of the ecumenical, mainline movement. As Prince Taylor Jr., a Methodist minister in Princeton, acknowledged, "Those of us who work for harmony and peaceful relations among the peoples of New Jersey will be seriously handicapped by having such a powerful medium of communication in such irresponsible hands."[78] By turning down the license transfer, the FCC could rid the Greater Philadelphia and New Jersey Council of Churches of a competitor.

Given the long-standing apathy of the NCC toward McIntire, it is not surprising that the Philadelphia diocese, synod, and council of every single NCC member denomination joined the complaint against McIntire. Even non-Protestant and nonreligious groups protested the transfer. The NAACP, Anti-Defamation League (ADL), and even the local committee for UNICEF sent complaints, although the AFL-CIO joined first. As with the WLBT case several months earlier, the AFL-CIO saw the WXUR transfer protest as a chance to take down another enemy of the labor movement. And this time, the AFL-CIO's national office would not have to back down under pressure from a segregationist state chapter as it had in Mississippi. The Pennsylvania AFL-CIO's letter to the FCC condemned McIntire's "determined campaign of division, of distrust, of hate and incitement against our democratic institutions."[79]

In a September 1963, two months after the FCC's Fairness Doctrine clarification was released, President George Meany sent a letter to all state chapters of the AFL-CIO asking them to report back on which stations aired conservative broadcasters like Carl McIntire, Billy James Hargis, and Clarence Manion. Meany asked them to respond within forty-five days so that they could "move forward on a nationwide program to insure fairness to the trade union movement on the air waves."[80] Using those reports, the AFL-CIO's Committee on Political Education (COPE) created an impressive map charting every station in the United States that aired one of the targeted conservatives. According to the AFL-CIO, "more than 6,000 rightist messages are broadcast weekly"; the only state spared was Maine. COPE provided excerpts of some of the more extreme messages, like those calling for the impeachment of the entire Supreme Court, labeling the income tax as a Marxist plot, and blaming the civil rights movement on outside agitators.[81] Four months later the AFL-CIO joined the UCC's attack on WLBT, and within the year, they had allied with the Greater Philadelphia Council of Churches against WXUR.

The ADL also filed with the FCC. The ADL had not always been at odds with McIntire; in 1948 McIntire had actually met with several ADL executives and the meeting ended with everyone convinced, more or less, that McIntire was not an anti-Semite.[82] That wary acceptance changed during the 1960 election, both because McIntire had by then become a major broadcaster and because the ADL supported John F. Kennedy, seeing the election of the first Catholic president as striking a blow for religious toleration.[83] In the next several years, the ADL published a barrage of material denouncing conservative, religious broadcasters, including the book *Danger on the Right* just before the election in 1964.[84] The ADL had always been friendly with the NCC, providing them with opposition research on McIntire back during the 1950s. Following suit, the Jewish Community Relations Council (JCRC)—representing thirty-three national Jewish organizations (including the ADL)—cast its support with the NCC as well. Usually, the JCRC protested anti-Semitic groups, which McIntire was not; he was an ardent Christian Zionist who often criticized anti-Semitic fundamentalists. Instead, the JCRC filed the complaint because it had become "aware of the extremely unfair, irresponsible and inaccurate accusations which have been made repeatedly by Rev. Carl McIntire against the National Council of Churches of America."[85] The support of allied liberal advocacy groups would be vital for the success of the NCC's campaign against conservative broadcasting, but the ultimate source of that campaign was the NCC.

McIntire was not entirely bereft of allies. For several years he had been courting South Carolina Senator Strom Thurmond. McIntire, not known for his subtlety, made a point of mentioning to Thurmond that the *Twentieth Century Reformation Hour* aired on seventeen stations in South Carolina. Thurmond had a great deal on his mind that March as he prepared to undertake his record-setting Senate filibuster against the Civil Rights Act of 1964, but he found the time to send McIntire a donation to assist him "in the tremendous work you are doing for God, humanity, and our Country." In McIntire's thank you note for the gift, he told the senator that he had "said a quiet prayer" for him at the five-and-a-half-hour mark of the filibuster (Thurmond would make it to twenty-four hours and eighteen minutes before he finished). He assured Thurmond that they were "holding up your hands in this fight," a biblical reference to Moses. In Exodus 17, so long as Moses's hands were uplifted, the Israelites had victory in their battle to exterminate the Amalekites. When Moses grew weary, Aaron and Hur held up his arms lest the people of God be defeated. McIntire offered to be Aaron to Thurmond's Moses. Given what Thurmond was filibustering, it was a horrifically ironic comparison. Eventually, even Thurmond's arms had to fall and the Civil Rights Act of 1964 passed. During the following months, McIntire routinely praised Thurmond and read excerpts from the senator's newsletters on the air.

Thurmond returned the favor, speaking to the FCC on behalf of the license transfer for WXUR and offering to give a pro-WXUR speech before the Senate.[86] In wooing Thurmond, McIntire had pursued the same strategy that the NCC had adopted against him in 1960, when John F. Kennedy had lambasted the Air Force manual on the Senate floor; in return, the NCC had distributed pro-JFK literature in West Virginia. The strategy was identical, but the NCC had better connections. For their pains, they won the president as an ally. McIntire just got a loud-mouthed but ineffective senator. In economics, this kind of behavior is known as "rent seeking," which is when a group lobbies the government to protect itself from competition; this action creates or protects profits, or "rent," for the group.[87] The NCC, outmatched in the marketplace of the airwaves by Carl McIntire, sought to protect its broadcasting division from competition by allying with John F. Kennedy (and a bevy of lesser government officials). McIntire then lobbied Strom Thurmond in a much less successful attempt to counter the NCC's rent-seeking behavior.

A House Divided

It is impossible to know whether Thurmond's appeal had any effect, but the FCC approved the transfer of WXUR to Carl McIntire (through the "front," as the AFL-CIO called it, of Faith Theological Seminary). This was the expected decision given that the FCC did not hold open hearings on license transfers, only on license renewals. Six commissioners supported the transfer, but Kenneth Cox vigorously dissented. Cox, a lifelong member of the UCC, wanted to delay the transfer and hold an open hearing where the opinions of the Greater Philadelphia Council of Churches and its allies would count. Cox noted that the strength of feeling against McIntire's application was "virtually unprecedented" and should not be "lightly overlooked."[88] Cox acknowledged that McIntire had promised to abide by FCC regulations but doubted that he actually would. Like the Greater Philadelphia Council of Churches, Cox believed that McIntire intended to violate the Fairness Doctrine. That potential violation outweighed his claim of free speech.

Cox's main antagonist on the commission, Lee Loevinger, had a very different response. The majority opinion of the court was rather vanilla, but Loevinger issued a stronger, separate concurrence. It is worth pitting the two statements against each other because they represent two sides of a real tension within the FCC. Loevinger had always been leery of the overeager application of the Fairness Doctrine, a concern he mooted in an exchange with the director of the American Civil Liberties Union earlier that year. He was concerned—presciently as it would turn out—that the doctrine could give "an incumbent federal administration" in the future "ample means to impose a pattern of ideational content acceptable to it." In English, Loevinger worried that a president could use the FCC to prevent his political opponents from airing their ideas. That was the worst-case scenario. Best-case scenario, the doctrine would simply tend "to impose a relatively mediocre conformity on broadcasters," what later journalists would call a "chilling effect."[89] Thus, in his concurrence, Loevinger approved the transfer, noting, "The only significant objection is based on the nature of the religious and political speeches" that would be made by McIntire. For Loevinger, the Fairness Doctrine "does not require fair presentation but requires only a fair opportunity for reply." It was immaterial whether McIntire told the "truth" about the NCC so long as he gave them opportunity to respond. Loevinger was scathing in his disapproval of Cox's dissent, implicitly accusing him of making "the FCC the moral proctor of the public or the den mother of the audience." Loevinger castigated Cox for hiding behind words like "'fairness,' or 'responsibility,' or 'reasonableness' or 'private purpose' as contrasted with 'public interest'" (scare quotes in the original). To Loevinger, "such terms are merely contemporary euphemisms for orthodoxy."[90]

The FCC approved the transfer on narrower grounds; McIntire had not yet violated the Fairness Doctrine and consequently the FCC could not deny him a license. McIntire took over the station in April 1965. WXUR's profits depended on both syndicated shows—including the *Twentieth Century Reformation Hour*, Hargis's *Christian Crusade*, and the *Manion Forum*—and local advertising by businesses in Media, Pennsylvania. The controversy around McIntire's purchase of WXUR scared off many of those advertisers, a problem made worse when the local chapter of the Women's International League for Peace and Freedom (WILPF) organized a boycott of any company that advertised on WXUR, a boycott that the local NAACP threatened to join as well.[91] WXUR's first annual report, sent to McIntire in May 1966, shows just how disastrous the boycott had become for the station. When McIntire took over, monthly commercial billings were approximately $6,000, a number that fell to around $500 during "the now infamous boycott" in December, which "normally one looks to . . . as their bright spot in the entire year." An increase in syndicated "Gospel broadcasts" made up for part of the difference, but to stay solvent, WXUR needed $2,500 more per month.[92] The amounts might seem small in comparison to McIntire's total revenue of around $2 million a year, but his operating margins were already paper thin without bleeding an additional $30,000 each year to WXUR. In addition, McIntire was forced to hire legal counsel to represent him before the FCC in subsequent lawsuits. Documentation for his lawyer's billings in 1965–1966 are missing, but in 1967 McIntire paid nearly $31,000 for legal advice alone, an expense that was nearly nonexistent prior to his purchase of WXUR.[93] Unless McIntire took some steps to shore up WXUR's financial position, he ran the risk of bankrupting his entire ministry given how much he had staked on its success.

In an attempt to stave off the boycott, McIntire commissioned two listener call-in shows, one titled *Freedom of Speech* and the other *Delaware County Today*, with the idea that doing so would fulfill his Fairness Doctrine obligation to represent a diversity of opinions on controversial issues of public importance. If people disagreed with WXUR's editorializing, they could call in and give their own point of view. That worked in theory, but WXUR's opponents accused the hosts of cutting off or insulting callers who disagreed with them. These shows were forerunners for the style of talk radio that would emerge in the 1980s and 1990s, with hosts who framed themselves as truth-telling voices of sanity swimming up-current against an insane culture while encouraging listeners to express their most inflammatory opinions.

These shows were not the impartial forums that WXUR had promised the FCC. Still, it was a stretch to claim that the shows violated the letter of the Fairness Doctrine. The WILPF admitted that "Livezey [the host of *Freedom of Speech*] himself says little that is objectionable; the objectionable matter comes from 'callers.'" The WILPF wondered if "our protesting groups [are] active in calling in and speaking on the program? Is there any proof that they have been denied the right or opportunity to do so?"[94] Actually engaging with the call-in hosts would be messy and might even provide support for McIntire's contention that he was allowing representation of a broad variety of views; complaining to the FCC would be simpler and more effective. During the winter of 1965–1966, the Media borough council held a public meeting for Media residents to air their concerns, sent a formal complaint to the FCC, and forced McIntire to drop the call-in shows.[95] Ironically, in court the FCC would use these call-in shows, instituted in an attempt to satisfy the requirements of the Fairness Doctrine, as an example of McIntire's failure to abide by the Fairness Doctrine.[96]

Censured and Monitored

Having the municipality of Media censure McIntire was embarrassment enough, but in the year following his purchase of WXUR, Democrats in both the Pennsylvania and New Jersey legislatures sent anti-McIntire resolutions to the FCC. In December 1965, five Democratic state representatives—all from Philadelphia or districts nearby—presented a resolution that was then passed by the Democratic-controlled House of Representatives. The resolution condemned McIntire for his "vicious attacks on the National Council of Churches," noting that McIntire "had little success until 1960 when his radio program . . . was established." The authors of the resolution got the date wrong, but the error is interesting because it points to the Air Force manual scandal and the first year that McIntire's show aired on more than a hundred stations. It was "self-evident," according to the resolution, that McIntire's "extremism" was dangerous and unwanted given that the Democrats had resoundingly won in the 1964 elections. If people in Philadelphia truly approved of McIntire, then why had a majority of them voted for Democrats?[97]

Democrats in the New Jersey state legislature, not to be outdone, proposed a law penalizing any person who in public uttered a "false and defamatory statement of fact, concerning a racial, religious or national group under circumstances tending to a breach of the peace" with a fine and possible prison time. Unlike their counterparts in Pennsylvania, the New Jersey authors did not name McIntire, although it was equally clear that they had McIntire and conservative broadcasters in mind. The definition of "public place" was extended "for the purposes of this act" alone to include radio and television studios. The authors assured the good people of New Jersey that "we are aware of this threat, that we do not have a liking for it and that we are doing something about it." It was vital that the legislature "expound brotherhood, not bigotry; love, not hate; [and] a united community and State, not a divided one." This they would accomplish by banning bigotry, commanding love, and forcibly uniting the people of New Jersey.[98] McIntire responded to the Pennsylvania and New Jersey resolutions predictably, accusing the two legislatures of trampling on his civil liberties and holding a rally for several thousand supporters on the Capitol steps in Harrisburg. McIntire also expressed his belief that "there has developed some kind of a working alliance by the Democratic Party leadership and the National Council of Churches."[99] There is not documentary evidence that any direct connection between the two groups existed. It is more likely that the state Democratic parties saw the potential for political gain in the 1966 midterm elections by painting all con-servative Republicans with the McIntire brush. Democratic legislators were ganging up on a vulnerable political foe; they were not pawns in a complex conspiracy involving the DNC and the NCC.

No doubt, the NCC welcomed all the help it could get in taking on McIntire. After the Greater Philadelphia Council of Churches proved unable to stop the license transfer, the NCC kept quiet for the rest of 1965. In December, the WILPF learned from the Philadelphia branch of the American Civil Liberties Union that WXUR's current license would expire in August 1966. The WILPF did not have the resources to carry on a full week of monitoring WXUR; they needed a liberal advocacy group with more heft to join in if they were to have any hope of success.[100] The Greater Philadelphia Council of Churches stepped up with the encouragement of the BFC. Francis Hines had kept the BFC apprised of the call-in show boycott.[101] In March 1966, Hines attended a meeting hosted by WILPF and the JCRC for "agencies fre-quently under attack by extremist groups" and offered the help of the Greater Philadelphia Council of Churches with monitoring a week's worth of WXUR broadcasts "in the expectation of finding material evidence that would war-rant a hearing before the FCC."[102]

For just $500 the Greater Philadelphia Council of Churches enlisted a professor and two graduate students at the University of Pennsylvania's Annenberg School for Communication. The project was in keeping with founder Walter Annenberg's vision for the new department in 1958, which was equipping students to defend the principle that "the right to free com-munication carries with it responsibility to respect the dignity of others."[103] Hines ran the plan by William Fore at the BFC and Fore gave the project his blessing, telling him that it "should be done locally" and "sounds like exactly what is needed."[104] Although the monitoring plan had won the eager support of both the NCC and local advocacy groups, Hines felt conflicted. He wanted "to stay away from the perspective of revoking WXUR licenses"; instead, the allied groups would simply "present evidence which will raise the question of WXUR licensees' responsibility in terms of exercising a public trust, and let the law take over."[105] Of course, the entire point of the endeavor was to get McIntire's license revoked; Hines just did not want to be the one directly responsible. His legal shillyshally betrays yet again the uneasy conscience of many involved in the campaign against conservative broadcasting. They were liberals who sincerely believed in the freedom of speech, but they put themselves in the awkward position of using illiberal methods to suppress the illiberal. They had the law on their side, but the resulting cognitive dissonance emerges repeatedly in their letters.

A Funny Thing Happened on the Way to the FCC Hearing

The Greater Philadelphia Council of Churches' monitoring campaign went ahead as scheduled, but the FCC delayed the license renewal hearing until January 1967. McIntire knew that a special, delayed hearing did not bode well for WXUR, so he petitioned a US court of appeals to deny the FCC hearing. The hearing could not take place before the court ruled, but in the meantime, the FCC passed a new clarification of the Fairness Doctrine. In July 1967, the FCC specified that stations that aired personal attacks "upon the honesty, character, integrity or like personal qualities of an identified person or group" while discussing "a controversial issue of public importance" had to notify the person or group attacked within a week of the broadcast with a copy of the offending tape or transcript. Failure to comply could mean as much as $10,000 in fines for each violation and the FCC would consider the number of violations while ruling on license renewals.[106]

One of the problems with the FCC's prior clarification of the Fairness Doctrine on July 26, 1963, was that it lacked an enforcement mechanism. Unless a person just happened to be listening to a show when attacked and had pen and paper to hand, he or she could not petition a station for response time. This is why groups like the Greater Philadelphia Council of Churches and the UCC started their own monitoring programs, but that was an expensive and arduous process. Now that stations were responsible for notifying victims of attacks, it would be significantly easier to respond. It shifted the entire burden for compliance to stations. Indeed, this gave the NCC and its allies a much better tool to use against conservative broadcasters. As mentioned previously, after the FCC's first clarification in 1963 Richard Goode had told Eugene Carson Blake that the goal of the NCC's campaign was to "add considerably to [McIntire's] overhead and expenses if he is forced into distributing scripts with his tapes."[107] Now, after the FCC's July 1967 ruling, the NCC could truly implement Goode's strategy. Station managers would be loath to air conservative programs that attacked people because of the cost of regulatory compliance. They would have to mail tapes to every offended party, air their responses, and keep track of all the paperwork generated lest they face fines or risk having their license renewal held up or even denied.

In October 1967, after more than a year delay, the US court of appeals allowed WXUR's license renewal hearing to proceed. It would not end until June 1968. As was customary with hearings, the FCC appointed an examiner to sift through the evidence, hear testimony, and make an initial finding. The examiner would then report the finding to the full commission. Ordinarily, the FCC acted in accordance with its hearing examiner, but this was no ordinary case. Most hearing reports were no longer than a few dozen pages; the WXUR hearing generated more than 7,800 pages of records. Understandably, it took the hearing examiner several months to compile his report, which the FCC released in December of 1968. The NCC was as shocked by the result as McIntire was delighted. FCC Examiner H. Gifford Irion ruled in favor of McIntire and WXUR. Nothing in Irion's biography provides any clues as to why he had ruled for McIntire. He was a member of the Virginia and District of Columbia bars, had worked as counsel for the Rural Electrification Commission during the New Deal, and had been a hearing examiner for the FCC since 1952. He was a New Deal liberal.[108]

In his finding, Irion acknowledged that McIntire had at times failed to abide by the Fairness Doctrine, but he decided for McIntire because it was "customary to examine the entire record of the applicant rather than dwell upon some singular deficiency." While McIntire had indeed failed to notify targets of personal attacks, for the FCC to deny a license for such a relatively minor infraction would be a "fell judgment." Such "Draconian justice" would discourage other stations from editorializing on controversial issues at all. And compared to other blander albeit fairer radio stations, Irion commented, "It is almost inconceivable that any station could have broadcast more variegated opinions upon so many issues." Irion admired McIntire's chutzpah even though he did not sympathize with his politics, preferring his "rough-and-tumble and fervent rhetoric" to the "diluted parlor chat" that characterized much of American broadcasting. Irion feared that strictly enforcing the Fairness Doctrine would have a chilling effect, thus undermining the very reason that the FCC instituted the Fairness Doctrine in the first place—to encourage robust editorializing. Irion had latched onto an inconsistency within the Fairness Doctrine itself. As McIntire attempted, "however inept, to allow wide-swinging utterance of all shades of thought," this one tenet of the Fairness Doctrine had come into conflict with another principle, that of "protecting persons and groups from attacks." Irion did not try to resolve this tension, but he believed WXUR's adherence to the former outweighed its failure in the latter.

In response to the complaints that McIntire did not serve the local need or public interest, Irion retorted that it was "fairly clear that the Philadelphia area contains an appreciable number of conservative fundamentalists," especially given how much money McIntire raised from his listeners. Furthermore, Irion believed that the call-in programs taken altogether showed a good-faith effort to represent a diversity of opinions. In particular, he praised *Delaware County Today*, the host of which would invite guests from across the political spectrum to debate him and would then conduct a question-and-answer session with listeners on topics ranging from the Vietnam War to Unitarianism. Irion's sly wit surfaces throughout the report (a rarity for the genre). When one Media citizen intimated that she would not feel comfortable as a guest on the call-in show, Irion wrote, "This was unquestionably her personal privilege but it does not follow that an agency of the government is, therefore, empowered to teach better manners to the program moderator."[109] Indeed, in the transcripts provided as exhibits to the report, *Delaware County Today* comes across as a kinder, gentler version of any number of cable news shows on the air in the twenty-first century.

The now familiar collection of liberal advocacy groups, including the Greater Philadelphia Council of Churches, asked the FCC to overturn Irion's decision. In July 1970, more than a year and a half after Irion's report, the FCC listened to their request and denied a license renewal to WXUR. The FCC very rarely overturned one of its own examiners, especially not a veteran like Irion. In disagreeing with Irion's assessment, the commission emphasized McIntire's failure to provide a variety of religious points of view, a nod to the primary role played by the Greater Philadelphia Council of Churches in the complaint against WXUR. McIntire had added an interview program titled *Interfaith Dialogue* to the schedule, but the show did not start airing until six months after the transfer and made little effort to invite clergy from nonfundamentalist denominations, and McIntire canceled it just over a year later. McIntire claimed that the show failed to take off because the Greater Philadelphia Council of Churches had boycotted the show despite the station's "virtually super-human efforts to obtain the cooperation of the GPCC." Irion had excused the failure, reasoning that the show "did appear, even if tardily."[110] The FCC was less forgiving. The vote had been unanimous, six to zero, short the usual dissenting vote of Lee Loevinger. (The Fairness Doctrine critic had resigned during the summer of 1968 to go into private practice.) McIntire appealed the FCC's decision to the US District Court of Appeals for the District of Columbia, but he would have to wait until 1972 for the court's decision to know the fate of WXUR.

7

The Radio Right in Decline

The WLBT and WXUR license denials were a red flag for independent station owners. Complying with the demands of the National Council of Churches (NCC), the United Church of Christ (UCC), and other liberal interest groups was both cheaper and safer than trying to win at a Federal Communications Commission (FCC) hearing. Furthermore, the NCC had received a helping hand from a well-timed US Senate Commerce Committee investigation into "radical" broadcasting, which placed additional pressure on noncompliant stations. The stage had been set for the mass eviction of conservative broadcasters from the airwaves. Given the sheer scale of the campaign and the hundreds of stations involved, it can be hard to get a sense of what it looked like on the local level. However, the NCC's efforts in Minnesota were particularly well documented; the state provides a useful case study for the success of the counterconservative campaign. The fatal blow did not land in Minnesota, however, but in the Intermountain West through the renewed efforts of the UCC.

By the early 1970s the combined efforts of Senate Democrats and the NCC left the Radio Right on fewer stations and with more tenuous finances than at any point in the previous decade. Carl McIntire wrote Richard Nixon asking him to intervene on his behalf with the FCC, but the president had no interest in helping conservatives who had long attacked him from the Right flank of the GOP. Furthermore, Nixon's staff quickly realized that they could, in imitation of Kennedy, harness the FCC and Internal Revenue Service (IRS) to advance the president's agenda by intimidating critical journalists and media outlets. With no relief coming from the White House, McIntire lost his station license for WXUR in 1972. By 1976 the program aired on only 30 radio stations, a 94% decline from its peak of 480 stations in 1964.[1] McIntire's listeners were, at first, bewildered by the decline, then enraged by what they saw as the federal government's complicity in suppressing their favorite broadcaster.

The Radio Right. Paul Matzko, © Oxford University Press (2020). Oxford University Press.
DOI: 10.1093/oso/9780190073220.001.0001

Senate Democrats Join the Fray

As the Greater Philadelphia Council of Churches prepared its monitoring campaign in 1966, a lawyer working for the US Senate Commerce Committee named Bob Lowe contacted the NCC. He asked for help with the Commerce Committee's effort to combat radicalism on the airwaves. The Senate Commerce Committee had oversight of the FCC, and its chair from 1961 to 1977 was powerful Democratic senator Warren Magnuson, who also happened to be FCC commissioner Kenneth Cox's former employer and mentor. Magnuson wanted to bulk up enforcement of the FCC's Fairness Doctrine and commissioned Lowe to go and gather evidence that enhanced regulations were needed.

In March 1966, Lowe met with William Fore, director of the NCC's Broadcasting and Film Commission (BFC). Afterward, Fore wrote Hines at the Greater Philadelphia Council of Churches, telling him that Lowe had encouraged the monitoring of WXUR to continue. Lowe had told Fore, "off the record," that he believed WXUR "ought to be clobbered" by the Greater Philadelphia Council of Churches when the station's license came up for renewal that summer.[2] In May, Lowe attended the BFC's annual meeting to update them on the Commerce Committee's plan, even giving them a scoop on the FCC's proposed revision of the personal attack rules. Just a year later, the FCC would follow through on that promise with additional clarification of the Fairness Doctrine in July 1967. Lowe's knowledge of a not-yet-public FCC proposal suggests that the Senate Commerce Committee had a hand in encouraging the FCC to issue that clarification. After hearing Lowe's presentation, the BFC voted to send Fore to the Commerce Committee's hearings "in support of the Commission's proposal," giving the Commerce Committee cover lest the public think the hearings were a narrowly partisan ploy.[3] The NCC aided Lowe's investigation in another way, helping him compile a list of every station in the United States that broadcast "radical" (conservative) programs. The BFC contacted every regional Council of Churches, asking them to survey their local stations and report back with which ones aired "attack programs."[4]

A Minnesota Case Study

Responses flooded in from all over the country, most of them singling out McIntire's *Twentieth Century Reformation Hour* or Hargis's *Christian*

Crusade.[5] Several regional councils also used this as an opportunity to pressure stations by asking them if they "make it possible for the *attacked* [emphasis original] to be heard." This pressure led many stations to reconsider airing conservative programming altogether. For example, Bruce Sifford, director of the Minnesota Church Committee on Radio-Television, sent a sample of his correspondence with local stations to the BFC. Sifford had contacted all 103 radio and television stations in Minnesota and heard back from 96 of them. Of those stations, four reported carrying either the *Twentieth Century Reformation Hour* or the *Christian Crusade*. Sifford then reported those stations to Bob Lowe. What is most interesting about the Minnesota Council of Churches' correspondence is the approach Sifford took when he contacted the stations. In the first paragraph of his letter, Sifford name-checked the Senate Commerce Committee and informed them that it was currently investigating Fairness Doctrine compliance. The implicit threat was not subtle. Sifford further asked the stations to air, without charge, one of the BFC-produced response interviews or an entire run of fourteen new, one-minute spots.[6]

The stations that did not carry McIntire or Hargis responded quickly; several aired the proffered programs anyways. Less forthcoming were the stations that did air McIntire or Hargis. One manager, Charles Woodward of station KSUM, agreed that "the tactics used by this man" (Billy James Hargis) were distasteful but defended airing Hargis's program because "a significant number of my listeners have indicated they want me to, and I am only attempting to live up to my promise to program 'in the public interest.'" Unfortunately for Woodward, local demand for a program did not equate with the public interest, at least not according to either the Minnesota Council of Churches or the FCC. However, Woodward did not go down without throwing a punch. Gifford had asked him if KSUM would make free time available to "any person or organization attacked on *Christian Crusade*." He responded, bitingly, that it was "terribly easy to get lost in a maze of semantics, but . . . we will make every effort to comply with the Fairness Doctrine," although it was unlikely that they would "honor a request from the Communist Party" should they be contacted. For a liberal organization like the Minnesota Council of Churches, which decried anti-Communist hysteria and McCarthyite witch hunting, Woodward's blow connected. Gifford admitted to the BFC that "Mr. Woodward caught me up short" although he himself had "exercised as much care as Eisenhower did his planning of the invasion of Normandy." Gifford believed that "Woodward's letter expresses the opinions of most Minnesota Broadcasters." Although Woodward had landed a blow, it was not a knockout and he tapped out immediately thereafter, noting that his station would stop carrying the *Christian Crusade*.[7]

In another case, a local ministerial association had asked Sifford to meet with Gene Koehn, the manager of radio station KWEB, which aired the *Twentieth Century Reformation Hour*. Koehn "admitted at the outset that he did not share" McIntire's views. Like Woodward at KSUM, Koehn aired the show because "a very vocal group in his market area" supported it and they were much "more vocal than the group opposing the program." McIntire's supporters had "flooded the station with letters and phone calls when he took the program off the air" for a time several months earlier. The overwhelming response convinced Koehn to put McIntire back on. Listener demand was strong, but it ultimately came down to dollars and cents. The *Twentieth Century Reformation Hour* "was a paid program" and "he had the responsibilities of his stockholders to show a profit." Koehn's response echoed that of station managers all across the nation when asked why they aired a program like McIntire's that they found disagreeable—it was popular and it paid. The director of radio and television for the Northern California-Nevada Council of Churches put it similarly, that "this is a tough market to make a buck in and the full gospel for the full buck 'schtick,' seems to be theirs at the moment."[8] Sifford did not report to the BFC what arguments he had marshaled against McIntire's program in speaking with Koehn, but whatever they were they worked. Koehn canceled the program. (It is impossible to say whether Koehn agreed with Sifford when he wrote afterward, "It was a most cordial meeting.")[9]

The Minnesota Council of Churches had very effectively used Bob Lowe's request for information to intimidate radio stations into compliance. Receiving a letter claiming the full force of a US Senate committee carried an unmistakable message: cross us and face congressional sanction. The pressure had an effect. Sifford's letters show that two stations, or a third of the stations in Minnesota that reported carrying conservative programs, had dropped McIntire because of the Minnesota Council of Churches' efforts. Staying in the good graces of the Minnesota Council of Churches, the FCC, and the US Senate Commerce Committee mattered more to radio station owners than popularity or payment. However, two stations may be an undercount. McIntire's records reveal that during the mid-1960s he broadcast on eight stations in Minnesota. Seven of those eight stations dropped him sometime before the start of 1967. The Minnesota Council of Churches' campaign to intimidate local broadcasters left McIntire with a single station in the state.

Most other regional councils simply sent a list of offending stations to the BFC without detailing what steps they took to find out. But while the Minnesota Council of Churches may have conducted a more sustained and expansive campaign than other regional councils, Bob Lowe's use of the NCC to gather information for Senate Democrats added to the pressure felt by many station owners across the nation. Formally, Bob Lowe's investigation fizzled out. The Senate Commerce Committee first postponed and then canceled the planned hearings. As Lowe told William Fore in September 1967, "The Senate simply was losing interest in the issue since they felt that the McIntire types were not gaining ground."[10] Although Fore framed his conversation with Lowe as a disappointment, it was actually an incredible victory in the campaign to push conservative broadcasting off the air. So many stations had dropped McIntire and fellow conservative broadcasters by 1967 that the Senate Commerce Committee could move on to the next target. The committee shifted its attention to the idea of government-funded public broadcasting as a centrist counterweight to radical voices from the Left and the Right. National Public Radio would be established four years later in 1971.

In August 1967, Lowe published his report about the state of radical broadcasting. Just weeks before, the FCC issued its July 1967 clarification of the Fairness Doctrine. (Lowe had sneaked a preview of his report to the FCC before it issued the clarification.) What Lowe found in his report showed that the situation in Minnesota was the story of conservative broadcasting in America writ large. In addition to Lowe's request for information from the NCC, he had also sent an eight-page questionnaire to all 6,787 stations in America asking about their compliance with the Fairness Doctrine and inquiring about which radical shows they aired. Unsurprisingly, given the context, a slim majority of respondents said that they supported the Fairness Doctrine as it then read, just over a fifth wanted it done away with entirely, and the remainder supported clarification, replying that the rules were either "too vague" or too onerous. Lowe then gave totals for each program, listing how many stations had dropped the show and how many continued to air it. According to Lowe, the *Twentieth Century Reformation Hour*'s count had gone from 398 stations to 183 in just two years. It was not just McIntire. Every conservative broadcaster had suffered, with the top secular shows like

Life Line declining at an average rate of 33%. Those programs most targeted by the NCC—counting the religious programs plus the *Citizens Council Forum*—declined by 59% that year, nearly double the rate of broadly conservative programming.[11] Conservative broadcasting in general and religious programming specifically had taken a body blow from which it would not fully recover until the 1980s and the end of the Fairness Doctrine.

United Church of Christ Redux

Although Bob Lowe, with the help of the NCC, had kicked off the final stage of the campaign against conservative broadcasting, the UCC would deliver the *coup-de-grâce*. Following Warren Burger's 1966 ruling that granted standing to the UCC in the WLBT case, Everett Parker and the UCC's Office of Communication expanded their efforts. Now that community groups had standing before the FCC, actions like that of the Greater Philadelphia Council of Churches against station WXUR could proceed. Indeed, Parker claimed WXUR as one of "the first major fruits of our victories before the commission and the court."[12] Nevertheless, while the Greater Philadelphia Council of Churches had the WXUR case well in hand, many communities lacked such influential, liberal organizations. To translate inchoate liberal indignation in towns across America into firm action against conservative broadcasters, the UCC offered help with monitoring expenses and legal advice. This way the UCC could remain in the background while newly organized community groups placed pressure on local radio and television stations to comply with the Fairness Doctrine.

The UCC's national monitoring campaign would not be cheap. Parker began soliciting funds immediately following Burger's ruling in 1966. First, he wrote George Meany, the president of the American Federation of Labor and Congress of Industrial Organizations (AFL-CIO), reminding him of the union's support for the WLBT case. Parker deftly avoided criticizing the Mississippi AFL-CIO's decision to pull its support from the case and offered the national AFL-CIO another chance "to bring an end to all forms of discrimination in broadcasting" against blacks and unions alike. Parker estimated that the UCC needed $75,000 to get the program off the ground.[13] The AFL-CIO offered $35,000 with the stipulation that the contribution remain anonymous.[14] The UCC needed another partner to make up the balance, which it found in the Marshall Field Foundation.

Speaking with the Field Foundation, Parker was much more explicit about the campaign's goals and expressed his frustration with the FCC's lackadaisical approach. As it was, "the FCC has functioned more as an umpire to prevent electrical interference among stations, than as a judge of compliance with the public interest." Since the FCC had failed in its duty, the UCC would pick up the slack. "We must do what the FCC should have been doing," Parker wrote, "pick out a few specific offenders, challenge their fitness for license renewal and thus set an example for others." Once they had had a few more victories, Parker believed that "even an indifferent or hostile FCC" would eventually "see the political hazard in letting the public do its job for it." Likewise, once stations realized that the Fairness Doctrine had bite, "the mere threat of license challenge, plus the ensuing costly proceedings, may invoke the profit motive to the extent that the station will decide that cooperation with the public is the better part of wisdom." Parker proposed a two-part campaign to the Field Foundation, one effort to address the continuing racism in broadcasting in the South, the other to address the growing influence of conservative broadcasters across the entire country. In the South, despite "demonstrable improvement in the treatment of racial issues" post-WLBT, "many pockets of resistance" remained, "especially in radio broadcasting." Clearing up those pockets remained a priority, but Parker believed that the conservative broadcasters—and he named McIntire and Hargis—were "equally disquieting and perhaps in the long run more significant."[15] The Field Foundation liked Parker's plan well enough to vote him $50,000, which, combined with the AFL-CIO's contribution, gave Parker his seed money.[16]

Parker focused his initial efforts on stations in the West, where "right wing extremist groups are also concentrating . . . in the hope of influencing the election results for the Senate and House of Representatives."[17] Lyndon Johnson had won the Intermountain West and West Coast handily in 1964; then again, he had won almost the entire nation (except the Deep South). In 1968, Democrats knew that the election would be much closer, especially given the potential for George Wallace to spoil the party's chances down south. The UCC wanted to put its thumb on the scale to counter the conservative broadcasters. In the West, the conservatives could buy a "high payoff for little money" because "a handful of TV and radio stations cover virtually all the population," allowing them "to saturate the air with propaganda."[18]

Parker immediately sent several field directors out west. They reported that the situation was just as bad as they had feared, if not worse. In towns like

Paradise, California, a "tranquil, orderly, friendly community" had "been corrupted by the corrupt use of local media." Paradise had only one radio station, KEWQ, which carried a "preponderance of fundamentalist religious programs" including Billy James Hargis. Even the moderator of the call-in program used his show as "a vehicle for waging a vendetta against individuals and organizations the right-wing would like to intimidate into silence." The moderator accused the local school superintendent of mismanagement of school funds and forced him to resign. The UCC offered to help him complain to the FCC. The conservative broadcasters had cloaked a once "happy pleasant town" in a "climate of fear and suspicion." Paradise no longer lived up to its name.

The UCC found the pattern in Paradise, California, repeated all across the West. Most of the offending stations were simply "shoestring operations at best," and since the Right had "the most money to buy air time it is the right-wing programs that stand the best chance of being aired." Conservatives used call-in programs for "organizing groups within a community for overt social action." For example, the moderator in Paradise had attacked a laundry list of liberal causes, including the civil rights movement, public schools, labor unions, welfare recipients, the NCC, the high school superintendent, and "the government generally."[19] This kind of conservative talk radio show would become commonplace in the 1980s, but it is important to remember that they were startling to a previous generation who assumed that the post–World War II era of relative political consensus would continue indefinitely.

The UCC responded by producing a program titled *EXTREMISM '67*, featuring a former FBI special agent who interviewed guests including a former president of the NCC, a Democratic US senator, and civil rights activist Bayard Rustin. More than five hundred radio stations agreed to air the program without charge. Later that year the UCC released *Let's Be Friends*, a series of forty short radio spots "puncturing the balloons of extremists," especially those "ministers who save souls on the radio for profit." The UCC also began contacting local community leaders and encouraging them to pressure the offending stations. Most stations quickly complied, although two citizens' groups sent complaints to the FCC with help from the UCC, including one for station KEWQ in Paradise, California. In response, the FCC held up KEWQ's license renewal and scheduled a special hearing. Fearing the worst, the station "moved swiftly to correct the abuses" by dropping its call-in show, firing its station manager, and giving equal airtime to all candidates for the next school board election.[20]

The UCC also went after groups other than fundamentalist Protestants. The Utah state chairman of the Democratic Party, Wally Sandack, requested the UCC's help in counteracting the conservatism of Mormon-controlled station KSL in Salt Lake City.[21] A local citizens' group petitioned the FCC to deny KSL a license renewal, but the FCC renewed the license with a four-to-three vote (Kenneth Cox was among the dissenters). The group then appealed to the US Circuit Court of Appeals for the District of Columbia. The back-and-forth continued until 1973 when the Department of Justice encouraged the FCC to adopt a ban preventing organizations from owning both a newspaper and a radio station. The Mormon Church sold KSL so that it could hold on to the *Deseret News*.[22]

The UCC's campaign in the West faced its strongest opposition from station KAYE in Seattle, Washington, which aired McIntire's *Twentieth Century Reformation Hour* and half a dozen other conservative programs. In 1968, a large group of prominent Seattle citizens who were bothered by the conservative message of KAYE formed the Puget Sound Committee (PSC) and led by a Congregational minister who was also the director of broadcasting for the Washington State Council of Churches. The following year, with the support of the UCC and the Anti-Defamation League (ADL), the PSC petitioned the FCC to deny a license renewal to KAYE. The petition listed forty-two complainants including the Democratic Governor of Washington Daniel J. Evans, who KAYE had criticized repeatedly. In addition, more than a dozen state senators and local government officials complained that they had not been consulted by "KAYE regarding ascertainment of community needs for the 1969 renewal application," one of the more common grievances listed.[23]

The PSC argued that the station had finally crossed the line during city council elections in the fall of 1967. The station had invited all of the council candidates to come on air, but it threw softballs in its interviews with the four candidates the station favored. Worse, the station's call-in program had made "some people expect a riot, expect to be assaulted on the streets, expect that their homes could be bulldozed at any given moment, accept that poverty programs and regional programs are communist inspired, and accept that schools teach children improper attitudes." In short, the station favored conservatism. The final straw was KAYE's support for Republican Mayor of Seattle James Braman and his proposal to strengthen the mayor's office by ending the city's council-manager form of government. The PSC arranged for the UCC to monitor a week of KAYE's programming; it reported thirty-three personal attacks, no replies, and "no effort on the part of sta-tion management to adhere to the FCC's Fairness Doctrine."[24] After a pro-longed legal battle, the FCC denied KAYE a license renewal and the station changed hands in 1974. The UCC often claimed that its monitoring program sought to "counterbalance right and left wing propaganda," but its actions belie the claim.[25] The only stations ever targeted were those that aired con-servative programming. Often, as with KSL and KAYE, the UCC aided the Democratic Party's attempts on the state and local level at silencing its pro-Republican competition.

The UCC's Office of Communication found itself in a tight spot finan-cially in the fall of 1967 when the Field Foundation's and the AFL-CIO's grants ended and were not renewed. To replace the funds, Everett Parker turned to the Ford Foundation. He sold the plan to Ford by appealing to the success of the WLBT case. Even if stations did "not view WLBT as prec-edent that applies to them," the "filing of a petition to deny renewal by a responsible local group—which would cost very little—would probably quickly convince them" otherwise and gain their cooperation.[26] The UCC's humble goal was to eliminate racism in broadcasting within five years.[27] Parker bragged how effective the UCC's campaign out west had been, men-tioning one station in Idaho that cleaned up its act the moment it found out the UCC had visited town. The Ford Foundation balked at the high cost, so Parker lowered his annual estimate to $110,700.[28] Gordon Henderson, the UCC's field director, wrote to Parker explaining what kind of program the Ford Foundation wanted.

I think the Ford people want something they can brag about. Ideally they would like to be able to picture themselves as financing a project that went into the deepest darknesses of the South where lynching occurs in every small town every Saturday night, and where every second word a white man speaks is "nigger," and brought light to the darkest corners. Perhaps we cannot meet that ideal but I certainly think we ought to be able to come up with something that approximates it. (I wouldn't be sur-prised if the *Field* people hoped they would get another WLBT case for their money and were disappointed that they didn't get it.) Let's make sure Ford gets whatever the devil it is that they are looking for; another WLBT case will do, I'm sure. . . . And then too, by damn, let us too, if we can swing it, make sure that we get publicity, credit and more grant money for our efforts.[29]

The relationship would prove profitable for both organizations. From 1968 to 1978, the Ford Foundation gave the UCC nearly $1 million to monitor the radio and television stations of the twenty-seven largest cities in the South. Because of a generous "multiplier effect," the Ford Foundation called it "one of the two or three most significant and effective civil rights efforts in the nation during that period," comparable in scale to the Voter Education Project.[30]

The UCC's southern monitoring program had great success, especially once the FCC finally denied WLBT's license renewal in 1969. Stations and community groups took notice. In 1970, the National Association for the Advancement of Colored People (NAACP) joined the UCC's campaign, and the two organizations convinced the FCC to delay renewal of all twenty-four station licenses in Atlanta, Georgia, for thirty days, which was long enough for the UCC to negotiate agreements regarding the number of black employees and the political balance of the programming.[31] In just six years, the UCC had gone from one unprecedented achievement to the next, from making WLBT the first station ever denied a license renewal on Fairness Doctrine grounds to convincing the FCC to take mass action in Atlanta. Along the way, the UCC had developed a formidable reputation. Once, Parker chanced upon a noncompliant station in Charlotte, North Carolina (it had the audacity to call anti–Vietnam War protestors "unwashed, long-haired hippies" and "commie sympathizers"). But when Parker "took up the cudgels" by complaining to the FCC, the commission immediately suspended the then in-process license renewal. The station caved at once.[32]

Internal Backlash: The Protestant Mainline in Decline

The UCC's campaign against conservative broadcasting out west and against racism in the South had been a rousing success. The BFC rewarded Everett C. Parker by electing him as its chairman in 1969.[33] But Parker's success with the monitoring campaign and his promotion masked an unpleasant reality. Despite multiple victories in the counter–Radio Right campaign, the NCC continued to struggle with lay discontentment stirred up by the likes of McIntire and Hargis. In a story that could be repeated across all the NCC's member denominations, Everett Parker's own UCC had started a half century of decline as parishioners left for conservative churches and denominations.

Parker's first job with the UCC in 1957 was to persuade recalcitrant congregations to join the new denomination after it was created by the merger of the Evangelical Reformed Church and the Congregational Christian Church. That merger had not gone smoothly. Many Congregationalist churches protested the merger, some because the leaders of the merger were theological liberals and others because they feared a loss of congregational autonomy.[34] That undercurrent of distrust of the denomination persisted into the 1960s. For example, during the 1964 election a member church in Illinois left the denomination in protest over the denominational magazine's anti-Goldwater editorializing. (Indeed, the church elder board contacted conservative broadcaster Edgar Bundy, who also ran a conservative file service, and asked him if the magazine's editorial staff contained any Communists. Bundy said no, which was undoubtedly a disappointment to the elders.) The offending magazine was an autonomous "instrumentality," meaning that the denomination had limited oversight over its officers and publications.[35] Everett Parker's own Office of Communication was another of these instrumentalities; there was little that congregations who disagreed with its campaign against conservative broadcasting could do about it. One regional UCC executive named Horace Sills worried that "the activities of some of the boards and agencies only add fuel to the fires that are burning in opposition to the denominational programs."[36]

By 1968, the congregational discontent had reached the tipping point. Church after church voted to leave the UCC. Some of them were small churches, like St. Peter's Reformed Church in Harmony, Pennsylvania, which voted fifty to zero to secede.[37] Others were large enough to be a worry, including Jackson Avenue UCC in New Orleans, which left with 624 members.[38] These congregations left because of the influence of conservative broadcasters. Horace Sills, the conference minister overseeing St. Peter's, reported that the church had "very strong leanings toward the fundamentalist attitude." Furthermore, "an abundance of propaganda against the National Council of Churches and the United Church of Christ" was "floating about" in his conference because "the radio audience of evangelists such as Carl McIntyre [sic], Bill Jo Hargis, and Kathryn Kuhlman is very large and the influence is felt in many of our churches." Sills had heard whispers that other local churches would soon follow St. Peter's example.[39] The UCC had the same problem as the NCC; an uncomfortably large group of its own laypeople trusted the likes of McIntire and Hargis over their own clergy.

Ben Herbster, the president of the UCC, called an executive meeting to discuss the "increasing number of churches which have either withdrawn or threatened to withdraw."[40] Herbster calculated that in the preceding year, 31 churches had joined the UCC, 52 had been consolidated down into 24 churches, and 59 withdrew in one form or another.[41] At the executive meeting, Herbster downplayed the problem and the denomination agreed on an anodyne list of measures to correct the trend, like informing pastors that the national staff would gladly field their questions.[42] In hindsight, they should have done more. The denomination peaked with 2,070,413 members and 6,960 churches in 1965, totals that would decline to 1,997,898 members and 6,803 churches in 1969 and continue to slide every year thereafter. By 2009, the UCC was down to 1,080,199 members and 5,287 churches, barely half of its peak.[43] While not enough to prove causation, there is a clear correlation between the UCC's attack on conservative broadcasters and the beginning of a long, slow decline for the UCC. Attacking the Radio Right had only further alienated disgruntled parishioners.

All Hands, Abandon Ship

Carl McIntire's *Twentieth Century Reformation Hour*, on the other hand, faced a quick, rapid decline. The campaigns of the NCC and its allies against conservative broadcasting had a cumulative effect. For example, multiple Seattle stations, leery of the ongoing battle between the UCC and station KAYE, dropped McIntire in 1970 as soon as the FCC had denied a license renewal to WXUR.[44] The crucial moment was not in 1970, however, but when the FCC clarified the Fairness Doctrine in July 1967. In the months following, letters from station managers poured into McIntire's office, either dropping the *Twentieth Century Reformation Hour* outright or asking him to go easy on the personal attacks. One station owner bluntly stated that "the FCC has got their teeth in my bread and butter" and accused the FCC of being "prosecutor, judge, and jury."[45]

Station WUNS, in the hamlet of Lewisburg, Pennsylvania, regretted dropping McIntire given their amiable relationship of six years, but compliance with the new regulations would cause "many, many man-hours of work over and above the regular weekly chores of an already-under-staffed small radio station." Furthermore, the station owner was in negotiations with a "very responsible group of citizens" and feared that a complaint—perhaps from said group of citizens who were looking to get a license on the cheap—might cause the FCC to balk at the transfer.[46] WUNS did get the chance to work out some of its frustrations a month later. The liberal Institute for American Democracy (IAD) had complained about an attack made by McIntire prior to the station's cancellation of his program. WUNS agreed to air the IAD's response, but "we were, possibly unfortunately . . . forced to put it in the first available spot which we deemed timely, that is to say right after the nine a.m. news this Sunday," one of the least desirable airtimes of the week.[47] A petty revenge was preferable to none at all.

There was a marked shift in the tenor of letters written by stations to Fairness Doctrine complainants between the early 1960s and the late 1960s. For example, when the Missouri Council of Churches sent station WQIZ in St. George, South Carolina, a warning in 1963 saying that "so-called 'religious broadcasters' " would face censure by the FCC, the station manager threw the warning back in the council's face, calling it "the track/junk from you about the National Council of Churches" and criticizing their "meddling" with broadcasting, "a place in which you have no business."[48] Two years later, after the beginning of the WLBT and WXUR cases, WQIZ's tune had changed. The FCC had notified the station of a formal complaint against it and the manager immediately wrote McIntire worrying that if they had "any trouble or a hearing over this complaint we will be forced to go off the air for bankruptcy reasons." He was "a small businessman" who could not "stand up under the financial strain."[49] The FCC's 1963 clarification of the Fairness Doctrine alone had not been enough to convince local stations that they had to adjust their programming. The NCC's use of the Fairness Doctrine had.

The FCC's 1967 clarification of the Fairness Doctrine increased the pressure to comply all the more. For example, in 1964 the American Civil Liberties Union (ACLU) sent a request—cosigned by the Congress of Racial Equality, the NAACP, the American Jewish Congress, and the National Urban League—for response time to station KONI in Spanish Fork, Utah, a country-western radio station that aired both Hargis and McIntire. KONI acknowledged that the two had attacked the ACLU, but brushed off the request.[50] After the FCC's 1967 clarification, however, KONI told McIntire that he needed to send the station verbatim transcripts of his broadcasts so that they could inform those whom he had attacked. Even so, the "tremendous additional work of pre-listening, dubbing copies for persons attacked, and the correspondence involved to comply" might force them to discontinue their "pro-American, conservative programs."[51]

This had been the NCC's plan all along. McIntire would be compelled "to sit down in front of a typewriter," as Richard Goode had crowed to Eugene Carson Blake back in 1963, thus adding "considerably to his overhead and expenses" when "forced into distributing scripts with his tapes."[52] KONI, un-like most stations, truly sympathized with Carl McIntire's political agenda, but even it had to bow to the FCC's regulations. But that did not mean they had to like it. In September 1967, Franklin Littel, of the IAD, had written an editorial calling for right-wingers—whose "stench is disloyalty"—to be "thrown out of whatever groups they are in," hoping that they could be quickly "muted and rendered ineffective." Littel had written in a newspaper, so it was protected free speech. Hargis responded on air, suggesting that Littel's thinking was a "short step from that of Hitler's in relation to the Jews in Germany," a pointed insult given that Littel was a respected scholar of the Holocaust. KONI faithfully complied with the letter of the clarified Fairness Doctrine and informed Littel of Hargis's criticism. The station's next sentence was, "We agree."[53]

No matter how witty the repartee, stations continued to drop McIntire's program. Figure 7.1 shows that McIntire's station count fell as quickly as it had risen. The story told by the archives matches what the raw numbers show. The rapid rise in the number of stations airing the *Twentieth Century Reformation Hour* spooked the NCC from 1960 to 1964. The station total then peaked the year the NCC began its counteroffensive against conserva-tive broadcasting. The greatest decline came in 1967, the year the FCC clari-fied the Fairness Doctrine's personal attack rules.[54] Figure 7.2 offers another way of visualizing the collapse of the *Twentieth Century Reformation Hour,* comparing the number of stations that added and dropped the program each year.

McIntire continued to look for new stations to arrest the slide, but more stations dropped him than he could add each year after 1964. Again, a dis-proportionate number of the drops came in 1967 with the FCC's clarification of the Fairness Doctrine. Figure 7.2 reveals something hidden from a simple station total count. Stations started dropping McIntire in significant num-bers for the first time in 1963, the year of the FCC's first clarification of the Fairness Doctrine.

As it lost stations, the *Twentieth Century Reformation Hour* began to struggle financially, as shown in Figure 7.3. McIntire kept irregular fi-nancial records. During the boom years of his ministry he recorded the

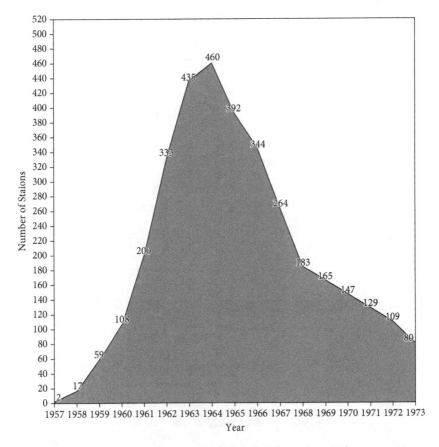

Figure 7.1. Number of stations airing the *Twentieth Century Reformation Hour*, 1957–1974.

daily total receipts (top grey line) but never provided a budget, so it is not possible to match revenue to expenses. He did calculate the minimum operating income (bottom grey line) needed to keep the radio show on the air and his newspaper afloat.[55] But beginning in 1967, he calculated actual operating income (black line) and compared it to the minimum income needed; it was also the last year that McIntire's income exceeded expenses.

Historian Nicole Hemmer has suggested that the complaints about the Fairness Doctrine were "a popular fund-raising tool."[56] Certainly, broadcasters made Fairness Doctrine–based fundraising appeals, but for McIntire this was an act of desperation, not a clever strategy for turning a

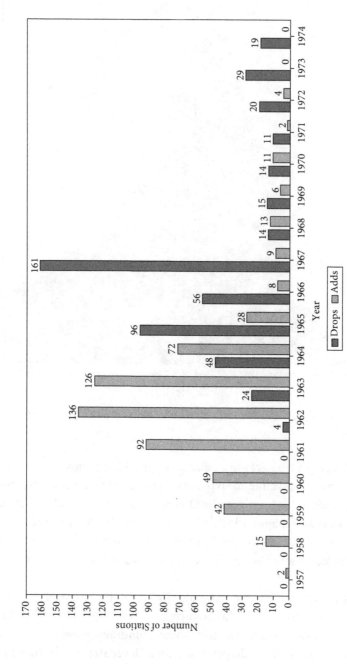

Figure 7.2. Number of stations dropping/adding the *Twentieth Century Reformation Hour*, 1957–1974.

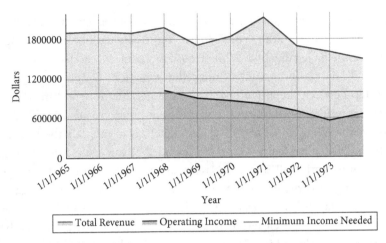

Figure 7.3. Financial statistics for the *Twentieth Century Reformation Hour.*

minor affliction into a boon. Losing stations hurt McIntire's bottom line. He kept total revenue high for a time by starting new ventures to excite donors— like a hotel and conference center in Cape Canaveral, Florida, rebranded as the "Gateway to the Stars"—but that was not a sustainable strategy. He also increased the number of fundraising appeals he made on air but only succeeded in annoying his backers. One station dropped him because it felt that the show had become "a vehicle for a pseudo-telethon for fund raising." Another accused him of spending "too much time talking about condominiums, raising funds for temple construction, etc."[57] WXUR also continued to be a drain on his finances; even his ability to borrow money against the station had dried up by 1969.[58] Because he had secured the loan for the station with a mortgage on his seminary property, he lost both when the FCC revoked the station license. By 1976 he could pay neither the electric bill nor his office manager's salary, a devoted employee who asked plaintively, "Brighter days *are* coming, aren't they?"[59] For Carl McIntire, they most certainly were not.

Nixon versus the Networks

McIntire appealed to President Nixon for relief from the FCC's denial of a license renewal for WXUR but was informed that "it would be wholly inappropriate for the President to attempt to influence the considered judgement of an independent regulatory commission."[60] Whatever McIntire had hoped for from his letters to the White House, it probably did not include a desire for a lecture on legality by a White House functionary less than five months prior to Nixon's own scandal-induced resignation. Despite a testy relationship between the ardently anti-Communist McIntire and the détente-seeking president—McIntire once played ping-pong on a jury-rigged table in front of the White House to protest Nixon's refusal to entertain the Taiwanese national ping-pong team—McIntire defended Nixon against the Watergate accusations until well into 1974, releasing a statement that McIntire, despite being "a consistent opponent of the President's policy in regard to the Communists," supported Nixon because the president had declared "his innocence," "his closest associates [had] lied to his face," he had been "betrayed . . . behind his back," and finally he had been left "at the mercy of pious political opponents and an increasingly determined press." News to the contrary was fake and not to be believed.[61]

Yet unlike Barry Goldwater in 1964 and George Wallace in 1968, Nixon had always had a frosty relationship with the Radio Right. That appears to have begun with the Kamp controversy of 1958 and attempts by Democrats to link Nixon to the radical Right in 1960. Despite those efforts, Nixon and the conservatives did not see eye to eye on a range of issues. Conservative broadcasters were overtly segregationist while Nixon preferred the dog whistle. They wanted to invade mainland China, not walk along the Great Wall with the Chinese premier. McIntire held pro–Vietnam War rallies as late as 1973 while Nixon was negotiating a peace settlement. Take the example of one of McIntire's listeners who, inspired after listening to his favorite broadcaster rip into the compromising Nixon, got a massive decal placed on the back of his family van and mailed a picture to McIntire. The decal read, in twelve-inch-tall letters, "UN=[Hammer & Sickle]=[Swastika]=Nixon."[62] Suffice it to say, there was plenty of ill will between the Radio Right and Richard Nixon.

While Richard Nixon may not have liked the Radio Right, he was very much a fan of the Fairness Doctrine. In the months after his inauguration in 1969, Nixon grew increasingly irate with the negative news coverage he was receiving, especially in regard to the Vietnam War. He ordered his in-house team of political operators to use a combination of regulatory pressure and good old-fashioned intimidation to shape network television coverage of his administration. The core of the team included Pat Buchanan, Chuck Colson, John Ehrlichman, Jeb Stuart Magruder, and team leader H. R. "Bob"

Photo 7.1. This picture was included in a piece of fan mail sent to Carl McIntire. It is a reminder that Nixon was not popular with the conservative grassroots.
Carl McIntire Papers, Special Collections, Princeton Theological Seminary Library.

Haldeman. If those names sound familiar, it may be because the final four men listed would eventually be convicted of crimes related to the Watergate burglary and cover-up. But years before Watergate, Nixon's dirty-tricks operatives cut their teeth by abusing executive power to undermine critical media coverage.

Nixon's initial strategy for dealing with critical news coverage had been ineffective. When Nixon saw journalists attacking him or his administration, he would send a note to one of his team and tell them to browbeat the offender about how inaccurate their coverage was. Other times they were asked to plant fake letters to the editor, commission hit pieces by sympathetic outlets, or demand equal response time under the Fairness Doctrine. Very quickly Nixon's aides grew frustrated with the ticky-tacky demands; as Magruder noted, he had "logged 21 requests from the President in the last 30 days."[63] It would be almost a pitiful mental image were it not one that involved the single most powerful person on the planet: Richard Nixon, a known night owl, sitting alone in his secret office in the Old Executive Office Building, brooding about how unfair the media was being to him and making unreasonable demands of his aides. This was before the age of online social media, so there was no other way for the notoriously paranoid president to exorcise his petty resentments.

Finally, during the fall of 1969 Jeb Magruder was commissioned to write a memorandum outlining a more effective way of guaranteeing Nixon more favorable news coverage. Magruder was tired of what he called Nixon's scattered "shot-gun" approach, preferring something more targeted like a "rifle." In Magruder's straightforward metaphor, the rifle represented action by the FCC and the IRS. Magruder's inspiration for his plan was none other than the Kennedy administration itself; he had a grudging admiration for the Kennedys, who lacked any "qualms" about using "the power available to them to achieve their objectives." He specifically mentioned how the Kennedys had sent Federal Bureau of Investigation (FBI) agents to interrogate steel industry executives in the middle of the night; although "it caused an uproar in certain cases," the president had "achieved his goal and the vast majority of the American public was with him." All Magruder needed to do was convince Nixon "to use the power at hand to achieve our long term goals," namely, "eight years of a Republican Administration."[64] After all, the overriding objective of any first-term president is becoming a second-term president.

Magruder recommended five action points for Nixon's Committee to Re-Elect the President (CRP; mockingly nicknamed CREEP by the press). First, after the appointment of Dean Burch as the new chairman of the FCC, they would set up an "official monitoring system" at the commission from which to "make official complaints." An official warning from the FCC would do more to intimidate journalists than a call from a random White House aide. Burch was a sound choice. As a former chairman of the Republican National Committee (RNC), Burch could be relied upon to do whatever Nixon asked of him.

Magruder's second and third recommendations were similar; he wanted to use the anti-trust division of the Department of Justice and the IRS to "look into" the affairs of the offending networks. Even the mere "threat of a IRS investigation" or "anti-trust action" would "be effective in changing their views." Fourth, Magruder suggested that the administration "show favorites within the media" and only give scoops and access to sympathetic journalists. Again, he recommended following the example of Kennedy, saying that "since they [the press] are basically not on our side let us pick the favorable ones as Kennedy did." Finally, Magruder tasked the RNC with starting a "major letter writing" campaign to the FCC. On his own initiative, he had already "set-up a situation" at the RNC for doing so.[65]

The recommendations in Magruder's memo are eerily similar to those in the Reuther Memorandum eight years before. In both cases, a sympathetic FCC chairman would target the president's critics in the media with Fairness Doctrine complaints. If that was not enough, threats of IRS tax audits might do the trick. And to make sure that the countermedia campaign did not appear to come from the White House itself, the party apparatus would run the letter-writing campaign presumably under false pretenses. I have found no evidence that Magruder was directly inspired by the Reuther plan nor that he had even heard of it (although he had worked for the Barry Goldwater campaign in late 1963 at the same time that the Reuther Memorandum was leaked to the public). But Magruder did not need knowledge of the Reuther Memorandum to see the latent potential in using these kinds of tactics on Nixon's behalf. It does not take a genius to realize that executive appointees can be manipulated into advancing the president's agenda or that executive abuse of the IRS and FCC generally escaped public attention.

The final question is whether Nixon acted on Magruder's recommendations. The broader history of Nixon's abuses of his office is beyond the scope of this book, but suffice it to say that Nixon did follow through.[66] The first target was prominent NBC News anchor Chet Huntley, who, in a free-ranging and seemingly well-lubricated interview on the eve of his retirement, had said of Nixon, "The shallowness of the man overwhelms me; the fact that he is President frightens me."[67] Nixon was furious, so Magruder wrote up a response "plan on press objectivity." The proximate goal of the effort was to get Huntley to claim he was "misquoted" and apologize, but the ultimate goal was to "extend these questions to cover the professional objectivity and ethics of the whole media and to generate a public re-examination of the role of the media in American life." If the Nixon administration could convince ordinary American voters to "question the motivation for such remarks" and consider them a "breach of professional ethics," it would set a precedent for how they would regard anybody in the mainstream media that might dare to criticize the president.[68] After all, as Lawrence Higby reminded Magruder, "We don't care about Huntley" since "he is going to leave anyway. What we are trying to do here is to tear down the institution," the institution being public trust in the media. While reflexive public distrust of the media is a commonplace today, it had to be learned.[69]

The CRP team had a multipronged response planned. They would arrange for a private donor to fund a primetime special showing "how TV newsmen can structure the news by innuendo," like "how a raised eyebrow or a tone of voice can convey criticism." Articles, books, and letters to the editor would be generated in defense of the president. In particular, they wanted to "plant a column . . . which raises the question of objectivity," naming Kevin Phillips as the preferred choice. (Phillips, if you will recall, had coined the term the "Southern Strategy" after working for Nixon during the 1968 campaign.) On the broadcasting front, they would have FCC Chairman Dean Burch "express concern" when asked about press objectivity in a stage-managed letter from a congressman. Then they could "form a blue-ribbon media 'watchdog' committee to report to the public on cases of biased reporting." Meanwhile, a senator would write a public letter to the FCC mooting the idea of "licensing" newsmen because, after all, "the airwaves belong to the public" and "therefore the public should be protected from the misuse of these airwaves by individual newsmen."[70] Nixon had turned the "public interest" clause of the Communications Act of 1934 into a mockery of itself. The public's interest on the airwaves was whatever Nixon's interests were; its misuse was any attempt to criticize Nixon.

It is a severe understatement to say that Nixon's CRP team had a novel understanding of "press objectivity," since it included coercing journalists, leveraging government power over the media, and misleading the public. But the results of the counternetwork campaign were everything CRP had hoped for. Within weeks, Huntley had publicly apologized to Nixon, saying he was "terribly embarrassed" by his words and expressing shock at the "audacity" of the *Life* reporter in trying to make him "responsible for the alleged statements." That must have felt viscerally satisfying for Nixon, but getting Huntley's apology was never really the point.[71]

Over the next several weeks, FCC Chairman Dean Burch took advantage of the controversy over press objectivity to revise the commission's equal time rule. Previously, the requirement that an outlet airing a message from one party's political candidate must offer equal time to the other party's candidate had been applied to televised presidential addresses. CBS in particular had a regular postaddress series called "Loyal Opposition," which featured a speech by a congressperson from the party opposite the president's. Burch, however, decided to rescind that rule, arguing that it was necessary to "separate the President from his office." When he spoke to the nation from the White House—no matter the topic—he was speaking as the president, not as

Richard Nixon. In a series of meetings with each of the major network heads, the CRP team made it clear that not only did the networks not have to air a Democratic response according to the FCC rule revision but they should not air a Democratic response according to CRP.[72] CBS immediately complied, though they challenged the rules in court.

More damaging to the networks than the equal time tweak was a new primetime access rule, which restricted how much network-created programming that local station affiliates could air during peak evening hours. This had the effect of weakening network control over affiliates and shrinking a major source of network revenue. In addition, the FCC had recently ruled that network television companies would not be allowed to expand into cable broadcasting, which was at the earliest stages of development in 1970 but was already seen as the future of television.[73] While scholars still debate whether all of the rule changes were directly ordered by Nixon, Charles Colson summed up the attitude of the CRP team immediately following their passage, that "the other side is really being hurt as they begin to understand the FCC decisions."[74]

In the end, as long as the networks thought the administration was responsible, it did not matter whether they were or not. The networks may have thought so because of leaks to journalists from within the FCC itself. Years later it was revealed that in 1970 Chairman Dean Burch had warrantlessly wiretapped the phones of several FCC employees because, he admitted, "I was, I suppose, more concerned about the leaks in the agency than I was about that particular gentleman's privacy." Burch in particular worried that "confidential matters before the commission" and other "agenda information" would be revealed, suggesting that the agenda was using the FCC's rule-making powers to ensure favorable press coverage of the administration.[75]

Either way, as Colson reported back to Haldeman, the network heads had become "accommodating, cordial and almost apologetic" in meetings. Colson believed it was because they were "terribly nervous over . . . the recent FCC decisions" and because "they are also apprehensive of us" since "they felt we could . . . through the FCC make any policies we wanted to. (This is worrying them all.)" CBS even expressed surprise, not that the Nixon administration had requested more favorable coverage since "every Administration had felt the same way," but that they had "been slower in coming to them to complain than our predecessors."[76] CRP had achieved the goals of its counternetwork campaign in an astonishingly short timeframe. It was less than a year from Magruder's original "Shotgun versus Rifle" memorandum in October 1969 to almost complete network acquiescence by September 1970. It would be the print media—with its stronger legal protections and no scarcity rule or public interest mandate—that would take the lead in challenging the administration over the next several years.

There are striking similarities between the Nixon and Kennedy countermedia campaigns. Both put reliable party men who could follow instructions in the chairmanship of the FCC. Both changed broadcasting rules to intimidate media outlets into adjusting their programming, Kennedy with the Fairness Doctrine and Nixon with the equal time and ownership rules. Both relied on their political party apparatus to organize letter-writing campaigns to the FCC. There were, however, key differences between Nixon's and Kennedy's campaigns. Nixon tried to use the IRS to target his enemies with tax audits, but his IRS commissioner refused to do so; the IRS under Kennedy successfully repealed tax-exempt status for several conservative broadcasters.[77] Whereas Nixon tackled the major television networks, Kennedy focused his efforts on independent radio station owners. And, of course, the particular political point of view being suppressed by each president differed substantially. Yet in the end, both countermedia campaigns were remarkably successful.

Indeed, the very success of Nixon's counternetwork campaign convinced some of Kennedy's operatives to regret their involvement in the counter–Radio Right campaign. In a two-party system, eventually the other side gets a chance to do to you what was done to them. Fred Friendly, the crusading former CBS producer, took his network's capitulation to Nixon's demands personally. As he researched *The Good Guys, the Bad Guys, and the First Amendment*, he interviewed Kennedy's team both on and off the record, including Wayne Phillips, Wesley McCune, and Fred Cook, among others. (McCune, however, would later write Friendly and complain that the book left him feeling "somehow shafted." McCune also downplayed station owners' complaints about Fairness Doctrine intimidation, saying, "It is my belief that anyone who says he lost stations through intimidation is like the girl who suddenly rips her dress and hollers 'rape.'")[78] It was Wayne Phillips who had slipped various DNC reports and other confidential documents to Friendly. He had gone from, in the words of Dewey Anderson, a "bedeviled zealot" in 1964 to someone willing to expose his own illicit behavior by 1974.[79] Phillips did not confide what prompted his change of heart, but the abuse of the FCC's powers by the Nixon administration must have played a role.

Some people met with Friendly because they were grappling with "serious questions of guilt" over their involvement, but others involved appealed to points of principle.[80] During a meeting with one unnamed source—during which Friendly took notes on a restaurant placemat—the source confided that the Fairness Doctrine, which was "one of [the] greatest things," would be, if "carried to its logical conclusion," utterly "disastrous."[81] This interview likely took place in 1971, which, given the rulings of Nixon's FCC a year prior, makes the speaker's concerns understandable. Friendly himself, in a speech to a broadcasters' association in February 1973, a month before the Watergate scandal broke, said, "One bad idea that I wouldn't give even a nickel for is the concept that presidential power be exerted on the regulatory process to create a less critical climate for any one political party." Friendly illustrated his point by pointing to political pressure not to cover the My Lai massacre, Rachel Carson's environmental exposés, and Ralph Nader's consumer activism.[82]

But there were others who saw the writing on the wall much earlier. FCC Commissioner Lee Loevinger, who had previously fought the New Frontier faction on the FCC over enhancing the Fairness Doctrine, warned the American Civil Liberties Union back in 1964 of the danger of using the rules to ensure "balanced programming." That was because, despite the "culturally elevating" intent of those supporting the rule changes, "under authorities determined to misuse this power . . . it will afford ample means to impose a pattern of ideational content acceptable to, and supportive of, an incumbent federal administration."[83] Loevinger said these words during the Johnson administration—and in the middle of the DNC's summer campaign to use Fairness Doctrine complaints to intimidate stations airing pro-Goldwater programming—but he said nothing about specific parties or politicians. As is clearly demonstrated by this book, the temptation to use these powers for partisan ends is politically and ideologically agnostic.

To the Bitter End

Nixon would do nothing to help the Radio Right, so in September 1972 the US Circuit Court of Appeals for the District of Columbia upheld the FCC's denial of a license renewal for WXUR. The court rejected McIntire's claim that his freedom of speech had been violated, stating, "The First Amendment was never intended to protect the few while providing them with a sacrosanct sword and shield with which they could injure the many." Tolerated minority groups should know their place. McIntire's on-air attacks on the NCC were not protected speech. The court's decision had been unanimous, but Justice David Bazelon changed his position two months later and issued a dissent. (Bazelon had served with Supreme Court Justice Warren Burger on the DC Circuit Court of Appeals for more than a decade before Burger's promotion. The two men hated each other as much personally as they disagreed professionally.) Bazelon retorted, "If we are to go after gnats with a sledgehammer like the Fairness Doctrine, we ought to at least look at what else is smashed beneath our blow." He believed that the denial of a license renewal to WXUR violated the First Amendment, since "the public has lost access to information and ideas," a "loss not to be taken lightly, however unpopular or disruptive we might judge these ideas to be."[84] Bazelon's dissent still left a vote of two to one for the FCC and against McIntire.

McIntire's last day on WXUR was July 4, 1973. The symbolism was not lost on him. In protest, he held a "funeral" for WXUR on the lawn behind Independence Hall in Philadelphia, shown below in Photo 7.2. Pallbearers wearing judicial robes and wigs laid a scale model of the station's antenna in a coffin marked "Freedom of Speech" while mourners bedecked in Founding Father garb listened to Carl McIntire pronounce WXUR's last rites.[85] The following month, McIntire purchased a surplus World War II minesweeper and outfitted it with a powerful radio transmitter and a banner reading, "Radio Free America." McIntire's pirate radio station sailed only for a single day from the international waters off Cape May, New Jersey, before the FCC shut it down with a court order, just long enough for the broadcast to interfere with radio signals from as far away as Salt Lake City.[86] McIntire usually got the last word, even in defeat.

Although the NCC's campaign against conservative broadcasting had muted Carl McIntire, his former listeners did not simply renounce their conservative political and religious beliefs. As stations dropped the *Twentieth Century Reformation Hour* one by one, listeners wrote to McIntire expressing their rage at those whom they held responsible for it all: the NCC and the federal government. One listener, from a tiny town in the southeast corner of Washington State, wrote, "I feel as tho [sic] my life-line had been cut," when her local station dropped McIntire.[87] This was not just hyperbole. For some of these listeners, every weekday for the prior five, ten, or fifteen years they had turned on the radio and heard Carl McIntire tell them that they were part of a national movement to reclaim America for God and the Constitution. One

Photo 7.2. In response to the Federal Communications Commission's decision on station WXUR's license renewal, Carl McIntire held a mock funeral for the station on the green behind Independence Hall in Philadelphia.
Carl McIntire Papers, Special Collections, Princeton Theological Seminary Library.

listener from eastern Kansas, Mrs. G. H. Owen, wrote McIntire her thanks in 1960 to say that she was "no longer alone and helpless." McIntire armed her with "facts at hand" and the knowledge that she had "a place along with many others who are listening."[88] As noted in the discussion of the Polish ham boycott, McIntire's message appealed disproportionately to women like Mrs. Owen. The typical listener was middle-aged, married or widowed, a mother, and a housewife. right-wing broadcasters like Carl McIntire were as much a part of their daily lives as their pastor or their neighbors. And now he was being taken away from them.

Listeners often struggled to put how deeply they felt the loss into words. Sister Clara Courtin compared McIntire's show going off the air to "a death in our family." Mrs. Burns felt physically ill when her station "took off the grand religious and patriotic programs" like the *Twentieth Century Reformation Hour*. Others despaired of finding a replacement. "Now I feel so hopeless," one wrote, "where is our voice of conservatism?" Given how personal the pain of losing McIntire's show was to these listeners, it is not surprising that their next reaction was rage. Most of the letter writers blamed either the FCC or the NCC for kicking McIntire off their station. Two asked the nearly identical question, "Was it because of the FCC's un-'Fairness Doctrine'?" Another, not having yet heard an explanation for the cancellation, "naturally suppose[d that] the FCC threatenings [sic] have overcome our station." Others blamed the NCC, for although McIntire was gone, the local NCC-affiliated preacher still droned on and on over the radio. Not all the letters came from fundamentalists or even Protestants. One man who was "deeply involved in the Goldwater for President campaign" called himself a loyal "conservative Catholic for McIntire."[89]

These listeners barraged the stations with complaints, enough that both stations reluctantly issued statements explaining why they had dropped McIntire. Others wrote or called the FCC to complain, including one caller who, when put on hold for an interminable period, assumed "they were tracing [her] phone call" and gave some poor FCC staff underling an earful about his violation of her freedom of speech. That readiness to blame the

Photo 7.3. Carl McIntire leading a children's march in protest of the Federal Communications Commission's WXUR decision. It illustrates the sense of government betrayal felt among conservative radio listeners.

Carl McIntire Papers, Special Collections, Princeton Theological Seminary Library.

FCC for the cancellations easily transferred into a distrust of the federal government as a whole. As Mrs. C. E. Hooks learned, "You cannot beat the Federal Government." Although most of the letter writers were middle-aged housewives, one male writer merits special attention. Fred C. Koch, millionaire founder of Koch Industries, had been a faithful listener of McIntire's program. He convinced all the members of his local chapter of the John Birch Society to write the station in protest at the cancellation. (Unlike the widows, Koch did not enclose any money with his letter.)[90] Conservatives had never been especially trustful toward the federal government, but the suppression of the Radio Right cemented their belief that the government was not merely

Photo 7.4. A cartoon included with a reprint of Fred Friendly's "What's Fair on the Air?" for Carl McIntire's *Twentieth Century Reformation Hour*.

Carl McIntire Papers, Special Collections, Princeton Theological Seminary Library.

wasteful or rapacious; no, now they could point to the Fairness Doctrine as evidence that the federal government was actively hostile to conservatism. That belief would fuel support for the coming conservative counterrevolution and reach its apotheosis in Ronald Reagan.

The NCC and its allies had won a major, if temporary, victory over their religious and political competition in the New Right. They had done so by leveraging their institutional and cultural influence to convince a sympathetic federal bureaucracy to deny licenses to stations that aired conservative broadcasters. This was not an exercise of impartial justice but a targeted effort to silence an intolerant opposition. McIntire and company were indeed intolerant given their support for segregation and the paranoid extremes to which they took their anti-Communism, but the central irony in this story is that a coalition of liberal advocacy groups had used deeply illiberal methods to combat illiberalism. As media historian Heather Hendershot notes of the WXUR case, "The idea of 'free speech' was used to shut down free speech."[91] The conflicted rhetoric in the letters of the various leaders of this campaign confirms Hendershot's observation. They felt the cognitive dissonance between their liberal beliefs and their illiberal acts. It was awkward being a liberal censor. That cognitive dissonance reflected the contradictory mandates of the Fairness Doctrine itself, both to promote rigorous debate on controversial issues and to enforce civility. The Fairness Doctrine was a mess—arbitrarily applied, ill conceived, and rooted in an inchoate idea of the public interest—yet it became a vital tool in one of the most successful episodes of censorship in modern American history, comparable in scale and effectiveness to the suppression of birth control advocates by the Comstock laws.

8

Conclusion

From Radio Ronald Reagan to Donald Trump's Tweets

Although the Radio Right reached its nadir in the early 1970s, a few years later a shift in the regulatory environment combined with the advent of new media technologies opened the door to a second wave of mass conservative broadcasting. Religious broadcasters like Jerry Falwell and Pat Robertson used radio, television, and cable broadcasting to build national followings that, while perhaps not so large as those of the top 1960s broadcasters, were large enough to form a base for growing political influence. Furthermore, as the Federal Communications Commission (FCC) relaxed its enforcement of the Fairness Doctrine, ex-California Governor Ronald Reagan would use his new radio show to build the army of campaign volunteers that would propel him into the White House.

It is nearly impossible to trace what happened to specific individuals like Mrs. Owen or Mrs. Burns or any of the twenty million people who had listened to the *Twentieth Century Reformation Hour* at its peak, but as a group they did not simply disappear. The campaign against conservative broadcasting had successfully muted Carl McIntire, Billy James Hargis, and other major right-wing broadcasters, but it could not erase the conservative grassroots that they had organized. Those who listened to conservative broadcasters in the 1960s would form the core audience for the next wave of right-wing broadcasting.

Two factors drove the resurgence of right-wing broadcasting in the late 1970s. First, the FCC began relaxing its enforcement of the Fairness Doctrine. The hardline FCC commissioners left one by one, first Frederick Ford (1964), then E. William Henry (1966), Kenneth Cox (1970), and Nicholas Johnson (1973). Their replacements, many of whom were appointed by Republican Presidents Richard Nixon and Gerald Ford, may not have been conservative per se, but they were certainly less interested in using the Fairness Doctrine to target right-wing stations. The Fairness Doctrine rules that had been clarified in 1963 and reinforced in 1967 still remained in place, but the commission's

The Radio Right. Paul Matzko, © Oxford University Press (2020). Oxford University Press.
DOI: 10.1093/oso/9780190073220.001.0001

willingness to support the Fairness Doctrine's application in politically controversial cases waned. Then, President Jimmy Carter appointed a new FCC
chairman in 1977 named Charles Ferris, who began a decade-long process
of deregulating the airwaves, ending with the official repeal of the Fairness
Doctrine in 1987.[1]

The second factor that fueled the resurgence of right-wing broadcasting
was a new technology, cable television. The concept of cable broadcasting
was not new to the 1970s—there were small wire cable networks as far
back as the 1940s, especially in mountainous areas with poor over-the-air
transmission—but FCC regulations that were designed to protect AT&T's
transmission line monopoly had stymied the technology's growth. That
changed from 1977 to 1980 when the FCC, again with the encouragement of
Chairman Ferris, streamlined the approval process for cable network startups
and removed some of the more onerous noncompetition restrictions.[2] As
cable companies sprouted up all over the country, the cost of running a television program fell dramatically. In a repeat of what had happened with the
radio industry in the 1950s, by the early 1980s television broadcasting had
become cheaper and newly accessible for previously niche political and religious interests.

And as with independent radio before, those two changes launched a
boom in right-wing television and cable broadcasting. A new crop of fundamentalist preachers took the reins from Carl McIntire and Billy James Hargis,
including Jerry Falwell and Pat Robertson. Both men were from Virginia, although Falwell was Baptist and Robertson was Pentecostal. Both had also
been involved in local radio and television broadcasting in the 1960s but had
generally avoided politics in their broadcasts. That changed in step with the
regulatory outlook. They also expanded their media footprint. Pat Robertson
had a substantial radio and television footprint in the 1960s and 1970s, but it
was cable that both turned Robertson into a national figure and freed him to
engage in overt political advocacy. In 1977, just as the FCC relaxed its cable
regulations, Robertson started a small satellite cable channel that grew rapidly; by 1983 his Christian Broadcasting Network claimed seventeen million
viewers (only three million fewer than Carl McIntire's listener count twenty
years prior).[3] Later, Robertson's network would provide him with the perfect
launching platform for his surprise 1988 presidential campaign.

Falwell may not have run for president like Robertson, but he helped
make a president by creating a conservative advocacy group called the Moral
Majority, which would throw its support behind Ronald Reagan's candidacy

in 1980. Interestingly, the idea for such an organization came to Falwell at an anti–Fairness Doctrine rally held in Dallas in February 1979. A television station that was worried about Fairness Doctrine complaints had dropped popular televangelist James Robison after he made homophobic remarks. After the rally, Robison and Falwell met with conservative political organizers Ed McAteer and Paul Weyrich to plan for what would become the Moral Majority.[4] The rally was a sign that the FCC's disinterest in enforcing the Fairness Doctrine had so emboldened conservative broadcasters that they dared to directly challenge the doctrine for the first time since the mid-1960s and the WLBT, Red Lion, and WXUR cases.

Falwell and Robertson were two of the founding figures of what historians have called the "New Christian Right," which is commonly dated to 1976 when *Time* magazine ran a cover article announcing the "Year of the Evangelical." That year, a seemingly new evangelical voter bloc helped Sunday school teacher, peanut farmer, and Georgia Governor Jimmy Carter win his dark horse presidential bid. Yet while Carter's "born again" street credentials helped him win in 1976, it also led to a sense of betrayal among increasingly pro-life evangelicals as the Carter administration appointed pro-abortion Supreme Court justices. As a result, evangelical voters abandoned Carter in droves in 1980, supporting instead Ronald Reagan who had the endorsement of Falwell, Robertson, and other conservative broadcasters.

Reagan was happy to return the favor. The same group of organizers and broadcasters who had hosted the anti–Fairness Doctrine rally in Dallas in 1979 hosted another rally in the city in August 1980. This time, Ronald Reagan spoke to the packed crowd of fifteen thousand evangelicals, telling them, "I know you can't endorse me . . . but I want you to know that I endorse you and what you are doing."[5] Nothing could better symbolize the rebirth of conservative, religious broadcasting in the late 1970s. However, the term "New Christian Right" is a misnomer. There was nothing truly "new" about fundamentalist preachers using the airwaves to advance conservative politics. It had been done before and on a similar scale; McIntire and Hargis were the Falwell and Robertson of the 1960s. It may be more accurate to say that Falwell and Robertson were representatives of the second wave of right-wing broadcasting.

Even so, the historiography of the New Christian Right in the late 1970s and 1980s proceeds from some of the same flawed assumptions as the literature on the rise of the New Right twenty years before. There is the same fixation on finding the right issue(s) that motivated conservative evangelicals to come out of the woodwork, although this time the issues are framed as products of the "culture wars." Was it abortion, segregation academies, or gay rights that energized conservative activism? Asking that same, old question, however, leaves historians looking for shifts in the *demand* for conservative solutions rather than changes in the *supply* of those ideas.

Like a generation before, expanded access to mass media turned Falwell, Robertson, and dozens of other second-wave broadcasters into national figures with the power to amplify local activism. For example, Jerry Falwell used his television show, the *Old-Time Gospel Hour,* to draw national attention to Anita Bryant's anti-LGBT campaign in Florida in 1977. Dade County had passed an anti-discrimination ordinance protecting gay job seekers. Bryant wanted the ordinance repealed; when her pastor told Falwell, he flew Bryant up to Virginia to tape the show and then returned with her to Florida, where they held a joint, televised rally for ten thousand people protesting the ordinance. Several weeks later the ordinance was overturned and Bryant became a national icon of the culture wars.[6] The connection between local activism and national broadcasting—as well as the involvement of a Florida housewife famous for singing in a 1972 ad selling the wholesome virtues of orange juice to consumers—echoes Carl McIntire's support for Polish ham-boycotting housewives in 1962. Right-wing television broadcasters played as vital a role in fomenting conservative activism in the 1970s and 1980s as their predecessors on the radio had in the 1960s.[7]

Radio Ronald Reagan

Although conservative broadcasting in the age of Reagan is commonly associated with televangelists and cable preachers, radio still had an important role to play, a fact placed in clear relief by none other than Ronald Reagan himself. When Reagan won the presidency in 1980, political pundits declared him the "Great Communicator" for his on-camera charisma. He was not the first televised president, but he was the first president who fully understood television's political potential. Both as a Hollywood actor and as a popular host for the 1950s television program the *General Electric Theater,* Reagan had learned how to connect with broadcast audiences and how to convey complicated concepts through pithy soundbites.[8] That gave him a unique advantage over less camera-ready political opponents.

Reagan's victory in 1980 also represented the culmination of a trend first noted by Republican Party operative Kevin Phillips in 1974. Phillips, the author of the infamous "Southern Strategy" that aided Nixon's victory in 1972, had posited, "In the age of the mass media, the old Republican and Democratic parties have lost their logic. Effective communications are replacing party organizations as the key to political success." Phillips called this phenomenon the rise of the "mediacracy."[9] He was thinking of the potential of television at the time, but the thought applies just as well to radio and the New Right a decade earlier. The boom in conservative broadcasting created a surge of grassroots, conservative activism in the early 1960s, which culminated in the surprise candidacy of Barry Goldwater and the temporary conservative takeover of the Republican Party. Ronald Reagan's media-savvy presidency was the culmination of two decades of grassroots activism fueled by right-wing broadcasting.

Without fail, the expansive literature on Ronald Reagan discusses his television experience at length, but many of his biographers omit the fact that Reagan's political career also involved the effective use of radio broadcasting.[10] Indeed, radio provided the crucial link between the end of Reagan's term as governor of California in 1975 and his successful run for the presidency in 1979–1980. During those four years, Reagan delivered over a thousand daily radio addresses on more than two hundred radio stations.[11] It was this masterful use of a seemingly outdated medium that propelled Reagan to the White House.

But radio was a part of Reagan's life long before he ever dreamed of being a politician. He began his career as a sports radio announcer in Iowa. This was the golden age of radio and Reagan's little station quickly became a major NBC affiliate in the Midwest. He covered Chicago sports teams and showed an uncanny knack for colorfully announcing games even though he was not in attendance and was forced to rely on scant, telegraphed descriptions of the action. On one notable case, the telegraph machine broke down and Reagan was forced to come up with a series of fictional plays on the spot until the machine could be fixed, an early lesson in impromptu speaking that would serve him well as a politician. Finally, it was through his radio contacts that Reagan got a Hollywood screen test. Television may have made Reagan a star, but radio got him in the door.[12] Under other circumstances, one might expect Reagan's radio experience to end there, as an interesting but small stepping stone on his way to Hollywood celebrity and later the gubernatorial mansion in California. By the 1970s he was both a former television personality and the governor of the most populous state in the country; what need did he have for radio?

Yet Reagan turned to radio in 1975 when he left the governorship to prepare for his 1976 presidential campaign. Most of Reagan's advisers had recommended that he take a lucrative sinecure on a corporate board with minimal commitment; after all, he would be spending most of his time working the after-dinner speech circuit (or as Reagan called it, the "mashed potato circuit") to connect with future campaign donors.[13] Instead, Reagan opted for a daily radio commentary program called *Viewpoint*. Each broadcast was short, just five minutes long, but required writing a multipage script and spending time in a recording studio (although Reagan cut down on studio visits by recording them in batches of fifteen at a time). Still, that meant coming up with dozens of pages of content every three weeks even while crisscrossing the country on the speech circuit, a particularly impressive feat given that Reagan wrote more than two-thirds of the broadcasts himself. Yet the payoff was immense: 286 stations aired his broadcasts and 226 newspapers carried the transcripts as a regular column. His estimated listening audience was twenty million. Every day, for four years, twenty million Americans heard Ronald Reagan give his take on public affairs.[14] Arguably, the typical American voter was more familiar with what Reagan thought about current events than they were with what the sitting US president believed. An annual State of the Union address and a handful of televised Oval Office speeches simply could not compare to the day-in, day-out messaging of *Viewpoint*.

Peter Hannaford, one of Reagan's campaign advisers, recounted how as Reagan traveled all over the country giving fundraising pitches, he constantly ran into *Viewpoint* listeners. A local radio program sponsor or even the driver shuttling Reagan from the airport would say, "Oh Governor, I heard your program today, and it was terrific. You were right on target." *Viewpoint* not only helped Reagan get his conservative message out to potential voters but also created, in Hannaford's words, "a volunteer army of campaign workers." This "huge recruitment device" energized local activists and helped them imagine that Reagan might be the first leader since Barry Goldwater back in 1964 able to champion the conservative cause on the national stage. It also led to a flood of campaign donations. Volunteers manned phone banks to make fundraising calls. Local activists, inspired by hearing Reagan on the radio, signed up for campaign training sessions and the chance to meet Reagan in person.[15] *Viewpoint* played such an important role in Reagan's campaign, especially during the lead-up to 1980, that Reagan waited to declare his candidacy until the last, possible moment, worried that he would "lose some valuable forums the day I declare, among them 300 radio stations (5 days a week), 100 newspapers (twice a week), to say nothing of the speaking engagements."[16] That is because as a candidate the FCC's equal time rules would have required stations that chose to air *Viewpoint* to also grant Jimmy Carter or one of his campaign staff equal speaking time without charge, not something many stations would have been interested in doing. Reagan stopped airing the program during his candidacy, but it was the foundation on which his campaign had been built.

Perhaps the best measure of the importance of radio to Reagan's campaigns in 1976 and 1980 is what he chose radio over. When he had stepped down as governor, national news anchor Walter Cronkite offered Reagan the chance to do two weekly televised commentaries for the CBS Evening News. If he had accepted, Reagan would have had roughly 40% of the total primetime television audience watching him twice a week. Yet Reagan turned it down. Then after losing to President Ford in the Republican primaries in 1976, Reagan was offered his pick of the chairmanship of the Republican National Committee, a cabinet position in the Ford administration, or an ambassadorship to Great Britain. Reagan said no to all three. His reason? By "remaining independent"—whether from CBS's editorial control or party priorities—Reagan believed he was "in a position to speak out in both those channels for the things we believe in as well as against those things our opponents may try to do." Radio offered Reagan a mass audience without the strings attached to television. And unlike a leadership position in the Republican Party or the Ford administration, radio allowed Reagan to connect with ordinary voters and grassroots activists.[17]

To illustrate how radio helped Reagan's presidential image, consider a series of talks he gave during his final months on *Viewpoint* in the fall of 1979. That summer Jimmy Carter had signed the Strategic Arms Limitation Treaty II (SALT II) with the Soviet Union, which promised the first ever major reductions in the two superpowers' nuclear stockpiles. Conservatives were opposed to the treaty, believing that continuing the nuclear arms race signaled to America's allies its determination to stand up to global Communism. Furthermore, they felt that the treaty did not provide for a robust enforcement mechanism that could verify whether the Soviets actually kept the terms of the treaty. The treaty required confirmation by the Senate but was delayed indefinitely after the Soviet invasion of Afghanistan in December 1979, which raised conservative hackles even further.[18]

Carter's accommodationist position on SALT II was a weak spot for his re-election campaign, so of course that is where Reagan aimed his final on-air blows. Reagan had attacked the idea of strategic arms limitations throughout his time on *Viewpoint*. He questioned the verification process and compared SALT II to the infamous Munich Agreement with Nazi Germany.[19] One of Reagan's primary reasons for starting *Viewpoint* back in 1975 was to "en-hance [his] foreign affairs credibility."[20] Given how unpopular SALT II had become by the fall of 1979, attacking the Carter administration for signing the treaty allowed Reagan to do just that. *Viewpoint* also helped Reagan shape the public perception of Carter as a weak president not committed to maintaining American military superiority, a key theme in Reagan's 1980 campaign.

There are fascinating parallels between Reagan's use of conservative radio to attack the SALT II treaty in 1979 and the attack on the Nuclear Test Ban Treaty by conservative broadcasters in 1963. In both cases conservatives worried that a nuclear arms treaty with the Soviet Union lacked adequate enforcement mechanisms. In both cases opposition to the treaty was also an excuse to criticize the Democratic administration's broader conduct of the Cold War. In both cases conservatives used radio to appeal directly to voters, surprising Washington powerbrokers with a sudden surge of grassroots opposition.

Yet there the similarities end. In 1963, conservative opposition to the Nuclear Test Ban Treaty convinced John F. Kennedy to fully implement the Reuther Memorandum strategy. Jimmy Carter, on the other hand, was the "Great Deregulator," softening federal regulation of everything from beer production to broadcast fairness. Carter's FCC appointees were too busy deregulating the airwaves to conduct any kind of illicit targeting of conservative broadcasting.[21] Reagan's radio broadcasts from 1975 to 1979 would certainly have run afoul of the Fairness Doctrine strictly interpreted. While it is unlikely that anything short of a miracle could have led to a Carter victory in 1980, Carter might have had a better showing had he imitated Kennedy or Nixon and organized a campaign of Fairness Doctrine complaints against stations airing *Viewpoint*.

Although Carter's FCC ceased most enforcement of the Fairness Doctrine, it was not until the Reagan administration that the rule would be officially repealed. In 1987 the FCC, under the leadership of a Reagan-appointed chairman, voted four to zero to abolish the Fairness Doctrine.[22] A short-lived attempt by congressional Democrats to pass new Fairness Doctrine legislation was promptly vetoed by Reagan. It should not be surprising that as a former conservative radio broadcaster Reagan would find the Fairness Doctrine "antagonistic to the freedom of expression guaranteed by the First Amendment" or that he believed it would inhibit "a diversity of viewpoints in the public forum."[23] The history of right-wing broadcasting in the 1960s suggests that Reagan was right. Reagan understood the continuing political possibilities of radio in the age of television. In that, he and John F. Kennedy agreed, though where Kennedy advanced his policy agenda by shutting down conservative broadcasting, Reagan won the White House by harnessing it to his own ends.

"Bad for Country!" Lessons from the Age of Trump

The end of the Fairness Doctrine sparked the resurgence of right-wing talk radio. It is impossible to tell the story of conservative politics over the last thirty years without mentioning Rush Limbaugh and other broadcasters who used newly unrestricted access to the airwaves to advocate for conservative causes and candidates. That these regulatory changes would disproportionately benefit the political Right was not initially obvious. Historian Brian Rosenwald has shown that left-wing AM talk radio had a meaningful presence in the early days of talk radio, but its growth was constrained because of competition for liberal listeners from National Public Radio, which enjoyed the privileges of being government subsidized and having the superior sound quality and reach of FM radio.[24] Right-wing AM talk radio had no such competition, leading to conservative dominance in the sector. That had profound political consequences, affecting Newt Gingrich's rollout of his "Contract with America" platform in 1994, the talk radio–fueled defeat of immigration reform in 2007, and the normalization of Donald Trump's candidacy in 2016.

Additionally, the introduction of lightly regulated cable broadcasting in the late 1970s—thanks again to the Carter administration—eventually led to the creation of expressly partisan television channels like Fox News and MSNBC. As a result, there is greater ideological diversity in American television today than at any moment in its history. Shows from across the political spectrum—from the *Daily Show* to the *Young Turks* to *Tucker Carlson*

Tonight—could not have existed had television in the 2010s been regulated like radio in the 1960s. Imagine if political comedy shows had to balance how many of their jokes targeted each side of the aisle or if the subjects of a host's scorn could demand free response time. Reinstituting Fairness Doctrine–style regulations on broadcasting would have a chilling effect and discourage radical political speech from both sides of the spectrum.

There are people today who call for a renewal of the Fairness Doctrine in broadcasting or its extension to cover online media. Ever since the 1980s the idea has periodically made the rounds in progressive circles, often out of a sense of frustration with the conservative dominance of talk radio.[25] More recently, the Trump administration and several prominent supporters have suggested the need for government intervention to guarantee equitable treatment of conservative articles by online platforms like Facebook and Twitter. Advocates of rules prohibiting "shadow-banning" merely claim an interest in promoting fairness, but critics suspect that the rules would actually function to advance certain voices at the expense of others.[26] It is also a reminder that in a functioning democracy, no party retains a permanent monopoly on the use or abuse of government power, a thought to keep in the back of one's mind when considering any new policy.

One of Trump's appeals for Fairness Doctrine–style scrutiny of broadcast licensees is a particularly strong echo of John F. Kennedy in the 1960s. During a meeting with his national security advisers in July 2017, Trump had proposed a "tenfold" boost in the US nuclear arsenal, which was an odd proposal to make nearly three decades after the end of the Cold War and which purportedly led Secretary of State Rex Tillerson to call his boss a "moron."[27] A few months later, NBC News reported the story based on anonymous leaks from the White House. Trump, angry over the coverage, tweeted, "With all of the Fake News coming out of NBC and the Networks, at what point is it appropriate to challenge their License? Bad for country!" A year later in September 2018, Trump renewed the call after NBC was forced to apologize for its coverage of an unrelated story, writing, "I have long criticized NBC and their journalistic standards—worse than even CNN. Look at their license?"[28]

The sitting president of the United States had openly called for an executive agency to flagrantly violate the law to mute journalistic criticism. Neither Richard Nixon nor John F. Kennedy had ever so overtly and publicly expressed their willingness to abuse the power of the executive. Yet Trump's tweets did not provoke any licensing scrutiny of NBC by the FCC.

A few days after the first Twitter salvo, FCC chairman Ajit Pai, a Trump appointee, responded by saying, "I believe in the First Amendment. The FCC, under my leadership, will stand for the First Amendment. Under the law, the FCC does not have the authority to revoke the license of a broadcast station based on the content of a particular newscast."[29] On one hand, this is not surprising given the newly learned national habit of taking the president "seriously, but not literally," to use the words of journalist Salena Zito.[30] People took from the tweet that Trump was seriously angry at NBC, not that he was literally calling for the FCC to revoke NBC's television broadcasting license.

But expecting bureaucrats to consistently discern the line between what counts as an actionable executive command and what should be considered meaningless venting is very fine indeed, too fine when the person involved holds the single most powerful political office in the world. While the FCC commissioner in this case interpreted the tweet one way, there is no guarantee that an overzealous government bureaucrat might not have interpreted it in the same spirit as Henry II of England's infamous exclamation, "Will no one rid me of this turbulent priest!"[31] Since the expiration of the Fairness Doctrine, the FCC no longer has the authority to deny license renewals based on politically unbalanced programming, but there were executive agencies that could in theory have acted on the spirit of Trump's Twitter appeals.

The US Department of Justice's (DOJ's) Antitrust Division has the power to break up merged companies after the fact. Comcast had merged with NBCUniversal in 2011 and thus owned NBC News. Much of the criticism of the proposed merger at the time had come from progressives who were worried about a new mega-corporation that had market dominance over two traditionally distinct sectors, internet access and television content. The DOJ had imposed more than 150 conditions on the merger; for example, Comcast was not allowed to block NBCUniversal competitors who wanted to stream their content to Comcast internet customers. Those conditions expired at the beginning of 2018, but critics called for the DOJ to reinstitute the conditions and even to open a new antitrust investigation into the merger given Comcast-NBCUniversal's alleged misbehavior.[32] Donald Trump joined the chorus of critics at this sensitive moment, just a few weeks after his second Twitter salvo against NBC News, writing, "[The] American Cable Association has big problems with Comcast. They say that Comcast routinely violates Antitrust Laws."[33]

Technically, Trump had not ordered a government agency to do any-thing in regard to the proposed antitrust investigation. But one could not have faulted the logic of a midlevel bureaucrat at the DOJ if he or she had concluded from the tweets that the president would prefer that the antitrust investigation took place and that he might look with favor upon the careers of any officials who made sure it did. It would not be difficult to concoct a technical excuse as a justification, leaving the public none the wiser to the actual motivations. In the end, the DOJ did not open a new investigation into Comcast's merger with NBCUniversal, but the appearance of presiden-tial pressure on the regulatory process was widely noted.[34] Indeed, imme-diately after the president said that Comcast had an antitrust problem, the company's stock price fell sharply, suggesting that the market was pricing in the small yet meaningful risk of a nameless bureaucrat taking Trump both seriously and literally for once.[35]

Something like that may have happened with another merger involving a media company that had been critical of the Trump administration. AT&T had filed to acquire Time Warner, which owned cable news net-work CNN. Throughout his term, Trump had repeatedly sparred with CNN journalists, calling the organization "terrible" and purveyors of "fake news."[36] According to journalist Jane Mayer, Trump went beyond mere public attacks on CNN. In an Oval Office meeting in 2017, Trump ordered Gary Cohn, the director of the National Economic Council, and Chief of Staff John Kelly to tell the DOJ to file a lawsuit and block the AT&T acquisition of Time Warner, saying, "I want that deal blocked!" As Mayer's unnamed source said of the meeting, "The President does not un-derstand the nuances of antitrust law or policy, but he wanted to bring down the hammer."[37] Cohn refused to do so, but several months later, the DOJ would file a lawsuit to block the merger, although the challenge even-tually failed in federal court. There is as yet no direct evidence that the DOJ's decision to file the lawsuit was ordered by Trump, but even the pos-sibility is a reminder of the many ways that a savvier president could settle political scores using the broad powers of the executive branch.

Trump had handled NBC's criticism of his nuclear weapons policy in a ham-fisted way, but he did so without any immediate, ill consequences for the broadcast network. That is a contrast with President Kennedy who had, when confronted with criticism of his proposed Nuclear Test Ban Treaty by conservative broadcasters in 1963, launched an incisive cen-sorship campaign. Trump relied on inference, Kennedy on direct action.

Trump proposed, Kennedy disposed. This is not to suggest that the difference in outcome is a matter of personal character or ideological predisposition. The only difference that matters here is that one had the power of the Fairness Doctrine at hand and the other did not. Fairness Doctrine–style regulation of broadcasting or internet content today could be, if "carried to its logical conclusion" by an unhinged executive, utterly "disastrous" for the nation.[38]

Chronological Timeline

February–March 1960	The Air Force manual scandal breaks.
April 1960	John F. Kennedy (JFK) wins the West Virginia Democratic primary.
April 16, 1961	The Pro-Blue curriculum controversy erupts.
April 17, 1961	General Edwin Walker is suspended. The Bay of Pigs disaster embarrasses the Kennedy administration.
Third week of April 1961	Robert F. Kennedy (RFK) and Walter Reuther meet to strategize for the 1964 re-election campaign.
May 1961	On the advice of RFK, Walter Reuther meets with JFK, who asks him for "whatever ideas you might have."
November 2, 1961	General Edwin Walker resigns his military commission.
Second week of November	Walter Reuther meets with RFK to discuss the Reuther Memorandum plan.
November 16, 1961	RFK's assistant John Seigenthaler contacts the Internal Revenue Service's (IRS's) Mitchell Rogovin to ask about the tax-exempt status of "four or five organizations generally considered to be right-wing."
November 18, 1961	JFK delivers the "man on horseback" speech.
November 28, 1961	Seigenthaler clarifies with Rogovin which right-wing broadcasters he is interested in.
November 29, 1961	JFK gives a press conference, says he is "sure the IRS examines [right-wing tax exemptions]."
November 30, 1961	A JFK press conference memo is circulated within the IRS; Mitchell Rogovin is ordered to compile list of groups for a targeted audit.
December 19, 1961	Final draft of the Reuther Memorandum is sent to RFK.
December 20, 1961	Rogovin circulates a list of eighteen conservative groups for the audit; a copy is sent to the attorney general's office.
January 1962	The Reuthers fund the creation of Group Research Inc.
March 1962	RFK signs off on the IRS's audit of right-wing broadcasters.
April 1962	The audit of Billy James Hargis's *Christian Crusade* begins.
July–December 1962	The Polish ham boycott reaches its peak.
Summer of 1963	The Radio Right begins a wave of attacks on the Nuclear Test Ban Treaty.

June 2, 1963	E. William Henry is confirmed as the chairman of the Federal Communications Commission (FCC). JFK tells him that "it is important that stations be kept fair."
July 16, 1963	The FCC's Henry testifies to Congress about tweaking the Fairness Doctrine rules, which are to be "applicable for the 1964 election."
July 26, 1963	The FCC issues a clarification of the Fairness Doctrine explicitly targeting right-wing rhetoric and political positions.
August 7, 1963	JFK, RFK, Walter Reuther, and Democratic National Committee (DNC) Chairman John Bailey create the Citizens Committee for a Nuclear Test Ban.
August 13, 1963	White House tapes record JFK asking for the FCC and IRS to "do something about Life Line."
August 15, 1963	White House aide Myer Feldman drafts memos on *Life Line* and the Radio Right.
August 20, 1963	RFK meets with the IRS's Rogovin and the FCC's E. William Henry at the IRS to ask for an accelerated audit of *Life Line*.
August 21, 1963	The IRS's Rogovin meets with Myer Feldman at the White House. He references a meeting with RFK.
August 22, 1963	The Citizens Committee for a Nuclear Test Ban starts sending threats of Fairness Doctrine complaints to radio stations airing conservative programs.
September 18, 1963	The FCC's Henry establishes the Cullman Doctrine in response to questions about the Fairness Doctrine from Right-wing radio stations.
October 17, 1963	Wayne Phillips is recruited by JFK assistant Kenneth O'Donnell.
January 1964	Phillips meets with Walter Reuther, John Bailey, and O'Donnell to plan an anti–Barry Goldwater Fairness Doctrine campaign.
March 1964	Phillips signs up the Ruder Finn public relations firm to create the National Council for Civic Responsibility. The United Church of Christ files a Fairness Doctrine complaint against station WLBT in Jackson, Mississippi.
July 1964	Charles Brackbill takes charge of the National Council of Churches' counter–Radio Right campaign.
Summer of 1964	Phillips oversees the DNC's anti-Goldwater campaign, ultimately securing 1,700 free broadcasts.
October 1964	The National Council for Civic Responsibility launches an anti-Goldwater ad campaign.
Fall 1964	The National Council of Churches encourages local churches to threaten Fairness Doctrine complaints against radio stations airing conservative programs during election season.
November 1964	The Greater Philadelphia Council of Churches challenges Carl McIntire's purchase of station WXUR in Media, Pennsylvania.

March 1965	McIntire's purchase of station WXUR is approved by the FCC.
May 1965	National Council of Churches representatives meet with the FCC.
December 1965	The Pennsylvania and New Jersey state legislatures censure Carl McIntire.
March 1966	The Greater Philadelphia Council of Churches hires a University of Pennsylvania professor to monitor Carl McIntire. The US Senate Commerce Committee sends Bob Lowe to meet with the National Council of Churches and to ask for help compiling a list of stations airing conservative programs. Lowe says he is "on their side" in regard to McIntire's ownership of WXUR. National Council contacts thousands of radio stations asking whether they air right-wing programming and implying future Senate action against those which do.
May 1966	Bob Lowe meets with the National Council of Churches again and informs them of the FCC's forthcoming (and not yet public) rule changes.
August 1966	The Greater Philadelphia Council of Churches files a Fairness Doctrine complaint against WXUR.
September 1966	The National Council of Churches produces the "EXTREMISM '67" radio ad campaign for the midterm elections.
July 1967	The FCC adds additional enforcement mechanisms to the Fairness Doctrine.
August 1967	Bob Lowe issues a Senate Commerce Committee report on the Radio Right.
September 1967	Everett Parker and the United Church of Christ start a new counter–Radio Right campaign in the West.
Fall of 1967	The United Church of Christ files a Fairness Doctrine complaint against station KAYE in Seattle, Washington.
December 1968	The FCC's hearing examiner finds for McIntire in the WXUR case; the commission overrules him and denies license renewal.
March 1970	The United Church of Christ convinces the FCC to delay the license renewals of all stations in Atlanta, Georgia.
September 1972	McIntire loses his final court appeal over the WXUR license.
July 4, 1973	McIntire holds a protest "funeral" for his last day on WXUR.
January 1975	Ronald Reagan starts a daily radio commentary show called *Viewpoint* on 286 radio stations.

Notes

Chapter 1

1. "West Virginia Polls," box 27, folder "Primary-West Virginia Schedules and Plans," David F. Powers Papers (DFPP), JFK Presidential Library, Boston.
2. Unsigned to David F. Powers, April 12, 1960, box 27, folder "Primary—West Virginia, Background Materials," DFPP.
3. EMK to RFK, January 25, 1960, box 17, folder "1960 Campaign: West Virginia," Lawrence F. O'Brien Papers (LFOP), JFK Presidential Library, Boston.
4. The three stations were WEPM in Martinsburg, WVAR in Richwood, and WKLC in St. Albans.
5. *Internationaletter* 2 (September 1960): 1–2. Published by the International Council of Christian Churches.
6. There is a hole in the historical literature on both conservative and religious broadcasting post–World War II, although there are excellent works covering the early years of radio during the 1920s–1940s, including Matthew Sutton's *Aimee Semple McPherson and the Resurrection of Christian America*, Tona Hangen's *Redeeming the Dial: Radio, Religion, and Popular Culture in America*, Douglas Carl Abrams's *Selling the Old-Time Religion: American Fundamentalists and Mass Culture, 1920–1940*, and chapter 7, "Tuning in the Gospel," in Joel Carpenter, *Revive Us Again: The Reawakening of American Fundamentalism* (Oxford: Oxford University Press, 1997). The standard work on broadcasting history during the period, Erik Barnouw's trilogy, particularly *The Image Empire: A History of Broadcasting in the United States from 1953*, barely mentions conservative broadcasting in the 1950s–1960s and then only to applaud its marginalization.
7. Gary Clabaugh, *Thunder on the Right: The Protestant Fundamentalists* (Chicago: Nelson-Hall, 1974): 91.
8. I have tabulated McIntire's station totals from a list of station payments and from a binder he kept, updated through 1966, listing every station he broadcast on, its frequency, location, and the start and end dates of his relationship with it. I would be glad to make my tabulations available upon request. See "Radio Maps," n.d., box 528, folder 52, Carl McIntire Papers (CMP), Princeton Theological Seminary Library, Princeton, New Jersey; Markku Ruotsila came up with a different total station figure of 619, but that number includes every station McIntire ever aired on at any point in his ministry, whereas my calculation is an attempt to specify how many stations McIntire was on during any given year. See footnote 10 in Markku Ruotsila, *Fighting Fundamentalist: Carl McIntire and the Politicization of American Fundamentalism* (New York: Oxford University Press, 2015): 299–300.

9. Ted Sorenson and Ralph Dungan to John F. Kennedy and Robert F. Kennedy, "Memorandum: Religion in West Virginia—Possible Approaches," April 18, 1960, Papers of John F. Kennedy, Pre-Presidential Papers, Presidential Campaign Files, 1960, http://www.jfklibrary.org/Asset-Viewer/Archives/JFKCAMP1960-0997-013.aspx.

10. "Election of 1960," The American Presidency Project, University of California, Santa Barbara, http://www.presidency.ucsb.edu/showelection.php?year=1960.

11. "The Radical Right in America Today," December 19, 1961, box 63, folder "Reuther Memorandum," Robert F. Kennedy Attorney General Papers (RFKP), John F. Kennedy Presidential Library, Boston, MA.

12. Ibid.

13. Ibid. The memorandum cites James Reston, "San Francisco: How the New Conservatives Help Kennedy," New York Times, November 19, 1961: E8 in re the "Republican problem."

14. Jonathan Schoenwald, A Time for Choosing: The Rise of Modern American Conservatism (New York: Oxford University Press, 2002): 96–97; Don Critchlow, The Conservative Ascendancy: How the GOP Right Made Political History (Cambridge, MA: Harvard University Press, 2007): 63–64; there is a substantial treatment of the IRS component of the counter-Right campaign in John A. Andrew, The Power to Destroy: The Political Uses of the IRS from Kennedy to Nixon (Lanham, MD: Ivan R. Dee, 2002).

15. Heather Hendershot, What's Fair on the Air? Cold War Right-Wing Broadcasting and the Public Interest (Chicago: University of Chicago Press, 2011). My interest in conservative broadcasting began as a master's student at Temple University when I stumbled across an article version of one of Hendershot's book chapters. I owe her a deep intellectual debt. See Heather Hendershot, "God's Angriest Man: Carl McIntire, Cold War Fundamentalism, and Right-Wing Broadcasting," American Quarterly 59 (June 2007): 373–396.

16. For example, see Laura Wittern-Keller, Freedom of the Screen: Legal Challenges to State Film Censorship, 1915–1981 (Lexington: University Press of Kentucky, 2008); Robert Hilliard and Michael Keith, Dirty Discourse: Sex and Indecency in Broadcasting (Hoboken, NJ: Wiley-Blackwell, 2006).

17. Nicole Hemmer, Messengers of the Right: Conservative Media and the Transformation of American Politics (Philadelphia: University of Pennsylvania Press, 2016): 67; Nicole Hemmer, "Messengers of the Right: Media and the Modern Conservative Movement" (PhD diss., Columbia University, 2010).

18. Theodore Sorensen, Kennedy (New York: Harper and Row, 1965); Arthur Schlesinger, A Thousand Days: John F. Kennedy in the White House (Boston: Houghton Mifflin, 1965).

19. Thomas Reeves, A Question of Character: A Life of John F. Kennedy (New York: Free Press, 1991): 331–332.

20. Nick Bryant, The Bystander: John F. Kennedy and the Struggle for Black Equality (New York: Basic Books, 2006); David Niven, The Politics of Injustice: The Kennedys, the Freedom Rides, and the Electoral Consequences of a Moral Compromise

(Knoxville: University of Tennessee Press, 2003); Jonathan Rosenberg and Zachary Karabell, *Kennedy, Johnson, and the Quest for Justice* (New York: W. W. Norton, 2003); David Garrow, *The FBI and Martin Luther King, Jr.* (New York: Penguin Books, 1983); James Hilty, *Robert Kennedy: Brother Protector* (Philadelphia: Temple University Press, 2000); Larry Tye, *Bobby Kennedy: The Making of a Liberal Icon* (New York: Random House, 2016).

21. Victor Navasky, *Kennedy Justice* (New York: Atheneum, 1971): 435–439.

22. Tye, *Bobby Kennedy*, 165–186.

23. James Giglio, *The Presidency of John F. Kennedy* (Lawrence: University Press of Kansas, 1991); Michael O'Brien, *Rethinking Kennedy: An Interpretive Biography* (Chicago: Ivan R. Dee, 2009); Richard Reeves, *President Kennedy: Profile of Power* (New York: Simon & Schuster, 1994); Robert Dallek, *An Unfinished Life: John F. Kennedy, 1917–1963* (New York: Back Bay Books, 2003).

24. Peter Ling, *John F. Kennedy* (New York: Routledge, 2013): 265.

25. Theodor Adorno, *The Authoritarian Personality* (New York: American Jewish Committee, 1950); Daniel Bell, *The Radical Right* (Garden City, NY: Doubleday, 1963). It was a revision of Bell's 1955 collection *The New American Right*, which had been meant as a postmortem on the Second Red Scare; Richard Hofstadter, *The Paranoid Style in American Politics and Other Essays* (New York: Knopf, 1966); there was a large body of popular literature in the 1960s sponsored by liberal organizations that adopted the status anxiety framework to advance partisan interests. For example, see Benjamin Epstein and Arnold Foster, *The Radical Right: Report on the John Birch Society and Its Allies* (New York: Random House, 1967). Also see Seymour Lipset and Earl Raab, *The Politics of Unreason: Right-Wing Extremism in America, 1790–1970* (New York: Harper and Row, 1970).

26. Alan Brinkley, "AHR Forum: The Problem of American Conservatism," *American Historical Review* 99, no. 2 (April 1994): 409–429.

27. Jerome Himmelstein, *To the Right: The Transformation of American Conservatism* (Berkeley: University of California Press, 1992): 3.

28. Lisa McGirr, *Suburban Warriors: The Origins of the New American Right* (Princeton, NJ: Princeton University Press, 2002): 7.

29. Though the status anxiety perspective may be making a comeback in the aftermath of the 2016 election. For example, Thomas B. Edsall, "The Paranoid Style in American Politics Is Back," *New York Times*, September 8, 2016, http://www.nytimes.com/2016/09/08/opinion/campaign-stops/the-paranoid-style-in-american-politics-is-back.html?_r=0.

30. Thomas Frank, *What's the Matter with Kansas? How Conservatives Won the Heart of America* (New York: Holt Paperbacks, 2005).

31. Janell Ross, "Obama Revives His 'Cling to Guns or Religion' Analysis—for Donald Trump Supporters," *Washington Post*, December 21, 2015, https://www.washingtonpost.com/news/the-fix/wp/2015/12/21/obama-dusts-off-his-cling-to-guns-or-religion-idea-for-donald-trump/.

32. Donald T. Critchlow and Nancy MacLean, *Debating the American Conservative Movement, 1945 to the Present* (New York: Rowman and Littlefield, 2009): vii–viii.

33. Lisa McGirr, *Suburban Warriors: The Origins of the New American Right* (Princeton, NJ: Princeton University Press, 2002); Darren Dochuk, *From Bible Belt to Sunbelt: Plain-Folk Religion, Grassroots Politics, and the Rise of Evangelical Conservatism* (New York: W. W. Norton, 2012); Edward Miller, *Nut Country: Right-Wing Dallas and the Birth of the Southern Strategy* (Chicago: University of Chicago Press, 2015).

34. Nancy MacLean, "Guardians of Privilege," in *Debating the American Conservative Movement, 1945 to the Present*, ed. Donald T. Critchlow and Nancy MacLean (New York: Rowman and Littlefield, 2009): 125–126.

35. Bethany Moreton, *To Serve God and Wal-Mart: The Making of Christian Free Enterprise* (Cambridge, MA: Harvard University Press, 2010); Kim Phillips-Fein, *Invisible Hands: The Businessmen's Crusade against the New Deal* (New York: W. W. Norton, 2010); Kevin Kruse, *One Nation under God: How Corporate America Invented Christian America* (New York: Basic Books, 2015); Benjamin Waterhouse, *Lobbying America: The Politics of Business from Nixon to NAFTA* (Princeton, NJ: Princeton University Press, 2013); Julian Zelizer and Kim Phillips-Fein, eds., *What's Good for Business: Business and Politics since World War II* (New York: Oxford University Press, 2012); Kathryn Olmstead, *Right Out of California: The 1930s and the Big Business Roots of Modern Conservatism* (New York: New Press, 2015).

36. I have borrowed this supply-demand framework from the "religious economies" model of religious adherence. The best entry point into that sociology of religion literature is Roger Finke and Rodney Stark, *The Churching of America, 1776–2005: Winners and Losers in Our Religious Economy* (New Brunswick, NJ: Rutgers University Press, 2005) and *Acts of Faith: Explaining the Human Side of Religion* (Berkeley: University of California Press, 2000).

37. Heather Hendershot uses a different metaphor to describe broadcasters' role in the New Right. They "till[ed] the ground for the electoral rejection of the Great Society and the eventual triumph of Reagan." Hendershot, *What's Fair on the Air?*, 7.

38. Critchlow, *The Conservative Ascendancy*, 76.

39. See chapter 4 of Daniel K. Williams, *Defenders of the Unborn: The Pro-Life Movement Before Roe v. Wade* (New York: Oxford University Press, 2016); Lou Cannon, *Governor Reagan: His Rise to Power* (New York: Public Affairs, 2003); Donald Critchlow, *Phyllis Schlafly and Grassroots Conservatism: A Woman's Crusade* (Princeton, NJ: Princeton University Press, 2008).

40. Elizabeth Tandy Shermer, ed., *Barry Goldwater and the Remaking of the American Political Landscape* (Tucson: University of Arizona Press, 2013): 1.

41. David Farber, *The Rise and Fall of Modern American Conservatism: A Short History* (Princeton, NJ: Princeton University Press, 2012): 5, 106; Robert Goldberg, *Barry Goldwater* (New Haven, CT: Yale University Press, 1997): x.

42. Rick Perlstein, *Before the Storm: Barry Goldwater and the Unmaking of the American Consensus* (New York: Nation Books, 2009): xv.

43. Nicole Hemmer, "The Dealers and the Darling: Conservative Media and the Candidacy of Barry Goldwater," in *Barry Goldwater and the Remaking of the American Political Landscape*, ed. Elizabeth Tandy Shermer (Tucson: University of Arizona Press, 2013): 114–143.

44. Shermer, *Barry Goldwater*, 4; John Micklethwait and Adrian Wooldridge, *The Right Nation: Conservative Power in America* (New York: Penguin Books, 2005); Godfrey Hodgson, *The World Turned Right Side Up: A History of the Conservative Ascendancy in America* (Boston: Houghton Mifflin, 1996).

45. Jonathan Schoenwald, *A Time for Choosing: The Rise of Modern American Conservatism* (New York: Oxford University Press, 2001).

46. Farber, *Rise and Fall*, 40.

47. William F. Buckley, "Our Mission Statement," *National Review*, November 19, 1955, http://www.nationalreview.com/article/223549/our-mission-statement-william-f-buckley-jr.

48. George H. Nash, *The Conservative Intellectual Movement in America Since 1945* (New York: Basic Books, 1976): xiii, xvii, 134–135. The book has since been reprinted by Intercollegiate Studies Institute, a conservative advocacy group of which William F. Buckley was once president; see also Bruce Frohnen, Jeremy Beer, and Jeffrey Nelson, eds., *American Conservatism: An Encyclopedia* (Wilmington, DE: Intercollegiate Studies Institute, 2006). You will find nary a mention of major conservative broadcasters, but you will find individual entries for each of Buckley's major publications; Nash also inspired Jerome Himmelstein, *To the Right: The Transformation of American Conservatism* (Oakland: University of California Press, 1992): 7; Paul Weyrich, "Blue Collar or Blue Blood?," in Robert Whitaker, *The New Right Papers* (New York: St. Martin's Press, 1982).

49. Heather Hendershot, "God's Angriest Man: Carl McIntire, Cold War Fundamentalism, and Right-Wing Broadcasting," *American Quarterly* 59, no. 2 (June 2007): 385, 390;

50. Rick Perlstein, "I Thought I Understood the American Right. Trump Proved Me Wrong," *New York Times*, April 11, 2017, https://www.nytimes.com/2017/04/11/magazine/i-thought-i-understood-the-american-right-trump-proved-me-wrong.html

51. The Radio Right should be studied along with other radical Right factions outside the Buckley-defined "mainstream." See George Hawley, *Right-Wing Critics of American Conservatism* (Lawrence: University Press of Kansas, 2016).

52. Schoenwald, *A Time for Choosing*, 98.

53. George Will quoted in Richard Brookhiser, *Right Time, Right Place: Coming of Age with William F. Buckley Jr. and the Conservative Movement* (New York: Basic Books, 2011): 1. It is notable that Brookhiser's first encounter with Buckley came while watching Buckley's television program, *Firing Line*, which began airing in 1966.

54. "Publications on the Right," box 492, folder 1, Group Research Inc. Records, 1955–1996 (GRI), Columbia University Libraries, New York City; Gary Clabaugh, *Thunder on the Right: The Protestant Fundamentalists* (Chicago: Nelson-Hall, 1974): 91.

55. There is a growing literature that attempts to do just that, starting with Leonard Moore's response to Alan Brinkley's 1994 article calling for more work on conservatism. Moore suggested that scholars respond with more social history of the New Right rather than more work on conservative leaders and intellectuals. See Leonard J. Moore, "Good Old-Fashioned New Social History and the Twentieth-Century

American Right," *Reviews in American History* 24 (December 1996): 555–573; David Farber and Jeff Roche, eds., *The Conservative Sixties* (New York: Peter Lang, 2003); D. J. Mulloy, *The World of the John Birch Society: Conspiracy, Conservatism, and the Cold War* (Nashville: Vanderbilt University Press, 2014); Williams, *Defenders of the Unborn*; Schoenwald, *A Time for Choosing*.

56. For a more detailed, blow-by-blow account from McIntire's perspective, see Patrick Farabaugh, "Carl McIntire and His Crusade against the Fairness Doctrine" (PhD diss., Pennsylvania State University, 2010).

57. Michael Lienesch, *Redeeming America: Piety and Politics in the New Christian Right* (Chapel Hill: University of North Carolina Press, 1993); Ruth Murray Brown, *For a Christian America: A History of the Religious Right* (New York: Prometheus Books, 2002); see chapter 10 of Laura Kalman, *Right Star Rising: A New Politics, 1974–1980* (New York: W. W. Norton, 2010).

58. "Born Again! The Evangelicals," *Newsweek,* October 25, 1976. The Google Ngram of "New Christian Right" and "Religious Right" shows a massive increase in usage starting in 1977.

59. Dochuk, *From Bible Belt to Sunbelt*, xxii. Dochuk references Jon Butler's influential article, "Jack-in-the-Box Faith: The Religion Problem in Modern American History," *Journal of American History* 90 (March 2004): 1357–1378.

60. James Davison Hunter, *Evangelicalism: The Coming Generation* (Chicago: University of Chicago Press, 1987).

Chapter 2

1. Paul Matzko, "Radio Politics, Origin Myths, and the Creation of New Evangelicalism," *Fides et Historia* 48, no. 1 (Winter/Spring 2016): 61–90; Elizabeth Fones-Wolf, *Waves of Opposition: Labor and the Struggle for Democratic Radio* (Urbana: University of Illinois Press, 2006).

2. Christopher Sterling and John Michael Kittross, *Stay Tuned: A History of American Broadcasting* (Mahway, NJ: Lawrence Erlbaum Associates, 2002): 283, 349, 862.

3. *Christian Beacon* 13, no. 11 (April 22, 1948): 1. *Christian Beacon* 13, no. 1 (February 12, 1948): 4.

4. I have tabulated McIntire's station totals from a list of station payments and from a binder he kept, updated through 1966, listing every station he broadcast on, its frequency, location, and the start and end dates of his relationship with it. I would be glad to make my tabulations available upon request. See "Radio Maps," n.d., box 528, folder 52, CMP; Markku Ruotsila came up with a different total station figure of 619, but that number includes every station McIntire ever aired on at any point in his ministry, whereas my calculation is an attempt to specify how many stations McIntire was on in any given year. See footnote #10 in Ruotsila, *Fighting Fundamentalist*, 299–300.

5. "International Radio Network of Evangelist Billy James Hargis," *Christian Crusade Magazine,* October 1960: 13. Hardbound annual copies in box 4, folder 51, BJHP; Gary K. Clabaugh, *Thunder on the Right: The Protestant Fundamentalists* (Chicago: Nelson-Hall, 1974): 101.

6. "Seventh Anniversary Progress Report: The Manion Forum," box 541, folder 5, CMP.

7. Arnold Forster and Benjamin Epstein, *Danger on the Right: The Attitudes, Personnel and Influence of the Radical Right and Extreme Conservatives* (New York: Random House, 1964): 136–137.

8. "Publications on the Right," box 492, folder 1, GRI. Group Research head Wesley McCune compiled the circulation statistics mostly from nonprofit tax forms. Using the same data, by 1965 combined circulation had swelled to nearly eight hundred thousand.

9. Clabaugh, *Thunder on the Right*, 91.

10. Nicole Hemmer, "The Dealers and the Darling: Conservative Media and the Candidacy of Barry Goldwater," in *Barry Goldwater and the Remaking of the American Political Landscape,* ed. Elizabeth Tandy Shermer (Tucson: University of Arizona Press, 2013): 127.

11. George Thayer, *The Farther Shores of Politics: The American Political Fringe Today* (New York: Simon and Schuster, 1967): 147.

12. Ibid., 157.

13. Mary C. Brennan, *Turning Right in the Sixties: The Conservative Capture of the GOP* (Chapel Hill: University of North Carolina Press, 2007): 13; see also Thomas Frank and David Mulcahey, *Boob Jubilee: The Cultural Politics of the New Economy* (New York: W. W. Norton, 2003): 350, who inaccurately dismiss the boycott as the product of a John Birch Society front group; despite most of the archival material about the boycott coming from the papers of Carl McIntire, it receives only the briefest mention in Markku Ruotsila's otherwise comprehensive and excellent biography. Markku Ruotsila, *Fighting Fundamentalist: Carl McIntire and the Politicization of American Fundamentalism* (New York: Oxford, 2015).

14. "Threats of Boycotts Force Many Stores to Drop Red Imports," *Journal of Physical Therapeutics* 2, no. 2 (March/April 1963): 22.

15. R. J. Crampton, *Eastern Europe in the Twentieth Century—And After*, 2nd ed. (New York: Routledge, 1997): 255–325.

16. John F. Kennedy, "Remarks of Senator John F. Kennedy at the Annual Awards Dinner of the Overseas Press Club," speech, New York City, May 6, 1957, John F. Kennedy Library, http://www.jfklibrary.org/Research/Research-Aids/JFK-Speeches/Overseas-Press-Club-NYC_19570506.aspx.

17. Henry W. Brands, "Redefining the Cold War: American Policy toward Yugoslavia, 1948–1960," *Diplomatic History* 11 (January 1987): 49, 52.

18. David Mayers, *George Kennan and the Dilemmas of US Foreign Policy* (New York: Oxford University Press, 1988): 212.

19. "Memorandum from the Executive Secretary of the Department of State (Battle) to the President's Special Assistant for National Security Affairs (Bundy)," in *Foreign Relations of the United States, 1961–1963,* vol. 26, *Eastern Europe; Cyprus; Greece; Turkey,* ed. James E. Miller and Glenn W. LaFantasie (Washington, DC: US Government Printing Office, 1994): 120; Eugene A. Theroux, "Congress and the Question of Most Favored Nation Status for the People's Republic of China," *Catholic University Law Review* 23 (Fall 1973): 36.

20. Louis Fischer, "Oral History Interview with George F. Kennan," in *Interviews with George F. Kennan*, ed. T. Christopher Jesperson (Jackson: University Press of Mississippi, 2002): 75.

21. Card, "Communist-Made Products," n.d., box 3, folder 12, CMP,. You can view an alternate version of the flier in card form at http://historiansworkshop.richmond.edu/items/show/222.

22. "Transcript of President John F. Kennedy's Inaugural Address," Washington, DC (January 20, 1961), https://www.ourdocuments.gov/doc.php?doc=91&page=transcript.

23. "F.H.D's around the Town," *Nashua Telegraph,* December 4, 1962: 4.

24. "TCTWOTAOCMOTLBS," *Newsweek,* December 3, 1962: 93–94; "Organizations: The Card Caper," *Time Magazine,* December 21, 1962: 23.

25. Obituary, "Dr. Jerome D. 'Jerry' Harold," *Ammen Family Cremation and Funeral Care,* http://www.afcfcare.com/obits/obituaries.php/obitID/1580. Florida Bible College was founded in 1962 by A. Ray Stanford, a Youth for Christ organizer and the pastor of Grove Community Church in Miami.

26. Card, "Communist-Made Products," n.d., box 3, folder 12, CMP.

27. Qtd. in Joseph Sullivan, "Threats of Boycotts Force Many Stores to Drop Red Imports," *Wall Street Journal,* December 20, 1962: 1.

28. Pamphlet, "The Shoppers Guide to Communist Imports," Committee to Warn of the Arrival of Communist Merchandise on the Local Business Scene, n.d., box 3, folder 1, Craig T. Sheldon Papers (CSP), Alabama Department of Archives and History, Montgomery, Alabama, http://digital.archives.alabama.gov/cdm/singleitem/collection/voices/id/2005/rec/4.

29. "The Bullet That Killed Your Son," Citizens Committee to Warn of Communist Imports, box 3, folder 15, CMP; Note, "F. Skrudland," n.d., stapled to Krakus advertisement, box 3, folder 2, CMP.

30. Edward S. Kaplan, *American Trade Policy: 1923–1995* (Westport, CT: Greenwood Press, 1996): 68–75.

31. James Reston, "What Ever Happened to Smoot and Hawley?," *New York Times,* January 26, 1962: 30; on Reston's ties to the Kennedy administration, see Stephen Kinzer, *The Brothers: John Foster Dulles, Allen Dulles, and Their Secret World War* (New York: Henry Holt and Company, 2013).

32. "Threats of Boycotts Force Many Stores to Drop Red Imports," *Journal of Physical Therapeutics,* 2, no. 2 (March/April 1963): 22.

33. "Foe of Card Campaign Didn't Lose Customers," *Alton Evening Telegraph,* November 14, 1962: 1.

34. Estrellita Capo to Carl McIntire, August 22, 1962, box 3, folder 14, CMP.

35. *Christian Beacon,* July 2, 1962: 1–2, 4; *Christian Beacon,* December 6, 1962: 2, 8; "Foe of Card Campaign Didn't Lose Customers," *Alton Evening Telegraph,* November 14, 1962: 1; Dale Crowley Jr. to Carl McIntire, September 21, 1962, box 3, folder 14, CMP.

36. C. Calvin Struth to Carl McIntire, July 20, 1962, box 3, folder 14, CMP.

37. Jack Cooper to Carl McIntire, September 18, 1962, box 3, folder 14, CMP.

38. Jerome D. Harold to Carl McIntire, October 22, 1965, box 3, folder 2, CMP.

39. You can see an example stapled to Dale Crowley Jr. to Carl McIntire, December 21, 1962, box 3, folder 14, CMP; "The Card Caper," *Time Magazine*, December 21, 1962: 23; while Polish ham boycotters were placing cards warning of Communist products in 1962, in the mid-1950s the owner of a small supermarket chain in New York had placed signs next to his own merchandise warning customers of which products might aid the spread of Communism. Kathryn Montgomery, *Target Prime Time: Advocacy Groups and the Struggle over Entertainment Television* (New York: Oxford University Press, 1989): 14.

40. Joseph Sullivan, "Threats of Boycotts Force Many Stores to Drop Red Imports," *Wall Street Journal*, December 20, 1962: 1.

41. "Bullock's Sues Anti-Red Merchandise Campaign," *Long Beach Press-Telegram*, January 10, 1963.

42. "Foe of Card Campaign Didn't Lose Customers," *Alton Evening Telegraph*, November 14, 1962: 1.

43. "The Card Caper," *Time Magazine*, December 21, 1962: 23.

44. "Foe of Card Campaign Didn't Lose Customers," *Alton Evening Telegraph*, November 14, 1962: 1.

45. Ibid.

46. Mrs. Roy B. Cook to Carl McIntire, September 23, 1967, box 3, folder 11, CMP; "Burning Communist-Made Baskets," *Atlanta Journal*, November 16, 1962: 9.

47. As opposed to the usual, made-in-America taste of aluminum, I suppose. H. D. Bamper to Anheuser Busch, February 15, 1964, box 3, folder 13, CMP.

48. Doug Heinsohn to George Morse, July 24, 1962, box 3, folder 14, CMP.

49. Millie Sakewicz to Carl McIntire, November 30, 1962, box 3, folder 14, CMP.

50. "Furlough Tip Wins $5," *Delaware County Daily Times*, August 26, 1963: 11. The Mrs. Mildred Sakewicz in the article shared a home address with the Mrs. Millie Sakewicz who wrote the letter to McIntire; she had previously contacted the paper in 1960 with a tip but failed to win more than a runners-up commendation. See "Daily Times Tips Contest," *Delaware County Daily Times*, July 4, 1960: 17.

51. Millie Sakewicz to Carl McIntire, November 30, 1962, box 3, folder 14, CMP; Consumer Price Index Inflation Calculator, US Department of Labor, Bureau of Labor Statistics, http://www.bls.gov/data/inflation_calculator.htm.

52. Joseph Sullivan, "Threats of Boycotts Force Many Stores to Drop Red Imports," *Wall Street Journal*, December 20, 1962: 1.

53. Bernard Gwertzman, "Poles Expect $5 Million Loss to Trade Boycott," *(Washington) Evening Star*, February 2, 1963: D6.

54. "Movement against Trade with Reds Grow," *Wanderer* (?), November 25, 1963. Copy in box 3, folder 13, CMP; "F.H.D's Around the Town," *Nashua Telegraph*, December 4, 1962: 4; Mrs. F. W. Sullinger to [Carl McIntire], December 18, 1962, box 3, folder 14, CMP. See attached letters from retailers, several of which are cited in the next footnote; for A&P figures, see William Walsh, *The Rise and Decline of I Great Atlantic and Pacific Tea Company* (Secaucus, NJ: Lyle Stuart, 1986): 90–91. The early 1960s were an inflection point for A&P, and it is interesting to hypothesize that the boycott played a role in the rather sudden decline of America's largest retailer.

55. "Sale of Red Items Urged, Store Says," *San Diego Union,* April 2, 1963: A12; Linda Morse to Jess Miniger, August 13, 1962, box 3, folder 14, CMP; Robert Greenburg to Mr. and Mrs. Thomas J. Snyder, September 25, 1962, ibid; Frank Stuckey to M. H. Hays, September 19, 1962, ibid; G. P. Fleming to Mr. and Mrs. Thomas J. Snyder, September 28, 1962, ibid.

56. "Ordinances Restricting the Sale of 'Communist Goods,'" *Columbia Law Review* 65 (February 1965): 310–311.

57. Chris Haire, "Gospel Swamp: A Legacy of Religion in Fountain Valley," *Orange County Register,* April 25, 2013, http://www.ocregister.com/articles/church-505577-valley-community.html; Jerry Hicks, "Shaping the Future," *Orange Coast Magazine,* September 2007: 160–164; Darren Dochuk, *From Bible Belt to Sunbelt: Plain-Folk Religion, Grassroots Politics, and the Rise of Evangelical Conservatism* (New York: W. W. Norton, 2011); "$1,000 License Required to Sell Red-Made Goods," *Los Angeles Times,* March 5, 1963: 22.

58. "$1,000 License Required to Sell Red-Made Goods," *Los Angeles Times,* March 5, 1963: 22; Paul Weeks, "Red-Made Products License Fee: $1,000," *Miami Herald,* March 10, 1963: 46A. The two articles give different business statistics, but the lower number appears to include only stores within city limits, while the higher number includes both fruit stands and stores in the surrounding area.

59. "Ordinances Restricting the Sale of 'Communist Goods,'" *Columbia Law Review* 65 (February 1965): 311. Also the source for the starred ordinances in Figure 2.2.

60. "Threats of Boycotts Force Many Stores to Drop Red Imports," *Journal of Physical Therapeutics,* 2, no. 2 (March/April 1963): 22.

61. "Todd Suspends Nearly ¾ Million Pounds of Foreign Meats," *Alabama Farmers' Bulletin* 31 (May 15, 1964): 1; "A.W. Todd: 1955–1959, 1963–1967, 1991–1995," Alabama Department of Archives and History, http://www.archives.alabama.gov/conoff/awtodd.html.

62. "Drive to Stop Buying Red Goods Hurts Communist Nations," *The Courier-Journal* (Louisville, Kentucky), February 19, 1963: 10.

63. Fifty-six years later this same legislation would be used to justify raising tariffs on imports from countries like Germany, China, and Canada by the Donald Trump administration. Ironically, the "national security" clause meant by the bill authors to justify lowering tariffs in the midst of the Cold War would be used for the opposite purpose after the Cold War was over. Jacob M. Schlesinger and William Mauldin, "Trump to Revive 1962 Law to Explore New Barriers on Steel Imports," *Wall Street Journal,* April 20, 2017, https://www.wsj.com/articles/trump-to-revive-1962-law-to-explore-new-barriers-on-steel-imports-1492661339.

64. Edward S. Kaplan, *American Trade Policy: 1923–1995* (Westport, CT: Greenwood Press, 1996): 68–75; David Mayers, *George Kennan and the Dilemmas of US Foreign Policy* (New York: Oxford University Press, 1988): 213.

65. Fischer, "Oral History Interview with George F. Kennan," 77.

66. Press Conference, John F. Kennedy, "546—The President's News Conference," December 12, 1962, http://www.presidency.ucsb.edu/ws/?pid=9054.

67. Alan P. Dobson, *US Economic Statecraft for Survival, 1933–1991* (New York: Routledge, 2003): 166.

68. "Ordinances Restricting the Sale of 'Communist Goods,'" *Columbia Law Review* 65 (February 1965): 312.

69. Dan T. Carter, *The Politics of Rage: George Wallace, the Origins of the New Conservatism, and the Transformation of American Politics* (Baton Rouge: Louisiana State University Press, 2000); Kevin Kruse, *White Flight: Atlanta and the Making of Modern Conservatism* (Princeton, NJ: Princeton University Press, 2005); Joseph Crespino, *In Search of Another Country: Mississippi and the Conservative Counterrevolution* (Princeton, NJ: Princeton University Press, 2009).

70. Michelle Nickerson, *Mothers of Conservatism: Women and the Postwar Right* (Princeton, NJ: Princeton University Press, 2012); Lisa McGirr, *Suburban Warriors: The Origins of the New American Right* (Princeton, NJ: Princeton University Press, 2002); William Martin, *With God on Our Side: The Rise of the Religious Right in America* (New York: Broadway Books, 2005); Donald Critchlow, *Phyllis Schlafly and Grassroots Conservatism: A Woman's Crusade* (Princeton, NJ: Princeton University Press, 2005); June Benowitz, *Challenge and Change: Right-Wing Women, Grassroots Activism, and the Baby Boom Generation* (Gainesville: University Press of Florida, 2015); Mary Brennan, *Wives, Mothers, and the Red Menace: Conservative Women and the Crusade against Communism* (Boulder: University Press of Colorado, 2008).

71. When citing boycotters, I have decided to defer to their own choice of honorific in recognition of that fact.

72. *Maude*, "The Grass Story," directed by Bill Hobin, written by Gordon Farr and Arnold Kane, CBS, December 5, 1972.

73. Betty Friedan, *The Feminine Mystique* (New York: W. W. Norton, 1997): 61. The first edition was published in February 1963; for more on the significance of the *Feminine Mystique*, see Stephanie Coontz, *A Strange Stirring: The Feminine Mystique and American Women at the Dawn of the 1960s* (New York: Basic Books, 2011).

74. Lizabeth Cohen, *A Consumers' Republic: The Politics of Mass Consumption in Postwar America* (New York: Vintage Books, 2003): 8, 35–38, 367–370. Cohen exclusively focuses on liberal female-led boycotts, but the principles she outlines apply equally to the Polish ham boycott.

75. Technically, the phrase "seal of approval" wasn't used. Instead, the seal said "Good Housekeeping Guaranteed." But it was commonly called a "seal of approval" and since that was the language used by the boycotter that is what I will go with here. For an example, see Krakus advertisement, box 3, folder 2, CMP.

76. Betty Friedan, "Women Are People, Too!," *Good Housekeeping*, August 9, 2010, http://www.goodhousekeeping.com/life/career/advice/a18890/1960-betty-friedan-article/.

77. Wade H. Nichols to Mrs. Alice J. Miller, September 5, 1962, box 3, folder 14, CMP.

78. See chapter 5, Adam Laats, *The Other School Reformers: Conservative Activism in American Education* (Cambridge, MA: Harvard University Press, 2015); see chapter 5, William Martin, *With God on Our Side: The Rise of the Religious Right in America* (New York: Broadway Books, 2005); see chapter 3, Michelle Nickerson, *Mothers of Conservatism*.

79. Memorandum, Myer Feldman, "Right-Wing Groups," August 15, 1963: 5, box 106, folder "Right Wing Movement, Part I," John F. Kennedy Presidential Papers;

Memorandum, Myer Feldman, "Financial Scope of the American Right-Wing," August 1963: 5, box 106, folder "Right Wing Movement, Part I," JFKP.

80. "Station KFDI, Wichita, KS," April 1965, "Station KFAX, San Francisco, CA, September 1964," box 526, folders 9 and 26, CMP.

81. "Correspondence Chronologically Arranged, July 1959–December 1960, Showing Check Donations," box 25, folders 12–13, CMP. Author's tabulation available upon request.

82. Mrs. Lila Hughes to Carl McIntire, December 9, 1960, box 25, folder 13, CMP.

83. Jeanne C. Thomas to Carl McIntire, July 19, 1962, box 3, folder 14, CMP.

84. Estrellita Capo to Carl McIntire, August 22, 1962, box 3, folder 14, CMP.

85. Dale Crowley Jr. to Carl McIntyre [sic], September 21, 1962, box 3, folder 14, CMP.

86. Jeanne C. Thomas to Carl McIntire, July 19, 1962, box 3, folder 14, CMP; see also C. Calvin Struth to Carl McIntire, July 20, 1962, box 3, folder 14, CMP; see over-view of "Willis E. Stone Papers, 1955–1982," University of Oregon Libraries, Special Collections and University Archives, Eugene, OR, http://archiveswest.orbiscascade.org/ark:/80444/xv22930.

87. Each of the listed authors encouraged the inclusion of conservative social movements as objects of analysis. Kathleen Blee and Kimberly Creasap, "Conservative and Right-Wing Movements," *Annual Review of Sociology* 36 (2010): 269–286; Kathleen Blee, "Ethnographies of the Far Right," *Journal of Contemporary Ethnography* 36 (2007): 119–128; Nelson Pichardo, "New Social Movements: A Critical Review," *Annual Review of Sociology* 23 (1997): 411–430; David Dietrich, "Rebellious Conservatives: Social Movements in Defense of Privilege" (PhD diss., Duke University, 2011).

88. Charles Tilly and Sidney Tarrow, *Contentious Politics*, 2nd ed. (New York: Oxford University Press, 2015): 120; Tilly's original work on resource mobilization came in a series of influential articles in the 1970s. There is a useful overview by John McCarthy and Mayer Zald, "Resource Mobilization and Social Movements: A Partial Theory," *American Journal of Sociology* 82 (May 1977): 1212–1241.

89. Pamela E. Oliver and Gerald Marwell, "Mobilizing Technologies for Collective Action," in *Frontiers in Social Movement Theory,* ed. Aldon D. Morris and Carol McClurg Mueller (New Haven, CT: Yale University Press, 1992): 251–272. Oliver and Marwell use "technology" in its cultural sense rather than material sense, but in this case the physical piece of technology—the radio—enabled the development of a new recipe of knowledge for increasing movement outreach and fundraising. Technology can beget "technology."

90. Elizabeth Gillespie McRae, *Mothers of Massive Resistance: White Women and the Politics of White Supremacy* (New York: Oxford University Press, 2018).

91. Joseph Crespino, "Goldwater in Dixie: Race, Region, and the Rise of the Right," in *Barry Goldwater and the Remaking of the American Political Landscape*, ed. Elizabeth Tandy Shermer (Tucson: University of Arizona Press, 2013): 146–147. Crespino splits the baby between the backlash thesis and its critics. See also Joseph Crespino, *In Search of Another Country: Mississippi and the Conservative Counterrevolution* (Princeton, NJ: Princeton University Press, 2009).

92. Michele Margolis, *From Politics to the Pews: How Partisanship and the Political Environment Shape Religious Identity* (Chicago: University of Chicago Press, 2018).

93. Kevin Phillips, *The Emerging Republican Majority* (New York: Arlington House, 1969).

94. *Christian Beacon* 5, no. 41 (November 28, 1940): 8.

95. "Student Survey (Filled Out)," (ca. 1925), box 304, folder 5, CMP.

96. Carl McIntire to Senator Tom Connally, July 30, 1948, box 652, folder 5, CMP.

97. Roy Reed, *Faubus: The Life and Times of an American Prodigal* (Fayetteville: University of Arkansas Press, 1999).

98. Carl McIntire to Governor Faubus, September 23, 1958, box 158, folder 6, CMP.

99. Emmetta Germaine to Carl McIntire, October 4, 1958, box 28, folder 7, CMP; Carl McIntire to Emmetta Germaine, October 7, 1958, box 28, folder 7, CMP.

100. "For Stricken Governor, A McIntire Serenade," *Philadelphia Daily News*, May 17, 1972: 4.

101. Strom Thurmond to Carl McIntire, March 6, 1964, Carl McIntire to Strom Thurmond, March 19, 1964, Carl McIntire to Strom Thurmond, April 3, 1964, Strom Thurmond to Carl McIntire, May 7, 1964, Strom Thurmond to Carl McIntire, December 18, 1964, box 243, folder 7, CMP.

102. "Certificate Signed by George Wallace," July 20, 1971, folder 6, box 634, CMP; "George C. Wallace Speech," August 1, 1969, folder 46, box 4, BJHP; Donald Janson, "Wallace Publicly Backs Hargis' Christian Crusade," *Courier-Journal & Times*, August 3, 1969: n.p.

103. "Open Letter to Martin Luther King," May 25, 1964, box 179, folder 1, CMP.

104. Carl McIntire, "Your Land Is Full of Violence: On the Assassination of Martin Luther King," box 547, folder 18, CMP.

105. The formal backlash literature includes Mary Edsall and Thomas Edsall, *Chain Reaction: The Impact of Race, Rights, and Taxes on American Politics* (New York: W. W. Norton, 1992); Jeremy Mayer, *Running on Race: Racial Politics in Presidential Campaigns* (New York: Random House, 2002); Kari Frederickson, *The Dixiecrat Revolt and the End of the Solid South, 1932–1968* (Chapel Hill: University of North Carolina Press, 2001); William Berman, *America's Right Turn: From Nixon to Clinton* (Baltimore: Johns Hopkins University Press, 1994); in the past decade there has been a new body of work updating the backlash literature by paying closer attention to local segregationist activism and including nuanced treatments of class. See Matthew Lassiter, *The Silent Majority: Suburban Politics in the Sunbelt South* (Princeton, NJ: Princeton University Press, 2007); Kevin Kruse, *White Flight: Atlanta and the Making of Modern Conservatism* (Princeton, NJ: Princeton University Press, 2007); Daniel HoSang, *Racial Propositions: Ballot Initiatives and the Making of Postwar California* (Oakland: University of California Press, 2010); Ronald Formisano, *Boston against Busing: Race, Class, and Ethnicity in the 1960s and 1970s* (Chapel Hill: University of North Carolina Press, 2004); for the counter-backlash literature, see Donald Critchlow, *The Conservative Ascendancy: How the GOP Right Made Political History* (Cambridge, MA: Harvard University Press, 2007); Lisa McGirr, *Suburban Warriors: The Origins of the New American Right* (Princeton, NJ: Princeton University Press, 2001); Byron Shafer and Richard

Johnston, *The End of Southern Exceptionalism: Class, Race, and Partisan Change in the Postwar South* (Cambridge, MA: Harvard University Press, 2009).

Chapter 3

1. Michael Coyne, "*Seven Days in May*: History, Prophecy and Propaganda," in *Windows on the Sixties: Exploring Key Texts of Media and Culture*, ed. Anthony Aldgate, James Chapman, and Arthur Marwick (New York: I. B. Tauris Publishers, 2000): 80.
2. Ibid., 76–80. My list and Coyne's line up on most of the characters, although he doesn't name Hargis as the inspiration for McPherson, possibly because I do not think Coyne was familiar with Walker and Hargis's collaboration in Operation Midnight Ride, which, as we will see, is quite similar to how the film portrays the relationship between Scott and McPherson.
3. Ibid., 74, 82–83.
4. Ibid., 76, 80, 83.
5. Edward Hunter, *Brainwashing in Red China* (New York: Vanguard Press, 1951).
6. Cabell Phillips, "Right-Wing Officers Worrying Pentagon," *New York Times*, June 18, 1961: 1, 56; Jonathan Schoenwald, *A Time for Choosing: The Rise of Modern American Conservatism* (Oxford: Oxford University Press, 2001); D. J. Mulloy, *The World of the John Birch Society: Conspiracy, Conservatism, and the Cold War* (Nashville, TN: Vanderbilt University Press, 2014).
7. Interview with James Wine, n.d., record group 17, box 7, folder 8, Papers of the National Council of the Churches of Christ (NCC), Presbyterian Historical Society, Philadelphia.
8. Air Reserve Center Training Manual, n.d., record group 17, box 6, folder 28, NCC.
9. In the 1960s, the National Council of Churches claimed some forty-five million members in its affiliated denominations. See "What Is This American Council?," n.d., record group 17, box 6, folder 2, NCC. Samuel McCrea Calvert, "Information about the American Council of Christian Churches," n.d., record group 17, box 6, folder 2, NCC.
10. "After Reds, Not Church Unit, AF Manual's Author Says," *Christian Crusade*, March 1960: 10–11, reproduced from the *New York Journal-American*, February 19, 1960.
11. Billy James Hargis, "Christian Crusade Threatened by National Council of Churches!," *Christian Crusade*, March 1960: 9.
12. Carl McIntire, *Twentieth Century Reformation* (Collingswood, NJ: Christian Beacon Press, 1944): ix.
13. For more on Soviet persecution of religious groups, and collaboration by the official Orthodox church, see Dimitry Pospielovsky's trilogy *History of Soviet Atheism in Theory and Practice and the Believers*; Richard Mouw, "Plus: You're Right, Dr. McIntire!," *Christianity Today*, May 21, 2002.
14. "A Letter from Carl McIntire about the ICCC," June 4, 1956, box 8, folder 12, Papers of Donald G. Barnhouse, Presbyterian Historical Society, Philadelphia.
15. Samuel McCrea Cavert, "Information about the American Council of Christian Churches," April 8, 1954, record group 17, box 6, folder 2, NCC; see also "What Is This American Council?," April 8, 1954, record group 17, box 6, folder 2, NCC.

16. Donald Janson and Bernard Eismann, *The Far Right* (New York: McGraw-Hill, 1963): 82.

17. Harold Kilpatrick to Clymer Wright, August 28, 1959, and Daniel F. Koon to James Wine, October 29, 1959, record group 17, box 7, folder 5, NCC.

18. Rev. Seleen sermon, "Apostles of Discord," April 3, 1960, First Presbyterian Church of Escanaba, Michigan, record group 17, box 6, folder 25, NCC.

19. George Laurent to Edwin T. Dahlberg, April 13, 1960, record group 17, box 7, folder 2, NCC.

20. Freedom of Information and Privacy Acts, "Subject: National Council of Churches" (HQ File: 100-50869, Section 9): 12, 41, 146, 150–151, 182.

21. Harold Kilpatrick to "Buck," March 22, 1960, record group 17, box 6, folder 22, NCC.

22. Harold E. Fey to James Wine, March 28, 1960, record group 17, box 6, folder 24, NCC.

23. Carl Cannon to James Wine, February 15, 1960, record group 17, box 7, folder 7, NCC.

24. James Wine to Lou Cassels, March 15, 1960, record group 17, box 6, folder 24, NCC.

25. "The Churches and the Air Force Manual Issue," record group 17, box 6, folder 22, NCC.

26. Roy G. Ross to G. Bromley Oxnam, March 25, 1960, record group 17, box 7, folder 6, NCC.

27. James Wine to Richard Bolling, April 1, 1960, record group 17, box 6, folder 22, NCC.

28. "Air Force Manual Decried: Kennedy Opposes Church—State Tie," *New York Times*, April 17, 1960: 1, 23.

29. Theodore C. Sorenson, "Memorandum on the Religious Issue," August 15, 1960, Papers of John F. Kennedy, Pre-Presidential Papers, Presidential Campaign Files, 1960, http://www.jfklibrary.org/Asset-Viewer/Archives/JFKCAMP1960-1015-021. aspx.

30. Biographical sheet, box 3, folder 56, BJHP.

31. Jonathan Schoenwald, *A Time for Choosing: The Rise of Modern Conservatism* (Oxford: Oxford University Press, 2001): 105–107.

32. "Walker Assigned to Pacific," *Washington Post,* October 14, 1961: n.p.

33. Walker's statement was immediately published in booklet form, Edwin Walker, *Censorship and Survival* (New York: Bookmailer, 1961): 1.

34. "Special Announcement, The Conservative Society of America Announces Publication of a 162-page book entitled: The Case of General Edwin A. Walker," box 384, folder 7, GRI.

35. Daniel Lowery to Edwin Walker, July 31, 1961, box 3, folder 57, BJHP.

36. "American Eagle Crusade for Truth, an Address by Edwin A. Walker," box 4, folder 1, BJHP.

37. Frederick G. Dutton quoted in Joseph Crespino, *Strom Thurmond's America* (New York: Hill and Wang, 2012): 4; there would be strong echoes of Kennedy's Palladium speech during the election of 2016 in Hillary Clinton's "Basket of Deplorables" speech. Katie Reilly, "Read Hillary Clinton's 'Basket of Deplorables' Remarks about Donald Trump Supporters," *Time*, September 10, 2016, http://time. com/4486502/hillary-clinton-basket-of-deplorables-transcript/. Clinton was raised in a conservative household and was a Goldwater supporter in 1964, so it is not impossible that she had Kennedy's speech in mind when saying that she could not

imagine Donald Trump riding in on a "white horse" to save America: https://www.youtube.com/watch?v=pbts0BKiomk.

38. John F. Kennedy, "Address at California Democratic Party Dinner" (speech, Los Angeles, CA, November 18, 1961), JFK Presidential Library, https://www.jfklibrary.org/Asset-Viewer/Archives/JFKPOF-036-020.aspx.

39. Aesop's "The Hunter and the Horseman," http://www.aesops-fables.com/the-hunter-and-the-horseman; Ross Winn, "The Man on Horseback," *Winn's Firebrand* 2, no. 7 (December 1903): 1–2.

40. Alan Brinkley, *John F. Kennedy: The American Presidents Series: The 35th President, 1961–1963* (New York: Times Books, 2012): 83.

41. "General Edwin Walker Information Concerning," November 8, 1961, FBI Files on Edwin Walker, 116-165494 File, Section 1, p. 28, https://www.maryferrell.org/mffweb/archive/viewer/showDoc.do?docId=145519&relPageId=28.

42. Lee White, a long-time aide to both John F. Kennedy and his father, was the man on the spot. Examples of his briefings can be found in box 12, folder "The Radical Right, November 1961–June 1962," White House Staff Files of Lee C. White, JFK Presidential Library, Boston, Massachusetts. The briefings frequently mention Hargis, Schwarz, and Walker.

43. "How the Independent American Plans to Help," *Independent American*, February 25, 1963: 4.

44. "Both Parties No-Win, Ex-General Charges," n.p., March 6, 1963. From a clippings scrapbook in the Hargis collection at the University of Arkansas.

45. "Walker Says Rockefeller and Kennedy 'Both the Same,'" *St. Louis Globe-Democrat*, March 20, 1963: 1; "Gen. Walker Calls for Third Party to Stop Kennedy and Rockefeller," *Colorado Springs Gazette Telegraph*, June 28, 1963: 9.

46. Victor Reuther, *The Brothers Reuther and the Story of the UAW: A Memoir* (Boston: Houghton Mifflin, 1976).

47. "Some Observations on the 1960 Campaign and Recommendations for 1962 and 1964," box 63, folder "Reuther," RFKP.

48. Walter Reuther to Robert Kennedy, April 16, 1961, box 377, folder 3, UAW President's Office: Walter P. Reuther Collection Papers (WRP), Wayne State University, Detroit.

49. Bobby to Walter, May 3, 1961, box 377, folder 3, WRP.

50. "A Clergyman's Testimony against the Closed Shop," n.d., box 175, folder 1, CMP.

51. See collection of Kamp's pamphlets in box 426, folder 4, WRP.

52. "Brown Says Knowland Has 'Fascist' Backers," *Evening Star* (Washington, DC), September 15, 1958.

53. Press Release from UAW President Walter P. Reuther, September 14, 1958, box 425, folder 15, WRP; Kamp had actually been imprisoned for refusing to reveal his donor list to an investigatory committee of the US House of Representatives in 1950. He was held in contempt along with Earl Browder of the Communist Party USA and William L. Patterson of the Civil Rights Congress, a rather strange set of bedfellows. John Morris, "Lobby Inquiry Asks Data of 166 Firms," *New York Times*, June 2, 1950: 16; "House Cites Kamp, Already in a Cell," *New York Times*, September 1, 1950: 13;

Harold Hinton, "Browder, Five Others Indicted in Contempt," *New York Times*, November 27, 1950: 1.

54. Nelson Lichtenstein, *Walter Reuther: The Most Dangerous Man in Detroit* (New York: University of Illinois Press, 1995): 167–168.

55. Victor Reuther, *The Brothers Reuther and the Story of the UAW* (Boston: Houghton Mifflin Company, 1976): 437–439.

56. "Brown Presses Attack," *New York Times*, September 17, 1958: 30.

57. Lawrence Davies, "President Asked to Condemn Kamp," *New York Times*, September 18, 1958: 13.

58. W. H. Lawrence, "Nixon Denounces Aid on Pamphlets," *New York Times*, October 5, 1958.

59. "Michigan—State of Ominous Warning," *Weekly Crusader* 1, no. 2 (November 4, 1960).

60. "This We Believe," advertisement, *New York Times*, October 25, 1960: 19.

61. Victor Reuther to Walter Reuther, November 8, 1961, box 17, folder 15, Victor G. Reuther Papers (VRP), Wayne State University, Detroit.

62. "Memorandum," November 8, 1961, folder 15, box 17, VRP.

63. Victor Reuther to Walter Reuther, November 22, 1961, folder 19, box 27, VRP.

64. For more on the defection of liberal Republicans, see Geoffrey Kabaservice, *Rule and Ruin: The Downfall of Moderation and Destruction of the Republican Party, from Eisenhower to the Tea Party* (Oxford: Oxford University Press, 2013).

65. Victor Reuther to Robert Kennedy, December 19, 1961, box 63, folder "Reuther Memorandum," RFKP.

66. Donald Janson, "Hargis Group to Back Goldwater Despite Some Members' Attacks," *New York Times*, August 9, 1964: 55.

67. "The Radical Right in America Today," box 63, folder "Reuther Memorandum," RFKP.

68. Lisa McGirr, *Suburban Warriors: The Origins of the New American Right* (Princeton, NJ: Princeton University Press, 2001): 60–61.

69. Victor Reuther probably got his information from Bill Becker, "Right-Wing Groups Multiplying Appeals in Southern California," *New York Times*, October 29, 1961: 43.

70. Jack Gould, "TV: Christian Anti-Communism Crusade Here," *New York Times*, November 3, 1961: 71.

71. "The Radical Right in America Today," box 63, folder "Reuther Memorandum," RFKP, 7–8.

72. Ibid., 15–18.

73. Ibid., 18–21.

74. "He Guards the Peace: Edwin Anderson Walker," *New York Times*, September 25, 1957: 18.

75. "The American Eagle Weapons for Freedom," folder 1, box 4, BJHP.

76. For a more detailed account of Walker's actions in Oxford, see Chris Cravens, "Edwin A. Walker and the Right Wing in Dallas, 1960–1966" (MA thesis, Southwest Texas State University, 1991).

77. "Walker Demands Vocal Protest," *New York Times*, September 30, 1962: 69.

78. Claude Sitton, "Negro at Mississippi U. As Barnett Yields; 3 Dead in Campus Riot, 6 Marshals Shot; Guardsmen Move In; Kennedy Makes Plea," *New York Times*, October 1, 1962: 1.

79. *The Associated Press v. Edwin A. Walker*, 389 U.S. 28 (1967); see David Halberstam, *Breaking News: How the Associated Press Has Covered War, Peace, and Everything Else* (New York: Princeton Architectural Press, 2007): 95–96.

80. Herbert J. Miller Jr. to Mrs. Helen D. Kay, October 10, 1962, BJHP.

81. William Mullen, "Gen. Walker Tells Own Story of Mississippi Tragedy," *Amarillo Daily News*, March 28, 1963: 29.

82. "The Mississippi Conflict and the Shameful Treatment of General Edwin Walker," *Weekly Crusader* 2, no. 50 (October 12, 1962).

83. Thomas Szasz, *Psychiatric Justice* (New York: Macmillan, 1965); see also Thomas Szasz, "The Shame of Medicine: The Case of General Edwin Walker," *The Freeman*, September 23, 2009.

84. "The American Eagle Weapons for Freedom," box 4, folder 1, BJHP.

85. Billy James Hargis, "The Children of Cuba, Communism, and a False Prophet," n.p., December 10, 1961, box 2, folder 21, BJHP.

86. For the FBI reports on Hargis's trip, see box 1, folder 5, BJHP.

87. Billy James Hargis, "No One Mourns the Death of a Dictator," June 5, 1961, box 2, folder 22, BJHP.

88. Sasha Issenberg, "The Wild Road Trip That Launched the Populist Conservative Movement: How a Fiery Preacher and a Maverick Army General Took the Nation by Storm," *Smithsonian*, August 31, 2018, https://www.smithsonianmag.com/history/wild-road-trip-rallied-conservatives-180970033.

89. Billy James Hargis, "Introduction of Edwin A. Walker, March 18, 1963," speech, n.p., March 18, 1963, http://www.pet880.com/images/19630318_Midnight_EAW_Intro_1.JPG.

90. Billy James Hargis to Mrs. Gerald Tanner, February 18, 1963, box 4, folder 13, BJHP.

91. Financial estimates and rally locations culled from "Operation Midnight Ride" records in box 4, BJHP. Figures available upon request.

92. UPI, "Gen. Walker Finds Miss Riot Just 'Lot of Fun,'" *Chicago Defender*, March 9, 1963: 1.

93. "Gen. Walker fires at Kennedy, U.N.," *Birmingham News*, March 9, 1963: 1.

94. Bob Jones III to Billy James Hargis, February 15, 1963, box 4, folder 23, BJHP.

95. Robert D. Dilley to Billy James Hargis, February 19, 1963, box 4, folder 31, BJHP.

96. Rosalind K. Frame to Billy James Hargis, n.d., box 4, folder 16, BJHP; "Rosalind Kress Frame Haley Obituary," *Savannah Morning News*, April 28, 2008.

97. *Report of the President's Commission on the Assassination of President Kennedy* (Washington, DC: Government Printing Office, 1964): 183–187; Philip Shenon, *A Cruel and Shocking Act: The Secret History of the Kennedy Assassination* (New York: Henry Holt and Company, 2013).

98. *Investigation of the Assassination of President John F. Kennedy, Hearings before the Select Committee on Assassinations of the US House of Representatives*, vol. 2 (Washington, DC: US Government Printing Office, 1979): 232–233.

99. For more on border radio, see Gene Fowler and Bill Crawford, *Border Radio: Quacks, Yodelers, Pitchmen, Psychics, and Other Amazing Broadcasts of the American Airwaves* (Austin: University of Texas Press, 2002).

100. "Summary of Information," August 28, 1957, box 1, folder 5, BJHP.

101. "To: Director, From: SAC Oklahoma City," December 21, 1961, box 1, folder 5, BJHP.

102. "To Director FBI, and SAC, Washington Field from Civil Rights Section General Investigative Division," August 5, 1963, box 1, folder 9, BJHP.

103. "Christian Crusade," August 5, 1963, box 1, folder 9, BJHP.

104. For example, here is an interview with Walker following the assassination of JFK: https://www.youtube.com/watch?v=mx_-K4jCpm8.

105. "Address by President John F. Kennedy to the UN General Assembly," September 25, 1961, http://www.state.gov/p/io/potusunga/207241.htm.

106. Hargis got his hands on copies of most of the booklets in the series. For example, see "Disarmament: The New U.S. Initiative," United States Arms Control and Disarmament Agency Publication 8 (Washington, DC: US Government Printing Office, 1962). Of all the publications, perhaps the most radical is "Toward a World without War: A Summary of United States Disarmament Efforts—Past and Present," United States Arms Control and Disarmament Agency Publication 10 (Washington, DC: Government Printing Office, 1962). Copies of these two booklets can be found in box 92, folder 37, BJHP.

107. "U.S. to Propose End of National Armies," *Los Angeles Times*, March 31, 1962: 1.

108. Ken Thompson, "One, Two, Three—Surrender," *Dallas Morning News*, January 23, 1962.

109. "Statement on Disarmament by Senator John G. Tower," April 19, 1962, box 92, folder 31, BJHP.

110. "Disarmament—Part I," *The Dan Smoot Report*, broadcast 403, May 6, 1963, box 92, folder 32, BJHP.

111. "National Committee against the Treaty of Moscow," August 16, 1963, box 93, folder 11, BJHP.

112. Craig Hosmer, "A Design for Suicide—Our Atomic Test Proposals at Geneva," *Manion Forum*, broadcast 414, September 2, 1962.

113. Fen Osler Hampson and Michael Hart, *Multilateral Negotiations: Lessons from Arms Control, Trade, and the Environment* (Baltimore: Johns Hopkins University Press, 1999): 72.

114. Erin Richardson, "SANE and the Limited Test Ban Treaty of 1963: Mobilizing Public Opinion to Shape U.S. Foreign Policy" (MA thesis, Ohio University, 2009): 85.

115. Theodore Sorenson, *Kennedy* (New York: Harper and Row, 1965): 737.

116. Donald Janson and Bernard Eismann, *The Far Right* (New York: McGraw-Hill, 1963): 227–230.

117. Dave Person, "Retired Journalist Sought to 'Make a Difference,'" *Kalamazoo Gazette*, February 5, 2009.

118. "Transmittal Slip," Jack Conway to Victor Reuther, August 27, 1963, box 17, folder 16, VRP.

119. A. Warren James Jr. to Robert Kennedy, August 4, 1963, box 63, folder "Reuther Memorandum," RFKP.

120. Jos. E. Rullestad to Walter Reuther, July 25, 1963, box 17, folder 16, VRP.

121. "Major Bundy Comments on Reuther Memorandum," July 23, 1963, box 17, folder 16, VRP.

122. Billy James Hargis, "Walter Reuther's Secret Memorandum," n.d., box 17, folder 17, VRP. Here is an example of Hargis's radio voice: https://www.youtube.com/watch?v=4ssybQg1ZAY. Listen to it and imagine him reading those lines. Jack Conway to Victor Reuther, August 8, 1963, box 17, folder 16, VRP.

123. Handwritten note on memorandum, "B" to Andy Oehmann," July 9, 1963, box 63, folder "Reuther Memorandum," RFKP.

124. Ed Guthman to Attorney General, June 20, 1963, box 63, RFKP; "Jack" to "Ed," June 24, 1963, box 63, RFKP.

125. "Jack" to "Ed," June 26, 1963, box 63, RFKP.

126. Andrew F. Oehmann to Mrs. Dan Stricker, July 12, 1963, box 63, RFKP. Oehmann was one of Robert F. Kennedy's executive assistants.

127. "AFO" to Attorney General, November 7, 1963, box 63, RFKP.

128. Andrew F. Oehmann to J. Edward Roush, November 15, 1963, box 63, RFKP.

129. Nelson Lichtenstein, *Walter Reuther: The Most Dangerous Man in Detroit* (New York: University of Illinois Press, 1995).

130. Victor Reuther, *The Brothers Reuther and the Story of the UAW* (Boston: Houghton Mifflin Company, 1976): 440.

Chapter 4

1. The lecture was the basis first of an article in *Harper's* and ultimately became the lead essay in one of Hofstadter's books. Richard Hofstadter, "The Paranoid Style in American Politics," *Harper's Magazine,* November 1964: 77–86.

2. Ibid., 84–85.

3. Philip Jenkins, "The Paranoid Style in Liberal Politics," *American Conservative,* November 6, 2013, http://www.theamericanconservative.com/the-paranoid-style-in-liberal-politics/.

4. "The Radical Right in America Today," p. 8, box 63, folder "Reuther Memorandum," RFKP.

5. "Memorandum," p. 3, Victor Reuther to Walter Reuther, November 8, 1961, box 17, folder 15, VRP. This is the early draft of the Reuther Memorandum mentioned in chapter 2 and was written to give Walter Reuther talking points for his upcoming meeting with Robert Kennedy.

6. Interview of Wesley McCune by Niel M. Johnson, September 15–16, 1988, Harry S. Truman Presidential Library, Independence, Missouri.

7. "Confidential Memorandum," Victor Reuther to Walter Reuther, January 31, 1962, box 27, folder 15, VRP; "Memorandum," Jacob Clayman to Walther Reuther, May 13, 1965, box 325, folder 12, WRP.

8. "Ronald Reagan," in "Directory, Group Research Inc," box 333, folder 1, WRP.

9. Inez Robb, "Keating's Dilemma," *Pittsburgh Press*, August 5, 1964: 21; "Republican Boos Won't Hurt Keating," *Lewiston Morning Tribune*, October 2, 1964: 4.

10. "Inquiries Received by Group Research, Inc., during 1964," p. 14, box 484, folder 7, GRI.

11. Joe Rauh, one of the authors of the Reuther Memorandum, was also general counsel for the Americans for Democratic Action and an executive committee member of GRI. Judith Smith, ed., *Political Brokers: People, Organizations, Money, and Power* (New York: Liveright, 1972): 17–18.

12. Martin Arnold, "Keating Mends Italian Fences," *New York Times*, October 11, 1964.

13. "We, the People! and Tax Repealers Meet," *Group Research Report* 1, no. 1 (September 19, 1962): 1.

14. David Burnham, *A Law unto Itself: Power, Politics, and the IRS* (New York: Random House, 1989): 261–262.

15. John A. Andrew III, *Power to Destroy: The Political Uses of the IRS from Kennedy to Nixon* (Chicago: Ivan R. Dee, 2002).

16. Victor Reuther to Walter Reuther, November 8, 1961, box 17, folder 15, VRP.

17. "Investigation of the Special Service Staff of the Internal Revenue Service," for the Joint Committee on Internal Revenue Taxation (Washington, DC: US Government Printing Office, June 5, 1975): 103.

18. Interview of John L. Seigenthaler by Ronald J. Grele, John F. Kennedy Oral History Collection, February 22, 1966, John F. Kennedy Presidential Library, Boston, Massachusetts, p. 299.

19. Ibid., 302–303, 322–326.

20. "Investigation of the Special Service Staff," 103.

21. The full name of the committee was the United States Senate Select Committee to Study Governmental Operations with Respect to Intelligence Activities and headed by Idaho Senator Frank Church. It was commissioned in 1975 to investigate abuse of powers and obstruction by the national security apparatus and the executive branch.

22. John Seigenthaler to Mitchell Rogovin, November 28, 1961, box 42, folder "Internal Revenue Service 7/1961-12/1961," RFKP.

23. "Transcript of the President's News Conference on World and Domestic Affairs," *New York Times*, November 30, 1961: 14.

24. David Burnham, *A Law unto Itself: Power, Politics, and the IRS* (New York: Random House, 1989): 98–99.

25. Elizabeth MacDonald, "The Kennedys and the IRS," *Wall Street Journal*, January 28, 1997: A18.

26. John Seigenthaler to Mitchell Rogovin and Dean J. Barron, December 20, 1961, box 42, folder "Internal Revenue Service 7/1961-12/1961," RFKP.

27. John A. Andrew III, *Power to Destroy: The Political Uses of the IRS from Kennedy to Nixon* (Chicago: Ivan R. Dee, 2002): 27. The reference to "mass media" was blotted out on the document when Andrew procured it with a Freedom of Information Act request, but he managed to find another copy with the reference intact. Curious.

28. Elizabeth MacDonald, "The Kennedys and the IRS," *Wall Street Journal,* January 28, 1997: A18.
29. "Investigation of the Special Service Staff," 104–105.
30. Burnham, *A Law unto Itself,* 271.
31. "Investigations of the Special Service Staff," 106–107.
32. "Ideological Organizations Proposed for First Phase of Audit Program," box 42, folder "Internal Revenue Service 1963," RFKP; "Investigation of the Special Service Staff," 108–109.
33. Andrew, *Power to Destroy,* 35; "Investigations of the Special Service Staff," 108.
34. Marquis Childs, "Kennedy Thinks Rightists Use Tax Exemption for Propaganda," *St. Louis Post-Dispatch,* October 10, 1963: 1, section 6B.
35. "Investigation of the Special Service Staff," 110.
36. Hargis sued the IRS and the case went to the US district court, which ruled in Hargis's favor. Hargis reprinted those records as "Christian Crusade vs. Internal Revenue Service, 'A Landmark Decision,'" box 4, folder 7, BJHP.
37. "Christian Crusade vs. Internal Revenue Service," 19–21.
38. "Religious Discrimination," *Christian Beacon,* box 252, folder 18, CMP.
39. "Religion and Politics," *Weekly Crusader* 8, no. 1 (November 17, 1967), box 5, folder 1, BJHP.
40. "Police State Brutality," backpage, *Weekly Crusader* 8, no. 15 (February 23, 1968), box 5, folder 1, BJHP.
41. Clyde L. Bickerstaff to Christian Echoes Ministry, Inc., September 22, 1966, reprinted in "Internal Revenue Service, Package," n.d., box 4, folder 7, BJHP.
42. "Christian Crusade vs. Internal Revenue Service," 22, 25–32.
43. "Religious Discrimination," *Christian Beacon,* box 252, folder 18, CMP.
44. "Fact Sheet on Life Line Foundation, Inc.," n.d. (1965?), box 490, folder 3, GRI.
45. For a detailed, laudatory history of the Blue Book, see Victor Pickard, *America's Battle for Media Democracy: The Triumph of Corporate Libertarianism and the Future of Media Reform* (New York: Cambridge University Press, 2014).
46. See 47 U.S.C. §315 "Facilities for Candidates for Public Office," http://transition.fcc.gov/mb/policy/political/candrule.htm.
47. Martha Minow to Attorney General, n.d., box 53, folder "Minow," RFKP; Kenneth Cox, interview by William Hartigan, October 19, 1977, transcript, JFK Oral History Collection, JFK Presidential Library, Boston, pp. 11–12.
48. The full text of Minow's "Vast Wasteland" speech is available online as is the audio of the address: http://www.americanrhetoric.com/speeches/newtonminow.htm.
49. Ayn Rand, "Check Your Premises: Have Gun, Will Nudge," *Objectivist Newsletter* 1, no. 3 (March 1962): 9–10, 12.
50. "The FCC," *Human Events* 20, no. 6 (February 9, 1963): 104.
51. Allison Perlman, *Public Interests: Media Advocacy and Struggles over U.S. Television* (New Brunswick, NJ: Rutgers University Press, 2016): 7.
52. The texts of both speeches were reprinted in Newton Minow, *Equal Time: The Private Broadcaster and the Public Interest* (New York: Atheneum, 1964).
53. Gerald V. Flannery, ed., *Commissioners of the FCC 1927–1994* (New York: University Press of America, 1995): 133.

54. "Hooray for Agnew" to Kenneth Cox, February 27, 1970, box 2, folder 4, Kenneth A. Cox Papers, Wisconsin Historical Society, Madison.

55. Christopher Lydon, "F.C.C. Man Bitter as Term is Ending," *New York Times*, June 15, 1970: 35.

56. Adam Bernstein, "Kenneth A. Cox, Lawyer, MCI Executive," *Washington Post*, November 3, 2011.

57. Kenneth A. Cox, interview by William Hartigan, October 19, 1977, transcript, JFK Oral History Collection, JFK Presidential Library, Boston, p. 2.

58. Cox, interview, 5; Seigenthaler, interview, 298.

59. E. William Henry, interview by Ronald J. Grele, March 14, 1966, transcript, JFK Oral History Collection, JFK Presidential Library, Boston, pp. 2–5.

60. E. William Henry to "Uncle Jake," December 17, 1962, box 10, folder "Chairman—Personal 1962," E. William Henry Papers (EWHP), Wisconsin Historical Society, Madison.

61. Harriet Van Horne, "Applause for E. William Henry, Courageous New FCC Chairman," *Houston Press*, July 8, 1963.

62. E. William Henry to Fritz Heneman, October 4, 1963, box 10, folder "Chairman—Personal 1962," EWHP. The bill was known as the Rogers bill after its sponsor Walter Rogers (D-Texas).

63. Lou Bryan to Commissioner Cox, June 1968, box 2, folder 4, Kenneth Cox Papers, Wisconsin Historical Society.

64. Handwritten note from Fred Friendly's interview with E. William Henry, box 81, folder 6, Fred Friendly Papers (FFP), Columbia University, New York.

65. "The Radical Right in America Today," box 63, folder "Reuther Memorandum," RFKP.

66. "Statement of E. William Henry, Chairman Federal Communications Commission," July 16, 1963, box 21, folder "Editorializing, 1963–1965," EWHP.

67. Ben F. Waple, "Stations' Responsibilities under Fairness Doctrine as to Controversial Issue Programming," July 26, 1963, MC #001, box 934, folder 7, Records of the American Civil Liberties Union (ACLU), Princeton University Library, Princeton, New Jersey.

68. Ibid.

69. "Application of the FCC Fairness Doctrine to Broadcast of Controversial Issues: The July 26th Public Notice," July 27, 1963, MC #001, box 934, folder 16, ACLU.

70. "*Your* Children's Teeth Contain Strontium-90," *New York Times*, April 7, 1963.

71. Erin Richardson, "SANE and the Limited Test Ban Treaty of 1963: Mobilizing Public Opinion to Shape U.S. Foreign Policy" (MA thesis, Ohio University, 2009): 80–82.

72. Ronald Terchek, *The Making of the Test Ban Treaty* (New York: Springer, 1970): 84–85.

73. Richardson, "SANE and the Limited Test Ban Treaty of 1963," 85, 88.

74. James Jeremiah Wadsworth, *The Silver Spoon: An Autobiography* (Geneva, NY: W. F. Humphrey Press, 1980).

75. James J. Wadsworth to Station Manager WQIZ Radio, August 23, 1963, box 499, folder 26, CMP; Rear Admiral Chester Ward, "The Unlimited Dangers of a Limited Test Ban," *Manion Forum*, August 4, 1963.

76. A full transcript of the response was attached to one of Wadsworth's letters to another station. See James J. Wadsworth to John M. Norris, September 9, 1963, box 93, folder 12, BJHP.

77. Clarence Jones to James J. Wadsworth, August 26, 1963, box 499, folder 26, CMP.

78. James J. Wadsworth to John M. Norris, September 9, 1963, box 93, folder 12, BJHP; John M. Norris to James J. Wadsworth, August 22, 1963, box 653, folder 2, CMP; John M. Norris to James J. Wadsworth, September 13, 1963, box 93, folder 12, BJHP.

79. Cullman Broadcasting Co., 40 F.C.C. 576 (1963). A copy of the ruling can be found in Carl McIntire's papers. "FCC Replies to Two Broadcast Station Inquiries about Program Series Critical of Nuclear Test Ban Treaty," box 496, folder 1, CMP.

80. "The Fairness Doctrine," August 7, 1964, box 3, folder 3, BJHP.

81. Clarence Manion, "Do You Want Federal Censorship for Your Local Radio Station?," *Manion Forum*, October 27, 1963. Copy found in box 46, folder "The Manion Forum," EWHP.

82. Ibid.

83. Edith Kermit Roosevelt, "The FCC and the Reuther Memo," *Suncoast News*, October 17, 1963. Roosevelt's article was reprinted by Carl McIntire's *Twentieth Century Reformation Hour* for a special, undated issue, "The Free Exercise of Religion and the FCC," box 496, folder 19, CMP.

84. Durward G. Hall to William Henry, September 9, 1963, box 14, folder "Congressional Letters," EWHP.

85. Unnamed to A. S. Herlong, July 29, 1963, box 14, folder "Congressional Letters," EWHP.

86. Bill Brock to William E. Henry, October 22, 1963, box 14, folder "Congressional Letters," EWHP.

87. "Fairness Caught Between," *Broadcasting*, October 21, 1963: 80–81. The article cited Edith Kermit Roosevelt's column.

88. E. William Henry to Clyde Patton, December 27, 1963, box 10, folder "Chairman—Personal 1963," EWHP.

89. E. William Henry to Joseph S. Clark, March 24, 1964, box 46, folder "Memoranda—1964," EWHP.

90. E. William Henry to Everett McKinley Dirksen, November 20, 1963, box 17, folder "Congressional Correspondence," EWHP; Everett McKinley Dirksen to E. William Henry, December 9, 1963, EWHP.

91. Henry's letter to Montana Republican representative Don L. Short was even denser and less helpful than his response to Dirksen. E. William Henry to Don L. Short, December 16, 1963, EWHP.

92. E. William Henry to Bill Brock, December 19, 1963, box 23, folder "Fairness Doctrine," EWHP.

93. E. William Henry to A. Sydney Herlong, August 2, 1963, box 14, folder "Congressional Letters," EWHP.

94. Gerald Flannery ed., *Commissioners of the FCC, 1927–1994* (New York: University Press of America, 1995): 138–140.

95. Robert Schlesinger, *White House Ghosts: Presidents and Their Speechwriters* (New York: Simon and Schuster, 2008): 116.
96. "Telephone Recordings: Dictation Belt 25C.2. Federal Communications Commission and 'Life Line,'" August 13, 1963, Presidential Recordings, JFK Presidential Library, Boston.
97. "Investigation of the Special Service Staff of the Internal Revenue Service," 108–109.
98. Myer Feldman, "Memorandum for the President," August 15, 1963, box 106, folder "Right Wing Movement, Part I," JFKP.
99. Myer Feldman, "Financial Scope of the American Right-Wing, August 1963," box 106, folder "Right Wing Movement, Part I," JFKP.
100. Ibid.
101. John M. Bailey, untitled speech, box 2, folder 1, John M. Bailey Papers, Thomas J. Dodd Research Center, University of Connecticut, Storrs.
102. Feldman, "Memorandum for the President," August 15, 1963, box 106, folder "Right Wing Movement, Part I," JFKP.
103. "Telephone Recordings: Dictation Belt 25C.2. Federal Communications Commission and 'Life Line,'" August 13, 1963, Presidential Recordings, JFK Presidential Library, Boston.

Chapter 5

1. Shaun Casey, *The Making of a Catholic President: Kennedy vs. Nixon 1960* (New York: Oxford University Press, 2009): 3–8.
2. For more on Bailey from a sympathetic point of view, see Joseph I. Lieberman, *The Legacy: Connecticut Politics 1930–1980* (Hartford, CT: Spoonwood Press, 1981).
3. Henry Steele Commager to John M. Bailey, April 12, 1968, box 9, folder 22, John M. Bailey Papers, Thomas J. Dodd Research Center, University of Connecticut, Storrs.
4. Sean Savage, *JFK, LBJ, and the Democratic Party* (Albany: State University of New York Press, 2004): 213.
5. Bailey mentioned this fact in his press conference at the Western States Democratic Conference. O. N. Malmquist, "Demo Sees Tax Cut: Boost of $16 Million for Utah," *Salt Lake Tribune*, September 19, 1963.
6. Benjamin Guthrie, *Statistics of the Presidential and Congressional Election of November 3, 1964* (Washington, DC: US Government Printing Office, 1965): 27
7. Gale McGee to Mike Feldman, August 14, 1963, folder "Right-Wing Movement, Part I," box 106, President's Office Files, JFK Presidential Library, Boston.
8. KBBS (Buffalo), KEVA (Evanston), KASL (Newcastle), KVOW (Riverton), KROE (Sheridan), KYCN (Wheatland), KVWO (Cheyenne); county population statistics from the 1960 US Census, https://www.census.gov/population/www/censusdata/cencounts/files/wy190090.txt.
9. Ibid.

10. O. N. Malmquist, "West to Up JFK Vote, Demos Say," *Salt Lake Tribune,* September 18, 1963.

11. M. Demar Teuscher, "Demos Loose Blast at GOP Right Wing," *Deseret News,* September 19, 1963.

12. The booklet was titled "Far Right in the Far West" but had no publication information. A photocopy can be found in box 99, folder "Democratic National Committee Weekly Reports 9/26/63," President's Office Files, JFK Presidential Library, Boston.

13. Helen O'Donnell and David Groff, *A Common Good: The Friendship of Robert F. Kennedy and Kenneth P. O'Donnell* (New York: William Morrow, 1998).

14. "Memorandum," Wayne Phillips to Fred Friendly, October 17, 1974, box 81, folder 6, FFP, p. 1.

15. William T. Lake to Richard Bodorff and Sue Wilson, May 8, 2014, http://transition.fcc.gov/Daily_Releases/Daily_Business/2014/db0508/DA-14-621A1.pdf.

16. Notes from meeting between Fred Friendly and Nicholas Zapple, "Additional Memo on Nick Zapple," October 14, 1975, box 81, folder 9, FFP.

17. "Memorandum," Wayne Phillips to Fred Friendly, October 17, 1974, box 81, folder 6, FFP, pp. 3–4.

18. Ibid.

19. Quotes from draft manuscripts in Cook's papers. Fred Cook, *Franklin D. Roosevelt: Valiant Leader,* box 6, folder 11, Fred J. Cook Papers, Syracuse University, Syracuse, p. 1; Fred Cook, *The Unfinished Story of Alger Hiss,* box 5, folder 4, Fred J. Cook Papers, Syracuse University, Syracuse, p. 177; Fred Cook, *The F.B.I. Nobody Knows,* box 3, folder 5, Fred J. Cook Papers, Syracuse University, Syracuse, p. 448.

20. Frank Winn to Walter Reuther, December 16, 1962, box 27, folder 23, VRP.

21. Letter reprinted in undated broadsheet, "Do You Want This Man to Have the Keys to the White House?," 1965, box 73, folder 6, BJHP.

22. Fred Cook, "The Ultras: Aims, Affiliations and Finances of the Radical Right," *The Nation,* June 30, 1962. Copy found in box 3, folder 4, BJHP. "Smear" was handwritten on the cover.

23. "Fred Cook Notes," undated, box 82, folder 1, FFP.

24. Fred Cook is on GRI's list of information requests for 1964. See p. 4, "Inquiries Received by Group Research, Inc., during 1964," box 484, folder 7, GRI.

25. Fred Cook, "Radio Right: Hate Clubs of the Air," *The Nation,* May 25, 1964. Reprinted by Carl McIntire in special packet, "The Democratic National Committee's Attack," box 108, folder 17, CMP.

26. Untitled notes from phone call between Fred Friendly and Carey McWilliams, October 3, 1974, box 82, folder 1, FFP.

27. Walter Pincus, "'Right-Wing' Broadcasts Protested," *Sunday Star,* October 18, 1964.

28. E. William Henry to Martin Firestone, February 26, 1964, box 10, folder "Chairman—Personal, 1964, Jan-July," EWHP.

29. "Local TV Programming Inquiries," in *Federal Communications Commission 29th Annual Report for the Fiscal Year 1963* (Washington, DC: US Government Printing Office, 1963): 60–61, https://apps.fcc.gov/edocs_public/attachmatch/DOC-308696A1.pdf.

30. "New Wrinkle in Hearings: Witness Hunt," *Broadcasting,* December 10, 1962: 102; "What Omaha Taught Henry," *Broadcasting,* October 28, 1963: 31–33.

31. Kitty Broman Putnam and William Lowell Putnam, *How We Survived in UHF Television: A Broadcasting Memoir, 1953–1984* (Jefferson, NC: McFarland and Company, 2011): 148, 181, 189–190.

32. Robert Hanyok, *Spartans in Darkness: American SIGINT and the Indochina War, 1945–1975* (Washington, DC: National Security Agency, 2002), http://fas.org/irp/nsa/spartans/index.html.

33. "Memorandum," Wayne Phillips to Fred Friendly, October 17, 1974, box 81, folder 6, FFP, pp. 5–9.

34. Martin Firestone to "Dear Sir," n.d., box 659, folder 13, CMP; for more on Rowan, see Dan Nimmo and Chevelle Newsome, *Political Commentators in the United States in the 20th Century: A Bio-Critical Sourcebook* (Westport, CT: Greenwood Press, 1997): 324.

35. "Confidential," Martin Firestone to Wayne Phillips, October 28, 1964, box 81, folder 2, FFP, p. 1.

36. Marvin R. Steffins to Ben F. Waple, March 1, 1965, box 16, folder 31, Papers of Eugene Bertermann, Billy Graham Center, Wheaton, Illinois.

37. Excerpt from Bailey's report included in "Memorandum," Wayne Phillips to Fred Friendly, October 17, 1974, box 81, folder 6, FFP, p. 10.

38. "Confidential," Martin Firestone to Wayne Phillips, October 28, 1964, box 81, folder 2, FFP, p. 1.

39. Excerpt from Phillips's report included in "Memorandum," Wayne Phillips to Fred Friendly, October 17, 1974, box 81, folder 6, FFP, pp. 9–10; Sean Savage, *JFK, LBJ, and the Democratic Party* (Albany: State University of New York Press, 2004): 155.

40. "Confidential," Martin Firestone to Wayne Phillips, October 28, 1964, box 81, folder 2, FFP, pp. 4–5.

41. Ibid., 6.

42. Jack Black to Carl McIntire, July 12, 1964, box 459, folder 4, CMP.

43. Fred W. Friendly, *The Good Guys, the Bad Guys, and the First Amendment: Free Speech vs. Fairness in Broadcasting* (New York: Random House, 1975).

44. Ralph Engelman, *Friendlyvision: Fred Friendly and the Rise and Fall of Television Journalism* (New York: Columbia University Press, 2009): 212–218.

45. "Memorandum on Lunch with Al Landa," May 29, 1975, box 82, folder 1, FFP.

46. List of Walter Reuthers Meetings during the JFK Administration, box 19, folder 3, VRP.

47. "Memorandum," Wayne Phillips to Fred Friendly, October 17, 1974, box 81, folder 6, FFP, p. 1.

48. Scheduler, March 6, 1964, box 26, folder 3, Paul F. Zucker Papers (PFZP), State Historical Society of Wisconsin, Madison.

49. David Finn, *The Way Forward: My First Fifty Years at Ruder Finn* (New York: Millwood Publishing, 1998): 92.

50. "Memorandum," Wayne Philips to Fred Friendly, October 17, 1974, box 81, folder 6, FFP, p. 4.

51. Paul B. Zucker to Wayne Phillips, April 15, 1964, box 6, folder 4, PFZP.

52. For more on Larson see David Stebenne, *Modern Republican: Arthur Larson and the Eisenhower Years* (Bloomington: Indiana University Press, 2006).

53. "Who's Responsible Now," *National Review* (March 23, 1965): 224.

54. "Memorandum on Lunch with Al Landa," May 29, 1975, box 82, folder 1, FFP; untitled interview notes from Fred Friendly meeting with Dewey Anderson, February 14, 1975, box 82, folder 1, FFP; Stuart Sucherman to Fred Friendly, April 8, 1975, box 82, folder 1, FFP.

55. Paul B. Zucker to Wayne Phillips, April 14, 1964, box 6, folder 4, PFZP; Advertisement, "Six Reasons Why You Should Worry about Extremism in the U.S. Today," *New York Times,* October 8, 1964: 13, section C.

56. Untitled interview notes from Fred Friendly meeting with Dewey Anderson, February 14, 1975, box 82, folder 1, FFP.

57. Advertisement, "Six Reasons Why You Should Worry about Extremism in the U.S. Today," *New York Times,* October 8, 1964: 13, section C.

58. Roy Parker Jr., "Right-Wing Programs to Be Monitored," *Winston-Salem Journal,* October 23, 1964: 12.

59. Newsletter, "The National Council for Civic Responsibility an Embryonic Gestapo," box 3, folder 6, BJHP; newsletter, Billy James Hargis, "I See the Hand of God in This," box 1, folder 19, BJHP.

60. "Who's Responsible Now?," *National Review,* March 23, 1965: 224–226.

61. Untitled interview notes from Fred Friendly meeting with Dewey Anderson, February 14, 1975, box 82, folder 1, FFP; Stuart F. Sucherman to Fred W. Friendly, April 8, 1975, box 82, folder 1, FFP.

62. Arthur Larson to Eugene Carson Blake, March 3, 1965, box 19, folder 9, Eugene Carson Blake Papers, Presbyterian Historical Society, Philadelphia.

63. David Stebenne, *Modern Republican: Arthur Larson and the Eisenhower Years* (Bloomington: Indiana University Press, 2006): 253–254.

64. Untitled interview notes from Fred Friendly meeting with Arthur Larson, February 20, 1975, box 199, folder 7, FFP.

65. Untitled interview notes from Fred Friendly meeting with Dewey Anderson, February 14, 1975, box 82, folder 1, FFP.

66. John A. Andrew, *Power to Destroy: The Political Uses of the IRS from Kennedy to Nixon* (Chicago: Ivan R. Dee, 2002): 40–44.

67. "Memo from Bill Ruder," February 19, 1975, box 82, folder 1, FFP.

68. Neil J. Young, "Sermonizing in Pearls: Phyllis Schlafly and the Women's History of the Religious Right," *Los Angeles Review of Books,* September 7, 2016, https://lareviewofbooks.org/article/sermonizing-pearls-phyllis-schlafly-womens-history-religious-right#.

69. Lawrence F. O'Brien to the President, October 3, 1964, box 3, folder 8, John M. Bailey Papers, Thomas J. Dodd Research Center, University of Connecticut, Storrs.

70. Richard Seaver to Jerry Workman, October 23, 1964, box 80, folder 3, FFP; Edward de Grazia to Milton Perlman, January 22, 1965, box 80, folder 3, FFP.

71. Untitled transcript of *Christian Crusade* broadcast, November 25, 1964, box 1, folder 13, Fred Cook Papers (FCP), Syracuse University, Syracuse, New York.

72. Fred Cook to Ben Waple, April 19, 1965, box 1, folder 3, FCP.

73. "Retreat of the Crusaders," *Newsweek,* December 7, 1959: 64; Frank S. Hogan to Fred J. Cook, December 9, 1964, box 1, folder 5, FCP.

74. Ben F. Waple to John M. Norris, October 6, 1965, box 1, folder 3, FCP. Waple included the relevant portion of the transcript of Hargis's personal attack on Cook.

75. Fred Cook to Wayne Phillips, January 25, 1965, box 1, folder 7, FCP.

76. Fred Cook to Wayne Phillips, February 9, 1965, box 81, folder 6, FCP.

77. "Dr. Billy James Hargis, His Christian Crusade, His Christian Echoes National Ministry, and Connections with Other Groups," October 10, 1962, box 1, folder 13, FCP; "Letter from Phillips," October 24, 1974, box 82, folder 3, FFP.

78. Fred Cook to Wayne Phillips, January 7 and 9, 1965, box 81, folder 6, FFP.

79. "Broadcast Action," September 19, 1963, box 81, folder 6, FFP.

80. Fred Cook to Ben Waple, February 7, 1965, box 1, folder 3, FCP; Ben Waple to Fred Cook, April 14, 1965, box 1, folder 3, FCP.

81. Wayne Moorehead to Fred J. Cook, December 28, 1964, box 1, folder 8, FCP; "List of Stations Canceling Hargis," undated, box 81, folder 6, FFP.

82. Jack Willis to Fred J. Cook, January 6, 1965, box 1, folder 11, FCP.

83. Jack Willis to Ben F. Waple, April 29, 1965, box 1, folder 6, FCP.

84. Ben F. Waple to Garrett Broadcasting, Inc., October 6, 1965, box 1, folder 3, FCP; Jack Willis to Fred J. Cook, October 26, 1965, box 1, folder 6, FCP.

85. Obituary of John Harden Norris, *York Daily Record & York Dispatch*, September 30, 2008; Gladys Titzck Rhoads and Nancy Titzck Anderson, *McIntire: Defender of Faith and Freedom* (Maitland, FL: Xulon Press, 2012): 200, 345–346.

86. Samuel Sauls, "Prelude to *Red Lion*: History and Analysis of the Proposed *Red Lion et al.,* v. *FCC and Democratic National Committee* Challenge of the Fairness Doctrine" (MA thesis, North Texas State University, 1980): 25–26.

87. Carl McIntire, "Brightman's Tape," *The Christian Beacon,* "The Power of the FCC," n.d., box 451, folder 83, CMP. McIntire published a transcript of Brightman's response tape in a special edition of the *Beacon.*

88. Sauls, "Prelude to Red Lion," 26–40.

89. John M. Norris to Martin E. Firestone, October 20, 1964, box 1, folder 11, FCP.

90. John M. Norris to John de J. Pemberton Jr., October 19, 1964, box 1, folder 11, FCP.

91. Sauls, "Prelude to Red Lion," 15–16, 49.

92. Ibid., 47–54; "Statement by Rev. John M. Norris, Red Lion, Pennsylvania, RE: Filing of Case of Red Lion Broadcasting Co.," September 21, 1965, box 497, folder 12, CMP.

93. John M. Norris to Fred J. Cook, January 7, 1965, box 1, folder 11, FCP.

94. Ben F. Waple to John H. Norris, December 9, 1965, box 1, folder 3, FCP.

95. Ibid.

96. Tammy W. Sun, "Equality by Other Means: The Substantive Foundations of the Vagueness Doctrine," *Harvard Civil Rights-Civil Liberties Law Review* 46 (2011): 150–151.

97. *Red Lion Broadcasting Co. v. FCC*, 381 F. 2d 922 (D.C. Cir. 1967).

98. *Red Lion*, 381 F. at 928.

99. *Red Lion*, 381 F. at 929.

100. *Red Lion Broadcasting Co. v. FCC*, 395 U.S. 394 (1969).

101. *Red Lion*, 395 U.S. at 390.

102. Erwin Krasnow and Lawrence Longley, *The Politics of Broadcast Regulation* (New York: St. Martin's Press, 1978): 99.

103. John Berresford, "The Scarcity Rationale for Regulating Traditional Broadcasting: An Idea Whose Time Has Passed," *Federal Communications Commission Media Bureau Staff Research Paper*, March 2005, https://transition.fcc.gov/ownership/materials/already-released/scarcity030005.pdf.

104. L. A. Powe Jr., "Red Lion and Pacifica: Are They Relics?," *Pepperdine Law Review* 36 (March 2009): 445–462; Thomas Hazlett, Sarah Oh, and Drew Clark, "The Overly Active Corpse of Red Lion," *Northwestern Journal of Technology and Intellectual Property* 9 (Fall 2010): 51–95.

105. *Red Lion*, 395 U.S. at 393.

106. Robert Horwitz, "Broadcast Reform Revisited: Reverend Everett C. Parker and the 'Standing Case,'" *Communications Review* 2 (1997): 23.

107. John Norris to Gale William McGee, November 16, 1965, box 23, folder "Fairness Doctrine Complaints," EWHP. See stapled note for the comment.

108. John M. Norris to the President, August 10, 1967, box 81, folder 2, FFP.

109. Robert Caro, *Means of Ascent: The Years of Lyndon Johnson* (New York: Vintage Books, 1990). See also Jack Shafer, "The Honest Graft of Lady Bird Johnson," *Slate*, July 16, 2007, http://www.slate.com/articles/news_and_politics/press_box/2007/07/the_honest_graft_of_lady_bird_johnson.html.

110. John M. Norris to the President, October 6, 1967, box 81, folder 2, FFP.

111. John M. Norris to Fred J. Cook, June 19, 1969, box 499, folder 16, CMP.

112. Fred J. Cook to John M. Norris, June 26, 1969, box 499, folder 16, CMP.

113. Horace R. Kornegay to Ralph V. Anderson, July 30, 1964, box 659, folder 13, CMP.

Chapter 6

1. See Jill K. Gill, *Embattled Ecumenism: The National Council of Churches, the Vietnam War, and the Trials of the Protestant Left* (Dekalb, IL: Northern Illinois University Press, 2011). David Hollinger, *After Cloven Tongues of Fire: Protestant Liberalism in Modern American History* (Princeton, NJ: Princeton University Press, 2013). Matthew S. Hedstrom, *The Rise of Liberal Religion: Book Culture and American Spirituality in the Twentieth Century* (Oxford: Oxford University Press, 2012). Leigh E. Schmidt and Sally M. Promey, eds., *American Religious Liberalism* (Bloomington: Indiana University Press, 2012).

2. Gary Dorrien, "The Protestant Mainline Makes a (Literary) Comeback," *Religion Dispatches*, August 5, 2013, http://www.religiondispatches.org/archive/atheologies/7233/the_protestant_mainline_makes_a_literary_comeback.

3. For another example of mainline Protestant illiberalism toward conservative religious competitors, see Elesha Coffman's description of how the editors of the ecumenical *Christian Century* magazine disseminated false rumors about evangelist Billy Graham. Elesha Coffman, *The Christian Century and the Rise of the Protestant Mainline* (Oxford: Oxford University Press, 2013).

4. *Historical Statistics of the United States, Colonial Times to 1970, Part 1* (Washington, DC: US Bureau of the Census, 1975): 391.

5. James Wine, "Report of James Wine to the General Board, National Council of Churches," June 1 1960, record group 95, box 9, folder 15, Papers of Eugene Carson Blake (ECB), Presbyterian Historical Society, Philadelphia.

6. "Extremists Try to Curb Clergy," *New York Times*, March 28, 1960.

7. "Changes in Audience Mail Operations," September 28, 1961, record group 16, box 3, folder 1, NCC.

8. "Comparison of Month-End Operating Balances," n.d., record group 16, box 1, folder 26, NCC; I pieced together McIntire's financial statistics from several account books and mail receipt ledgers in his papers. A detailed tabulation is available upon request.

9. "Comparison of Month-End Operating Balances," n.d., record group 16, box 1, folder 26, NCC; Rome A. Betts, "Report to the Board of Managers of the Broadcasting and Film Commission," February 17, 1959, record group 16, box 1, folder 25, NCC.

10. Lowell Saunders, "The National Religious Broadcasters and the Availability of Commercial Radio Time" (PhD diss., University of Illinois, 1968): 192–193.

11. "What Is This American Council?," n.d., record group 17, box 6, folder 2, NCC. Samuel McCrea Calvert, "Information about the American Council of Christian Churches," n.d., record group 17, box 6, folder 2, NCC.

12. Coffman, *The Christian Century*, 181.

13. Louis Cassels, "American Baptists May Leave National Council of Churches," *Lodi News-Sentinel* (Lodi, CA), May 27, 1960; See chapter 5 of Roger L. Frederickson, *The Church That Refused to Die: A Powerful Story of Reconciliation and Renewal* (Wheaton, IL: Victor Books, 1991).

14. "Notes on the Consultation between Members of the General Public Interpretation Committee and the Broadcasting and Film Commission," February 26, 1963, record group 303.2, box 17, folder 22, Papers of the United Presbyterian Church (UPC), Presbyterian Historical Society, Philadelphia, Pennsylvania.

15. James Wine to Patrick E. Lee, June 9, 1960, record group 17, box 7, folder 8, NCC.

16. Eugene Carson Blake to Roe H. Johnston, March 22, 1960, record group 17, box 7, folder 1, NCC.

17. James Wine to Donald F. Beisswenger, May 23, 1960, record group 17, box 16, folder 28, NCC.

18. James Wine to Paul C. Combs, March 14, 1960, record group 17, box 7, folder 8, NCC.

19. "Draft of Letter from Local Council of Churches, or Similar Group, to Owner of Local Radio Station," n.d., record group 17, box 7, folder 8, NCC.

20. James Wine to Harlan M. Frost, April 28, 1960, record group 17, box 7, folder 6, NCC.

21. George E. Korn, "Everett C. Parker and the Citizen Media Reform Movement: A Phenomenological Life History" (PhD diss., Southern Illinois University at Carbondale, 1991): 89.

22. Ibid., 102–103.

23. Everett C. Parker, interview by William C. Winslow, *United Church of Christ, a Four-Part DVD Collection*, December 15, 2006.

24. The full text of the "Call to Christian Action in Society" can be found online at the Baylor Institute of Church-State Studies, http://digitalcollections.baylor.edu/cdm/ref/collection/cs-vert/id/12757.

25. Horwitz, "Broadcast Reform Revisited," 5.

26. Bryan Burrough, *The Big Rich: The Rise and Fall of the Greatest Texas Oil Fortunes* (New York: Penguin Books, 2009).

27. Fred Friendly, *The Good Guys, the Bad Guys, and the First Amendment: Free Speech vs. Fairness in Broadcasting* (New York: Vintage Books, 1977): 90.

28. Horwitz, "Broadcast Reform Revisited," 23.

29. The best two works on the WLBT case and its connection to the civil rights movement are Kay Mills, *Changing Channels: The Civil Rights Case That Transformed Television* (Jackson: University of Mississippi, 2004) and Steven Classen, *Watching Jim Crow: The Struggles over Mississippi TV, 1955–1969* (Durham, NC: Duke University Press, 2004).

30. Ibid., 6, 9.

31. Mississippi AFL-CIO, "Petition Protesting Grant of Application Requesting Hearing and for Other Relief," March 1964, Papers of the United Church of Christ Office of Communications (2002.19.15, item 4), United Church of Christ Archives, Cleveland, Ohio.

32. Fred A. Lewis to Claude Ramsey, "Re: Storkline Corporation Case No. 15-RC-2327," July 12, 1962, UCC Office of Communications, United Church of Christ Archives, Cleveland, Ohio.

33. The locals' resolutions of support for WLBT are stapled to the UCC's petition. "Petition to Intervene and to Deny Application for Renewal," April 8, 1964, UCC Office of Communications, United Church of Christ Archives, Cleveland, Ohio.

34. "Brief for American Civil Liberties Union, Amicus Curiae," UCC Office of Communications (2002.19.15, item 18), United Church of Christ Archives, Cleveland, Ohio.

35. Korn, "Everett C. Parker and the Citizen Media Reform Movement," 143–144.

36. *Office of Communications of the United Church of Christ v. Federal Communications Commission*, 359 F.2d 994 (D.C. Cir. 1966); *Office of Communication of the United Church of Christ v. Federal Communications Commission*, 425 F.2d. 543 (D.C. Cir. 1969).

37. Horwitz, "Broadcast Reform Revisited," 34.

38. Lew Powell and Edwin E. Meek, "Mississippi's WLBT: After the License Challenge," *Columbia Journalism Review,* May/June 1973: 55.

39. Minutes, "Broadcasting and Film Commission's Executive Committee," May 5, 1966, record group 16, box 3, folder 1, NCC, p. 5.

40. "Personnel Announcement," July 15, 1964, record group 95, box 6, folder 8, ECB.

41. Charles Brackbill Jr., "Comprehensive Statement of Synod Radio-Television Work," April 27, 1961, record group 303.2, box 5, folder 11, UPC.

42. David Gockley to James Wine, March 17, 1960, record group 17, box 7, folder 8, NCC; the Greater Philadelphia and New Jersey Council of Churches worked closely together on broadcasting issues. Note the references to Charles Brackbill, Carl Cannon to James Wine, March 3, 1960, record group 17, box 7, folder 8, NCC.

43. Charles Brackbill to James Wine, March 11, 1960, record group 17, box 7, folder 8, NCC.

44. Board of Managers minutes, February 7–9, 1961, record group 16, box 1, folder 25, NCC.

45. Charles Brackbill Jr., "A Critique of Religious Radio," November 29, 1961, record group 303.2, box 13, folder 11, UPC.

46. "Summary of Consultation with Local Broadcasters," February 20, 1961, record group 303.2, box 13, folder 11, UPC.

47. Frederick W. Ford, "Radio Regulation and Government Ethics," February 8, 1961, record group 16, box 1, folder 25, NCC.

48. "Personnel Announcement," July 15, 1964, record group 95, box 6, folder 8, ECB.

49. Minutes, "Broadcasting and Film Commission Board of Managers," May 6–7, 1965, record group 16, box 1, folder 26, NCC. Parker and Brackbill were also elected to the BFC's executive committee; Minutes, "Broadcasting and Film Commission Board of Managers," February 17, 1964, record group 16, box 1, folder 26, NCC.

50. William F. Fore, "Report of the Executive Director to the Organizational Meeting of the Broadcasting and Film Commission," May 6–7, 1965, record group 16, box 1, folder 26, NCC.

51. William F. Fore, "Report of the Executive Director to BFC Executive Committee," May 5, 1966, record group 16, box 3, folder 1, NCC.

52. Kim A. Smith, "Why Ascertainment Failed," *Communications and the Law* 11, no. 2 (June 1989): 49–60.

53. Charles Brackbill Jr., "To: All Local Broadcasting Committees," November 7, 1960, record group 303.2, box 5, folder 11, UPC.

54. William F. Fore to Members of the BFC Executive Committee, June 5, 1964, record group 16, box 2, folder 29, UPC.

55. Arthur P. DeLuca, "FCC Broadcast Standards for Ascertaining Community Needs," *Fordham Urban Law Journal* 5, no. 1 (1976): 55–81.

56. Charles Brackbill, "A Critique of Religious Radio," November 29, 1961, record group 303.2, box 13, folder 11, United Presbyterian Church.

57. William F. Fore to Burton Marvin, May 10, 1967, record group 16, box 1, folder 13, NCC.

58. Richard Goode to Eugene Carson Blake, April 6, 1964, record group 95, box 6, folder 8, Papers of Eugene Carson Blake.

59. Minutes, "National Council of the Churches of Christ in the U.S.A. Broadcasting and Film Commission Board of Managers," September 22–23, 1966, record group 16, box 1, folder 26, NCC.

60. W. James Richards to William F. Fore, July 17, 1964, and William F. Fore to W. James Richards, August 13, 1964, record group 16, box 1, folder 13, NCC.

61. Don Hall, "Fairness in Broadcasting," *Newspulse: Weekly Newspaper for Methodists* 1, no. 6 (September 25, 1964): 2.

62. William F. Fore, "Response to NCC Radio Attacks," April 5, 1965, record group 16, box 1, folder 13, NCC.

63. W. James Richards to William F. Fore, August 4, 1965, record group 16, box 1, folder 13, NCC. W. James Richards to Lee Pemberton, July 21, 1965, record group 16, box 1, folder 13, NCC.

64. Garnett E. Phibbs to O. H. Bertram, November 9, 1966, record group 16, box 1, folder 13, NCC; obituary, "Lutheran Pastor Known for Media Ministry," *Toledo Blade*, May 29, 1979: 14.

65. Gerald Gause to Sam Lawder, November 16, 1965, record group 16, box 1, folder 13, NCC.

66. David Hollinger, *After Cloven Tongues of Fire: Protestant Liberalism in Modern American History* (Princeton, NJ: Princeton University Press, 2013): xiii; it is actually quite striking how much less analytical attention has been paid to the social construction and definition of the word "mainline" as opposed to the deep and divisive literature on the word "evangelical."

67. Ward Allan Howe, "Railroads Getting Off the Passenger Track," *New York Times*, September 14, 1958: X35.

68. Search terms "mainline churches" and "mainline Protestant" at http://books.google.com/ngrams.

69. John Wicklein, "Extremists Try to Curb Clergy," *New York Times*, March 28, 1960: 1.

70. Jack Black to Carl McIntire, July 12, 1964, box 459, folder 4, CMP.

71. Martin E. Firestone to George Huddleston Jr., October 12, 1964, box 659, folder 46, CMP. Carl McIntire to George Huddleston Jr., November 12, 1964, box 659, folder 46, CMP.

72. Ibid.

73. Carl McIntire, "20th Century Reformation Hour: 20 Years," 1975, box 178, folder 80, CMP, p. 5; Fred Friendly, *The Good Guys and the Bad Guys and the First Amendment: Free Speech vs. Fairness in Broadcasting* (New York: Vintage Books, 1977): 79.

74. Mary Dudziak, *Cold War Civil Rights: Race and the Image of American Democracy* (Princeton, NJ: Princeton University Press, 2011).

75. H. Francis Hines to William Henry, November 20, 1964, box 507, folder 1, CMP.

76. Frederick L. Fritsch to Federal Communications Commission, November 19, 1964, box 507, folder 1, CMP.

77. Frank H. Stroup to William Henry, November 23, 1964, box 507, folder 1, CMP.

78. Prince A. Taylor Jr. to Federal Communications Commission, November 24, 1964, box 507, folder 1, CMP.

79. Harry Boyer to E. William Henry, December 28, 1964, box 936, folder 10, ACLU.

80. George Meany, "To Local Central Bodies," September 6, 1963, MC #001, box 934, folder 7, ACLU.

81. "Political Memo from COPE," December 16, 1963, box 659, folder 46, CMP.

82. Meier Steinbrink to Carl McIntire, October 15, 1948, box 86, folder 12, CMP.

83. "The Religious Issue in the Presidential Campaign," *Facts* 13, no. 9 (June–July 1960).

84. Arnold Forster and Benjamin Epstein, *Danger on the Right: The Attitudes, Personnel and Influence of the Radical Right and Extreme Conservatives* (New York: Random House, 1964); William F. Buckley, "Professional Smear Job Done by Anti-Defamation League," *Chattanooga News-Free Press,* September 30, 1964.

85. Robert K. Greenfield and I. David Pincus to William Henry, November 20, 1964, box 507, folder 1, CMP.

86. Strom Thurmond to Carl McIntire, March 6, 1964, Carl McIntire to Strom Thurmond, March 19, 1964, Carl McIntire to Strom Thurmond, April 3, 1964, Strom Thurmond to Carl McIntire, May 7, 1964, Strom Thurmond to Carl McIntire, December 18, 1964, box 243, folder 7, CMP.

87. David R. Henderson, "Rent Seeking," *Concise Encyclopedia of Economics,* http://www.econlib.org/library/Enc/RentSeeking.html.

88. Kenneth A. Cox, "Dissenting Statement of Commissioner Kenneth A. Cox," FCC 65-207, box 936, folder 10, ACLU.

89. John J. Pemberton Jr. to William H. Ferry, July 20, 1964, box 935, folder 9, ACLU.

90. Lee Loevinger, "Concurring Opinion of Commissioner Loevinger," FCC 65-207, box 936, folder 10, ACLU.

91. Patrick Farabaugh, "Carl McIntire and His Crusade against the Fairness Doctrine" (PhD diss., Pennsylvania State University, 2010): 87–88.

92. John H. Norris, "First Annual Report of Radio Stations WXUR-AM and WXUR-FM," May 24, 1966, box 496, folder 2, CMP.

93. Joseph A. Fanelli and Benedict P. Cottone to Carl McIntire, December 1, 1967, box 507, folder 3, CMP.

94. "Statement and Recommendations of the Committee on Civil Liberties of WLIPF re Station WXUR, Media, PA," February 17, 1966, box 936, folder 10, ACLU.

95. Farabaugh, "Carl McIntire and His Crusade against the Fairness Doctrine," 80–85.

96. *Brandywine-Main Line Radio Inc. v. F.C.C.,* 473 F.2d 16 (US Court of Appeal, DC, 1972).

97. General Assembly of Pennsylvania, House Resolution No. 160, December 14, 1965, box 643, folder 10, CMP.

98. General Assembly of the State of New Jersey, Bill No. 376, February 14, 1966, box 656, folder 21, CMP.

99. Carl McIntire, "Statement by Dr. Carl McIntire," n.d., box 1, folder 12, CMP.

100. "Statement and Recommendations of the Committee on Civil Liberties of WILPF re Station WXUR, Media, PA," February 17, 1966, box 936, folder 10, ACLU.

101. Francis Hines to William F. Fore, February 23, 1966, record group 16, box 1, folder 13, NCC.

102. Francis Hines to William F. Fore, March 14, 1966, record group 16, box 1, folder 13, NCC.

103. Walter H. Annenberg, October 16, 1958. This quote from Annenberg's speech is on the Annenberg's School website: http://www.asc.upenn.edu/About/Default.aspx.

104. William Fore to Francis Hines, March 30, 1966, record group 16, box 1, folder 13, NCC.

105. Francis Hines to William F. Fore, March 25, 1966, record group 16, box 1, folder 13, NCC.

106. Farabaugh, "Carl McIntire and His Crusade against the Fairness Doctrine," 99.

107. Richard Goode to Eugene Carson Blake, April 6, 1964, record group 95, box 6, folder 8, Papers of Eugene Carson Blake, Presbyterian Historical Society, Philadelphia, Pennsylvania.

108. H. Gifford Irion, "The Legal Status of the Conscientious Objector," *George Washington Law Review* 8, no. 2 (December 1939): 125; "Closed Circuit," *Broadcasting,* December 1, 1952: 5.

109. H. Gifford Irion, "Report No. 4846, WXUR, WXUR-FM, Media, Pa., License Renewal Proposed in Initial Decision," December 13, 1968. McIntire reprinted and distributed the full document as "Historic Decision WXUR," box 455, folder 27, CMP.

110. Farabaugh, "Carl McIntire and His Crusade against the Fairness Doctrine," 113–115.

Chapter 7

1. Station tabulation available upon request.

2. William F. Fore to H. Francis Hines, March 23, 1966, record group 16, box 1, folder 13, NCC.

3. Minutes, "Broadcasting and Film Commission Executive Committee," May 5–6, 1966, record group 16, box 3, folder 1, NCC.

4. Bruce Sifford to Robert Norris, March 2, 1966, record group 16, box 1, folder 13, NCC.

5. T. C. Whitehouse to E. Robert Norris, March 4, 1966, record group 16, box 1, folder 13, NCC.

6. Bruce Sifford to Fred King, March 1, 1966, record group 16, box 1, folder 13, NCC.

7. Charles Woodward to Bruce Sifford, March 2, 1966. Bruce Sifford to Robert Norris, 3 March 1966, record group 16, box 1, folder 13, NCC.

8. George C. Conklin Jr. to Robert Norris, March 18, 1966, record group 16, box 1, folder 13, NCC.

9. Bruce Sifford to Robert Norris, March 2, 1966, record group 16, box 1, folder 13, NCC.

10. William F. Fore to Burton Marvin, September 27, 1967, record group 16, box 1, folder 13, NCC.

11. "One Man's Ideas on Regulation," *Broadcasting,* May 13, 1968: 58–61.

12. Everett C. Parker to Leslie Dunbar, August 17, 1966, Records of the United Church of Christ (UCC) (2002.19.03).

13. Everett C. Parker to George Meany, April 1, 1966, UCC (2002.19.15, item 4).

14. George Meany to Everett C. Parker, November 17, 1966, UCC (2002.19.03).

15. Everett C. Parker to Leslie Dunbar, July 1, 1966, UCC (2002.19.03).

16. Press Release, United Church of Christ Office of Communication, January 2, 1967, UCC (2002.19.02, item 22).

17. Minutes, United Church of Christ Office of Communication Board of Directors, September 11, 1967, UCC (2002.19.22, item 11).

18. J. Martin Bailey, untitled draft of press release, November 14, 1967, UCC (2002.19.02, item 2).

19. Gordon G. Henderson to Everett C. Parker, January 10, 1968, UCC (2002.19.03).

20. Ibid.

21. Ibid.; "In Defense of Fairness," n.d., box 197, folder 2, ACLU, pp. 10–12.

22. Adam Candeub, "Media Ownership Regulation, the First Amendment, and Democracy's Future," *UC Davis Law Review,* April 2007: 1566–1567, footnote 88.

23. Information regarding the UCC's KAYE campaign is from a single, massive binder. UCC (2002.19.04, item 1).

24. Ibid.

25. J. Martin Bailey, untitled draft of press release, November 14, 1967, UCC (2002.19.02, item 2).

26. Everett C. Parker to Thomas E. Cooney Jr., August 21, 1967, UCC (2002.19.02, item 22).

27. Everett C. Parker to Thomas E. Cooney Jr., October 3, 1969, UCC (2002.19.02, item 22).

28. Everett C. Parker to Thomas E. Cooney Jr., September 23, 1967, UCC (2002.19.02, item 22).

29. Gordon G. Henderson to Everett C. Parker, May 29, 1968, UCC (2002.19.02, item 22).

30. Thomas E. Conney Jr., to Everett C. Parker, January 26, 1979, UCC (2002.19.02, item 22); Donald Critchlow, *Intended Consequences: Birth Control, Abortion, and the Federal Government in Modern America* (New York: Oxford University Press, 2001): 97–98; for more on the unintended consequences of foundation work on the civil rights movement, see Megan Ming Francis, "The Price of Civil Rights: Black Lives, White Funding, and Movement Capture," *Law and Society Review* 53, no. 1 (January 29, 2019): 275–309.

31. Everett C. Parker to Thomas E. Cooney Jr., March 4, 1970, UCC (2002.19.02, item 22).

32. Everett C. Parker to Thomas E. Cooney Jr., January 29, 1970, UCC (2002.19.02, item 22).

33. Minutes, National Council of the Churches of Christ in the USA Broadcasting and Film Commission Board of Managers, September 25, 1969, record group 16, box 1, folder 27, NCC.

34. For a brief description of Congregationalist opposition to the merger, see Louis Gunnemann, *The Shaping of the United Church of Christ* (Cleveland: United Church Press, 1977), although a definitive account of the controversy remains unwritten.

35. Lester M. Barritt, "Report on the United Church Herald," Review Committee of the First Congregation Church of Western Springs, UCC (90.2, item 4).

36. Horace S. Sills to Ben M. Herbster, November 11, 1968, UCC (90.2, item 5).

37. G. Ray Robinson to the United Church of Christ, October 21, 1968, UCC (90.2, item 5).
38. Carl Burkle to Ben Herbster, August 9, 1968, UCC (90.2, item 5).
39. Horace S. Sills to Ben M. Herbster, October 30, 1968, UCC (90.2, item 5).
40. Ben Herbster to Everett Barrows, Harry Bredeweg, et al., November 26, 1968, UCC (90.2, item 5).
41. Joseph H. Evans to Ben M. Herbster, April 29, 1969, UCC (90.2, item 5).
42. "Report of the President of the United Church of Christ to the Executive Council, March 3–5, 1969, UCC (90.2, item 17).
43. The Association of Religion Data Archives, "United Church of Christ Membership Data," http://www.thearda.com/Denoms/D_1463.asp.
44. George W. Boucher to Robert Anderson, September 21, 1970. Don Bevillacqua to Tri County McIntire Committee, September 21, 1970, box 496, folder 2, CMP.
45. Emmett Alleman to Carl McIntire, September 25, 1967. Lamar A. Newcomb to Carl McIntire, September 11, 1967, box 499, folder 22, CMP.
46. Carl Miller and Gloria Bailey to Carl McIntire, September 8, 1967, box 175, folder 18, CMP.
47. G. M. Bailey to Carl McIntire, October 13, 1967, box 509, folder 19, CMP.
48. Stanley I. Stuber, "Memo: RE FCC Fairness Doctrine as to Controversial Issue Programming," 1963. Clarence Jones to Stanley I. Stuber, October 28, 1963, box 659, folder 47, CMP.
49. Clarence Jones to Carl McIntire, February 16, 1965, box 645, folder 16, CMP.
50. George K. Culbertson to John de J. Pemberton Jr., October 26, 1964, MC #001, box 937, folder 13, ACLU.
51. George K. Culbertson to Carl McIntire, August 14, 1967, box 179, folder 2, CMP.
52. Richard Goode to Eugene Carson Blake, April 6, 1964, record group 95, box 6, folder 8, Papers of Eugene Carson Blake.
53. George K. Culbertson to Franklin Little, September 15, 1967, box 659, folder 10, CMP.
54. The totals for 1968–1970 are estimates. McIntire kept track of his station totals up until 1966, Bob Lowe's report gives the total for 1967, and McIntire again kept track from 1971 to 1974.
55. He calculated the minimum income needed at just under $82,000 a month, prorated to $984,000 a year. This was not enough to sustain his entire operation long term, only enough to keep the lights on. "Radio & Beacon—Cost Per Month," box 472, folder 1, CMP. The note is a loose piece of paper kept in the back of the ledger titled "1-1-68 to 12-31-70," which also is probably an indication of when it was written.
56. Hemmer, Messengers of the Right, 109.
57. Gerald E. Meloon to Twentieth Century Reformation Hour, October 10, 1978, box 270, folder 7, CMP; "8 Inch Loose Leaf Binders—Records of Payments to Radio Stations Nationwide," box 268, CMP. The comment is on the final page for WYFI-FM in Norfolk, Virginia, dated February 25, 1972.
58. Robert J. Crudden to John H. Norris, June 17, 1969, box 499, folder 16, CMP.
59. Peggy Powell to Bryson, Bialoskurski, and Sialoskurski, March 22, 1976, box 421, folder 40, CMP.

60. Roland L. Elliott to Carl McIntire, March 20, 1974, box 19, folder 5, CMP; Carl McIntire to Richard Nixon, March 7, 1974, box 19, folder 5, CMP.

61. "Statement by Dr. Carl McIntire," June 15, 1973, box 19, folder 5, CMP.

62. Bud and Mary Daley to Carl McIntire, March 15, 1972, box 175, folder 17, CMP.

63. "The Shot-gun versus the Rifle," J. S. Magruder to H. R. Haldeman, October 17, 1969, box 81, folder 2, FFP.

64. Ibid.

65. Ibid.

66. John Farrell, *Nixon: The Life* (New York: Doubleday, 2017); Douglas Brinkley and Luke Nichter, *The Nixon Tapes: 1971–1972* (New York: Houghton Mifflin Harcourt, 2014); Evan Thomas, *Being Nixon: A Man Divided* (New York: Random House, 2015).

67. Thomas Thompson, "Chet Heads for the Hills," *Life,* July 17, 1970: 36.

68. Memorandum, Jeb S. Magruder to Mr. Haldeman and Mr. Klein, July 17, 1970, box 19, folder 5, CMP.

69. L. Higby to Mr. Magruder, July 16, 1970, box 19, folder 5, CMP.

70. Ibid.

71. "Huntley Voices Regret to Nixon Over Article," *New York Times,* August 7, 1970: 61.

72. Robert Walters, "Untangling the FCC Ruling," *Evening Star,* August 17, 1970, box 80, folder 4, FFP; Robert Samuelson, "CBS Cites FCC Ruling, Suspends 'Loyal Opposition' Series," *Washington Post,* August 21, 1970, box 80, folder 4, FFP.

73. Fred Ferretti, "F.C.C. Bars 3 Major Networks from Ownership of Cable TV," *New York Times,* June 26, 1970: 83.

74. "Memorandum for H. R. Haldeman," Charles Colson, August 26, 1970, box 19, folder 5, CMP; Mara Einstein, *Media Diversity: Economics, Ownership, and the FCC* (Mahwah, NJ: Lawrence Erlbaum Associates, 2004): 67.

75. Sanford Ungar, "FCC Bugged Employees' Phone Calls," *Washington Post,* January 7, 1973, box 80, folder 4, FFP.

76. "Memorandum for H. R. Haldeman," Charles Colson, September 25, 1970, box 19, folder 5, CMP.

77. David Dykes, "Former IRS Chief Recalls Defying Nixon," *USA Today,* May 26, 2013.

78. Wes McCune to Fred Friendly, April 18, 1975, box 19, folder 5, FFP.

79. Untitled interview with Dewey Anderson by Fred Friendly, n.d., box 80, folder 1, FFP.

80. "Memorandum on Lunch with Al Landa," Fred Friendly, May 29, 1975, box 82, folder 1, FFP.

81. Placemat from the Monocle on Capitol Hill, dated 1971, box 81, folder 6, FFP.

82. Fred Friendly, "Remarks Prepared for Delivery at the Silver Anniversary Banquet of the Northwest Broadcast News Association," Minneapolis, Minnesota, February 2, 1973, box 93, folder 5, FFP.

83. John de Pemberton Jr to Dr. William H. Ferry, July 20, 1964, box 935, folder 9, ACLU.

84. *Brandywine-Main Line Radio, Inc. v. F.C.C.,* 473 F.2d 16 (D.C. Cir. 1972).

85. Photos of the event are in an envelope marked WXUR Funeral, July 4, 1973, box 613, folder 51, CMP.

86. Edward E. Plowman, "McIntire's Navy," *Liberty* 69, no. 1 (January–February 1974): 2–9.

87. Nellie Jackson to Friends of McIntire, August 13, 1974, box 175, folder 17, CMP.

88. G. H. Owen to Carl McIntire, November 1, 1960, box 25, folder 12, CMP.

89. Ibid.; C. E. Hooks to Carl McIntire, January 29, 1974, box 496, folder 32, CMP.

90. Ibid.; Fred C. Koch to Carl McIntire, April 7, 1965, box 526, folder 9, CMP.

91. Heather Hendershot, *What's Fair on the Air? Cold War Right-Wing Broadcasting and the Public Interest* (Chicago: University of Chicago Press, 2011): Kindle loc. 1842 of 3419.

Chapter 8

1. Reed W. Smith, "Charles Ferris: Jimmy Carter's FCC Innovator," *Journal of Radio & Audio Media* 21 (2014): 149–162.

2. Christopher Sterling and John Michael Kittross, *Stay Tuned: A History of American Broadcasting* (Mahway, NJ: Lawrence Erlbaum Associates, 2002): 467–470.

3. David Harrell, *Pat Robertson: A Life and Legacy* (Grand Rapids, MI: William B. Eerdmans, 2010): 42–44, 46–47, 79–82; Alec Foege, *The Empire God Built: Inside Pat Robertson's Media Machine* (New York: John Wiley & Sons, 1996).

4. Robert Wuthnow, *Rough Country: How Texas Became America's Most Powerful Bible-Belt State* (Princeton, NJ: Princeton University Press, 2014): 335–337; for more on Falwell, see Susan Harding, *The Book of Jerry Falwell: Fundamentalist Language and Politics* (Princeton, NJ: Princeton University Press, 2000); Michael Sean Winters, *God's Right Hand: How Jerry Falwell Made God a Republican and Baptized the American Right* (New York: Harper Collins, 2012).

5. Ronald Reagan, "National Affairs Campaign Address on Religious Liberty," *American Rhetoric*, August 22 1980, Dallas, Texas, http://www.americanrhetoric.com/speeches/ronaldreaganreligiousliberty.htm.

6. Winters, *God's Right Hand*, 103; Andrew Hartman, *A War for the Soul of America: A History of the Culture Wars* (Chicago: University of Chicago Press, 2015): 94–95.

7. However, not all of the major televangelists were involved in overt political activity, especially those from the prosperity gospel tradition. They were more concerned with monetary prosperity as a marker of divine favor than they were political influence. See John Wigger, *The Rise and Fall of Jim and Tammy Faye Bakker's Evangelical Empire* (New York: Oxford University Press, 2017).

8. Thomas W. Evans, *The Education of Ronald Reagan: The General Electric Years and the Untold Story of His Conversion to Conservatism* (New York: Columbia University Press, 2008).

9. Robert E. Denton, *The Primetime Presidency of Ronald Reagan: The Era of the Television Presidency* (Santa Barbara, CA: Praeger, 1988): xii, 5.

10. Lou Cannon, *Governor Reagan: His Rise to Power* (New York: Public Affairs, 2003): 437. Cannon discusses Reagan's time as a sports announcer at length, but his use of the radio in the 1970s gets only the briefest mention, that it "kept him in the public eye."

11. Kiron K. Skinner, Annelise Anderson, and Martin Anderson, eds., *Reagan, in His Own Hand: The Writings of Ronald Reagan That Reveal His Revolutionary Vision for America* (New York: Free Press, 2001): xiv.
12. Ronald Reagan and Richard Hubler, *Where's the Rest of Me?* (New York: Duell, Sloan, and Pearce, 1965): 44–71.
13. Kiron Skinner, Annelise Anderson, and Martin Anderson, "Reagan's Path to Victory," *New York Times,* October 31, 2004.
14. Skinner, *Reagan in His Own Hand*, xv.
15. Peter Hannaford, interview by Stephen F. Knott and Russell Riley, January 10, 2003, Ronald Reagan Oral History Project, Miller Center of Public Affairs at the University of Virginia, Charlottesville, Virginia, http://web1.millercenter.org/poh/transcripts/ohp_2003_0110_hannaford.pdf.
16. Skinner, Anderson, and Anderson, "Reagan's Path to Victory."
17. Kiron Skinner, Annelise Anderson, and Martin Anderson, eds., *Reagan's Path to Victory: The Shaping of Ronald Reagan's Vision: Selected Writings* (New York: Free Press, 2004): xiv–xvii, 58–59.
18. Kalman, *Right Star Rising*, 323.
19. Skinner, *Reagan in His Own Hand*, 62–63.
20. Skinner, "Reagan's Path to Victory."
21. Reed W. Smith, "Charles Ferris: Jimmy Carter's FCC Innovator," *Journal of Radio & Audio Media* 21 (2014): 149–162.
22. Robert D. Hershey, "F.C.C. Votes Down Fairness Doctrine in a 4-0 Decision," *New York Times,* August 5, 1987: C26; Donald Jung, *The Federal Communications Commission, the Broadcast Industry, and the Fairness Doctrine: 1981–1987* (Lanham, MD: University Press of America, 1993).
23. Ronald Reagan, "Message to the Senate Returning without Approval the Fairness in Broadcasting Bill," June 19, 1987, Reagan Library, Simi Valley, California, https://www.reaganlibrary.archives.gov/archives/speeches/1987/061987h.htm.
24. Brian Rosenwald, "Mount Rushmore: The Rise of Talk Radio and Its Impact on Politics and Public Policy" (PhD diss., University of Virginia, 2015).
25. Jim Puzzanghera, "Democrats Speak Out for Fairness Doctrine," *Los Angeles Times,* July 23, 2007, http://articles.latimes.com/2007/jul/23/business/fi-fairness23.
26. Nancy Scola, "Could Trump Bring Back the Fairness Doctrine?," *Politico,* November 21, 2016, https://www.politico.com/tipsheets/morning-tech/2016/11/could-trump-bring-back-the-fairness-doctrine-217507; Eric Peterson, "The Internet Doesn't Need a Fairness Doctrine," *National Review,* September 4, 2018, https://www.nationalreview.com/2018/09/internet-censorship-fairness-doctrine-not-needed/.
27. Courtney Kube, Kristen Welker, Carol Lee, and Savannah Guthrie, "Trump Wanted Tenfold Increase in Nuclear Arsenal, Surprising Military," *NBC News,* October 11, 2017), https://www.nbcnews.com/news/all/trump-wanted-dramatic-increase-nuclear-arsenal-meeting-military-leaders-n809701.

28. Donald J. Trump, Twitter post, October 11, 2017, 9:55 a.m., https://twitter.com/realdonaldtrump/status/918112884630093825?lang=en; Donald J. Trump, Twitter post, September 4, 2018, 10:58 a.m., https://twitter.com/realDonaldTrump/status/1036991866124861440.

29. Brian Fung, "FCC Chair on Trump's NBC Tweet: 'The FCC will stand for the First Amendment,'" *Washington Post,* October 17, 2017, https://www.washingtonpost.com/news/the-switch/wp/2017/10/17/trumps-fcc-chair-has-finally-addressed-the-nbc-license-issue/.

30. Salena Zito, "Taking Trump Seriously, Not Literally," *The Atlantic,* September 23, 2016, https://www.theatlantic.com/politics/archive/2016/09/trump-makes-his-case-in-pittsburgh/501335/.

31. Former FBI director James Comey thought of the same historical comparison after Trump suggested that Comey ought to suspend the FBI probe into disgraced former national security adviser Michael Flynn. Sarah Pulliam Bailey, "Why Did James Comey Say, 'Will No One Rid Me of This Meddlesome Priest?,'" *Washington Post,* June 8, 2017, https://www.washingtonpost.com/news/acts-of-faith/wp/2017/06/08/why-did-comey-say-will-no-one-rid-me-of-this-meddlesome-priest/.

32. Kim Hart, "Comcast-NBC Merger Conditions Expire, Raising Anti-Competitive Fears," *Axios,* January 22, 2018, https://www.axios.com/comcast-nbm-1516393866-a394d1c7-abc5-4f51-879e-3fcab1c0de89.html.

33. Donald J. Trump, Twitter post, November 12, 2018, 1:13 p.m., https://twitter.com/realDonaldTrump/status/1062045654711713792.

34. Josh Kosman, "Justice Department Backs Off Comcast-NBCUniversal Merger Probe," *New York Post,* December 27, 2018, https://nypost.com/2018/12/27/justice-department-backs-off-comcast-nbcuniversal-merger-probe/.

35. Sarah Salinas, "Comcast Shares Slip after Trump Tweets about a Call for Antitrust Investigation," *CNBC,* November 12, 2018, https://www.cnbc.com/2018/11/12/comcast-shares-slip-after-trump-alleges-company-routinely-violates-antitrust-laws.html.

36. Philip Bump, "How CNN Became Trumpworld's Most-Hated Network," *Washington Post,* October 26, 2018, https://www.washingtonpost.com/politics/2018/10/26/how-cnn-became-trumpworlds-most-hated-network/.

37. Jane Mayer, "The Making of the Fox News White House," *New Yorker,* March 11, 2019, https://www.newyorker.com/magazine/2019/03/11/the-making-of-the-fox-news-white-house.

38. Placemat from the Monocle on Capitol Hill, dated 1971, box 81, folder 6, FFP.

Selected Bibliography

For the sake of readers who are interested in further study, I have cut the bibliography down into a list of consulted manuscript collections and a list of cited books and scholarly articles. Newspaper articles are not included, but those citations can be found in the footnotes.

Manuscript Collections

Athens, Georgia
University of Georgia Hargrett Rare Book & Manuscript Library
   Files of the Arbitron Ratings Company
   John J. Flynt, Jr. Papers
   Herman Talmadge Papers

Boston, Massachusetts
John F. Kennedy Presidential Library & Museum
   John F. Kennedy Pre-Presidential Papers
   Robert F. Kennedy Attorney General Papers
   Lawrence F. O'Brien Papers
   David F. Powers Papers
   James Wine Papers

Chicago, Illinois
Chicago History Museum
   Clarence Manion Papers

Cleveland, Ohio
United Church of Christ Archives
   Files of the UCC Office of Communications

Detroit, Michigan
Walter P. Reuther Library
   Victor G. Reuther Collection
   Walter P. Reuther Records
   UAW Community Action Program Department Collection

Fayetteville, Arkansas
University of Arkansas Libraries Special Collections Department
   Billy James Hargis Papers

Greenville, South Carolina
Bob Jones University Fundamentalism File
   W. O. H. Garman Papers
   Gilbert Stenholm Papers
   G. Archer Weniger Papers

Madison, Wisconsin
Wisconsin Historical Society
   Kenneth A. Cox Papers
   E. William Henry Papers
   Paul B. Zucker Papers

New York City, New York
Columbia University Rare Book & Manuscript Library
   Fred Friendly Papers
   Group Research Inc. Records

Philadelphia, Pennsylvania
Presbyterian Historical Society
   Donald Grey Barnhouse Papers
   Eugene Carson Blake Papers
   Files of the National Council of the Churches of Christ
   Files of the United Presbyterian Church

Princeton, New Jersey
Princeton Theological Seminary Libraries Special Collections
   Carl McIntire Papers
Princeton University Seeley G. Mudd Manuscript Library
   American Civil Liberties Union Records

Storrs, Connecticut
University of Connecticut Thomas J. Dodd Research Center
   John M. Bailey Papers

Syracuse, New York
Syracuse University Library Special Collections
   Fred J. Cook Papers

Wheaton, Illinois
Billy Graham Center Archives
   National Religious Broadcasters Records

Books and Journal Articles

Abrams, Douglas Carl. *Selling the Old-Time Religion: American Fundamentalists and Mass Culture, 1920–1940.* Athens: University of Georgia Press, 2001.

Adorno, Theodor. *The Authoritarian Personality.* New York: American Jewish Committee, 1950.

Aldgate, Anthony, and James Chapman, eds. *Windows on the Sixties: Exploring Key Texts of Media and Culture*. New York: I. B. Tauris Publishers, 2000.

Andrew, John A. *The Power to Destroy: The Political Uses of the IRS from Kennedy to Nixon*. Lanham, MD: Ivan R. Dee, 2002.

Barnouw, Erik. *The Image Empire: A History of Broadcasting in the United States from 1953*. New York: Oxford University Press, 1970.

Bell, Daniel. *The Radical Right*. Garden City, NY: Doubleday, 1963.

Benowitz, June. *Challenge and Change: Right-Wing Women, Grassroots Activism, and the Baby Boom Generation*. Gainesville: University Press of Florida, 2015.

Berman, William. *America's Right Turn: From Nixon to Clinton*. Baltimore: Johns Hopkins University Press, 1994.

Blee, Kathleen. "Ethnographies of the Far Right." *Journal of Contemporary Ethnography* 36 (2007): 119–128.

Blee, Kathleen, and Kimberly Creasap. "Conservative and Right-Wing Movements." *Annual Review of Sociology* 36 (2010): 269–286.

Brands, Henry W. "Redefining the Cold War: American Policy toward Yugoslavia, 1948–1960." *Diplomatic History* 11 (January 1987): 41–53.

Brennan, Mary C. *Turning Right in the Sixties: The Conservative Capture of the GOP*. Chapel Hill: University of North Carolina Press, 2007.

———. *Wives, Mothers, and the Red Menace: Conservative Women and the Crusade against Communism*. Boulder: University Press of Colorado, 2008.

Brinkley, Alan. "AHR Forum: The Problem of American Conservatism." *American Historical Review* 99 (April 1994): 409–429.

———. *John F. Kennedy: The American Presidents Series: The 35th President, 1961–1963*. New York: Times Books, 2012.

Brinkley, Douglas, and Luke Nichter. *The Nixon Tapes: 1971–1972*. New York: Houghton Mifflin Harcourt, 2014.

Brookhiser, Richard. *Right Time, Right Place: Coming of Age with William F. Buckley, Jr. and the Conservative Movement*. New York: Basic Books, 2011.

Brown, Ruth Murray. *For a Christian America: A History of the Religious Right*. Amherst, NY: Prometheus Books, 2002.

Burnham, David. *A Law unto Itself: Power, Politics, and the IRS*. New York: Random House, 1989.

Burrough, Bryan. *The Big Rich: The Rise and Fall of the Greatest Texas Oil Fortunes*. New York: Penguin Books, 2009.

Butler, Jon. "Jack-in-the-Box Faith: The Religion Problem in Modern American History." *Journal of American History* 90 (March 2004): 1357–1378.

Candeub, Adam. "Media Ownership Regulation, the First Amendment, and Democracy's Future." *UC Davis Law Review*, April 2007: 1547–1611.

Cannon, Lou. *Governor Reagan: His Rise to Power*. New York: Public Affairs, 2003.

Caro, Robert. *Means of Ascent: The Years of Lyndon Johnson*. New York: Vintage Books, 1990.

Carter, Dan T. *The Politics of Rage: George Wallace, the Origins of the New Conservatism, and the Transformation of American Politics*. Baton Rouge: Louisiana State University Press, 2000.

Casey, Shaun. *The Making of a Catholic President: Kennedy vs. Nixon 1960*. New York: Oxford University Press, 2009.

Clabaugh, Gary. *Thunder on the Right: The Protestant Fundamentalists*. Chicago: Nelson-Hall, 1974.

Classen, Steven. *Watching Jim Crow: The Struggles over Mississippi TV, 1955–1969*. Durham, NC: Duke University Press, 2004.

Coffman, Elesha. *The Christian Century and the Rise of the Protestant Mainline*. Oxford: Oxford University Press, 2013.

Cohen, Lizabeth. *A Consumers' Republic: The Politics of Mass Consumption in Postwar America*. New York: Vintage Books, 2003.

Crampton, R. J. *Eastern Europe in the Twentieth Century—And After*. New York: Routledge, 1997.

Cravens, Chris. "Edwin A. Walker and the Right Wing in Dallas, 1960–1966." MA thesis, Southwest Texas State University, 1991.

Crespino, Joseph. "Goldwater in Dixie: Race, Region and the Rise of the Right." In Shermer, 144–169.

———. *In Search of Another Country: Mississippi and the Conservative Counterrevolution*. Princeton, NJ: Princeton University Press, 2009.

———. *Strom Thurmond's America*. New York: Hill and Wang, 2012.

Critchlow, Donald T. *The Conservative Ascendancy: How the GOP Right Made Political History*. Cambridge, MA: Harvard University Press, 2007.

———. *Intended Consequences: Birth Control, Abortion, and the Federal Government in Modern America*. New York: Oxford University Press, 2001.

———. *Phyllis Schlafly and Grassroots Conservatism: A Woman's Crusade*. Princeton, NJ: Princeton University Press, 2008.

Critchlow, Donald T., and Nancy MacLean. *Debating the American Conservative Movement, 1945 to the Present*. New York: Rowman and Littlefield, 2009.

Denton, Robert E. *The Primetime Presidency of Ronald Reagan: The Era of the Television Presidency*. Santa Barbara, CA: Praeger, 1988.

Dietrich, David. "Rebellious Conservatives: Social Movements in Defense of Privilege." PhD diss., Duke University, 2011.

Dobson, Alan P. *US Economic Statecraft for Survival, 1933–1991*. New York: Routledge, 2003.

Dochuk, Darren. *From Bible Belt to Sunbelt: Plain-Folk Religion, Grassroots Politics, and the Rise of Evangelical Conservatism*. New York: W. W. Norton, 2012.

Dowland, Seth. *Family Values and the Rise of the Christian Right*. Philadelphia: University of Pennsylvania Press, 2015.

Dudziak, Mary. *Cold War Civil Rights: Race and the Image of American Democracy*. Princeton, NJ: Princeton University Press, 2011.

Edsall, Mary, and Thomas Edsall. *Chain Reaction: The Impact of Race, Rights, and Taxes on American Politics*. New York: W. W. Norton, 1992.

Engelman, Ralph. *Friendlyvision: Fred Friendly and the Rise and Fall of Television Journalism*. New York: Columbia University Press, 2009.

Epstein, Benjamin, and Arnold Forster. *Danger on the Right: The Attitudes, Personnel and Influence of the Radical Right and Extreme Conservatives*. New York: Random House, 1964.

———. *The Radical Right: Report on the John Birch Society and Its Allies*. New York: Random House, 1967.

Evans, Thomas W. *The Education of Ronald Reagan: The General Electric Years and the Untold Story of His Conversion to Conservatism*. New York: Columbia University Press, 2008.

Farabaugh, Patrick. "Carl McIntire and His Crusade against the Fairness Doctrine." PhD diss., Pennsylvania State University, 2010.

Farber, David. *The Rise and Fall of Modern American Conservatism: A Short History*. Princeton, NJ: Princeton University Press, 2012.

Farber, David, and Jeff Roche, eds. *The Conservative Sixties*. New York: Peter Land, 2003.

Farrell, John. *Richard Nixon: The Life*. New York: Vintage, 2017.

Finke, Roger, and Rodney Stark. *The Churching of America, 1776–2005: Winners and Losers in Our Religious Economy*. New Brunswick, NJ: Rutgers University Press, 2005.

Finn, David. *The Way Forward: My First Fifty Years at Ruder Finn*. New York: Millwood Publishing, 1998.

Flannery, Gerald, ed. *Commissioners of the FCC, 1927–1994*. New York: University Press of America, 1995.

Foege, Alec. *The Empire God Built: Inside Pat Robertson's Media Machine*. New York: John Wiley & Sons, 1996.

Fones-Wolf, Elizabeth. *Waves of Opposition: Labor and the Struggle for Democratic Radio*. Urbana: University of Illinois Press, 2006.

Formisano, Ronald. *Boston against Busing: Race, Class, and Ethnicity in the 1960s and 1970s*. Chapel Hill: University of North Carolina Press, 2004.

Fowler, Gene, and Bill Crawford. *Border Radio: Quacks, Yodelers, Pitchmen, Psychics, and Other Amazing Broadcasts of the Americans Airwaves*. Austin: University of Texas Press, 2002.

Frank, Thomas. *What's the Matter with Kansas? How Conservatives Won the Heart of America*. New York: Holt Paperbacks, 2005.

Frank, Thomas, and David Mulcahey. *Boob Jubilee: The Cultural Politics of the New Economy*. New York: W. W. Norton, 2003.

Frederickson, Kari. *The Dixiecrat Revolt and the End of the Solid South, 1932–1968*. Chapel Hill: University of North Carolina Press, 2001.

Frederickson, Roger L. *The Church That Refused to Die: A Powerful Story of Reconciliation and Renewal*. Wheaton, IL: Victor Books, 1991.

Friendly, Fred W. *The Good Guys, the Bad Guys, and the First Amendment: Free Speech vs. Fairness in Broadcasting*. New York: Random House, 1975.

Frohnen, Bruce, Jeremy Beer, and Jeffrey Nelson, eds. *American Conservatism: An Encyclopedia*. Wilmington, DE: Intercollegiate Studies Institute, 2006.

Gill, Jill K. *Embattled Ecumenism: The National Council of Churches, the Vietnam War, and the Trials of the Protestant Left*. Dekalb: Northern Illinois University Press, 2011.

Goldberg, Robert. *Barry Goldwater*. New Haven, CT: Yale University Press, 1997.

Gunnemann, Louis. *The Shaping of the United Church of Christ*. Cleveland: United Church Press, 1977.

Halberstam, David. *Breaking News: How the Associated Press Has Covered War, Peace, and Everything Else*. New York: Princeton Architectural Press, 2007.

Hamburger, Philip. *Is Administrative Law Unlawful?* Chicago: University of Chicago Press, 2014.

Hampson, Fen Osler, and Michael Hart, *Multilateral Negotiations: Lessons from Arms Control, Trade, and the Environment*. Baltimore: Johns Hopkins University Press, 1999.

Hangen, Tona. *Redeeming the Dial: Radio, Religion, and Popular Culture in America*. Chapel Hill: University of North Carolina Press, 2003.

Harding, Susan. *The Book of Jerry Falwell: Fundamentalist Language and Politics*. Princeton, NJ: Princeton University Press, 2000.

Harrel, David. *Pat Robertson: A Life and Legacy*. Grand Rapids, MI: William B. Eerdmans, 2010.

Hartman, Andrew. *A War for the Soul of America: A History of the Culture Wars.* Chicago: University of Chicago Press, 2015.

Hawley, George. *Right-Wing Critics of American Conservatism.* Lawrence: University Press of Kansas, 2016.

Hazlett, Thomas, Sarah Oh, and Drew Clark. "The Overly Active Corpse of Red Lion." *Northwestern Journal of Technology and Intellectual Property* 9 (Fall 2010): 51–95.

Hedstrom, Matthew S. *The Rise of Liberal Religion: Book Culture and American Spirituality in the Twentieth Century.* Oxford: Oxford University Press, 2012.

Hemmer, Nicole. "The Dealers and the Darling: Conservative Media and the Candidacy of Barry Goldwater." In Shermer, 114–143.

———. *Messengers of the Right: Conservative Media and the Transformation of American Politics.* Philadelphia: University of Pennsylvania Press, 2016.

———. "Messengers of the Right: Media and the Modern Conservative Movement." PhD diss., Columbia University, 2010.

Hendershot, Heather. "God's Angriest Man: Carl McIntire, Cold War Fundamentalism, and Right-Wing Broadcasting." *American Quarterly* 59 (June 2007): 373–396.

———. *What's Fair on the Air? Cold War Right-Wing Broadcasting and the Public Interest.* Chicago: University of Chicago Press, 2011.

Hilliard, Robert, and Michael Keith. *Dirty Discourse: Sex and Indecency in Broadcasting.* Hoboken, NJ: Wiley-Blackwell, 2006.

Himmelstein, Jerome. *To the Right: The Transformation of American Conservatism.* Berkeley: University of California Press, 1992.

Hodgson, Godfrey. *The World Turned Right Side Up: A History of the Conservative Ascendancy in America.* Boston: Houghton Mifflin, 1996.

Hofstadter, Richard. "The Paranoid Style in American Politics." *Harper's Magazine,* November 1964: 77–86.

———. *The Paranoid Style in American Politics and Other Essays.* New York: Knopf, 1966.

Hollinger, David. *After Cloven Tongues of Fire: Protestant Liberalism in Modern American History.* Princeton, NJ: Princeton University Press, 2013.

Horwitz, Robert. "Broadcast Reform Revisited: Reverend Everett C. Parker and the 'Standing Case.'" *Communications Review* 2 (1997): 311–348.

Hosang, Daniel. *Racial Propositions: Ballot Initiatives and the Making of Postwar California.* Oakland: University of California Press, 2010.

Hunter, James Davison. *Evangelicalism: The Coming Generation.* Chicago: University of Chicago Press, 1987.

Janson, Donald, and Bernard Eismann. *The Far Right.* New York: McGraw-Hill, 1963.

Jesperson, T. Christopher, ed. *Interviews with George F. Kennan.* Jackson: University Press of Mississippi, 2002.

Jung, Donald. *The Federal Communications Commission, the Broadcast Industry, and the Fairness Doctrine, 1981–1987.* Lanham, MD: University Press of America, 1993.

Kabaservice, Geoffrey. *Rule and Ruin: The Downfall of Moderation and Destruction of the Republican Party, From Eisenhower to the Tea Party.* Oxford: Oxford University Press, 2013.

Kalman, Laura. *Right Star Rising: A New Politics, 1974–1980.* New York: W. W. Norton, 2010.

Kaplan, Edward S. *American Trade Policy: 1923–1995.* Westport, CT: Greenwood Press, 1996.

Kinzer, Stephen. *The Brothers: John Foster Dulles, Allen Dulles, and Their Secret World War.* New York: Henry Holt and Company, 2013.

Korn, George E. "Everett C. Parker and the Citizen Media Reform Movement: A Phenomenological Life History." PhD diss., Southern Illinois University at Carbondale, 1991.

Krasnow, Erwin, Lawrence Longley, and Herbert Terry. *The Politics of Broadcast Regulation*. New York: Palgrave Macmillan, 1982.

Kruse, Kevin. *One Nation under God: How Corporate America Invented Christian America*. New York: Basic Books, 2015.

———. *White Flight: Atlanta and the Making of Modern Conservatism*. Princeton, NJ: Princeton University Press, 2007.

Laats, Adam. *The Other School Reformers: Conservative Activism in American Education*. Cambridge, MA: Harvard University Press, 2015.

Lassiter, Matthew. *The Silent Majority: Suburban Politics in the Sunbelt South*. Princeton, NJ: Princeton University Press, 2007.

Lichtenstein, Nelson. *Walter Reuther: The Most Dangerous Man in Detroit*. New York: University of Illinois Press, 1995.

Lichtman, Allan J. *White Protestant Nation: The Rise of the American Conservative Movement*. New York: Grove Press, 2009.

Lieberman, Joseph I. *The Legacy: Connecticut Politics 1930–1980*. Hartford, CT: Spoonwood Press, 1981.

Lienesch, Michael. *Redeeming America: Piety and Politics in the New Christian Right*. Chapel Hill: University of North Carolina Press, 1993.

Lipset, Seymour, and Earl Raab. *The Politics of Unreason: Right-Wing Extremism in America, 1790–1970*. New York: Harper and Row, 1970.

Martin, William. *With God on Our Side: The Rise of the Religious Right in America*. New York: Broadway Books, 2005.

Matzko, Paul. "No Uncertain Trumpet: Carl McIntire and the Politicization of Fundamentalism." MA thesis, Temple University, 2010.

———. "Radio Politics, Origin Myths, and the Creation of New Evangelicalism." *Fides et Historia* 48:1 (Winter/Spring 2016): 61–90.

Mayer, Jeremy. *Running on Race: Racial Politics in Presidential Campaigns*. New York: Random House, 2002.

Mayers, David. *George Kennan and the Dilemmas of US Foreign Policy*. New York: Oxford University Press, 1988.

McCarthy, Anna. *The Citizen Machine: Governing by Television in 1950s America*. New York: New Press, 2010.

McGirr, Lisa. *Suburban Warriors: The Origins of the New American Right*. Princeton, NJ: Princeton University Press, 2002.

McRae, Elizabeth Gillespie. *Mothers of Massive Resistance: White Women and the Politics of White Supremacy*. New York: Oxford University Press, 2018.

Micklethwait, John, and Adrian Wooldridge. *The Right Nation: Conservative Power in America*. New York: Penguin Books, 2005.

Miller, Edward. *Nut Country: Right-Wing Dallas and the Birth of the Southern Strategy*. Chicago: University of Chicago Press, 2015.

Miller, James E., and Glenn W. LaFantasie, eds. *Foreign Relations of the United States, 1961–1963*, vol. 26, *Eastern Europe; Cyprus; Greece; Turkey*. Washington, DC: United States Government Printing Office, 1994.

Mills, Kay. *Changing Channels: The Civil Rights Case That Transformed Television*. Jackson: University of Mississippi Press, 2004.

Minow, Newton. *Equal Time: The Private Broadcaster and the Public Interest*. New York: Atheneum, 1964.

Mintz, Frank. *The Liberty Lobby and the American Right: Race, Conspiracy, and Culture*. Westport, CT: Praeger, 1985.

Montgomery, Kathryn. *Target: Prime Time: Advocacy Groups and the Struggle over Entertainment Television*. New York: Oxford University Press, 1990.

Moore, Leonard J. "Good Old-Fashioned New Social History and the Twentieth-Century American Right." *Reviews in American History* 24 (December 1996): 555–573.

Moreton, Bethany. *To Serve God and Wal-Mart: The Making of Christian Free Enterprise*. Cambridge, MA: Harvard University Press, 2010.

Morris, Aldon D., and Carol McClurg Mueller, eds. *Frontiers in Social Movement Theory*. New Haven, CT: Yale University Press, 1992.

Mulloy, D. J. *The World of the John Birch Society: Conspiracy, Conservatism, and the Cold War*. Nashville: Vanderbilt University Press, 2014.

Nash, George H. *The Conservative Intellectual Movement in America Since 1945*. New York: Basic Books, 1976.

Nickerson, Michelle. *Mothers of Conservatism: Women and the Postwar Right*. Princeton, NJ: Princeton University Press, 2012.

Nimmo, Dan, and Chevelle Newsome. *Political Commentators in the United States in the 20th Century: A Bio-Critical Sourcebook*. Westport, CT: Greenwood Press, 1997.

O'Donnell, Helen, and David Groff. *A Common Good: The Friendship of Robert F. Kennedy and Kenneth P. O'Donnell*. New York: William Morrow, 1998.

Olmstead, Kathryn. *Right Out of California: The 1930s and the Big Business Roots of Modern Conservatism*. New York: New Press, 2015.

Perlman, Allison. *Public Interests: Media Advocacy and Struggles over U.S. Television*. New Brunswick, NJ: Rutgers University Press, 2016.

Perlstein, Rick. *Before the Storm: Barry Goldwater and the Unmaking of the American Consensus*. New York: Nation Books, 2009.

Phillips-Fein, Kim. *Invisible Hands: The Businessmen's Crusade against the New Deal*. New York: W. W. Norton, 2010.

Pickard, Victor. *America's Battle for Media Democracy: The Triumph of Corporate Libertarianism and the Future of Media Reform*. New York: Cambridge University Press, 2014.

Powe, L. A. "Red Lion and Pacifica: Are They Relics?" *Pepperdine Law Review* 36 (March 2009): 445–462.

Putnam, Kitty Broman, and William Lowell Putnam. *How We Survived in UHF Television: A Broadcasting Memoir, 1953–1984*. Jefferson, NC: McFarland and Company, 2011.

Reagan, Ronald, and Richard Hubler. *Where's the Rest of Me?* New York: Duell, Sloan, and Pearce, 1965.

Reed, Roy. *Faubus: The Life and Times of an American Prodigal*. Fayetteville: University of Arkansas Press, 1999.

Reuther, Victor. *The Brothers Reuther and the Story of the UAW: A Memoir*. Boston: Houghton Mifflin, 1976.

Rhoads, Gladys Titzck, and Nancy Titzck Anderson. *McIntire: Defender of Faith and Freedom*. Maitland, FL: Xulon Press, 2012.

Richardson, Erin. "SANE and the Limited Test Ban Treaty of 1963: Mobilizing Public Opinion to Shape U.S. Foreign Policy." MA thesis, Ohio University, 2009.

Ruotsila, Markku. *Fighting Fundamentalist: Carl McIntire and the Politicization of American Fundamentalism*. New York: Oxford University Press, 2015.

Sauls, Samuel. "Prelude to *Red Lion*: History and Analysis of the Proposed *Red Lion et al., v. FCC and Democratic National Committee* Challenge of the Fairness Doctrine." MA thesis, North Texas State University, 1980.

Savage, Sean. *JFK, LBJ, and the Democratic Party*. Albany: State University of New York Press, 2004.

Schlesinger, Robert. *White House Ghosts: Presidents and Their Speechwriters*. New York: Simon and Schuster, 2008.

Schmidt, Leigh E., and Sally M. Promey, eds. *American Religious Liberalism*. Bloomington: Indiana University Press, 2012.

Schoenwald, Jonathan. *A Time for Choosing: The Rise of Modern American Conservatism*. New York: Oxford University Press, 2002.

Shafer, Bryon, and Richard Johnston. *The End of Southern Exceptionalism: Class, Race, and Partisan Change in the Postwar South*. Cambridge, MA: Harvard University Press, 2009.

Shenon, Philip. *A Cruel and Shocking Act: The Secret History of the Kennedy Assassination*. New York: Henry Holt and Company, 2013.

Shermer, Elizabeth Tandy, ed. *Barry Goldwater and the Remaking of the American Political Landscape*. Tucson: University of Arizona Press, 2013.

Skinner, Kiron K., Annelise Anderson, and Martin Anderson, eds. *Reagan, in His Own Hand: The Writings of Ronald Reagan That Reveal His Revolutionary Vision for America*. New York: Free Press, 2001.

———. *Reagan's Path to Victory: The Shaping of Ronald Reagan's Vision: Selected Writings*. New York: Free Press, 2004.

Smith, Reed W. "Charles Ferris: Jimmy Carter's FCC Innovator." *Journal of Radio & Audio Media* 21 (2014): 149–162.

Stebenne, David. *Modern Republican: Arthur Larson and the Eisenhower Years*. Bloomington: Indiana University Press, 2006.

Sterling, Christopher, and John Michael Kittross. *Stay Tuned: A History of American Broadcasting*. Mahway, NJ: Lawrence Erlbaum Associates, 2002.

Sun, Tammy W. "Equality by Other Means: The Substantive Foundations of the Vagueness Doctrine." *Harvard Civil Rights-Civil Liberties Law Review* 46 (2011): 150–151.

Sutton, Matthew. *Aimee Semple McPherson and the Resurrection of Christian America*. Cambridge, MA: Harvard University Press, 2009.

Szasz, Thomas. *Psychiatric Justice*. New York: Macmillan, 1965.

Terchek, Ronald. *The Making of the Test Ban Treaty*. New York: Springer, 1970.

Thayer, George. *The Farther Shores of Politics: The American Political Fringe Today*. New York: Simon and Schuster, 1967.

Theroux, Eugene A. "Congress and the Question of Most Favored Nation Status for the People's Republic of China." *Catholic University Law Review* 23 (Fall 1973): 28–60.

Thomas, Evan. *Being Nixon: A Man Divided*. New York: Random House, 2015.

Tilly, Charles, and Sidney Tarrow. *Contentious Politics*. New York: Oxford University Press, 2015.

Wadsworth, James Jeremiah. *The Silver Spoon: An Autobiography*. Geneva, NY: W. F. Humphrey Press, 1980.

Walsh, William. *The Rise and Decline of the Great Atlantic and Pacific Tea Company*. Secaucus, NJ: Lyle Stuart, 1986.

Waterhouse, Benjamin. *Lobbying America: The Politics of Business from Nixon to NAFTA*. Princeton, NJ: Princeton University Press, 2013.

Wigger, John. *PTL: The Rise and Fall of Jim and Tammy Faye Bakker's Evangelical Empire*. New York: Oxford University Press, 2017.

Williams, Daniel K. *Defenders of the Unborn: The Pro-Life Movement Before Roe v. Wade*. New York: Oxford University Press, 2016.

Winters, Michael Sean. *God's Right Hand: How Jerry Falwell Made God a Republican and Baptized the American Right*. New York: Harper Collins, 2012.

Wittern-Keller, Laura. *Freedom of the Screen: Legal Challenges to State Film Censorship, 1915–1981*. Lexington: University Press of Kentucky, 2008.

Wuthnow, Robert. *Rough Country: How Texas Became America's Most Powerful Bible-Belt State*. Princeton, NJ: Princeton University Press, 2014.

Zelizer, Julian, and Kim Phillips-Fein, eds. *What's Good for Business: Business and Politics Since World War II*. New York: Oxford University Press, 2012.

Index

Note: Figures are indicated by *f* following the page number

For the benefit of digital users, indexed terms that span two pages (e.g., 52–53) may, on occasion, appear on only one of those pages.